CliffsNotes®

Math Review for Standardized Tests

3RD EDITION

by
BTPS Testing

Contributing Authors:

Jerry Bobrow, Ph.D.

Ed Kohn, M.S.

Carol Ameche Nicholson, Ed.D.

Peter Z Orton, Ph.D.

Consultants:

Ron Podrasky, M.A.

Joy Mondragon-Gilmore, Ph.D.

Houghton Mifflin Harcourt
Boston • New York

About the Authors

BTPS Testing is a national authority in the field of test preparation. BTPS Testing has offered test-preparation workshops at the California State Universities for over 35 years. The faculty at BTPS Testing has authored more than 30 test-preparation guides sold nationwide, including *CliffsNotes* preparation guides for the GRE, CSET, GMAT, CBEST, Praxis, RICA, SAT, and ACT. Each year, the authors of this study guide conduct lectures to thousands of students preparing for graduate, college, and teacher credentialing exams.

Acknowledgements

The authors at BTPS Testing are indebted to senior editor, Christina Stambaugh, for her attention to detail and accuracy during the production process.

Editorial

Executive Editor: Greg Tubach
Senior Editor: Christina Stambaugh
Production Editor: Erika West
Copy Editor: Donna Wright
Technical Editors: Mary Jane Sterling and Tom Page
Proofreader: Lynn Northrup

CliffsNotes® Math Review for Standardized Tests, 3rd Edition

Library of Congress Control Number: 2016938932
ISBN: 978-0-544-63102-1 (pbk)

Printed in the United States of America

DOC 10 9 8 7 6 5 4 3

4500722334

For information about permission to reproduce selections from this book, write to trade.permissions@hmhco.com or to Permissions, Houghton Mifflin Harcourt Publishing Company, 3 Park Avenue, 19th Floor, New York, New York 10016.

www.hmhco.com

Table of Contents

Table of Contents

Table of Contents

Table of Contents

Introduction

Why You Need This Guide

Are you planning to take the ...

GRE	SAT
GMAT	Praxis Core
CSET	CBEST
PSAT	ACT

or any other standardized test or state teacher's certification test with a math section?

This study guide is the most unique math guide available today. It is much more than simply a math review book. It is concise, easy to use, and full of insights into the types of questions to increase your test-taking success by focusing squarely on a test-oriented math review. It demonstrates how to avoid the common and costly errors that will trap those unprepared for the kinds of questions on standardized tests.

Our unique approach will bring back memories of mathematical rules and concepts previously learned but since forgotten through lack of use or understanding. This guide will not only review the essential basic skills, but also show you how to apply them *effectively and specifically* on standardized tests aligned with the Common Core Standards. Math topics in this guide introduce the critical areas that are part of a conceptually larger set of Common Core ideas that ask you to interpret, explain, and make sense of real-life quantitative scenarios.

Throughout this guide, language is nontechnical but consistent with the terminology used on most standardized tests.

What This Guide Contains

CliffsNotes Math Review for Standardized Tests, 3rd Edition, provides an excellent and extensive overview of the areas of concern for test-takers:

- Arithmetic
- Algebra
- Statistics and probability
- Geometry
- Word application problems
- Strategies and sample questions for common problem types:
  - Mathematical reasoning
  - Quantitative comparison
  - Data sufficiency

Each chapter includes a diagnostic test, explanations of rules and concepts with examples, practice problems with explanations, a review test with answers, and a glossary.

If you're taking the GRE, GMAT, SAT, PSAT, ACT, CSET, CBEST, Praxis Core, or any other exam with a math section, this book was designed for YOU!

Range of Difficulty and Scope

The range of difficulty and scope of problem types on standardized tests vary significantly, depending upon which exam is taken and if the exam is aligned with the Common Core Standards. In addition, many exams are administered by computer while others are administered by paper and pencil. For example,

- The ACT includes math problems drawing from arithmetic, algebra I, geometry, and algebra II.
- The GMAT includes math problems from only arithmetic, algebra I, statistics, and geometry, but it is heavily laden with word and data analysis problems (and a section called integrated reasoning). It also includes a section or two of data sufficiency problems, a unique problem type covered in Chapter 8.
- The GRE includes math reasoning problems drawing from arithmetic, algebra I, statistics, geometry, data analysis, and graph interpretation. GRE questions appear in four formats: quantitative comparison, multiple-choice "select one answer," multiple-choice "select one or more answers," and numeric entry "fill-in." The unique format of quantitative comparison questions is covered in Chapter 7.
- The SAT and PSAT are aligned to the Common Core Standards and include multistep math reasoning problems in arithmetic, basic statistics, algebra I, algebra II, geometry, and trigonometry. Questions can appear as multiple-choice "select one answer" or student-produced response "fill-in the answer grid."
- The Praxis Core and CBEST are aligned to the Common Core Standards and emphasize math reasoning skills. Problems include basic arithmetic, simple algebra I concepts, basic geometry (congruence and similarity), basic statistics, and probability. The CBEST has many word-type problems, whereas the Praxis Core has longer word application problems. The Praxis Core has selected-response questions that appear as "select one answer" or "select one or more answers," as well as numeric entry questions. Although these tests draw upon the more basic mathematical concepts, procedure problems are quite common. (Procedure problems do not ask for a final numerical answer, but rather "how" a problem should be worked to be solved.)
- The CSET: Multiple Subjects is aligned with the Common Core Standards and California's Subject Matter Requirements (SMRs) and is similar in nature to the tests given for the Praxis Core and CBEST. The mathematics section on the CSET, however, contains more algebra and geometry concepts. The format of the CSET has two components. One part is the standard multiple-choice format. The other part requires an essay constructed response that addresses a specific math topic prompt. Problems come from basic arithmetic, algebra I, geometry, and data analysis, including probability and statistics.

Focus on Reasoning

The Common Core Mathematics initiative defines what you should know and what you should be able to perform using a quantitative reasoning approach. Most standardized tests ask that you demonstrate Common Core quantitative reasoning competence. Math reasoning skills extend beyond memorizing math formulas and terms to find the correct solution to a problem. Math reasoning starts with making sense of foundational arithmetic topics so that you can solve problems of higher-level mathematics in algebra, geometry, statistics, and probability. To be a *math problem solver,* you must apply critical thinking skills to everyday scenarios as you reason abstractly and quantitatively to solve multistep math problems.

Common Core math reasoning problem solvers:

- Make sense of problems and persevere in solving them.
- Reason abstractly and quantitatively to explain, justify, and draw conclusions.
- Construct viable arguments and analyze the mathematical reasoning of others.
- Model with mathematics in everyday math application scenarios.
- Use electronic devices strategically (i.e., calculators, software, and so on).
- Attend to precision and thoughtful, mathematical, step-by-step processes.
- Look for structure or patterns in numeric and graphic problems.
- Repeat and express math reasoning regularly.

Mathematical reasoning application problems appear in a word problem format that combines numbers, descriptive text, and visual diagrams. Sometimes word problems can be confusing because you are required to take words and translate them into a quantitative problem. Try not to overthink math reasoning problems. Focus on the words used, their meaning, and how they are connected to solve the problem.

To help you deconstruct and translate word problems into numeric equations, Chapter 5 contains a list of key words that signal a math operation (pp. 289–290), along with numerous examples that you can refer to again and again during your math preparation.

A General Guideline

From a strictly mathematical perspective, the ACT and SAT require the greatest range and highest level of math skills of the exams mentioned. Although the GMAT does not require algebra II, its problems tend to be more complex, more rigorous, and more demanding of insights and techniques than, say, the Praxis Core, CBEST, or CSET. The GRE would probably fall in the middle category of difficulty because the questions tend to require reasoning skills, but are less difficult than the ACT, SAT, and GMAT. Still, GRE questions are more difficult than those on the Praxis Core, CBEST, or CSET.

As you work through this book, keep in mind which questions will be appropriate for you. The practice problems in each area are generally arranged so that the first few are the easiest and the last few are the most difficult. Therefore, an ACT, SAT, or GMAT candidate should work all the practice problems, whereas a Praxis Core candidate will probably not have to be concerned with the most difficult problem in each set. Be sure to check the official website for the specific exam you'll take to determine the level of difficulty for your math questions. Make use of the online information from the test-makers. *Review the appropriate level of math, and use your time effectively!*

How to Use This Guide

Start your preparation by identifying question types, assessing your skills, reviewing content material, understanding strategies, and practicing what you have learned. For optimal results, take detailed notes on the pages of this book to highlight important information.

1. Review the materials concerning your test provided by the testing company. This information is usually available at no charge and will detail the areas and question types for your particular exam.

   GMAT: http://www.mba.com/us

   GRE: http://www.ets.org/gre/

   SAT: https://sat.collegeboard.org/

   ACT: http://www.actstudent.org/

   CBEST: http://www.ctcexams.nesinc.com

   CSET: http://www.ctcexams.nesinc.com

   Praxis Core: http://www.ets.org/praxis/about/core/

   PSAT: https://collegereadiness.collegeboard.org/psat-nmsqt-psat-10

2. Take the arithmetic diagnostic test in Chapter 1.

3. Check your answers on the arithmetic diagnostic test in Chapter 1.

4. If your results on the diagnostic test warrant extensive arithmetic study, work through all of the arithmetic review and practice problems. If your results on the diagnostic test do not warrant extensive arithmetic review but you have some weakness in that area, concentrate on the review sections pertinent to your weaknesses. (The diagnostic test answers are cross-referenced to the appropriate review pages.)

5. Take the arithmetic review test at the end of Chapter 1.

6. Based on your results on the arithmetic review test, review any sections still requiring improvement.

7. Follow the same process (steps 2 through 6) for the remaining review chapters (algebra, statistics and probability, geometry, and word problems).

8. Notice that chapters 6–8 of this guide contain test strategies and special problem types appearing on some standardized tests—mathematical reasoning (all exams), quantitative comparison (GRE), and data sufficiency (GMAT). The particular exam you're taking will determine which of these areas are important for you to study. The questions will help "fine tune" your general math review and improve your problem-solving skills for your test.

9. Even if a unique problem type (say, quantitative comparison or data sufficiency) will not appear on your exam, you should also work these practice problems in chapters 7 and 8. The questions will help broaden your understanding of the particular math skill and give insight that may help solve the question types that will be on the test you'll take.

Chapter 1

Arithmetic

Arithmetic is represented on the Common Core Standards in all mathematical concepts and shares the basic properties of counting (adding, subtracting, multiplying, and dividing). The importance of understanding the basic concepts of arithmetic numbers and quantities cannot be overstated. These foundational concepts interrelate with all higher-level math reasoning skills aligned with the Common Core Standards. Knowing how to perform arithmetic operations will help you perform complex critical reasoning problems in algebra, geometry, and statistics.

Connecting Arithmetic and the Common Core Standards

This chapter is organized by arithmetic topics that are part of a conceptually larger set of Common Core ideas. The following table highlights elements of the Common Core Standards that connect to the domain topics covered in this chapter.

Arithmetic Common Core Connections

The Real Number System and Complex Numbers	Identify properties of rational and irrational numbers.
	Understand basic math operations: addition, subtraction, multiplication, and division.
	Perform arithmetic operations with complex numbers.
Quantities and Reasoning	Use logic and reasoning to solve problems.
	Reason quantitatively and use units to solve problems.
	Use multiple methods to solve real-world problems.
Ratios and Proportional Relationships	Perform arithmetic problems with ratios and proportions to make informed decisions about real-life events.
	Use ratios to understand proportional relationships.

Arithmetic Diagnostic Test

Questions

1. Which of the following are integers?
   $\frac{1}{2}, -2, 0, 4, 3.2$

2. Graph the following on a number line.
   $\frac{1}{2}, -2, 0, 4, 3.2$

3. Which of the following are rational numbers?
   $5.8, 6, \frac{1}{4}, \sqrt{4}, \sqrt{7}, \pi$

4. What are the prime factors of 30?

5. Which of the following are perfect cubes?
   1, 6, 8, 9, 27

6. The commutative property of addition is represented by

   Ⓐ $2 + (3 + 4) = (2 + 3) + 4$
   Ⓑ $2 + (-2) = 0$
   Ⓒ $(3 + 5) = (5 + 3)$

7. $(6 \times 10^4) + (3 \times 10^2) + (4 \times 10^{-1}) =$

8. Simplify $3[3^2 + 2(4 + 1)]$.

9. Round 4.4584 to the nearest thousandth.

10. $-4 + 8(2 - 3) =$

11. $-12 - 6(-4) =$

12. $(-6)(-8) =$

13. 2,730 is divisible by which of the following?
    3, 4, 8

14. Change $5\frac{3}{4}$ to an improper fraction.

15. Change $\frac{32}{6}$ to a mixed number in lowest terms.

16. $\frac{2}{7} + \frac{3}{5} =$

17. $1\frac{3}{8} + 2\frac{5}{6} =$

18. Carissa would like to add a border edge to a flower planter. The length of the planter requires 11 feet of border. If Carissa already has $\frac{2}{3}$ feet of border left over from a different flower planter, how much more border will she need to purchase?

19. $6\frac{1}{8} - 3\frac{3}{4} =$

20. $-\frac{7}{8} - \frac{5}{9} =$

21. $-\frac{1}{6} \times \frac{1}{3} =$

22. $2\frac{3}{8} \times 1\frac{5}{6} =$

23. $-\frac{1}{4} \div \frac{9}{14} =$

24. A second-grade teacher has a total of $18\frac{1}{8}$ yards of yarn for a class project. Each of the 30 students needs exactly $1\frac{1}{4}$ yards of the yarn. How much more yarn must the teacher purchase in order to complete the class project?

25. $\dfrac{1}{3 + \dfrac{2}{1 + \frac{1}{3}}} =$

26. $0.08 + 1.3 + 0.562 =$

27. $0.45 - 0.003 =$

28. $8.001 \times 2.4 =$

29. $-0.147 \div -0.7 =$

30. Change $\dfrac{3}{20}$ to a decimal.

31. Change 7% to a decimal.

32. What is 79% of 64?

33. 40% of what is 20?

34. Change $\dfrac{1}{8}$ to a percent.

35. What is the percent increase of a rise in temperature from 80° to 100°?

36. If 1 kilometer equals 0.6 mile, then 25 kilometers equal how many miles?

37. Express 0.00000023 in scientific notation.

38. $(3.2 \times 10^3)(2.4 \times 10^8) =$

39. $(5.1 \times 10^6) \div (1.7 \times 10^2) =$

40. $8^3 \times 8^7 =$

41. $9^5 \div 9^2 =$

42. $(5^3)^2 =$

43. Approximate $\sqrt{30}$ to the nearest tenth.

44. Simplify $\sqrt{80}$.

45. $-\sqrt{9} =$

46. $\sqrt[3]{64} =$

Answers

Page numbers following each answer refer to the review section applicable to the problem type.

1. −2, 0, 4 (p. 8)

2. (p. 16)

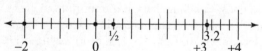

3. 5.8, 6, $\dfrac{1}{4}$, $\sqrt{4}\left(\sqrt{4}=2\right)$ (p. 9)

4. 2, 3, 5 (pp. 9, 26)

5. 1, 8, 27 (p. 9)

6. C (p. 10)

7. 60,300.4 (p. 12)

8. 57 (p. 13)

9. 4.458 (p. 15)

10. −12 (p. 17)

11. 12 (p. 18)

12. 48 (p. 19)

13. 3 (p. 20)

14. $\dfrac{23}{4}$ (p. 22)

15. $5\dfrac{2}{6} = 5\dfrac{1}{3}$ (p. 22)

16. $\dfrac{31}{35}$ (p. 31)

17. $4\dfrac{5}{24}$ (p. 31)

18. $10\dfrac{1}{3}$ (p. 35)

19. $2\dfrac{3}{8}$ (p. 37)

20. $-\dfrac{103}{72} = -1\dfrac{31}{72}$ (p. 34)

21. $-\dfrac{1}{18}$ (p. 38)

22. $\dfrac{209}{48} = 4\dfrac{17}{48}$ (pp. 39–40)

23. $-\dfrac{7}{18}$ (p. 41)

24. $19\dfrac{3}{8}$ (p. 39)

25. $\dfrac{2}{9}$ (p. 43)

26. 1.942 (pp. 45–46)

27. 0.447 (pp. 45–46)

28. 19.2024 (p. 46)

29. 0.21 (p. 47)

30. 0.15 (p. 47)

31. 0.07 (p. 49)

32. 50.56 (p. 52)

33. 50 (p. 53)

34. $12\dfrac{1}{2}\%$ or 12.5% (p. 49)

35. 25% (p. 56)

36. 15 miles (p. 68)

37. 2.3×10^{-7} (pp. 59–60)

38. 7.68×10^{11} (pp. 60–61)

39. 3×10^{4} (pp. 61–62)

40. 8^{10} (p. 58)

41. 9^{3} (p. 58)

42. 5^{6} (p. 58)

43. 5.5 (pp. 64–65)

44. $4\sqrt{5}$ (pp. 65–66)

45. -3 (p. 64)

46. 4 (p. 64)

Arithmetic Review

A critical component of the Common Core Standards is the ability to understand that numbers represent quantities and are used to calculate and solve equations. To understand numbers, it is important to grasp the various math terms and numeric relationships. To begin, you should be familiar with the operations of addition, subtraction, multiplication, and division of whole numbers (0, 1, 2 , 3, . . .). The following is a review of signed numbers, fractions, decimals, and important additional topics for arithmetic and data analysis.

Preliminaries

Groups of Numbers

In doing arithmetic and algebra, we work with several groups of numbers.

- **Natural or counting numbers:** The numbers 1, 2, 3, 4, . . . are called *natural or counting numbers.*
- **Whole numbers:** The numbers 0, 1, 2, 3, . . . are called *whole numbers.* Whole numbers are counting numbers plus 0.
- **Integers:** The numbers . . . –2, –1, 0, 1, 2, . . . are called *integers.*
- **Negative integers:** The numbers . . . –3, –2, –1 are called *negative integers.*
- **Positive integers:** The natural numbers are sometimes called the *positive integers.*

- **Rational numbers:** The numbers that can be expressed as fractions using integers are called *rational numbers*. Values such as $1\frac{1}{2} = \frac{3}{2}$ or $0.875 = \frac{7}{8}$ are called rational numbers. Since every integer can be expressed as that integer over 1, all integers are rational numbers. ***Note:*** Zero is a rational number since $\frac{0}{1} = 0$.

- **Irrational numbers:** The numbers whose exact values cannot be expressed as fractions are called *irrational numbers*. Two examples of irrational numbers are $\sqrt{3}$ and π.

- **Real numbers:** *Real numbers* consist of all rational and irrational numbers. Typically, most standardized exams use only real numbers, which are the commonly used numbers in everyday math calculations.

- **Prime numbers:** A *prime number* is a natural number greater than 1 that can be evenly divided only by itself and 1. For example, 19 is a prime number because it can be evenly divided only by 19 and 1, but 21 is not a prime number because 21 can be evenly divided by other numbers (3 and 7). The only even prime number is 2; thereafter, any even number may be divided evenly by 2. Therefore, any even number greater than 2 is not prime. Zero and 1 are *not* prime numbers. The first ten prime numbers are 2, 3, 5, 7, 11, 13, 17, 19, 23, and 29.

- **Composite numbers:** A *composite number* is a natural positive number greater than 1, and divisible by more than just 1 and itself: 4, 6, 8, 9, 10, 12, 14, 15, . . .

- **Odd numbers:** *Odd numbers* are integers not divisible by 2: $\pm 1, \pm 3, \pm 5, \pm 7, \ldots$

- **Even numbers:** *Even numbers* are integers divisible by 2: $0, \pm 2, \pm 4, \pm 6, \ldots$

  Notice that both even and odd numbers are two digits apart. This is an important detail when working with word problems that may only use odd or even numbers.

- **Squares:** *Squares* are the result when numbers are raised to the second power: $(2^2 = 2 \times 2 = 4)$, $(3^2 = 3 \times 3 = 9)$; 1, 4, 9, 16, 25, 36 . . .

- **Cubes:** *Cubes* are the result when numbers are raised to the third power: $(2^3 = 2 \times 2 \times 2 = 8)$, $(3^3 = 3 \times 3 \times 3 = 27)$; 1, 8, 27, 64, 125, 216 . . .

Practice: Groups of Numbers

1. Using only the digits 2, 3, and 5, how many ways can these numbers be rearranged to form a prime three-digit number?

Answers: Groups of Numbers

1. The digits 2, 3, and 5 can be rearranged as 235, 253, 325, 352, 523, or 532. After reviewing the six possibilities, immediately rule out any number ending in 2 or 5. After checking the two remaining numbers, 253 and 523, to see if they are divisible by 7, 11, 13, 17 . . . , you will find that 253 is divisible by 11. Since 253 is divisible by 11, this leaves 523 as the only prime number.

Ways to Show Multiplication

There are several ways to show multiplication:

$4 \times 3 = 12$	$(4)(3) = 12$	$(4)3 = 12$
$4 \cdot 3 = 12$	$4(3) = 12$	

Common Math Symbols

= is equal to	< is less than	⊥ is perpendicular to
≠ is not equal to	≥ is greater than or equal to	≅ is congruent to
≈ is approximately equal to	≤ is less than or equal to	
> is greater than	‖ is parallel to	

Properties of Basic Mathematical Operations

Some Properties (Axioms) of Addition

Closure is when all answers fall into the original set. If you add two even numbers, the answer is still an even number; therefore, the set of even numbers *is closed* (has closure) under addition ($2 + 4 = 6$). If you add two odd numbers, the answer is not an odd number; therefore, the set of odd numbers *is not closed* (does not have closure) under addition ($3 + 5 = 8$).

Commutative means that the *order* does not make any difference:

$$2 + 3 = 3 + 2 \qquad a + b = b + a$$

Note: Commutative does *not* hold for subtraction:

$$3 - 1 \neq 1 - 3 \qquad a - b \neq b - a$$

Associative means that the *grouping* does not make any difference:

$$(2 + 3) + 4 = 2 + (3 + 4) \qquad (a + b) + c = a + (b + c)$$

The grouping has changed (parentheses moved), but the sides are still equal.

Note: Associative does *not* hold for subtraction:

$$4 - (3 - 1) \neq (4 - 3) - 1 \qquad a - (b - c) \neq (a - b) - c$$

The *identity element* for addition is 0. Any number added to 0 gives the original number:

$$3 + 0 = 3 \qquad a + 0 = a$$

The *additive inverse* is the opposite (negative) of the number. Any number plus its additive inverse equals 0 (the identity):

$$3 + (-3) = 0; \text{ therefore, 3 and } -3 \text{ are additive inverses.}$$
$$-2 + 2 = 0; \text{ therefore, } -2 \text{ and 2 are additive inverses.}$$
$$a + (-a) = 0; \text{ therefore, } a \text{ and } -a \text{ are additive inverses.}$$

Some Properties (Axioms) of Multiplication

Closure is when all answers fall into the original set. If you multiply two even numbers, the answer is still an even number; therefore, the set of even numbers *is closed* (has closure) under multiplication ($2 \times 4 = 8$). If you multiply two odd numbers, the answer is an odd number; therefore, the set of odd numbers *is closed* (has closure) under multiplication ($3 \times 5 = 15$).

Commutative means that the *order* does not make any difference:

$$2 \times 3 = 3 \times 2 \qquad a \times b = b \times a$$

Note: Commutative does *not* hold for division:

$$2 \div 4 \neq 4 \div 2$$

Associative means that the *grouping* does not make any difference:

$$(2 \times 3) \times 4 = 2 \times (3 \times 4) \qquad (a \times b) \times c = a \times (b \times c)$$

The grouping has changed (parentheses moved), but the sides are still equal.

Note: Associative does *not* hold for division:

$$(8 \div 4) \div 2 \neq 8 \div (4 \div 2)$$

The *identity element* for multiplication is 1. Any number multiplied by 1 gives the original number:

$$3 \times 1 = 3 \qquad a \times 1 = a$$

The *multiplicative inverse* is the reciprocal of the number. Any number multiplied by its reciprocal equals 1:

$$2 \times \frac{1}{2} = 1; \text{ therefore, 2 and } \frac{1}{2} \text{ are multiplicative inverses.}$$

$$a \times \frac{1}{a} = 1; \text{ therefore, } a \text{ and } \frac{1}{a} \text{ are multiplicative inverses.}$$

Since 0 multiplied by any value can never equal 1, the number 0 has no multiplicative inverse.

A Property of Two Operations

The *distributive property* is the process of distributing the number on the outside of the parentheses to each term on the inside:

$$2(3 + 4) = 2(3) + 2(4) \qquad 2(3 - 4) = 2(3) - 2(4)$$

$$a(b + c) = a(b) + a(c) \qquad a(b - c) = a(b) - a(c)$$

Note: You cannot use the distributive property with the same operation:

$$3(4 \times 5 \times 6) \neq 3(4) \times 3(5) \times 3(6)$$

$$a(bcd) \neq a(b) \times a(c) \times a(d) \text{ or } (ab)(ac)(ad)$$

$$2 + (3 + 4) \neq (2 + 3) + (2 + 4)$$

Place Value

Each position in any number has *place value*. For instance, in the number 485, the 4 is in the hundreds place, the 8 is in the tens place, and the 5 is in the ones place. Thus, place value is as follows:

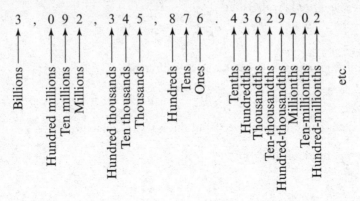

Practice: Place Value

1. Which digit is in the tens place in 483?

2. In 36,548, which digit is in the thousands place?

3. The digit 7 is in which place in 45,328.769?

4. Which digit is in the hundredths place in 25.0671?

5. Which digit is in the ten millions place in 867,451,023.79?

Answers: Place Value

1. 8

2. 6

3. tenths

4. 6

5. 6

Expanded Notation

Sometimes numbers are written in expanded notation to point out the place value of each digit. The more common forms of expanded notation—one with exponents, one without exponents—are shown in the last two lines of each example below. Notice that, in these, the digit is multiplied times its place value—1's, 10's, 100's, and so on.

Examples:

345 can be written as

$300 + 40 + 5$

$(3 \times 100) + (4 \times 10) + (5 \times 1)$

$(3 \times 10^2) + (4 \times 10^1) + (5 \times 10^0)$

43.25 can be written as

$40 + 3 + 0.2 + 0.05$

$(4 \times 10) + (3 \times 1) + \left(2 \times \frac{1}{10}\right) + \left(5 \times \frac{1}{100}\right)$

$(4 \times 10^1) + (3 \times 10^0) + (2 \times 10^{-1}) + (5 \times 10^{-2})$

Notice that the tenths place is 10^{-1} and the hundredths place is 10^{-2}, and so on.

Practice: Expanded Notation

Write in expanded notation using exponents.

1. 576

2. 1,489

3. 3.581

4. 302,400

Answers: Expanded Notation

1. $(5 \times 10^2) + (7 \times 10^1) + (6 \times 10^0)$

2. $(1 \times 10^3) + (4 \times 10^2) + (8 \times 10^1) + (9 \times 10^0)$

3. $(3 \times 10^0) + (5 \times 10^{-1}) + (8 \times 10^{-2}) + (1 \times 10^{-3})$

4. $(3 \times 10^5) + (0 \times 10^4) + (2 \times 10^3) + (4 \times 10^2) + (0 \times 10^1) + (0 \times 10^0)$ or $(3 \times 10^5) + (2 \times 10^3) + (4 \times 10^2)$

Grouping Symbols: Parentheses, Brackets, and Braces

Parentheses ( )

Parentheses are used to group numbers or variables. Everything inside parentheses must be done before any other operations.

Example:

$$50(2 + 6) = 50(8) = 400$$

When a parenthesis is preceded by a minus sign, remove the parentheses and change the sign of each term within the parentheses.

Example:

$$6 - (-3 + a - 2b + c) = 6 + 3 - a + 2b - c = 9 - a + 2b - c$$

The rule that everything inside the parentheses must be done before any other operation has one exception because of the *distributive property*.

Example:

$$50(2 + 6) = 50(2) + 50(6)$$
$$= 100 + 300$$
$$= 400$$

Brackets [ ] and Braces { }

Brackets and *braces* are also used to group numbers or variables. Technically, they're used after parentheses. Parentheses are to be used first, then brackets, then braces: $\{[( )]\}$. These are all grouping symbols. When solving problems, always start with the innermost grouping symbol. Sometimes, instead of brackets or braces, you'll see the use of larger parentheses:

$$((3 + 4) \cdot 5) + 2$$

A number using all three grouping symbols would look like this:

$$2\{1+[4(2+1)+3]\}$$

and would be simplified as follows (notice that you work from the inside out):

$$2\{1+[4(2+1)+3]\}=$$
$$2\{1+[4(3)+3]\}=$$
$$2\{1+[12+3]\}=$$
$$2\{1+[15]\}=$$
$$2\{16\}=32$$

Order of Operations

If multiplication, division, exponents, addition, parentheses, and so on are all contained in one problem, the *order of operations* is as follows:

1. Parentheses (includes all grouping symbols, working from the inside out)
2. Exponents and square roots
3. Multiplication and division (start with whichever comes first, left to right)
4. Addition and subtraction (start with whichever comes first, left to right)

Examples:

$$6+4\times3=\quad \text{(multiplication)}$$
$$6+12=\quad \text{(then addition)}$$
$$=18$$

$$10-3\times6+10^2+(6+1)\times4=$$
$$10-3\times6+10^2+(7)\times4=\quad \text{(parentheses first)}$$
$$10-3\times6+100+(7)\times4=\quad \text{(exponents next)}$$
$$10-18+100+28=\quad \text{(multiplication)}$$
$$-8+100+28=\quad \text{(addition/subtraction left to right)}$$
$$92+28=120$$

An easy way to remember the order of operations is <u>P</u>lease <u>E</u>xcuse <u>M</u>y <u>D</u>ear <u>A</u>unt <u>S</u>ally (Parentheses, Exponents, Multiplication or Division, Addition or Subtraction) or PEMDAS.

Practice: Order of Operations

Simplify.

1. $6+4\times3^2$

2. $3^2+6(4+1)$

3. $12-2(8+2)+5$

4. $8[3(3^2-8)+1]$

5. $6\{4[2(3+2)-8]-8\}$

6. $6(12+8)\div2+1$

Answers: Order of Operations

1. $6+4\times 3^2 =$
$6+4\times 9 =$
$6+36 = 42$

2. $3^2 + 6(4+1) =$
$9+6(5) =$
$9+30 = 39$

3. $12-2(8+2)+5 =$
$12-2(10)+5 =$
$12-20+5 =$
$-8+5 = -3$

4. $8\left[3(3^2-8)+1\right] =$
$8[3(9-8)+1] =$
$8[3(1)+1] =$
$8[3+1] =$
$8[4] = 32$

5. $6\{4[2(3+2)-8]-8\} =$
$6\{4[2(5)-8]-8\} =$
$6\{4[10-8]-8\} =$
$6\{4[2]-8\} =$
$6\{8-8\} =$
$6\{0\} = 0$

6. $6(12+8)\div 2+1 =$
$6(20)\div 2+1 =$
$120\div 2+1 =$
$60+1 = 61$

Rounding Off

To *round off* any number, follow these steps:

1. Underline the place value to which you're rounding off.
2. Look to the immediate right (one place) of your underlined place value.
3. Identify the number (the one to the right). If it's 5 or higher, round your underlined place value up by one number. If the number (the one to the right) is 4 or less, leave your underlined place value as is and change all the other numbers to its right to zeros.

Examples:

Round to the nearest thousand:
34<u>5</u>,678 becomes 346,000
92<u>8</u>,499 becomes 928,000

This works with decimals as well. Round to the nearest hundredth:

Examples:

3.4<u>6</u>78 becomes 3.47
298,435.0<u>8</u>3 becomes 298,435.08

Notice that the numbers to the right of the rounded digit are dropped when working with decimals.

Practice: Rounding Off

1. Round off 137 to the nearest ten.

2. Round off 4,549 to the nearest hundred.

3. Round off 0.4758 to the nearest hundredth.

4. Round off 99.483 to the nearest whole number (one's place).

5. Round off 6,278.38512 to the nearest thousandth.

Answers: Rounding Off

1. 140

2. 4,500

3. 0.48

4. 99

5. 6,278.385

Signed Numbers: Positive Numbers and Negative Numbers

Number Line

On a *number line,* numbers to the right of 0 are positive and numbers to the left of 0 are negative, as follows:

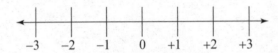

Given any two numbers on a number line, the one on the right is always larger, regardless of its sign (positive or negative). Note that fractions may also be placed on a number line:

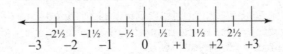

Practice: Number Line

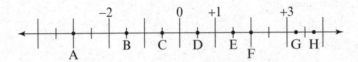

Review the number line above, then locate which letters correspond with the following numbers.

1. +2

2. −3

3. $+1\frac{1}{2}$

4. $-\frac{1}{2}$

5. $+3\frac{1}{4}$

Answers: Number Line

1. F
2. A
3. E

4. C
5. G

Addition of Signed Numbers

When adding two numbers with the same sign (either both positive or both negative), add the numbers and keep the same sign.

Examples:

$$\begin{array}{r} +5 \\ ++7 \\ \hline +12 \end{array} \qquad \begin{array}{r} -8 \\ +-3 \\ \hline -11 \end{array}$$

When *adding two numbers with different signs* (one positive and one negative), subtract the numbers and keep the sign of the number farthest from zero on the number line.

Examples:

$$\begin{array}{r} +5 \\ +-7 \\ \hline -2 \end{array} \qquad \begin{array}{r} -59 \\ ++72 \\ \hline +13 \end{array}$$

Signed numbers may also be added "horizontally."

Examples:

$+9 + 6 = +15$

$-12 + 9 = -3$

$8 + (-5) = 3$

Practice: Addition of Signed Numbers

1. $+25 + 8 =$

2. $-10 + 15 =$

3. $\begin{array}{r} -7 \\ +-3 \\ \hline \end{array}$

4. $\begin{array}{r} -82 \\ ++60 \\ \hline \end{array}$

5. $-18 + (+5) =$

Answers: Addition of Signed Numbers

1. $+33$
2. $+5$
3. -10

4. -22
5. -13

Subtraction of Signed Numbers

To subtract positive and/or negative numbers, just change the sign of the number being subtracted and then add.

Examples:

$$\begin{array}{r} +12 \\ \underline{-+4} \end{array} \qquad \begin{array}{r} -14 \\ \underline{--4} \end{array} \qquad \begin{array}{r} -19 \\ \underline{-+6} \end{array} \qquad \begin{array}{r} +20 \\ \underline{--3} \end{array}$$

$$\begin{array}{r} +12 \\ \underline{+-4} \\ +8 \end{array} \qquad \begin{array}{r} -14 \\ \underline{++4} \\ -10 \end{array} \qquad \begin{array}{r} -19 \\ \underline{+-6} \\ -25 \end{array} \qquad \begin{array}{r} +20 \\ \underline{++3} \\ +23 \end{array}$$

This may also be done "horizontally."

Examples:

$+12 - (+4) = +12 + (-4) = 8$

$-14 - (-4) = -14 + (+4) = -10$

$-19 - (+6) = -19 + (-6) = -25$

$+20 - (-3) = +20 + (+3) = +23$

Practice: Subtraction of Signed Numbers

1. $\begin{array}{r} +9 \\ \underline{-+3} \end{array}$

2. $\begin{array}{r} +25 \\ \underline{--9} \end{array}$

3. $+36 - (-5) =$

4. $-27 - (+4) =$

5. $-30 - (-2) =$

Answers: Subtraction of Signed Numbers

1. $+6$

2. $+34$

3. $+41$

4. -31

5. -28

Minus Preceding Parenthesis

If a minus precedes a parenthesis, it means that each term within the parentheses is to be subtracted. Therefore, using the same rule as in subtraction of signed numbers, simply change every sign within the parentheses to its opposite, and then add. Another option is to simplify everything within the parentheses first. Use the order of operations and then distribute the negative sign.

Examples:

$$9 - (+3 - 5 + 7 - 6) =$$
$$9 + (-3 + 5 - 7 + 6) =$$
$$9 + (+1) = 10$$

or

$$9 - (+3 - 5 + 7 - 6) =$$
$$9 - (-1) =$$
$$9 + 1 = 10$$

$$20 - (+35 - 50 + 100) =$$
$$20 + (-35 + 50 - 100) =$$
$$20 + (-85) = -65$$

or

$$20 - (+35 - 50 + 100) =$$
$$20 - (85) = -65$$

Practice: Minus Preceding Parenthesis

1. $2 - (+5 - 3) =$

2. $6 - (+8 - 5 + 10) =$

3. $10 - (-12 - 5 + 3) =$

4. $25 - (-4 + 7 - 8 - 5 + 6) =$

Answers: Minus Preceding Parenthesis

1. $2 - (+2) = 2 - 2 = 0$

2. $6 - (+13) = 6 - 13 = -7$

3. $10 - (-14) = 10 + 14 = 24$

4. $25 - (-4) = 25 + 4 = 29$

Multiplying and Dividing Signed Numbers

To multiply or divide signed numbers, treat them just like regular numbers but remember this rule: An odd number of negative signs will produce a negative answer. An even number of negative signs will produce a positive answer.

Examples:

$$(-3)(+8)(-5)(-1)(-2) = +240$$
$$(-3)(+8)(-1)(-2) = -48$$

$$\frac{-64}{-2} = +32$$

$$\frac{-64}{+2} = -32$$

Practice: Multiplying and Dividing Signed Numbers

1. $(-3)(+9) =$

2. $-8 \div -2 =$

3. $(-8)(+3)(-2) =$

4. $\frac{-10}{+5} =$

5. $\frac{(-4)(+2)(-6)}{-12} =$

Answers: Multiplying and Dividing Signed Numbers

1. -27

2. $+4$

3. $+48$

4. -2

5. -4

Multiplying and Dividing Using Zero

Zero times any number equals zero.

Examples:

$$0 \times 5 = 0$$
$$0 \times (-3) = 0$$
$$8 \times 9 \times 3 \times (-4) \times 0 = 0$$

Likewise, zero divided by any nonzero number is zero.

Examples:

$$0 \div 5 = 0$$
$$\frac{0}{3} = 0$$
$$0 \div (-6) = 0$$

Important note: Dividing by zero is "undefined" and is not permitted. For example, $\frac{6}{0}$ and $\frac{0}{0}$ are not permitted because there is no such answer. The answer is *not* zero.

Divisibility Rules

The following set of rules can help you save time in trying to check the divisibility of numbers:

A number is divisible by	If
2	the number ends in 0, 2, 4, 6, or 8 (the number must be even)
3	the sum of its digits is divisible by 3
4	the number formed by the last two digits is divisible by 4
5	it ends in 0 or 5
6	it is divisible by 2 and 3 (use the rules for both)
7	N/A (no simple rule)
8	the number formed by the last three digits is divisible by 8
9	the sum of its digits is divisible by 9

Examples:

Is 126 divisible by 3?

The sum of the digits $1 + 2 + 6 = 9$. Because 9 is divisible by 3, 126 is divisible by 3.

Is 1,648 divisible by 4?

Because 48 is divisible by 4, you know that 1,648 is divisible by 4.

Is 186 divisible by 6?

Because 186 ends in 6, it is divisible by 2. The sum of digits $1 + 8 + 6 = 15$. Because 15 is divisible by 3, 186 is divisible by 3. 186 is divisible by 2 and 3; therefore, it is divisible by 6.

Is 2,488 divisible by 8?

Because 488 is divisible by 8, you know that 2,488 is divisible by 8.

Is 2,853 divisible by 9?

The sum of the digits $2 + 8 + 5 + 3 = 18$. Because 18 is divisible by 9, you know that 2,853 is divisible by 9.

Practice: Divisibility

1. 4,620 is divisible by which of the following numbers?

2, 3, 4, 5, 6, 7, 8, 9

2. 13,131 is divisible by which of the following numbers?

2, 3, 4, 5, 6, 7, 8, 9

Answers: Divisibility

1. 2, 3, 4, 5, 6, 7

2: The number is even.

3: The sum of the digits $4 + 6 + 2 + 0 = 12$, which is divisible by 3.

4: The number formed by the last two digits, 20, is divisible by 4.

5: The number ends in 0.

6: The number is divisible by 2 and 3.

7: Divide 4,620 by 7 and you get 660.

8: The number formed by the last three digits, 620, is not divisible by 8.

9: The sum of the digits $4 + 6 + 2 + 0 = 12$, which is not divisible by 9.

2. 3, 9

2: The number is not even.

3: The sum of the digits $1 + 3 + 1 + 3 + 1 = 9$, which is divisible by 3.

4: The number formed by the last two digits, 31, is not divisible by 4.

5: The number does not end in 0 or 5.

6: The number is not even.

7: The number is not divisible by 7. Divide and you'll see that there is a remainder.

8: The number formed by the last three digits, 131, is not divisible by 8.

9: The sum of the digits $1 + 3 + 1 + 3 + 1 = 9$, which is divisible by 9.

Common Fractions

Numerator and Denominator

Fractions consist of two numbers: a *numerator* (which is above the line) and a *denominator* (which is below the line). The line dividing the numerator and denominator is called a *fraction bar*.

$$\frac{1}{2} \quad \begin{array}{l} \text{numerator} \\ \text{denominator} \end{array} \quad \text{or numerator 1/2 denominator}$$

The denominator lets you know the number of equal parts into which something is divided. The numerator tells you how many of these equal parts are being considered. Thus, if the fraction is $\frac{3}{5}$ of a pie, then the denominator, 5, tells you that the pie has been divided into 5 equal parts, of which 3 (the numerator) are in the fraction. Sometimes it helps to think of the dividing bar (in the middle of a fraction) as meaning "out of." In other words, $\frac{3}{5}$ would also mean 3 "out of" 5 equal pieces from the whole pie. All rules for signed numbers also apply to fractions.

Negative Fractions

Fractions may be *negative* as well as positive (see the number line on p. 16). However, negative fractions are typically written $-\frac{3}{4}$ not $\frac{-3}{4}$ or $\frac{3}{-4}$ (although they are all equal):

$$-\frac{3}{4} = \frac{-3}{4} = \frac{3}{-4}$$

Proper Fractions and Improper Fractions

A fraction like $\frac{3}{5}$, where the numerator is smaller than the denominator, is less than one. This kind of fraction is called a *proper fraction.*

Examples:

$$\frac{4}{7}, \frac{2}{5}, \frac{1}{9}, \frac{10}{12}$$

But sometimes a fraction may be more than or equal to one. This is when the numerator is larger than or equal to the denominator. Thus, $\frac{12}{7}$ is more than one. This is called an *improper fraction.*

Examples:

$$\frac{7}{4}, \frac{3}{2}, \frac{10}{3}, \frac{16}{15}, \frac{8}{8}$$

Mixed Numbers

When a term contains both a whole number and a fraction, it is called a *mixed number.* For example, $5\frac{1}{4}$ and $290\frac{3}{4}$ are both mixed numbers. To change an improper fraction to a mixed number, you divide the denominator into the numerator and write the remainder as a fraction with the divisor in the denominator.

Examples:

$$\frac{18}{5} = 3\frac{3}{5}$$

$$5 \overline{)18}$$
$$\underline{15}$$
$$3$$

To change a mixed number to an improper fraction, you multiply the denominator times the whole number, add in the numerator, and put the total over the original denominator.

Example:

$$4\frac{1}{2} = \frac{9}{2} = (2 \times 4) + 1 = 9$$

Practice: Mixed Numbers and Improper Fractions

Change the improper fractions to mixed numbers.

1. $\dfrac{3}{2}$

2. $\dfrac{7}{4}$

3. $\dfrac{10}{3}$

4. $\dfrac{16}{5}$

5. $\dfrac{23}{4}$

Change the mixed numbers to improper fractions.

6. $1\dfrac{3}{4}$

7. $4\dfrac{1}{2}$

8. $5\dfrac{3}{4}$

9. $21\dfrac{3}{4}$

10. $8\dfrac{4}{5}$

Answers: Mixed Numbers and Improper Fractions

1. $1\dfrac{1}{2}$

2. $1\dfrac{3}{4}$

3. $3\dfrac{1}{3}$

4. $3\dfrac{1}{5}$

5. $5\dfrac{3}{4}$

6. $\dfrac{7}{4}$

7. $\dfrac{9}{2}$

8. $\dfrac{23}{4}$

9. $\dfrac{87}{4}$

10. $\dfrac{44}{5}$

Equivalent Fractions

Simplifying Fractions

A fraction must be *reduced to lowest terms.* This is done by dividing both the numerator and denominator by the largest number that will divide evenly into both. For example, $\dfrac{10}{25}$ is reduced to $\dfrac{2}{5}$ by dividing both the numerator and denominator by 5.

Examples:

$$\frac{30}{50} = \frac{30 \div 10}{50 \div 10} = \frac{3}{5}$$

$$\frac{8}{40} = \frac{8 \div 8}{40 \div 8} = \frac{1}{5}$$

$$\frac{9}{15} = \frac{9 \div 3}{15 \div 3} = \frac{3}{5}$$

Practice: Simplifying Fractions

Simplify the fractions.

1. $\dfrac{6}{8}$

2. $\dfrac{15}{20}$

3. $\dfrac{18}{36}$

4. $\dfrac{40}{90}$

5. $\dfrac{75}{30}$

Answers: Simplifying Fractions

1. $\dfrac{3}{4}$

2. $\dfrac{3}{4}$

3. $\dfrac{1}{2}$

4. $\dfrac{4}{9}$

5. $\dfrac{5}{2}$

Enlarging Denominators

The denominator of a fraction may be *enlarged* by multiplying both the numerator and the denominator by the same number. *Note:* Even though the numbers of the numerator and denominator are larger, the *value* of the fraction is still the same.

Examples:

$$\frac{1}{2} = \frac{1 \times 5}{2 \times 5} = \frac{5}{10}$$

$$\frac{3}{4} = \frac{3 \times 10}{4 \times 10} = \frac{30}{40}$$

Practice: Enlarging Denominators

1. Change $\dfrac{3}{5}$ to tenths.

2. Express $\dfrac{3}{4}$ as eighths.

3. $\dfrac{5}{7} = \dfrac{?}{21}$

4. $\dfrac{2}{15} = \dfrac{?}{45}$

5. Change the fraction $\dfrac{3}{8}$ to an equivalent fraction with a denominator of 24.

Answers: Enlarging Denominators

1. $\dfrac{6}{10}$

2. $\dfrac{6}{8}$

3. $\dfrac{15}{21}$

4. $\dfrac{6}{45}$

5. $\dfrac{9}{24}$

Factors

Factors of a number are those whole numbers that, when multiplied together, yield the number.

Examples:

What are the factors of 8?

$8 = 2 \times 4 \qquad 8 = 1 \times 8$

Therefore, the factors of 8 are 1, 2, 4, and 8, because $4 \times 2 = 8$ and $1 \times 8 = 8$.

What are the factors of 24?

$24 = 1 \times 24 \qquad 24 = 2 \times 12 \qquad 24 = 3 \times 8 \qquad 24 = 4 \times 6$

Therefore, the factors of 24 are 1, 2, 3, 4, 6, 8, 12, and 24.

Practice: Factors

Find the factors.

1. 6

2. 9

3. 12

4. 48

Answers: Factors

1. 1, 2, 3, and 6

2. 1, 3, and 9

3. 1, 2, 3, 4, 6, and 12

4. 1, 2, 3, 4, 6, 8, 12, 16, 24, and 48

Common Factors

Common factors are those factors that are the same for two or more numbers.

Example:

What are the common factors of 6 and 8?

6: 1, 2, 3, 6
8: 1, 2, 4, 8

1 and 2 are common factors of 6 and 8.

Some numbers may have many common factors.

Example:

What are the common factors of 24 and 36?

24: 1, 2, 3, 4, 6, 8, 12, 24
36: 1, 2, 3, 4, 6, 9, 12, 18, 36

Thus, the common factors of 24 and 36 are 1, 2, 3, 4, 6, and 12.

Practice: Common Factors

Find the common factors.

1. 10 and 30

2. 12 and 18

3. 6 and 15

4. 70 and 80

Answers: Common Factors

1. 1, 2, 5, and 10

2. 1, 2, 3, and 6

3. 1 and 3

4. 1, 2, 5, and 10

Prime Factorization

When working with large numbers, it is often easier to use prime factorization and rewrite the number as a product of its primes. Remember that neither 0 nor 1 are prime numbers.

Example:

What is the prime factorization of 50?

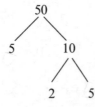

Write the factors in order: $2 \times 5 \times 5$ or 2×5^2.

Note: No matter how you split up the numbers, you will always end up with the same prime factorization.

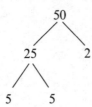

The prime factorization remains $2 \times 5 \times 5$.

Greatest Common Factor

The greatest common factor is the largest factor common to two or more numbers.

Example:

What is the greatest common factor of 12 and 30?

12: 1, 2, 3, 4, 6, 12
30: 1, 2, 3, 5, 6, 10, 15, 30

Notice that while, 1, 2, 3, and 6 are all common factors of 12 and 30, only 6 is the greatest common factor.

Practice: Greatest Common Factor

Find the greatest common factor.

1. 6 and 12

2. 24 and 40

3. 24 and 60

4. 40 and 100

Answers: Greatest Common Factor

1. 6

2. 8

3. 12

4. 20

Multiples

Multiples of a number are found by multiplying that number by 1, by 2, by 3, by 4, by 5, and so on.

Examples:

Multiples of 3 are 3, 6, 9, 12, 15, 18, 21, and so on.
Multiples of 4 are 4, 8, 12, 16, 20, 24, 28, 32, and so on.
Multiples of 7 are 7, 14, 21, 28, 35, 42, 49, 56, and so on.

Practice: Multiples

Name the first seven multiples.

1. 2

2. 5

3. 6

4. 8

5. 10

Answers: Multiples

1. 2, 4, 6, 8, 10, 12, 14

2. 5, 10, 15, 20, 25, 30, 35

3. 6, 12, 18, 24, 30, 36, 42

4. 8, 16, 24, 32, 40, 48, 56

5. 10, 20, 30, 40, 50, 60, 70

Common Multiples

Common multiples are those multiples that are the same for two or more numbers.

Example:

What are the common multiples of 2 and 3?

$2 \longrightarrow$ 2 4 6 8 10 12 14 16 18 etc.
$3 \longrightarrow$ 3 6 9 12 15 18 etc.

Notice that common multiples go on indefinitely.

Practice: Common Multiples

Find the first three common multiples.

1. 2 and 6

3. 4 and 6

2. 3 and 4

Answers: Common Multiples

1. 6, 12, 18

3. 12, 24, 36

2. 12, 24, 36

Least Common Multiple

The *least common multiple* is the smallest multiple that is common to two or more numbers.

Examples:

What is the least common multiple of 2 and 3?

$2 \longrightarrow 2\ 4\ \boxed{6}\ 8\ 10\ \boxed{12}$ etc.
$3 \longrightarrow\ \ \ 3\ \boxed{6}\ \ \ 9\ \ \ \boxed{12}$ etc.

The smallest multiple common to both 2 and 3 is 6.

What is the least common multiple of 2, 3, and 4?

$2 \longrightarrow 2\ 4\ 6\ 8\ 10\ \boxed{12}$ etc.
$3 \longrightarrow\ \ \ 3\ 6\ 9\ \ \ \boxed{12}$ etc.
$4 \longrightarrow\ \ \ \ 4\ \ \ 8\ \ \ \ \boxed{12}$ etc.

The least common multiple of 2, 3, and 4 is 12.

Practice: Least Common Multiple

Find the least common multiple.

1. 3 and 4

2. 4 and 6

3. 3, 4, and 5

4. Let X be the greatest common factor of 104 and 64, and Y the greatest common factor of 54 and 81. What is the least common multiple of X and Y?

Answers: Least Common Multiple

1. 12

2. 12

3. 60

4. Use prime factorization to find the greatest common factor of 104 and 64. Draw a prime factorization chart to determine the common prime factors.

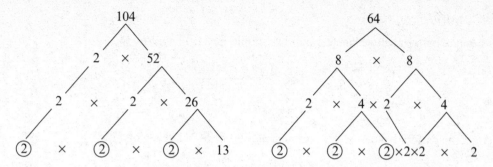

The prime factors that these numbers have in common are 2 × 2 × 2 = 8. Therefore, X = 8.

Repeat the process for 54 and 81.

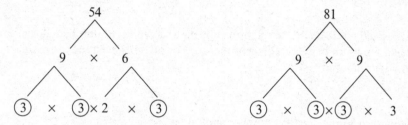

Common prime numbers are 3 × 3 × 3 = 27. Therefore, Y = 27.

XY = (8)(27) = 216. The least common multiple of 8 and 27 is 216 because 8 is a product of multiples of 2 and 27 is a product of multiples of 3. Therefore, these numbers have nothing in common.

Number Sequences

Progressions of numbers are *sequences* with some patterns. Unless the sequence has a simple repeat pattern (1, 2, 4, 1, 2, 4, . . . or 1, 1, 2, 2, 2, 3, 3, 3, 3, . . .), you should first look for a common difference between the numbers to solve the problem.

Example:

Based on the pattern below, the next number should be 24: 20 + 4 or 24.

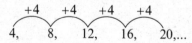

In some sequences, you may need to take a closer look at the difference between the numbers to see if a pattern arises there.

Example:

Based on the pattern below, the next number should be 22: 16 + 6 or 22.

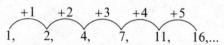

In other sequence patterns, the numbers themselves are being added, multiplied, or squared (subtracted or divided is also possible but not as common) to get the next number.

Examples:

Based on the pattern below, the next number should be 34: 13 + 21 or 34.

$$(2 + 3 = 5) \qquad (5 + 8 = 13)$$
$$2, \qquad 3, \qquad 5, \qquad 8, \qquad 13, \qquad 21,...$$
$$(3 + 5 = 8)$$

Based on the pattern below, the next number should be 512: 128 × 4 or 512.

$$(2 \times 4 = 8)$$
$$2, \qquad 8, \qquad 32, \qquad 128,...$$
$$(8 \times 4 = 32)$$

Finally, if using the actual numbers or the relationships between adjacent numbers doesn't solve the pattern, you should try to find a pattern between adjacent numbers or possibly even the use of more than one operation between adjacent numbers.

Examples:

Based on the pattern below, the next number should be 7: 5 + 2 or 7.

$$\overset{+2 \quad +2 \quad +2 \quad +2}{1, \quad 5, \quad 3, \quad 7, \quad 5, \quad 9}$$

Another common-sense method is to follow the repeating pattern. For example,

1,	5,	3,	7,	5,	9,	=	7
(add 4)	(subtract 2)	(add 4)	(subtract 2)	(add 4)	(subtract 2)	=	

Based on the pattern below, the next number should be 155: 7 × 22 + 1, or 155. Multiply adjacent numbers and add 1.

$$(0 \times 1) + 1 = 1 \qquad (1 \times 2) + 1 = 3$$
$$0, \qquad 1, \qquad 1, \qquad 2, \qquad 3, \qquad 7, \qquad 22,...$$
$$(1 \times 1) + 1 = 2 \qquad (2 \times 3) + 1 = 7$$

Practice: Number Sequence

Find the next number in each sequence.

1. 37, 35, 32, 28, 23, _____

2. 31, 33, 29, 35, 27, 37, 25, _____

3. 2, 6, 18, 54, _____

4. 0, 10, 19, 27, 34, 40, _____

5. 49, 64, 81, 100, 121, _____

6. 3, 9, 4, 8, 5, 7, 6, _____

7. 1, 3, 2, 5, 9, 44, _____

Answers: Number Sequence

1. 17 (−2, −3, −4, and so on)
2. 39 (+2, −4, +6, −8, and so on)
3. 162 (multiplying by 3)
4. 45 (+10, +9, +8, +7, and so on)
5. 144 (consecutive perfect squares)
6. 6 (alternate numbers up 1, down 1) (+6, −5, +4, −3, +2, −1)
7. 395 (multiply consecutive numbers and subtract 1)

Adding and Subtracting Fractions

Adding Fractions

To add fractions, you must first change all denominators to their *lowest common denominator* (LCD), the lowest number that can be divided evenly by all the denominators in the problem. When you have all the denominators the same, you may add fractions by simply adding the numerators (the denominator remains the same).

Examples:

$$\frac{3}{8} = \frac{3}{8}$$
$$+\frac{1}{2} = \frac{4}{8}$$
$$\frac{7}{8}$$

One-half is changed to four-eighths.

$$\frac{1}{4} = \frac{3}{12}$$
$$+\frac{1}{3} = \frac{4}{12}$$
$$\frac{7}{12}$$

Change both fractions to LCD of 12.

In the first example, we changed the $\frac{1}{2}$ to $\frac{4}{8}$ because 8 is the lowest common denominator, and then we added the numerators 3 and 4 to get $\frac{7}{8}$. In the second example, we had to change both fractions to get the lowest common denominator of 12, and then we added the numerators to get $\frac{7}{12}$.

Of course, if the denominators are already the same, just add the numerators.

Example:

$$\frac{6}{11}$$
$$+\frac{3}{11}$$
$$\frac{9}{11}$$

Note that fractions may be added across as well.

Example:

$$\frac{3}{8} + \frac{1}{2} = \frac{3}{8} + \frac{4}{8} = \frac{7}{8}$$

Practice: Adding Fractions

1. $\dfrac{1}{4} + \dfrac{3}{8} =$

2. $\dfrac{1}{2}$
$+\dfrac{3}{10}$

3. $\dfrac{7}{8} + \dfrac{3}{10} =$

4. $\dfrac{4}{15}$
$+\dfrac{2}{5}$

Answers: Adding Fractions

1. $\dfrac{1}{4} + \dfrac{3}{8} = \dfrac{2}{8} + \dfrac{3}{8} = \dfrac{5}{8}$

2. $\dfrac{1}{2} + \dfrac{3}{10} = \dfrac{5}{10} + \dfrac{3}{10} = \dfrac{8}{10} = \dfrac{4}{5}$

3. $\dfrac{7}{8} + \dfrac{3}{10} = \dfrac{35}{40} + \dfrac{12}{40} = \dfrac{47}{40}$ or $1\dfrac{7}{40}$

4. $\dfrac{4}{15} + \dfrac{2}{5} = \dfrac{4}{15} + \dfrac{6}{15} = \dfrac{10}{15} = \dfrac{2}{3}$

Adding Positive and Negative Fractions

The rules for signed numbers (pp. 16–18) apply to fractions as well.

Examples:

$$-\dfrac{1}{2} + \dfrac{1}{3} = -\dfrac{3}{6} + \dfrac{2}{6} = -\dfrac{1}{6}$$

$+\dfrac{3}{4} = +\dfrac{9}{12}$
$+-\dfrac{1}{3} = -\dfrac{4}{12}$
$+\dfrac{5}{12}$

Practice: Adding Positive and Negative Fractions

1. $+\dfrac{4}{5}$
$-\dfrac{1}{10}$

2. $-\dfrac{9}{10}$
$+\dfrac{4}{15}$

3. $\left(+\dfrac{3}{4}\right) + \left(-\dfrac{1}{2}\right) =$

4. $\left(-\dfrac{3}{4}\right) + \dfrac{1}{3} + \left(-\dfrac{1}{6}\right) =$

Answers: Adding Positive and Negative Fractions

1.
$$\left(+\frac{4}{5}\right)=\left(+\frac{8}{10}\right)$$
$$\underline{-\frac{1}{10}=-\frac{1}{10}}$$
$$\frac{7}{10}$$

2.
$$\left(-\frac{9}{10}\right)=\left(-\frac{27}{30}\right)$$
$$\underline{\left(+\frac{4}{15}\right)=\left(\frac{8}{30}\right)}$$
$$-\frac{19}{30}$$

3. $+\frac{3}{4}+\left(-\frac{1}{2}\right)=+\frac{3}{4}+\left(-\frac{2}{4}\right)=\frac{1}{4}$

4. $\left(-\frac{3}{4}\right)+\left(\frac{1}{3}\right)+\left(-\frac{1}{6}\right)=\left(-\frac{9}{12}\right)+\left(\frac{4}{12}\right)+\left(-\frac{2}{12}\right)=-\frac{7}{12}$

Subtracting Fractions

To subtract fractions, the same rule (find the LCD) given on p. 31 applies, except that you subtract the numerators.

Examples:

$$\frac{7}{8}=\frac{7}{8}$$
$$\underline{-\frac{1}{4}=-\frac{2}{8}}$$
$$\frac{5}{8}$$

$$\frac{3}{4}=\frac{9}{12}$$
$$\underline{-\frac{1}{3}=-\frac{4}{12}}$$
$$\frac{5}{12}$$

Again, a subtraction problem may be done across as well as down.

Example:

$$+\frac{7}{8}-\left(+\frac{1}{4}\right)=+\frac{7}{8}+\left(-\frac{2}{8}\right)=\frac{5}{8}$$

Practice: Subtracting Fractions

1. $\dfrac{3}{4}$

$-\dfrac{1}{2}$

2. $\dfrac{5}{6}$

$-\dfrac{1}{3}$

3. $\dfrac{3}{8}$

$-\dfrac{1}{9}$

4. $\dfrac{5}{12}-\dfrac{2}{5}$

Answers: Subtracting Fractions

1. $\dfrac{3}{4}=\dfrac{3}{4}$

$-\dfrac{1}{2}=-\dfrac{2}{4}$

$\dfrac{1}{4}$

2. $\dfrac{5}{6}=\dfrac{5}{6}$

$-\dfrac{1}{3}=-\dfrac{2}{6}$

$\dfrac{3}{6}=\dfrac{1}{2}$

3. $\dfrac{3}{8}=\dfrac{27}{72}$

$-\dfrac{1}{9}=-\dfrac{8}{72}$

$\dfrac{19}{72}$

4. $\dfrac{5}{12}-\dfrac{2}{5}=\dfrac{25}{60}-\dfrac{24}{60}=\dfrac{1}{60}$

Subtracting Positive and Negative Fractions

The rule for subtracting signed numbers (p. 18) applies to fractions as well.

Examples:

$+\dfrac{9}{10}=+\dfrac{9}{10}=+\dfrac{9}{10}$

$--\dfrac{1}{5}=++\dfrac{1}{5}=+\dfrac{2}{10}$

$+\dfrac{11}{10}=1\dfrac{1}{10}$

$+\dfrac{2}{3}-\left(-\dfrac{1}{5}\right)=\dfrac{10}{15}-\left(-\dfrac{3}{15}\right)=\dfrac{10}{15}+\dfrac{3}{15}=\dfrac{13}{15}$

$+\dfrac{1}{3}-\dfrac{3}{4}=+\dfrac{4}{12}-\dfrac{9}{12}=+\dfrac{4}{12}+\left(-\dfrac{9}{12}\right)=-\dfrac{5}{12}$

Practice: Subtracting Positive and Negative Fractions

1. $+\dfrac{3}{4}$

$-\dfrac{1}{3}$

2. $+\dfrac{1}{6}-\left(-\dfrac{1}{3}\right)=$

3. $-\dfrac{1}{4}-\left(+\dfrac{2}{3}\right)=$

4. $-\dfrac{7}{12}-\left(+\dfrac{5}{6}\right)=$

Answers: Subtracting Positive and Negative Fractions

1. $+\dfrac{3}{4}=+\dfrac{9}{12}$

$-\dfrac{1}{3}=-\dfrac{4}{12}$

$\phantom{+-\dfrac{1}{3}=}\ +\dfrac{5}{12}$

2. $+\dfrac{1}{6}-\left(-\dfrac{1}{3}\right)=+\dfrac{1}{6}-\left(-\dfrac{2}{6}\right)=+\dfrac{1}{6}+\dfrac{2}{6}=\dfrac{3}{6}=\dfrac{1}{2}$

3. $-\dfrac{1}{4}-\left(+\dfrac{2}{3}\right)=-\dfrac{3}{12}-\left(+\dfrac{8}{12}\right)=-\dfrac{3}{12}+\left(-\dfrac{8}{12}\right)=-\dfrac{11}{12}$

4. $-\dfrac{7}{12}-\left(+\dfrac{5}{6}\right)=-\dfrac{7}{12}-\left(+\dfrac{10}{12}\right)=-\dfrac{7}{12}+\left(-\dfrac{10}{12}\right)=-\dfrac{17}{12}$ or $-1\dfrac{5}{12}$

Adding and Subtracting Mixed Numbers

Adding Mixed Numbers

To add mixed numbers, the same rule (find the LCD) shown on p. 31 applies, but make sure that you always add the whole numbers to get your final answer.

Example:

$2\dfrac{1}{2}=2\dfrac{2}{4}$ ← $\left\{\begin{array}{l}\text{One-half is changed}\\ \text{to two-fourths.}\end{array}\right.$

$+3\dfrac{1}{4}=3\dfrac{1}{4}$

$\phantom{+3\dfrac{1}{4}=}\ 5\dfrac{3}{4}$ $\left\{\begin{array}{l}\text{Remember to add the}\\ \text{whole numbers.}\end{array}\right.$

Sometimes you may end up with a mixed number that includes an improper fraction. In that case, you must change the improper fraction to a mixed number and combine it with the sum of the integers.

Example:

$$2\frac{1}{2} = 2\frac{2}{4}$$

$$+5\frac{3}{4} = 5\frac{3}{4}$$

$$7\frac{5}{4}$$

And since $\frac{5}{4} = 1\frac{1}{4}$, $7\frac{5}{4} = 7 + 1\frac{1}{4} = 8\frac{1}{4}$.

Remember: The rules for adding signed numbers (p. 17) apply for mixed numbers as well.

Practice: Adding Mixed Numbers

1.
$$3\frac{1}{2}$$
$$+1\frac{2}{6}$$

2.
$$4\frac{3}{5}$$
$$+2\frac{1}{10}$$

3. $+4\frac{5}{6} + \left(-2\frac{1}{3}\right) =$

4.
$$-14\frac{3}{4}$$
$$+21\frac{7}{8}$$

Answers: Adding Mixed Numbers

1.
$$3\frac{1}{2} = 3\frac{3}{6}$$
$$+1\frac{2}{6} = +1\frac{2}{6}$$
$$4\frac{5}{6}$$

2.
$$4\frac{3}{5} = 4\frac{6}{10}$$
$$+2\frac{1}{10} = +2\frac{1}{10}$$
$$6\frac{7}{10}$$

3. $+4\frac{5}{6} + \left(-2\frac{1}{3}\right) = +4\frac{5}{6} + \left(-2\frac{2}{6}\right) = +4\frac{5}{6} - 2\frac{2}{6} = 2\frac{3}{6} = 2\frac{1}{2}$

4.
$$-14\frac{3}{4} = -14\frac{6}{8}$$
$$+21\frac{7}{8} = +21\frac{7}{8}$$
$$7\frac{1}{8}$$

Subtracting Mixed Numbers

When you subtract mixed numbers, sometimes you may have to "borrow" from the whole number, just as you sometimes borrow from the next column when subtracting ordinary numbers.

Examples:

$$\begin{array}{r} 6\overset{4}{\cancel{6}}\overset{11}{\cancel{1}} \\ -129 \\ \hline 522 \end{array}$$

$$\begin{array}{r} \overset{3}{\cancel{4}}\overset{\frac{7}{6}}{\cancel{\tfrac{1}{6}}} \\ -2\frac{5}{6} \\ \hline 1\frac{2}{6}=1\frac{1}{3} \end{array}$$

You borrowed 1 from the 10's column.

You borrowed 1 in the form $\frac{6}{6}$ from the 1's column, and added it to the $\frac{1}{6}$ to get $\frac{7}{6}$.

To subtract a mixed number from a whole number, you have to "borrow" from the whole number.

Example:

$$\begin{array}{r} 6 = 5\frac{5}{5} \\ -3\frac{1}{5} = 3\frac{1}{5} \\ \hline 2\frac{4}{5} \end{array}$$

← { Borrow 1 in the form of $\frac{5}{5}$ from the 6.

↙ { Remember to subtract the remaining whole numbers.

Remember that the rules for signed numbers (p. 18) apply here also, and that subtracting can be done across as well as down.

Practice: Subtracting Mixed Numbers

1. $\begin{array}{r} 3\frac{7}{8} \\ -1\frac{2}{8} \\ \hline \end{array}$

2. $4\frac{3}{4} - 1\frac{1}{2} =$

3. $\begin{array}{r} 15\frac{1}{4} \\ -6\frac{1}{2} \\ \hline \end{array}$

4. $24\frac{1}{8} - 16\frac{3}{4} =$

5. $\begin{array}{r} 102\frac{3}{6} \\ --53\frac{1}{2} \\ \hline \end{array}$

6. Sarah needs $22\frac{3}{4}$ yards of fabric for a project. If she currently has $12\frac{2}{3}$ yards of fabric, how much more fabric, in yards, does she need to purchase?

Answers: Subtracting Mixed Numbers

1.

$$3\frac{7}{8}$$
$$-1\frac{2}{8}$$
$$\overline{2\frac{5}{8}}$$

2. $4\frac{3}{4} - 1\frac{1}{2} = 4\frac{3}{4} - 1\frac{2}{4} = 3\frac{1}{4}$

3. $15\frac{1}{4} = 15\frac{1}{4} = 1\cancel{5}\frac{\overset{5}{\cancel{4}}}{\cancel{4}}$

$$-6\frac{1}{2} = -6\frac{2}{4} = -6\frac{2}{4}$$
$$\overline{\phantom{-6\frac{2}{4}=}8\frac{3}{4}}$$

4. $24\frac{1}{8} - 16\frac{3}{4} = 24\frac{1}{8} - 16\frac{6}{8} = 2\cancel{4}\,\overset{3}{}\overset{\frac{9}{8}}{\cancel{\frac{1}{8}}} - 16\frac{6}{8} = 7\frac{3}{8}$

5.
$$102\frac{3}{6} = \quad 102\frac{3}{6} = \quad 102\frac{3}{6}$$
$$--53\frac{1}{2} = --53\frac{3}{6} = +53\frac{3}{6}$$
$$\overline{\phantom{--53\frac{1}{2}=--53\frac{3}{6}=+}155\frac{6}{6} = 156}$$

6.
$$22\frac{3}{4} = 22\frac{9}{12}$$
$$-12\frac{2}{3} = 12\frac{8}{12}$$
$$\overline{\phantom{-12\frac{2}{3}=}\, = 10\frac{1}{12}} \text{ yards of fabric}$$

Multiplying Fractions and Mixed Numbers

Multiplying Fractions

To multiply fractions, simply multiply the numerators, and then multiply the denominators. Simplify to the lowest terms if necessary.

Example:

$$\frac{2}{3} \times \frac{5}{12} = \frac{10}{36} = \frac{5}{18}$$

This answer had to be reduced because it wasn't in lowest terms. You could first have "canceled," which would have eliminated the need to reduce your answer. To cancel, find a number that divides evenly into one numerator and one denominator. In this case, 2 will divide evenly into 2 in the numerator (it goes in one time) and 12 in the denominator (it goes in six times).

Example:

$$\frac{\overset{1}{\cancel{2}}}{3} \times \frac{5}{\underset{6}{\cancel{12}}} = \frac{5}{18}$$

Remember: You may cancel only when multiplying fractions. The rules for multiplying signed numbers hold here, too (p. 19).

Examples:

$$\frac{1}{4} \times \frac{2}{7} = \frac{1}{\overset{}{\underset{2}{4}}} \times \frac{\overset{1}{2}}{7} = \frac{1}{14}$$

$$\left(-\frac{\overset{1}{3}}{\underset{2}{8}} \right) \times \left(-\frac{\overset{1}{4}}{\underset{3}{9}} \right) = \frac{1}{6}$$

Because whole numbers can also be written as fractions ($3 = \frac{3}{1}$, $4 = \frac{4}{1}$, and so on), the problem $3 \times \frac{3}{8}$ would be worked by changing 3 to $\frac{3}{1}$.

Example:

$$3 \times \frac{3}{8} = \frac{3}{1} \times \frac{3}{8} = \frac{9}{8} = 1\frac{1}{8}$$

Practice: Multiplying Fractions

1. $\dfrac{3}{5} \times \dfrac{1}{2} =$

2. $\dfrac{7}{8} \times \dfrac{2}{3} =$

3. $-\dfrac{4}{7} \times \dfrac{14}{3} =$

4. $\dfrac{7}{10} \times \dfrac{5}{6} \times \dfrac{1}{3} =$

5. $7 \times \dfrac{2}{14} =$

Answers: Multiplying Fractions

1. $\dfrac{3}{5} \times \dfrac{1}{2} = \dfrac{3}{10}$

2. $\dfrac{7}{8} \times \dfrac{2}{3} = \dfrac{7}{\underset{4}{8}} \times \dfrac{\overset{1}{2}}{3} = \dfrac{7}{12}$

3. $-\dfrac{4}{7} \times \dfrac{14}{3} = -\dfrac{4}{\underset{1}{7}} \times \dfrac{\overset{2}{14}}{3} = -\dfrac{8}{3} = -2\dfrac{2}{3}$

4. $\dfrac{7}{10} \times \dfrac{5}{6} \times \dfrac{1}{3} = \dfrac{7}{\underset{2}{10}} \times \dfrac{\overset{1}{5}}{6} \times \dfrac{1}{3} = \dfrac{7}{36}$

5. $7 \times \dfrac{2}{14} = \dfrac{\overset{1}{7}}{1} \times \dfrac{2}{\underset{2}{14}} = \dfrac{2}{2} = 1$

Multiplying Mixed Numbers

To multiply mixed numbers, first change any mixed number to an improper fraction, and then multiply as previously shown (p. 19).

Example:

$$3\frac{1}{3} \times 2\frac{1}{4} = \frac{10}{3} \times \frac{9}{4} = \frac{90}{12} = 7\frac{6}{12} = 7\frac{1}{2} \quad \text{or} \quad 3\frac{1}{3} \times 2\frac{1}{4} = \frac{\overset{5}{\cancel{10}}}{\underset{1}{\cancel{3}}} \times \frac{\overset{3}{\cancel{9}}}{\underset{2}{\cancel{4}}} = \frac{15}{2} = 7\frac{1}{2}$$

If the answer is in improper fraction form, change it back to a mixed number and cancel as needed. *Remember:* The rules for multiplication of signed numbers apply here as well (p. 19).

Practice: Multiplying Mixed Numbers

1. $2\frac{1}{2} \times 3\frac{1}{4} =$

2. $3\frac{1}{5} \times 6\frac{1}{2} =$

3. $-5\frac{1}{4} \times 3\frac{3}{7} =$

4. $\left(-4\frac{9}{10}\right) \times \left(-3\frac{3}{7}\right) =$

5. Adlai's writing assignment fills half $\left(\frac{1}{2}\right)$ of a typewritten page. To save space, Adlai changes the font to three-quarters $\left(\frac{3}{4}\right)$ of the original font size. With the new font size, how much space will the writing assignment take up on the page?

Answers: Multiplying Mixed Numbers

1. $2\frac{1}{2} \times 3\frac{1}{4} = \frac{5}{2} \times \frac{13}{4} = \frac{65}{8} = 8\frac{1}{8}$

2. $3\frac{1}{5} \times 6\frac{1}{2} = \frac{16}{5} \times \frac{13}{2} = \frac{\overset{8}{\cancel{16}}}{5} \times \frac{13}{\underset{1}{\cancel{2}}} = \frac{104}{5} = 20\frac{4}{5}$

3. $-5\frac{1}{4} \times 3\frac{3}{7} = -\frac{21}{4} \times \frac{24}{7} = -\frac{\overset{3}{\cancel{21}}}{\underset{1}{\cancel{4}}} \times \frac{\overset{6}{\cancel{24}}}{\underset{1}{\cancel{7}}} = -18$

4. $\left(-4\frac{9}{10}\right) \times \left(-3\frac{3}{7}\right) = \left(-\frac{49}{10}\right) \times \left(-\frac{24}{7}\right) = \left(-\frac{\overset{7}{\cancel{49}}}{\underset{5}{\cancel{10}}}\right) \times \left(-\frac{\overset{12}{\cancel{24}}}{\underset{1}{\cancel{7}}}\right) = \frac{84}{5} = 16\frac{4}{5}$

5. The assignment will take up $\frac{3}{8}$ of the page, $\frac{1}{2} \times \frac{3}{4} = \frac{3}{8}$. A quick check to see if this answer is reasonable will show you that $\frac{3}{8}$ is less than Adlai's $\frac{1}{2}$ of a page before the font was reduced.

Dividing Fractions, Complex Fractions, and Mixed Numbers

Dividing Fractions

To divide fractions, invert (turn upside down) the second fraction (the one "divided by") and multiply. Cancel (if need be) before multiplying.

Examples:

$$\frac{1}{6} \div \frac{1}{5} = \frac{1}{6} \times \frac{5}{1} = \frac{5}{6}$$

$$\frac{1}{6} \div \frac{1}{3} = \frac{1}{\underset{2}{\cancel{6}}} \times \frac{\overset{1}{\cancel{3}}}{1} = \frac{1}{2}$$

Here, too, the rules for division of signed numbers apply (p. 19).

Practice: Dividing Fractions

1. $\dfrac{1}{2} \div \dfrac{1}{3} =$

2. $\dfrac{3}{4} \div \dfrac{1}{2} =$

3. $\dfrac{3}{7} \div \dfrac{3}{14} =$

4. $\dfrac{3}{4} \div \left(-\dfrac{5}{8}\right) =$

5. When Julie, Anya, Kiara, Francesca, and Nicole traveled on vacation, their hotel bill for 5 nights was $750. All of the girls arrived the first night, but Julie only stayed 1 night. Anya and Kiara left after 3 nights. Francesca and Nicole stayed all 5 nights. If the total bill of $750 is divided equally among all five girls based on the number of nights stayed at the hotel, how much will Francesca and Nicole owe at the end of their vacation?

Answers: Dividing Fractions

1. $\dfrac{1}{2} \div \dfrac{1}{3} = \dfrac{1}{2} \times \dfrac{3}{1} = \dfrac{3}{2} = 1\dfrac{1}{2}$

2. $\dfrac{3}{4} \div \dfrac{1}{2} = \dfrac{3}{\underset{2}{\cancel{4}}} \times \dfrac{\overset{1}{\cancel{2}}}{1} = \dfrac{3}{2} = 1\dfrac{1}{2}$

3. $\dfrac{3}{7} \div \dfrac{3}{14} = \dfrac{\overset{1}{\cancel{3}}}{\underset{1}{\cancel{7}}} \times \dfrac{\overset{2}{\cancel{14}}}{\underset{1}{\cancel{3}}} = \dfrac{2}{1} = 2$

4. $\dfrac{3}{4} \div \left(-\dfrac{5}{8}\right) = \dfrac{3}{4} \times \left(-\dfrac{8}{5}\right) = \dfrac{3}{\underset{1}{\cancel{4}}} \times \left(-\dfrac{\overset{2}{\cancel{8}}}{5}\right) = -\dfrac{6}{5} = -1\dfrac{1}{5}$

5. $750 ÷ 5 nights = $150 per night.

Night	Number of Girls in the Room	Cost per Girl
1	5	$150 \times \dfrac{1}{5} = \$30.00$
2	4	$150 \times \dfrac{1}{4} = \$37.50$
3	4	$150 \times \dfrac{1}{4} = \$37.50$
4	2	$150 \times \dfrac{1}{2} = \$75.00$
5	2	$150 \times \dfrac{1}{2} = \$75.00$

Since Francesca and Nicole stayed 5 nights, they each owe $30.00 + $37.50 + $37.50 + $75.00 + $75.00 = $255.00.

Dividing Complex Fractions

Sometimes a division-of-fractions problem may appear in the following form:

$$\frac{\frac{3}{4}}{\frac{7}{8}}$$

These are called *complex fractions*. If so, consider the line separating the two fractions to mean "divided by." Therefore, this problem may be rewritten as

$$\frac{3}{4} \div \frac{7}{8}$$

Now, you can follow the same procedure as shown on p. 41.

$$\frac{3}{4} \div \frac{7}{8} = \frac{3}{\cancel{4}_1} \times \frac{\cancel{8}^2}{7} = \frac{6}{7}$$

Practice: Dividing Complex Fractions

1. $\dfrac{\frac{3}{4}}{\frac{1}{2}}$

2. $\dfrac{\frac{5}{6}}{\frac{1}{3}}$

3. $\dfrac{\frac{1}{2}}{\frac{3}{8}}$

4. $\dfrac{\frac{7}{8}}{\frac{1}{2}}$

Answers: Dividing Complex Fractions

1. $\dfrac{\frac{3}{4}}{\frac{1}{2}} = \frac{3}{4} \div \frac{1}{2} = \frac{3}{\cancel{4}_2} \times \frac{\cancel{2}^1}{1} = \frac{3}{2} = 1\frac{1}{2}$

2. $\dfrac{\frac{5}{6}}{\frac{1}{3}} = \frac{5}{6} \div \frac{1}{3} = \frac{5}{\cancel{6}_2} \times \frac{\cancel{3}^1}{1} = \frac{5}{2} = 2\frac{1}{2}$

3. $\dfrac{\frac{1}{2}}{\frac{3}{8}} = \frac{1}{2} \div \frac{3}{8} = \frac{1}{\cancel{2}_1} \times \frac{\cancel{8}^4}{3} = \frac{4}{3} = 1\frac{1}{3}$

4. $\dfrac{\frac{7}{8}}{\frac{1}{2}} = \frac{7}{8} \div \frac{1}{2} = \frac{7}{\cancel{8}_4} \times \frac{\cancel{2}^1}{1} = \frac{7}{4} = 1\frac{3}{4}$

Dividing Mixed Numbers

To divide mixed numbers, first change them to improper fractions (p. 22), and then follow the rule for dividing fractions (p. 41).

Examples:

$$3\frac{3}{5} \div 2\frac{2}{3} = \frac{18}{5} \div \frac{8}{3} = \frac{\overset{9}{\cancel{18}}}{5} \times \frac{3}{\underset{4}{\cancel{8}}} = \frac{27}{20} = 1\frac{7}{20}$$

$$2\frac{1}{5} \div 3\frac{1}{10} = \frac{11}{5} \div \frac{31}{10} = \frac{11}{\cancel{5}} \times \frac{\overset{2}{\cancel{10}}}{31} = \frac{22}{31}$$

Notice that after you invert and have a multiplication-of-fractions problem, you may then cancel when appropriate.

Practice: Dividing Mixed Numbers

1. $3\frac{1}{2} \div \frac{3}{4} =$

2. $1\frac{1}{6} \div 4\frac{1}{2} =$

3. $\left(-5\frac{4}{5}\right) \div \left(2\frac{1}{2}\right) =$

4. $\left(-3\frac{1}{5}\right) \div \left(-3\frac{1}{3}\right) =$

Answers: Dividing Mixed Numbers

1. $3\frac{1}{2} \div \frac{3}{4} = \frac{7}{2} \div \frac{3}{4} = \frac{7}{\underset{1}{\cancel{2}}} \times \frac{\overset{2}{\cancel{4}}}{3} = \frac{14}{3} = 4\frac{2}{3}$

2. $1\frac{1}{6} \div 4\frac{1}{2} = \frac{7}{6} \div \frac{9}{2} = \frac{7}{\underset{3}{\cancel{6}}} \times \frac{\overset{1}{\cancel{2}}}{9} = \frac{7}{27}$

3. $\left(-5\frac{4}{5}\right) \div \left(2\frac{1}{2}\right) = \left(-\frac{29}{5}\right) \div \frac{5}{2} = \left(-\frac{29}{5}\right) \times \left(\frac{2}{5}\right) = -\frac{58}{25} = -2\frac{8}{25}$

4. $\left(-3\frac{1}{5}\right) \div \left(-3\frac{1}{3}\right) = \left(-\frac{16}{5}\right) \div \left(-\frac{10}{3}\right) = \left(-\frac{\overset{8}{\cancel{16}}}{5}\right) \times \left(-\frac{3}{\underset{5}{\cancel{10}}}\right) = \frac{24}{25}$

Simplifying Fractions and Complex Fractions

If either the numerator or the denominator consists of several numbers (or fractions), these numbers must be combined into one number; reduce the fractions if necessary.

Examples:

$$\frac{28+14}{26+17} = \frac{42}{43}$$

$$\frac{\frac{1}{4}+\frac{1}{2}}{\frac{1}{3}+\frac{1}{4}} = \frac{\frac{1}{4}+\frac{2}{4}}{\frac{4}{12}+\frac{3}{12}} = \frac{\frac{3}{4}}{\frac{7}{12}} = \frac{3}{4} \div \frac{7}{12} = \frac{3}{\underset{1}{\cancel{4}}} \times \frac{\overset{3}{\cancel{12}}}{7} = \frac{9}{7} = 1\frac{2}{7}$$

$$\frac{2+\frac{1}{2}}{3+\frac{1}{4}} = \frac{2\frac{1}{2}}{3\frac{1}{4}} = \frac{\frac{5}{2}}{\frac{13}{4}} = \frac{5}{2} \div \frac{13}{4} = \frac{5}{\cancel{2}} \times \frac{\overset{2}{\cancel{4}}}{13} = \frac{10}{13}$$

$$\frac{3-\frac{3}{4}}{-4+\frac{1}{2}} = \frac{2\frac{1}{4}}{-3\frac{1}{2}} = \frac{\frac{9}{4}}{-\frac{7}{2}} = \frac{9}{4} \div -\frac{7}{2} = \frac{9}{\underset{2}{\cancel{4}}} \times -\frac{\overset{1}{\cancel{2}}}{7} = -\frac{9}{14}$$

$$\frac{1}{1+\frac{1}{1+\frac{1}{4}}} = \frac{1}{1+\frac{1}{\frac{5}{4}}} = \frac{1}{1+\left(1 \div \frac{5}{4}\right)} = \frac{1}{1+\left(1 \times \frac{4}{5}\right)} = \frac{1}{1+\frac{4}{5}} = \frac{1}{1\frac{4}{5}} = \frac{1}{\frac{9}{5}} = 1 \div \frac{9}{5} = \frac{1}{1} \times \frac{5}{9} = \frac{5}{9}$$

Practice: Simplifying Fractions and Complex Fractions

1. $\dfrac{-3-2}{-6+5} =$

3. $\dfrac{2-\frac{7}{8}}{1+\frac{3}{4}} =$

2. $\dfrac{3+\frac{1}{2}}{5+\frac{5}{6}} =$

4. $\dfrac{1+\frac{1}{2+\frac{1}{2}}}{3} =$

Answers: Simplifying Fractions and Complex Fractions

1. $\dfrac{-3-2}{-6+5} = \dfrac{-5}{-1} = 5$

2. $\dfrac{3+\frac{1}{2}}{5+\frac{5}{6}} = \dfrac{3\frac{1}{2}}{5\frac{5}{6}} = \dfrac{7}{2} \div \dfrac{35}{6} = \dfrac{\overset{1}{\cancel{7}}}{\underset{1}{\cancel{2}}} \times \dfrac{\overset{3}{\cancel{6}}}{\underset{5}{\cancel{35}}} = \dfrac{3}{5}$

3. $\dfrac{2-\frac{7}{8}}{1+\frac{3}{4}} = \dfrac{1\frac{1}{8}}{1\frac{3}{4}} = \dfrac{9}{8} \div \dfrac{7}{4} = \dfrac{9}{\underset{2}{\cancel{8}}} \times \dfrac{\overset{1}{\cancel{4}}}{7} = \dfrac{9}{14}$

4. $\dfrac{1+\frac{1}{2+\frac{1}{2}}}{3} = \dfrac{1+\frac{1}{\frac{5}{2}}}{3} = \dfrac{1+\left(1 \div \frac{5}{2}\right)}{3} = \dfrac{1+\left(1 \times \frac{2}{5}\right)}{3} = \dfrac{1+\left(\frac{2}{5}\right)}{3} = \dfrac{1\frac{2}{5}}{3} = \dfrac{\frac{7}{5}}{3} = \dfrac{7}{5} \div \dfrac{3}{1} = \dfrac{7}{5} \times \dfrac{1}{3} = \dfrac{7}{15}$

Decimals

Changing Decimals to Fractions

Fractions may also be written in *decimal* form (decimal fractions) by using a symbol called a *decimal point*. All numbers to the left of the decimal point are whole numbers. All numbers to the right of the decimal point are fractions with denominators of only 10, 100, 1,000, 10,000, and so on. To change decimals to fractions, follow these three steps:

1. Read it: 0.8 (eight-tenths)
2. Write it: $\frac{8}{10}$
3. Simplify it: $\frac{4}{5}$

All rules for signed numbers also apply to decimals.

Examples:

$0.6 = \frac{6}{10} = \frac{3}{5}$

$0.7 = \frac{7}{10}$

$0.07 = \frac{7}{100}$

$0.007 = \frac{7}{1,000}$

$0.0007 = \frac{7}{10,000}$

$0.00007 = \frac{7}{100,000}$

$0.25 = \frac{25}{100} = \frac{1}{4}$

Practice: Changing Decimals to Fractions

Change the decimals to fractions; simplify if necessary.

1. 0.4
2. 0.09
3. 0.75
4. 0.062

Answers: Changing Decimals to Fractions

1. 0.4 (four-tenths) $= \frac{4}{10} = \frac{2}{5}$
2. 0.09 (nine-hundredths) $= \frac{9}{100}$
3. 0.75 (75-hundredths) $= \frac{75}{100} = \frac{3}{4}$
4. 0.062 (62-thousandths) $= \frac{62}{1,000} = \frac{31}{500}$

Adding and Subtracting Decimals

To add or subtract decimals, just line up the decimal points and then add or subtract in the same manner you would add or subtract regular numbers.

Example:

$$23.6 + 1.75 + 300.002 = \quad\begin{array}{r} 23.6 \\ 1.75 \\ +\,300.002 \\ \hline 325.352 \end{array}$$

Adding in zeros can make the problem easier to work.

Examples:

$$\begin{array}{r} 23.600 \\ 1.750 \\ +\,300.002 \\ \hline 325.352 \end{array} \qquad 54.26 - 1.1 = \begin{array}{r} 54.26 \\ -\,1.10 \\ \hline 53.16 \end{array} \qquad 78.9 - 37.43 = \begin{array}{r} \overset{8}{7\!\!8.\cancel{9}{}^{1}0} \\ -\,37.4\,3 \\ \hline 41.4\,7 \end{array}$$

A whole number has an understood decimal point to its right.

Example:

$$17 - 8.43 = \begin{array}{r} \overset{6\;\;\;9}{1\cancel{7}.\cancel{0}{}^{1}0} \\ -\,8.4\,3 \\ \hline 8.5\,7 \end{array}$$

Practice: Adding and Subtracting Decimals

1. $19.6 + 5.02 =$

2. $108 + 71.04 =$

3. $0.16 - 0.043 =$

4. $12 - 0.061 =$

Answers: Adding and Subtracting Decimals

1. 24.62

2. 179.04

3. 0.117

4. 11.939

Multiplying Decimals

To multiply decimals, just multiply as usual. Then count the total number of digits above the line that are to the right of all decimal points. Place your decimal point in your answer so the same number of digits are to the right of the decimal point as there are above the line.

Example:

$$\begin{array}{r} 40.012 \leftarrow 3\text{ digits} \\ \times \quad 3.1 \leftarrow 1\text{ digit} \\ \hline 40012 \\ 120036 \\ \hline 124.0372 \leftarrow 4\text{ digits} \end{array}$$

$\left\{\begin{array}{l} \text{Total of 4 digits above the line} \\ \text{that are to the right of the decimal point.} \end{array}\right.$

$\left\{\begin{array}{l} \text{Decimal point placed so there is} \\ \text{same number of digits to the right} \\ \text{of the decimal point.} \end{array}\right.$

Practice: Multiplying Decimals

1. $\begin{array}{r} 30.1 \\ \times 2.65 \\ \hline \end{array}$

3. $(0.906) \times (-0.1) =$

4. $(-0.012) \times (-0.003) =$

2. $30 \times 9.061 =$

Answers: Multiplying Decimals

1. 79.765

2. 271.83

3. -0.0906

4. 0.000036

Dividing Decimals

Dividing decimals is the same as dividing other numbers, except that if the *divisor* (the number you're dividing by) has a decimal, you need to move it to the right as many places as necessary until it's a whole number. Then move the decimal point in the *dividend* (the number being divided into, which is inside the division sign) the same number of places. Sometimes you may have to add zeros to the dividend.

Examples:

$$1.25\overline{)5.} = 125\overline{)500.} \qquad (4.) \qquad 0.002\overline{)26.} = 2\overline{)26000.} \ (13000.)$$

Practice: Dividing Decimals

1. Divide 8 by 0.4.

2. $0.2\overline{)6.84}$

3. Divide 30.6 by 0.05.

4. $90.804\overline{)181.608}$

Answers: Dividing Decimals

1. 20

2. 34.2

3. 612

4. 2

Changing Fractions to Decimals

To change a fraction to a decimal, simply do what the operation says. In other words, $\dfrac{13}{20}$ means "13 divided by 20" with decimal points and zeros inserted as needed.

Examples:

$$\frac{13}{20} = 20\overline{)13.00} = 0.65 \ (0.65) \qquad \frac{5}{8} = 8\overline{)5.000} = 0.625 \ (0.625)$$

Practice: Changing Fractions to Decimals

Change each fraction to a decimal.

1. $\dfrac{1}{4}$

2. $\dfrac{3}{10}$

3. $\dfrac{3}{8}$

4. $\dfrac{7}{11}$

Answers: Changing Fractions to Decimals

1. 0.25

2. 0.3

3. 0.375

4. 0.6363 . . . (Repeating decimals can also be written as $0.\overline{63}$. The bar over 63 means that the number 63 is continuously repeated.)

Percents

A fraction whose denominator is 100 is called a *percent*. The word "percent" means hundredths (per hundred).

Example:

$$37\% = \frac{37}{100}$$

Changing Decimals to Percents

To change decimals to percents, follow these two steps:

1. Move the decimal point two places to the right.
2. Insert a percent sign.

Examples:

0.75 = 75%

0.05 = 5%

1.85 = 185%

20.3 = 2,030%

0.003 = 0.3%

Practice: Changing Decimals to Percents

Change each decimal to percent.

1. 0.32

2. 0.8

3. 0.006

4. 1.75

Answers: Changing Decimals to Percents

1. 32%

2. 80%

3. 0.6%

4. 175%

Changing Percents to Decimals

To change percents to decimals, follow these two steps:

1. Eliminate the percent sign.
2. Move the decimal point two places to the left (sometimes adding zeros will be necessary).

Examples:

75% = 0.75   5% = 0.05

23% = 0.23   0.2% = 0.002

Practice: Changing Percents to Decimals

Change each percent to a decimal.

1. 25%   **4.** 0.4%

2. 80%   **5.** 300%

3. 2%

Answers: Changing Percents to Decimals

1. 0.25   **4.** 0.004

2. 0.80 or 0.8   **5.** 3.00 or 3

3. 0.02

Changing Fractions to Percents

To change a fraction to a percent, follow these two steps:

1. Convert the fraction to a decimal.
2. Convert the decimal to a percent.

Examples:

$$\frac{1}{2} = 0.5 = 50\%$$ $$\frac{5}{2} = 2.5 = 250\%$$

$$\frac{2}{5} = 0.4 = 40\%$$ $$\frac{1}{20} = 0.05 = 5\%$$

Practice: Changing Fractions to Percents

Change each fraction to a percent.

1. $\dfrac{1}{4}$

2. $\dfrac{3}{8}$

3. $\dfrac{7}{20}$

4. $\dfrac{7}{2}$

5. To construct an erupting volcano science project, a student uses a formula of $2\dfrac{3}{4}$ cups of water, $\dfrac{1}{2}$ of a cup of vinegar, and $\dfrac{1}{8}$ of a cup of baking soda. What percent of baking soda is used in this formula?

Answers: Changing Fractions to Percents

1. 25%

2. $37\dfrac{1}{2}\%$ or 37.5%

3. 35%

4. 350%

5. Step 1: Rewrite the equations as improper fractions with a common denominator.

$$2\dfrac{3}{4} \text{ cups of water} = \dfrac{22}{8}$$

$$\dfrac{1}{2} \text{ cup of vinegar} = \dfrac{4}{8}$$

$$\dfrac{1}{8} \text{ cup of baking soda} = \dfrac{1}{8}$$

$$\dfrac{22}{8} + \dfrac{4}{8} + \dfrac{1}{8} = \dfrac{27}{8} \text{ cups of solution}$$

Step 2: Now, write an equation to find the percent of baking soda. Remember that fractions are:

$$\dfrac{\text{part}}{\text{whole}} : \dfrac{\dfrac{1}{8}}{\dfrac{27}{8}}$$

Simplify the complex fraction:

$$\dfrac{1}{8} \div \dfrac{27}{8} = \dfrac{1}{8} \times \dfrac{8}{27} = \dfrac{1}{27}$$

Step 3: Convert the fraction into a decimal, and then to a percent.

$$1 \div 27 = 0.\overline{037} \approx 0.04 \approx 4\%$$

Approximately 4% of baking soda is used in the formula.

Changing Percents to Fractions

To change a percent to a fraction, follow these steps:

1. Drop the percent sign.
2. Write over 100.
3. Simplify if necessary.

Examples:

$$60\% = \frac{60}{100} = \frac{3}{5} \qquad 230\% = \frac{230}{100} = \frac{23}{10} \qquad 13\% = \frac{13}{100}$$

Practice: Changing Percents to Fractions

Change each percent to a fraction.

1. 30%

2. 5%

3. 125%

4. 19%

Answers: Changing Percents to Fractions

1. $30\% = \frac{30}{100} = \frac{3}{10}$

3. $125\% = \frac{125}{100} = \frac{5}{4} = 1\frac{1}{4}$

2. $5\% = \frac{5}{100} = \frac{1}{20}$

4. $19\% = \frac{19}{100}$

Important Equivalents That Can Save You Time

Memorizing the following can eliminate unnecessary computations:

$$\frac{1}{100} = 0.01 = 1\%$$

$$\frac{3}{5} = \frac{6}{10} = 0.6 = 0.60 = 60\%$$

$$\frac{1}{10} = 0.1 = 10\%$$

$$\frac{7}{10} = 0.7 = 0.70 = 70\%$$

$$\frac{1}{5} = \frac{2}{10} = 0.2 = 0.20 = 20\%$$

$$\frac{4}{5} = \frac{8}{10} = 0.8 = 0.80 = 80\%$$

$$\frac{3}{10} = 0.3 = 0.30 = 30\%$$

$$\frac{9}{10} = 0.9 = 0.90 = 90\%$$

$$\frac{2}{5} = \frac{4}{10} = 0.4 = 0.40 = 40\%$$

$$\frac{1}{4} = \frac{25}{100} = 0.25 = 25\%$$

$$\frac{1}{2} = \frac{5}{10} = 0.5 = 0.50 = 50\%$$

$$\frac{3}{4} = \frac{75}{100} = 0.75 = 75\%$$

$$\frac{1}{3} = 0.33\frac{1}{3} = 33\frac{1}{3}\%$$

$$\frac{1}{6} = 0.16\frac{2}{3} = 16\frac{2}{3}\%$$

$$\frac{2}{3} = 0.66\frac{2}{3} = 66\frac{2}{3}\%$$

$$\frac{5}{6} = 0.83\frac{1}{3} = 83\frac{1}{3}\%$$

$$\frac{1}{8} = 0.125 = 0.12\frac{1}{2} = 12\frac{1}{2}\%$$

$$1 = 1.00 = 100\%$$

$$\frac{3}{8} = 0.375 = 0.37\frac{1}{2} = 37\frac{1}{2}\%$$

$$2 = 2.00 = 200\%$$

$$\frac{5}{8} = 0.625 = 0.62\frac{1}{2} = 62\frac{1}{2}\%$$

$$3\frac{1}{2} = 3.5 = 3.50 = 350\%$$

$$\frac{7}{8} = 0.875 = 0.87\frac{1}{2} = 87\frac{1}{2}\%$$

Finding Percent of a Number

To determine percent of a number, change the percent to a fraction or decimal (whichever is easier for you) and multiply. Remember, the word *of* means multiply.

Examples:

What is 20% of 80?

$$\frac{20}{100} \times 80 = \frac{1,600}{100} = 16 \text{ or } 0.20 \times 80 = 16.00 = 16$$

What is 12% of 50?

$$\frac{12}{100} \times 50 = \frac{600}{100} = 6 \text{ or } 0.12 \times 50 = 6.00 = 6$$

What is $\frac{1}{2}$% of 18?

$$\frac{\frac{1}{2}}{100} \times 18 = \frac{1}{200} \times 18 = \frac{18}{200} = \frac{9}{100} \text{ or } 0.005 \times 18 = 0.09$$

Practice: Finding Percent of a Number

1. What is 10% of 30?

3. What is $\frac{1}{4}$% of 1,000?

2. What is 70% of 20?

4. What is 250% of 12?

Answers: Finding Percent of a Number

1. $(0.10)(30) = 3$

2. $(0.70)(20) = 14$

3. $(0.0025)(1,000) = 2.5$

4. $(2.50)(12) = 30$

Other Applications of Percent

Turn the question word-for-word into an equation. For *what,* substitute the letter x; for *is,* substitute an *equal sign;* for *of,* substitute a *multiplication sign.* Change percents to decimals or fractions, whichever you find easier. Then solve the equation.

Examples:

18 is what percent of 90?

$$18 = x(90)$$
$$\frac{18}{90} = x$$
$$\frac{1}{5} = x$$
$$20\% = x$$

What is 15% of 60?

$$x = \frac{15}{100} \times 60 = \frac{90}{10} = 9$$
$$\text{or}$$
$$0.15(60) = 9$$

10 is 50% of what number?

$$10 = 0.50(x)$$
$$\frac{10}{0.50} = x$$
$$20 = x$$

Practice: Other Applications of Percent

1. 20 is what percent of 80?

2. 15 is 20% of what number?

3. 18 is what percent of 45?

4. What is 65% of 20?

Answers: Other Applications of Percent

1. $20 = x(80)$
$$\frac{20}{80} = x$$
$$\frac{1}{4} = x$$
$$x = 25\%$$

2. $15 = (0.20)x$
$$\frac{15}{0.20} = x$$
$$x = 75$$

3. $18 = x(45)$
$$\frac{18}{45} = x$$
$$\frac{2}{5} = x$$
$$x = 40\%$$

4. $x = (0.65)20$
$$x = 13$$

Percent—Proportion Method

A *proportion* is a statement that says that two values expressed in fraction form are equal. Since $\frac{5}{10}$ and $\frac{4}{8}$ both have values of $\frac{1}{2}$, it can be stated that $\frac{5}{10} = \frac{4}{8}$. In a proportion, the *cross products* (multiplying across the equal sign) always produce equal answers. In the example of $\frac{5}{10} = \frac{4}{8}$, $5 \times 8 = 10 \times 4$.

You can use this cross-products fact in order to solve a proportion. Suppose $\frac{x}{6} = \frac{4}{15}$. Applying the cross-products fact, you get

$$15x = 6 \times 4$$
$$15x = 24$$
$$x = \frac{24}{15} = \frac{8}{5} \text{ or } 1\frac{3}{5} \text{ or } 1.6$$

You can now apply this to percentage problems using the "is/of" method:

$$\frac{\text{percent number}}{100} = \frac{\text{"is" number}}{\text{"of" number}}$$

Example:

30 is what percent of 50?

Because the percent is the unknown, put an x over the 100. The number 30 is next to the word "is," so it goes on top of the next fraction, and 50 is next to the word "of," so it goes on the bottom of the next fraction. You now have the following proportion:

$$\frac{x}{100} = \frac{30}{50}$$

At this point, if you recognize that $\frac{30}{50} = \frac{60}{100}$, then you could quickly arrive at the answer of 60%. If you don't recognize this fact, you can continue using the cross-products approach:

$$50x = 3,000$$
$$x = 60$$

Hence, 30 is 60% of 50.

This method works for the three basic types of percent questions:

- 30 is what percent of 50?
- 30 is 20% of what number?
- What number is 30% of 50? (In this type of percent question, it's probably easier to simply multiply the numbers.)

Practice: Percent—Proportion Method

1. 40 is what percent of 200?

2. What percent of 25 is 10?

3. What number is 15% of 30?

4. 60 is 20% of what number?

5. 70% of what number is 35?

Answers: Percent—Proportion Method

1. $\dfrac{x}{100} = \dfrac{40}{200}$

   $\dfrac{x}{100} = \dfrac{20}{100}$

   $x = 20$

   Answer: 20%

   You don't have to work this problem out mechanically, because you can simplify $\dfrac{40}{200}$ to $\dfrac{20}{100}$.

2. $\dfrac{x}{100} = \dfrac{10}{25}$

   $25x = 1,000$

   $\dfrac{25x}{25} = \dfrac{\overset{40}{1,000}}{25}$

   $x = 40$

   Answer: 40%

   You could solve this problem by observing that $4 \times 25 = 100$, so $\dfrac{40}{100} = \dfrac{10}{25}$.

3. $\dfrac{15}{100} = \dfrac{x}{30}$

   $450 = 100x$

   $\dfrac{450}{100} = \dfrac{100x}{100}$

   $x = 4.5$

   Answer: 4.5

4. $\dfrac{20}{100} = \dfrac{60}{x}$

   $20x = 6,000$

   $\dfrac{20x}{20} = \dfrac{6,000}{20}$

   $x = 300$

   or

   $\dfrac{20}{100} = \dfrac{60}{x}$

   $\dfrac{1}{5} = \dfrac{60}{x}$

   $x = 300$

   Answer: 300

5. $\dfrac{70}{100} = \dfrac{35}{x}$

   $70x = 3,500$

   $\dfrac{70x}{70} = \dfrac{3,500}{70}$

   $x = 50$

   or

   $\dfrac{70}{100} = \dfrac{35}{x}$

   $\dfrac{7}{10} = \dfrac{35}{x}$

   $7x = 350$

   $x = 50$

   Answer: 50

   Again, this problem could be solved by observing that $\dfrac{70}{100}$ can be simplified to $\dfrac{35}{50}$.

Finding Percent Increase or Percent Decrease

To find the *percent change* (increase or decrease), use percent change $= \dfrac{\text{change}}{\text{starting point}}$, and then convert to a percentage.

Examples:

What is the percent decrease of a $500 item on sale for $400?

You know that the starting point is 500 and the change is $500 - 400 = 100$.

So, percent change $= \dfrac{\text{change}}{\text{starting point}} = \dfrac{100}{500} = \dfrac{1}{5} = 0.20 = 20\%$ decrease.

What is the percent increase of Jon's salary if it went from $1,500 a month to $2,000 a month?

You know that the starting point is 1,500 and the change is $2,000 - 1,500 = 500$.

So, percent change $= \dfrac{\text{change}}{\text{starting point}} = \dfrac{500}{1,500} = \dfrac{1}{3} = 33\dfrac{1}{3}\%$ increase.

Note: The terms *percentage rise* and *percentage difference* are the same as *percent change.*

Practice: Finding Percent Increase or Percent Decrease

1. Find the percent decrease from 200 to 180.

2. What is the percent difference between a first month's rent of $750 and a second month's rent of $1,000?

3. What is the percent increase in rainfall from January (2.5 inches) to February (4.0 inches)?

4. What is the percent change from 2,100 to 1,890?

5. Bianca purchased a dress that was originally priced at $90. The dress was reduced 40% and then reduced another 30%. What is the percent change of the original price to the price Bianca paid for the dress?

6. What is the percent increase (in area) if you resize a rectangular photograph from 3 in × 5 in to 5 in × 7 in?

Answers: Finding Percent Increase or Percent Decrease

1. $\dfrac{\text{change}}{\text{starting point}} = \dfrac{20}{200} = \dfrac{1}{10} = 10\%$

2. $\dfrac{\text{change}}{\text{starting point}} = \dfrac{250}{750} = \dfrac{1}{3} = 33\dfrac{1}{3}\%$

3. $\dfrac{\text{change}}{\text{starting point}} = \dfrac{1.5}{2.5} = \dfrac{15}{25} = \dfrac{3}{5} = 60\%$

4. $\dfrac{\text{change}}{\text{starting point}} = \dfrac{210}{2,100} = \dfrac{1}{10} = 10\%$

5. To solve this problem, use one of the following two methods.

Method 1: Longer Method

Step 1: Calculate the first discount by changing the percentage to a decimal. $90 × 40% = $90 × .40 = $36.

Step 2: Deduct the amount of the first discount from the original price. $90 – $36 = $54.

Step 3: Find the second reduction, 30% of $54. $54 × .30 = $16.20.

Step 4: Deduct the second discount from the adjusted price.

$54 – $16.20 = $37.80 (final price of dress)

Now, calculate the percent change from the original price.

$$\frac{\text{change}}{\text{original amount}} = \frac{90 - 37.80}{90} = \frac{52.20}{90} = .58 = 58\%$$

Method 2: Shorter Method

Step 1: Since the dress is on sale for 40% off $90, you can simply find the adjusted price by calculating 60% of the original sales price. Remember to change the percentage to a decimal.

$90 × .60 = $54

Step 2: Calculate 70% of the adjusted price.

$54 × .70 = $37.80 (final price of dress)

Now, calculate the percent change from the original price.

$$\frac{\text{change}}{\text{original amount}} = \frac{90 - 37.80}{90} = \frac{52.20}{90} = .58 = 58\%$$

6. Find the area of both photographs.

Photograph 1: 3 in × 5 in = 15 square inches

Photograph 2: 5 in × 7 in = 35 square inches

35 – 15 = 20 (amount of change)

$$\frac{\text{change}}{\text{original amount}} = \frac{35 - 15}{15} = \frac{20}{15} = 1\frac{1}{3} = 133\frac{1}{3}\%$$

Powers and Exponents

An *exponent* is a positive or negative number or zero placed above and to the right of a quantity. It expresses the power to which the quantity is to be raised or lowered. In 4^3, 3 is the exponent. It shows that 4 is to be used as a factor three times: $4 × 4 × 4$: 4^3 is read as *four to the third power* (or *four cubed*).

Examples:

$$2^4 = 2 \times 2 \times 2 \times 2 = 16$$
$$3^2 = 3 \times 3 = 9$$
$$3^5 = 3 \times 3 \times 3 \times 3 \times 3 = 243$$

Remember that $x^1 = x$ and $x^0 = 1$ when x is any number (other than 0).

Examples:

$$2^1 = 2 \quad 3^1 = 3 \quad 4^1 = 4$$
$$2^0 = 1 \quad 3^0 = 1 \quad 4^0 = 1$$

If the exponent is negative, such as 3^{-2}, then the number and exponent may be dropped under the number 1 in a fraction to remove the negative sign. The number can be simplified as follows:

$$3^{-2} = \frac{1}{3^2} = \frac{1}{9}$$

Examples:

$$2^{-3} = \frac{1}{2^3} = \frac{1}{8} \qquad\qquad 3^{-4} = \frac{1}{3^4} = \frac{1}{81} \qquad\qquad 4^{-2} = \frac{1}{4^2} = \frac{1}{16}$$

Operations with Powers and Exponents

To multiply two numbers with exponents, if the base numbers are the same, simply keep the base number and add the exponents.

Examples:

$$2^3 \times 2^5 = 2^8 \quad (2 \times 2 \times 2) \times (2 \times 2 \times 2 \times 2 \times 2) = 2^8$$
$$3^2 \times 3^4 = 3^6 \quad (3 \times 3) \times (3 \times 3 \times 3 \times 3) = 3^6$$
$$5^4 \times 5^3 = 5^7 \quad (5 \times 5 \times 5 \times 5) \times (5 \times 5 \times 5) = 5^7$$

To divide two numbers with exponents, if the base numbers are the same, simply keep the base number and subtract the second exponent from the first.

Examples:

$$3^4 \div 3^2 = 3^2 \qquad\qquad 4^8 \div 4^5 = 4^3 \qquad\qquad \frac{9^6}{9^2} = 9^4$$

To multiply or divide numbers with exponents, if the base numbers are different, you must simplify each number with an exponent first and then perform the operation.

Examples:

$$3^2 \times 2^2 = 9 \times 4 = 36 \qquad\qquad 6^2 \div 2^3 = 36 \div 8 = 4\frac{4}{8} = 4\frac{1}{2}$$

To add or subtract numbers with exponents, whether the base numbers are the same or different, you must simplify each number with an exponent first and then perform the indicated operation.

Examples:

$$3^2 - 2^3 = 9 - 8 = 1 \qquad\qquad 4^3 + 3^2 = 64 + 9 = 73$$

If a number with an exponent is taken to another power, $(4^2)^3$, simply keep the original base number and multiply the exponents.

Examples:

$$(4^2)^3 = 4^6 \qquad\qquad (3^3)^2 = 3^6$$

Practice: Operations with Powers and Exponents

Simplify, but leave with a number and one exponent when possible:

1. $2^4 \times 2^7 =$
2. $3^6 \times 3^4 =$
3. $5^3 \times 5 =$
4. $2^9 \div 2^4 =$
5. $4^6 \div 4^2 =$
6. $5^2 \div 5^4 =$

7. $4^2 \times 3^3 =$
8. $2^4 \div 3^2 =$
9. $(4^2)^4 =$
10. $(5^3)^5 =$
11. $(3^4)^3 =$
12. $(6^2)^3 =$

Answers: Operations with Powers and Exponents

1. 2^{11}
2. 3^{10}
3. $5^3 \times 5 = 5^3 \times 5^1 = 5^4$
4. 2^5
5. 4^4
6. 5^{-2} or $\dfrac{1}{5^2}$

7. $16 \times 27 = 432$
8. $16 \div 9 = 1\dfrac{7}{9}$
9. 4^8
10. 5^{15}
11. 3^{12}
12. 6^6

Scientific Notation

Very large or very small numbers are sometimes written in *scientific notation*. A number written in scientific notation is a number between 1 and 10 and multiplied by a power of 10.

Examples:

2,100,000 written in scientific notation is 2.1×10^6. Simply place the decimal point to get a number between 1 and 10 and then count the digits to the right of the decimal to get the power of 10.

2.100,000.   Moved 6 digits to the left

0.0000004 written in scientific notation is 4×10^{-7}. Simply place the decimal point to get a number between 1 and 10 and then count the digits from the original decimal point to the new one.

.0000004,   Moved 7 digits to the right

Notice that numbers greater than 1 have positive exponents when expressed in scientific notation, and positive numbers less than 1 have negative exponents when expressed in scientific notation. That is, if a number expressed in scientific notation has a positive exponent, its value is greater than 1, and if it has a negative exponent, it is a positive number but is less than 1.

Practice: Scientific Notation

Change to scientific notation.

1. 35,000

2. 1,112,000,000

3. 0.00047

4. 0.00000000327

Change from scientific notation.

5. 2.6×10^4

6. 3.11×10^7

7. 6.1×10^{-4}

8. 7.22×10^{-6}

Answers: Scientific Notation

1. 3.5×10^4

2. 1.112×10^9

3. 4.7×10^{-4}

4. 3.27×10^{-9}

5. 26,000

6. 31,100,000

7. 0.00061

8. 0.00000722

Multiplication in Scientific Notation

To multiply numbers in scientific notation, simply multiply the numbers together to get the first number and add the powers of 10 to get the second number.

Examples:

$(2 \times 10^2)(3 \times 10^4) =$

$(2 \times 10^2) \, (3 \times 10^4) = 6 \times 10^6$

$(6 \times 10^5)(5 \times 10^7) =$

$(6 \times 10^5) \, (5 \times 10^7) = 30 \times 10^{12}$

The answer must be changed to scientific notation (the first number must be between 1 and 10).
$30 \times 10^{12} = 3.0 \times 10^{13}$

$(4 \times 10^{-4})(2 \times 10^5) =$

$(4 \times 10^{-4}) \, (2 \times 10^5) = 8 \times 10^1$

Practice: Multiplication in Scientific Notation

1. $(3 \times 10^5) \, (2 \times 10^7) =$

2. $(3.5 \times 10^2) \, (2.1 \times 10^4) =$

3. $(5 \times 10^4) \, (9 \times 10^2) =$

4. $(6 \times 10^8) \, (4 \times 10^{-2}) =$

5. $(2 \times 10^2) \, (4 \times 10^4)(5 \times 10^6) =$

6. $(1.6 \times 10^{-3}) \, (4.2 \times 10^{-4}) =$

Answers: Multiplication in Scientific Notation

1. 6×10^{12}

2. 7.35×10^6

3. $45 \times 10^6 = 4.5 \times 10^7$

4. $24 \times 10^6 = 2.4 \times 10^7$

5. $40 \times 10^{12} = 4 \times 10^{13}$

6. 6.72×10^{-7}

Division in Scientific Notation

To divide numbers in scientific notation, simply divide the numbers to get the first number and subtract the powers of 10 to get the second number.

Examples:

$(8 \times 10^5) \div (2 \times 10^2) =$

$(8 \times 10^5) \div (2 \times 10^2) = 4 \times 10^3$

$\dfrac{7 \times 10^9}{4 \times 10^3} = 1.75 \times 10^6$

$(6 \times 10^7) \div (3 \times 10^9) =$

$(6 \times 10^7) \div (3 \times 10^9) = 2 \times 10^{-2}$

$(2 \times 10^4) \div (5 \times 10^2) =$

$(2 \times 10^4) \div (5 \times 10^2) = .4 \times 10^2$

The answer must be changed to scientific notation.

$0.4 \times 10^2 = 4 \times 10^1$

$(8.4 \times 10^5) \div (2.1 \times 10^{-4}) =$

$(8.4 \times 10^5) \div (2.1 \times 10^{-4}) = 4 \times 10^{5-(-4)} = 4 \times 10^9$

Practice: Division in Scientific Notation

1. $(8 \times 10^7) \div (4 \times 10^3) =$

2. $\dfrac{9.3 \times 10^8}{3.1 \times 10^5} =$

3. $(7.5 \times 10^{12}) \div (1.5 \times 10^{15}) =$

4. $(1.2 \times 10^5) \div (4 \times 10^3) =$

5. $(9 \times 10^2) \div (2 \times 10^8) =$

6. $(6 \times 10^4) \div (2 \times 10^{-3}) =$

7. The speed of light is approximately 1.86×10^5 miles per second. If the average distance from Earth to Mars is 1.4×10^8 miles, how many seconds will it take a light shining from Earth to reach Mars?

Answers: Division in Scientific Notation

1. 2×10^4

2. 3×10^3

3. 5×10^{-3}

4. $0.3 \times 10^2 = 3 \times 10^1$

5. 4.5×10^{-6}

6. $3 \times 10^{4-(-3)} = 3 \times 10^7$

7. $(1.4 \times 10^8) \div (1.86 \times 10^5) \approx .753 \times 10^3 \approx 753$ seconds

Squares and Cubes

Two specific types of powers should be noted: *squares* and *cubes*. To *square a number,* just multiply it by itself (the exponent would be 2).

Example:

6 squared (written 6^2) is 6×6, or 36

The square of a whole number is called a *perfect square*. The following is a list of the first 13 perfect squares.

$0^2 = 0$ $5^2 = 25$ $10^2 = 100$

$1^2 = 1$ $6^2 = 36$ $11^2 = 121$

$2^2 = 4$ $7^2 = 49$ $12^2 = 144$

$3^2 = 9$ $8^2 = 64$

$4^2 = 16$ $9^2 = 81$

To *cube a number,* just multiply it by itself twice (the exponent would be 3).

Example:

5 cubed (written 5^3) is $5 \times 5 \times 5$, or 125

The cube of a whole number is called a *perfect cube*. The following is a list of the first eight perfect cubes.

$0^3 = 0$ $3^3 = 27$ $6^3 = 216$

$1^3 = 1$ $4^3 = 64$ $7^3 = 343$

$2^3 = 8$ $5^3 = 125$

Practice: Powers and Exponents

Provide answers without exponents.

1. $5^4 =$

2. $2^5 =$

3. $6^1 =$

4. $7^0 =$

5. $5^{-2} =$

Answers: Powers and Exponents

1. $5^4 = 5 \times 5 \times 5 \times 5 = 625$

2. $2^5 = 2 \times 2 \times 2 \times 2 \times 2 = 32$

3. $6^1 = 6$

4. $7^0 = 1$

5. $5^{-2} = \dfrac{1}{5^2} = \dfrac{1}{25}$

Square Roots and Cube Roots

Note that square roots and cube roots, and operations with them, are often included in algebra sections. The following information will be discussed further in Chapter 2, "Algebra."

Square Roots

To find the *square root* of a number, you need to find a number that, when multiplied by itself, gives you the original number. In other words, to find the square root of 25, you should find the number that, when multiplied by itself, gives you 25. So the square root of 25 is 5, because $5 \times 5 = 25$. The symbol for square root is $\sqrt{}$.

The following is a list of the first 11 perfect (whole number) square roots.

$\sqrt{0} = 0$	$\sqrt{16} = 4$	$\sqrt{64} = 8$
$\sqrt{1} = 1$	$\sqrt{25} = 5$	$\sqrt{81} = 9$
$\sqrt{4} = 2$	$\sqrt{36} = 6$	$\sqrt{100} = 10$
$\sqrt{9} = 3$	$\sqrt{49} = 7$	

Special note: If no sign (or a positive sign) is placed in front of the square root, then a positive answer is required. Only if a negative sign is in front of the square root is a negative answer required. This notation is used on most standardized exams and will be adhered to in this book.

Examples:

$\sqrt{9} = 3$　　　　　　　　　　　　　　　　$-\sqrt{16} = -4$

$-\sqrt{9} = -3$　　　　　　　　　　　　　　$\sqrt{-16}$ is not a real number

$\sqrt{16} = 4$

Cube Roots

To find the *cube root* of a number, you need to find a number that, when multiplied by itself twice, gives you the original number. In other words, to find the cube root of 8, you should find the number that, when multiplied by itself twice, gives you 8. So the cube root of 8 is 2, because $2 \times 2 \times 2 = 8$. Notice that the symbol for cube root is the square root sign with a small three (called the *index*) above and to the left: $\sqrt[3]{}$. Other roots are similarly defined and identified by the index given. (In square root, an index of two is understood and usually not written.)

Following is a list of the first five perfect (whole number) cube roots:

$$\sqrt[3]{0} = 0 \qquad \sqrt[3]{1} = 1 \qquad \sqrt[3]{8} = 2 \qquad \sqrt[3]{27} = 3 \qquad \sqrt[3]{64} = 4$$

Note: The cube root of a negative number is a real number; however, the square root of a negative number is not a real number:

$$\sqrt[3]{-8} = -2, \text{ which is a real number because } (-2)(-2)(-2) = -8$$

Approximating Square Roots

To mentally find the square root of a number that is not an exact square, you need to find an approximate answer by using the procedure explained in the following example.

Example:

Approximate $\sqrt{42}$.

The $\sqrt{42}$ is between $\sqrt{36}$ and $\sqrt{49}$: $\sqrt{36} < \sqrt{42} < \sqrt{49}$.

$\sqrt{36} = 6$ and $\sqrt{49} = 7$

Therefore, $6 < \sqrt{42} < 7$, and since 42 is halfway between 36 and 49, $\sqrt{42}$ is approximately halfway between $\sqrt{36}$ and $\sqrt{49}$. To check, multiply: $6.5 \times 6.5 = 42.25$, or about 42.

Square roots of nonperfect squares can be approximated, looked up in tables, or found by using a calculating device.

$$\sqrt{2} \approx 1.414 \qquad \sqrt{3} \approx 1.732$$

Practice: Approximating Square Roots

1. $\sqrt{22}$

2. $\sqrt{71}$

3. $\sqrt{13}$

4. $\sqrt{\dfrac{400}{24}}$

Answers: Approximating Square Roots

1. 4.7

$\sqrt{16} < \sqrt{22} < \sqrt{25}$ Check: 4.7
$4 < \sqrt{22} < 5$ ×4.7
$4 < 4.7 < 5$ 329
                    188
              $22.09 \approx 22$

2. 8.4

$\sqrt{64} < \sqrt{71} < \sqrt{81}$ Check: 8.4
$8 < \sqrt{71} < 9$ ×8.4
$8 < 8.4 < 9$ 336
                    672
              $70.56 \approx 71$

3. 3.6

$\sqrt{9} < \sqrt{13} < \sqrt{16}$ Check: 3.6
$3 < \sqrt{13} < 4$ ×3.6
$3 < 3.6 < 4$ 216
                    108
              $12.96 \approx 13$

4. 4.1

$\sqrt{\dfrac{400}{24}} \approx \sqrt{16.7}$ Check: 4.1
$\sqrt{16} < \sqrt{16.7} < \sqrt{25}$ −   ×4.1
$4 < \sqrt{16.7} < 5$ 41
$4 < 4.1 < 5$ 164
            $16.81 \approx 16.7$

Simplifying Square Roots

Sometimes you will have to simplify square roots or write them in simplest form. In fractions, $\frac{2}{4}$ can be simplified to $\frac{1}{2}$. In square roots, $\sqrt{32}$ can be simplified to $4\sqrt{2}$. To simplify a square root, first factor the number under the $\sqrt{}$ into a counting number times the largest perfect square number that will divide into the number without leaving a remainder. (Perfect square numbers are 1, 4, 9, 16, 25, 36, 49 . . .). Then take the square root of the perfect square number. Finally, write as a single expression.

Example:

Simplify $\sqrt{32}$.

Factor: $\sqrt{32} = \sqrt{16 \times 2}$

Take the square root of the perfect square number: $\sqrt{16 \times 2} = \sqrt{16} \times \sqrt{2} = 4 \times \sqrt{2}$

Write as a single expression: $4\sqrt{2}$.

Remember that some square roots cannot be simplified, as they are already in simplest form—for example, $\sqrt{7}$, $\sqrt{10}$, or $\sqrt{15}$.

Practice: Simplifying Square Roots

Simplify.

1. $\sqrt{18}$

2. $\sqrt{75}$

3. $\sqrt{96}$

4. $\sqrt{50}$

5. Solve for x: $\sqrt{\sqrt{\sqrt{x}}} = 3$

Answers: Simplifying Square Roots

1. $\sqrt{18} = \sqrt{9 \times 2}$
   $= \sqrt{9} \times \sqrt{2}$
   $= 3 \times \sqrt{2}$
   $= 3\sqrt{2}$

2. $\sqrt{75} = \sqrt{25 \times 3}$
   $= \sqrt{25} \times \sqrt{3}$
   $= 5 \times \sqrt{3}$
   $= 5\sqrt{3}$

3. $\sqrt{96} = \sqrt{16 \times 6}$
   $= \sqrt{16} \times \sqrt{6}$
   $= 4 \times \sqrt{6}$
   $= 4\sqrt{6}$

4. $\sqrt{50} = \sqrt{25 \times 2}$
   $= \sqrt{25} \times \sqrt{2}$
   $= 5 \times \sqrt{2}$
   $= 5\sqrt{2}$

5. $\sqrt{\sqrt{\sqrt{x}}} = 3$. This means that
   $\sqrt{\sqrt{x}} = 9$ (because $3^2 = 9$), and
   $\sqrt{x} = 81$ (because $9^2 = 81$). Therefore,
   $x = 6{,}561$ (because $81^2 = 6{,}561$).

Measures

Measurement Systems

Customary System or English System

Length

12 inches (in) = 1 foot (ft)

3 feet = 1 yard (yd)

36 inches = 1 yard

1,760 yards = 1 mile (mi)

5,280 feet = 1 mile

Area

144 square inches (sq in) = 1 square foot (sq ft)

9 square feet = 1 square yard (sq yd)

Weight

16 ounces (oz) = 1 pound (lb)

2,000 pounds = 1 ton (T)

Capacity

2 cups (c) = 1 pint (pt)

2 pints = 1 quart (qt)

4 quarts = 1 gallon (gal)

4 pecks = 1 bushel

Time

365 days = 1 year

52 weeks = 1 year

10 years = 1 decade

100 years = 1 century

Metric System

Length—meter

Kilometer (km) = 1,000 meters (m)

Hectometer (hm) = 100 meters

Decameter (dam) = 10 meters

10 decimeters (dm) = 1 meter

100 centimeters (cm) = 1 meter

1,000 millimeters (mm) = 1 meter

Volume—liter

1,000 milliliters (ml, or mL) = 1 liter (1, or L)

1,000 liters = 1 kiloliter (kl, or kL)

Mass—gram

1,000 milligrams (mg) = 1 gram (g)

1,000 grams = 1 kilogram (kg)

1,000 kilograms = 1 metric ton (t)

Some approximations

A meter is a little more than a yard.

A kilometer is about 0.6 mile.

A kilogram is about 2.2 pounds.

A liter is slightly more than a quart.

Converting Units of Measure

Examples:

If 36 inches equals 1 yard, then 3 yards equals how many inches?

Intuitively: $3 \times 36 = 108$ inches

By proportion: $\dfrac{\text{yards}}{\text{inches}} : \dfrac{3}{x} = \dfrac{1}{36}$

Remember to set the same units across from each other—inches across from inches, yards across from yards—and then solve:

$$\frac{3}{x} = \frac{1}{36}$$
$$108 = x$$
$$x = 108 \text{ inches}$$

If 2.2 pounds equals 1 kilogram, then 10 pounds equals approximately how many kilograms?

Intuitively: $10 \div 2.2 = 4.5$ kilograms

By proportion: $\dfrac{\text{kilograms}}{\text{pounds}} : \dfrac{1}{2.2} = \dfrac{x}{10}$

$$2.2x = 10$$
$$\frac{2.2x}{2.2} = \frac{10}{2.2}$$
$$x \approx 4.5 \text{ kilograms}$$

How many weeks are there in 3 decades ?

Since 1 decade equals 10 years and 1 year equals 52 weeks, then 3 decades equal 30 years.

30 years × 52 weeks = 1,560 weeks in 30 years or 3 decades

Notice that this was converted step-by-step. It could have been done in one step:

$3 \times 10 \times 52 = 1,560$ weeks

Practice: Simple Conversion

1. If 1,760 yards equal 1 mile, how many yards are in 5 miles?

2. If 1 kilometer equals approximately 0.6 mile, approximately how many kilometers are there in 3 miles?

3. How many cups are in 3 gallons?

4. How many ounces are in 6 pounds?

5. If 1 kilometer equals 1,000 meters and 1 decameter equals 10 meters, how many decameters are in

   (a) 1 kilometer

   (b) 3 kilometers

Answers: Simple Conversion

1. $1,760 \times 5 = 8,800$ yards in 5 miles.

$$\frac{\text{yards}}{\text{miles}} : \frac{x}{5} = \frac{1,760}{1}$$
$$x = 1,760 \times 5$$
$$x = 8,880 \text{ yards}$$

2.
$$\frac{1}{0.6} = \frac{x}{3}$$
$$\frac{\text{kilometers}}{\text{miles}} : \frac{x}{3} = \frac{1}{0.6}$$
$$0.6x = 3$$
$$\frac{0.6x}{0.6} = \frac{3}{0.6}$$
$$x = 5 \text{ kilometers}$$

3. $4 \times 3 \times 2 \times 2 = 48$ cups in 3 gallons.

1 gallon = 4 quarts

Therefore, 3 gallons = 3(4) =12 quarts

1 quart = 4 cups

Therefore, 12 quarts = 12(4) = 48 cups

4. $6 \times 16 = 96$ ounces in 6 pounds.

$$\frac{\text{ounces}}{\text{pounds}} : \frac{x}{6} = \frac{16}{1}$$
$$x = 6 \times 16$$
$$x = 96 \text{ ounces}$$

5. (a) $\dfrac{1}{10} = \dfrac{x}{1,000}$

1 kilometer = 1,000 meters

1 decameter = 10 meters

$$\frac{\text{decameters}}{\text{meters}} : \frac{1}{10} = \frac{x}{1,000}$$
$$10x = 1,000$$
$$\frac{10x}{10} = \frac{1,000}{10}$$
$$x = 100 \text{ decameters}$$

(b) $\dfrac{1}{10} = \dfrac{x}{3,000}$

1 kilometer = 1,000 meters

Therefore, 3 kilometers = 3,000 meters

1 decameter = 10 meters

$$\frac{\text{decameters}}{\text{meters}} : \frac{1}{10} = \frac{x}{3,000}$$
$$10x = 3,000$$
$$\frac{10x}{10} = \frac{3,000}{10}$$
$$x = 300 \text{ decameters}$$

Arithmetic Review Test

Questions

1. The numbers 1, 2, 3, 4, . . . are called _____.

2. The numbers 0, 1, 2, 3, . . . are called _____.

3. The numbers . . . –2, –1, 0, 1, 2, . . . are called _____.

4. Fractions and integers fall into a category called _____.

5. $\sqrt{3}$ and π are examples of _____.

6. A prime number is a number that can be divided evenly only by _____.

7. A composite number is divisible by _____.

8. The first four square numbers greater than zero are _____, _____, _____, _____.

9. The first four cube numbers greater than zero are _____, _____, _____, _____.

10. Give the symbol or symbols for each of the following.

   (a) is equal to _____
   (b) is not equal to _____
   (c) is greater than _____
   (d) is less than _____
   (e) is greater than or equal to _____
   (f) is less than or equal to _____
   (g) is parallel to _____

11. "5 times 4" can be written a number of ways. Name three of them. _____, _____, _____

12. List the properties that are represented by each of the following.

   (a) $3 + 0 = 3$
   (b) $4 \times 1 = 4$
   (c) $3 + 6 = 6 + 3$
   (d) $4 + (6 + 2) = (4 + 6) + 2$
   (e) $3 + (-3) = 0$
   (f) $4(3 + 5) = 4(3) + 4(5)$
   (g) $7 \times \dfrac{1}{7} = 1$
   (h) $6 \times 8 = 8 \times 6$
   (i) $(2 \times 6) \times 3 = 2 \times (6 \times 3)$

13. In the number 543,216, which digit is in the ten-thousands place?

14. Express 367 in expanded notation.

15. $(4 \times 10^2) + (3 \times 10^0) + (2 \times 10^{-2}) =$

16. Simplify $3[5 + 2(3 - 1)]$.

17. Simplify $2 + 3\{2 + 4[6 + 4(2 + 1)]\}$.

18. Simplify $8 + 2 \times 6 + 10^2 + (2 + 3) \times 5$.

19. Round off 7.1779 to the nearest thousandth.

20. Complete the number line below for A, B, C, and D:

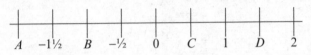

21. $-8 + 5 =$

22. $8 - 17 =$

23. Write a numeric sentence for the following. Jay owes six dollars and borrowed another five dollars.

24. $12 - (-6) =$

25. $\begin{array}{r} -19 \\ \underline{- + 24} \end{array}$

26. $12 - (4 - 7 + 6) =$

27. $(-18)(5) =$

28. $-15 \div -3 =$

29. $0 \div 5 =$

30. $\dfrac{8}{0} =$

31. The number 8,424 is divisible by which numbers between 1 and 10?

32. An improper fraction has _____.

33. Change $\dfrac{17}{3}$ to a mixed number.

34. Change $9\dfrac{1}{4}$ to an improper fraction.

35. Simplify $\dfrac{14}{35}$.

36. Change $\dfrac{1}{4}$ to twelfths.

37. List all the factors of 30.

38. Find the greatest common factor of 18 and 24.

39. List the prime factorization of 320.

40. Find the least common multiple of 6 and 8.

41. $\dfrac{3}{7} + \dfrac{4}{5} =$

42. $-\dfrac{6}{7} + \dfrac{1}{4} =$

43. $\dfrac{5}{8} - \dfrac{1}{3} =$

44. $\dfrac{1}{4} - \dfrac{2}{3} =$

45. $3\dfrac{1}{5} + 4\dfrac{3}{8} =$

46. $-5\dfrac{1}{2} + 4\dfrac{1}{4} =$

47. $6\dfrac{1}{4} - 3\dfrac{3}{5} =$

48. $\dfrac{3}{5} \times \dfrac{25}{36} =$

49. $-\dfrac{1}{6} \times -\dfrac{2}{7} =$

50. $8 \times \dfrac{1}{6} =$

51. $-6\dfrac{1}{2} \times 2\dfrac{4}{13} =$

52. $\dfrac{4}{9} \div \dfrac{5}{8} =$

53. Kaylie is making wreaths out of ribbon to sell at the county fair. She has 30 yards of ribbon and wants to make 15 wreaths. What is the maximum length of ribbon, in feet, that she can use for each wreath if each wreath has to be identical?

54. $\dfrac{\dfrac{3}{4}}{\dfrac{4}{5}}$

55. $4\dfrac{1}{3} \div 3\dfrac{3}{4} =$

56. Simplify $\dfrac{1}{2 + \dfrac{1}{4 + \dfrac{1}{2}}}$.

57. Change 0.35 to a fraction in lowest terms.

58. $4.6 + 3.924 + 1.88 =$

59. $6.009 - 4.11 =$

60. $8.9 \times 0.32 =$

61. $23.44 \div 0.4 =$

62. Change $\dfrac{5}{8}$ to a decimal.

63. Change 0.66 to a fraction in lowest terms.

64. Change 0.6 to a percent.

65. Change 57% to a decimal.

66. Change $\dfrac{7}{25}$ to a percent.

67. Change 78% to a fraction in lowest terms.

68. What is 45% of 30?

69. 15 is what percent of 120?

70. 21 is 30% of what number?

71. What is the percent increase from 120 to 150?

72. Express 360,000 in scientific notation.

73. Express 0.0002 in scientific notation.

74. $(3 \times 10^5)(2 \times 10^7) =$

75. $(7 \times 10^3)(5 \times 10^8) =$

76. $(1.5 \times 10^{-6})(3 \times 10^8) =$

77. $(9 \times 10^8) \div (3 \times 10^3) =$

78. $\dfrac{9 \times 10^2}{5 \times 10^8} =$

79. $(3 \times 10^7) \div (5 \times 10^{-4}) =$

80. $4^3 =$

81. $8^0 =$

82. $5^{-2} =$

83. $7^3 \times 7^5 =$ (with exponent)

84. $5^8 \div 5^3 =$ (with exponent)

85. $8^2 \times 3^2 =$

86. $2^6 - 5^2 =$

87. $(4^3)^2 =$ (with exponent)

88. $\sqrt{64} =$

89. $\sqrt[3]{27} =$

90. $\sqrt{-25} =$

91. $\sqrt[3]{-64} =$

92. Approximate $\sqrt{50}$ to the nearest tenth.

93. Simplify $\sqrt{60}$.

94. What is the sum of the cubes of the first three prime numbers minus the sum of two perfect squares between 25 and 64?

Answers

Page numbers following each answer refer to the review section applicable to the problem type.

1. natural or counting numbers (p. 8)

2. whole numbers (p. 8)

3. integers (p. 8)

4. rational numbers (p. 9)

5. irrational numbers (p. 9)

6. 1 and itself (p. 9)

7. more than just 1 and itself (p. 9)

8. 1, 4, 9, 16 (p. 9)

9. 1, 8, 27, 64 (p. 9)

10. **(a)** =, **(b)** ≠, **(c)** >, **(d)** <, **(e)** ≥, **(f)** ≤, **(g)** ∥ (p. 10)

11. 5×4, $5 \cdot 4$, $5(4)$ (p. 9)

12. **(a)** additive identity (p. 10)

(b) multiplicative identity (pp. 10–11)

(c) commutative property of addition (p. 10)

(d) associative property of addition (p. 10)

(e) additive inverse (p. 10)

(f) distributive property of multiplication and addition (p. 11)

(g) multiplicative inverse (p. 11)

(h) commutative property of multiplication (p. 11)

(i) associative property of multiplication (p. 11)

13. 4 (p. 12)

14. $(3 \times 10^2) + (6 \times 10^1) + (7 \times 10^0)$ (p. 12)

15. 403.02 (p. 12)

16. 27 (p. 13)

17. 224 (p. 13)

18. 145 (p. 14)

19. 7.178 (p. 15)

20. $A = -2$, $B = -1$, $C = \frac{1}{2}$, $D = 1\frac{1}{2}$ (p. 16)

21. -3 (p. 17)

22. -9 (p. 18)

23. $-6 + -5 = -11$ (p. 18)

24. $+18$ (pp. 18–19)

25. -43 (p. 18)

26. 9 (p. 18)

27. -90 (p. 19)

28. 5 (p. 19)

29. 0 (p. 20)

30. undefined (p. 20)

31. 2, 3, 4, 6, 8, 9 (p. 20)

32. a numerator that is larger than or equal to the denominator (p. 22)

33. $5\frac{2}{3}$ (p. 22)

34. $\frac{37}{4}$ (p. 22)

35. $\frac{2}{5}$ (p. 23)

36. $\frac{3}{12}$ (p. 24)

37. 1, 2, 3, 5, 6, 10, 15, 30 (p. 25)

38. 6 (p. 26)

39. $2^6 \times 5$ (p. 26)

40. 24 (p. 28)

41. $\frac{43}{35} = 1\frac{8}{35}$ (p. 31)

42. $-\frac{17}{28}$ (p. 32)

43. $\frac{7}{24}$ (p. 33)

44. $-\frac{5}{12}$ (p. 33)

45. $7\frac{23}{40}$ (p. 35)

46. $-1\frac{1}{4}$ (p. 35)

47. $2\frac{13}{20}$ (p. 37)

48. $\frac{5}{12}$ (p. 38)

49. $\frac{1}{21}$ (p. 38)

50. $\frac{4}{3} = 1\frac{1}{3}$ (p. 38)

51. -15 (p. 39)

52. $\frac{32}{45}$ (p. 41)

53. 6 feet (p. 41)

54. $\frac{15}{16}$ (p. 42)

55. $\frac{52}{45} = 1\frac{7}{45}$ (p. 42)

56. $\frac{9}{20}$ (p. 43)

57. $\frac{7}{20}$ (p. 45)

58. 10.404 (pp. 45–46)

59. 1.899 (p. 46)

60. 2.848 (p. 46)

61. 58.6 (p. 47)

62. 0.625 (p. 47)

63. $\dfrac{33}{50}$ (p. 45)

64. 60% (p. 48)

65. 0.57 (p. 49)

66. 28% (p. 49)

67. $\dfrac{39}{50}$ (p. 51)

68. 13.5 or $13\dfrac{1}{2}$ (p. 52)

69. 12.5% (p. 53)

70. 70 (p. 53)

71. 25% (p. 56)

72. 3.6×10^5 (pp. 59–60)

73. 2×10^{-4} (pp. 59–60)

74. 6×10^{12} (pp. 60–61)

75. $35 \times 10^{11} = 3.5 \times 10^{12}$ (pp. 60–61)

76. 4.5×10^2 (pp. 60–61)

77. 3×10^5 (pp. 61–62)

78. 1.8×10^{-6} (pp. 61–62)

79. $0.6 \times 10^{11} = 6 \times 10^{10}$ (pp. 61–62)

80. 64 (pp. 57–58)

81. 1 (p. 58)

82. $\dfrac{1}{25}$ or $\dfrac{1}{5^2}$ (p. 58)

83. 7^8 (p. 58)

84. 5^5 (p. 58)

85. 576 (p. 58)

86. 39 (p. 58)

87. 4^6 (p. 58)

88. 8 (p. 63)

89. 3 (p. 64)

90. not a real number (p. 64)

91. –4 (p. 64)

92. 7.1 (p. 65)

93. $2\sqrt{15}$ (pp. 65–66)

94. 75. The sum of the cubes of the first three prime numbers ($2^3 = 8$, $3^3 = 27$, $5^3 = 125$) is 160. The two perfect squares between 25 and 64 are 36 and 49; their sum is 49 + 36 = 85. Thus, 160 – 85 = 75. (pp. 9, 64)

Arithmetic Glossary of Terms

additive inverse: The opposite (negative) of the number. Any number plus its additive inverse equals 0.

associative property: Grouping of elements does not make any difference in the outcome. Only true for multiplication and addition.

braces: Grouping symbols used after the use of brackets. Also used to represent a set. { }

brackets: Grouping symbols used after the use of parentheses. [ ]

canceling: In simplifying fractions, divide the common factor into both a numerator and a denominator to make it easier to work with fractions.

closure property: When all answers fall into the original set.

combinations: The total number of possible choices when the order in which they occur does not matter.

common denominator: A number that can be divided evenly by all denominators in the problem.

common factors: Factors that are the same for two or more numbers.

common multiples: Multiples that are the same for two or more numbers.

commutative property: Order of elements does not make any difference in the outcome. Only true for multiplication and addition.

complex fraction: A fraction having a fraction or fractions in the numerator and/or denominator.

composite number: A number divisible by more than just 1 and itself (4, 6, 8, 9, . . .). 0 and 1 are *not* composite numbers.

counting number: *See* **natural (or counting) number.**

cube (of a number): The result when a number is used as factor three times or when the number is raised to the third power.

cube root: The value that when raised to the third power gives the original number. For example, the cube root of 125 is 5. The cube root symbol is $\sqrt[3]{}$, $\sqrt[3]{125} = 5$.

decimal fraction: Fraction with a denominator 10, 100, 1,000, and so on, written using a decimal point—for example, 0.3, 0.275.

decimal point: A point used to distinguish decimal fractions from whole numbers.

denominator: The bottom symbol or number of a fraction.

difference: The result of subtraction.

distributive property: The process of distributing the number on the outside of the parentheses to each number on the inside: $a(b + c) = ab + ac$.

even number: An integer (positive whole numbers, zero, and negative whole numbers) divisible by 2 with no remainder.

expanded notation: Pointing out the place value of each digit in a number by writing the number as the digit times its place value: $342 = (3 \times 10^2) + (4 \times 10^1) + (2 \times 10^0)$.

exponent: A positive or negative number or zero placed above and to the right of a number. Expresses the power to which the quantity is to be raised or lowered.

factor (noun): A number or symbol that divides without a remainder into another number. For example, 6 is a factor of 24, but 7 is not a factor of 24. 4 is a factor of 4. *b* is a factor of 5*ab*.

factor (verb): To find two or more quantities whose product equals the original quantity.

fraction: A symbol expressing part of a whole. Consists of a numerator and a denominator—for example, $\frac{3}{5}$ or $\frac{9}{4}$.

fraction bar: The line that divides the numerator from the denominator.

greatest common factor: The largest factor common to two or more numbers.

hundredth: The second decimal place to the right of the decimal point. For example, 0.08 is eight-hundredths.

identity element for addition: 0. Any number added to 0 gives the original number.

identity element for multiplication: 1. Any number multiplied by 1 gives the original number.

improper fraction: A fraction in which the numerator is greater than or equal to the denominator. For example, $\frac{5}{5}$ and $\frac{3}{2}$ are improper fractions.

integer: A whole number, either positive, negative, or zero.

invert: Turn upside down. If you are asked to invert $\frac{2}{3}$, the result is $\frac{3}{2}$.

irrational number: A number that is not rational (cannot be written as a fraction $\frac{x}{y}$, with x a natural number and y an integer)—for example, $\sqrt{3}$ or π.

least common multiple: The smallest multiple that is common to two or more numbers.

lowest common denominator: The smallest number that can be divided evenly by all denominators in the problem. It is the least common multiple of the denominators.

mixed number: A number containing both a whole number and a fraction—for example, $5\frac{1}{2}$.

multiples: Numbers found by multiplying a number by 1, by 2, by 3, by 4, and so on.

multiplicative inverse: The reciprocal of the number. Any nonzero number multiplied by its multiplicative inverse equals 1.

natural (or counting) number: A counting number: 1, 2, 3, 4, and so on. Zero is not a natural number.

negative number: A number less than zero.

number line: A visual representation of the positive and negative numbers and zero. The line may be thought of as an infinitely long ruler with negative numbers to the left of zero and positive numbers to the right of zero.

number sequence: A sequence of numbers with some pattern. One number follows another in some defined manner.

numerator: The top symbol or number of a fraction.

odd number: An integer (whole number) not divisible evenly by 2.

operation: Any arithmetic process that can be performed with numbers. This includes, but is not limited to, addition, subtraction, multiplication, division, raising to exponents, finding roots, and finding absolute value.

order of operations: The priority given to an operation relative to other operations. For example, multiplication takes precedence (is performed) before addition.

parentheses: Grouping symbols. ( )

percentage: A common fraction with 100 as its denominator. For example, 37% is $\frac{37}{100}$.

place value: The value given a digit by the position of a digit in the number.

positive number: A number greater than zero.

power: A product of equal factors. $4 \times 4 \times 4 = 4^3$, read "four to the third power" or "the third power of four." *Power* and *exponent* are sometimes used interchangeably.

prime factorization: Breaking a nonprime number into its prime factors.

prime number: A number that can be divided by only itself and 1—for example, 2, 3, 5, 7, and so on. 0 and 1 are *not* prime.

product: The result of multiplication.

proper fraction: A fraction in which the numerator is less than the denominator—for example, $\frac{2}{3}$.

proportion: Written as two equal ratios. For example, 5 is to 4 as 10 is to 8, or $\frac{5}{4} = \frac{10}{8}$.

quotient: The result of division.

ratio: A comparison between two numbers or symbols. May be written $x:y$, $\frac{x}{y}$, or x is to y.

rational number: Any value that can be exactly expressed as a fraction $\frac{x}{y}$, with x an integer and y a natural number.

real number: Any rational or irrational number.

reciprocal: The multiplicative inverse of a number. For example, $\frac{2}{3}$ is the reciprocal of $\frac{3}{2}$.

reducing: Changing a fraction into its lowest terms. For example, $\frac{2}{4}$ is reduced to $\frac{1}{2}$.

rounding off: Changing a number to a nearest place value as specified. A method of approximating.

scientific notation: A number between 1 and 10 and multiplied by a power of 10. Used for writing very large or very small numbers—for example, 2.5×10^4.

simplifying: In an equation (or expression) that has multiples of the same term, simplifying is the combining of like terms. Examples: 3 + 4 simplifies to 7; $4x - x$ simplifies to $3x$; and $7 + x + 3x + 9$ simplifies to $4x + 16$. *See also* **reducing.**

square (of a number): The result when a number is used as a factor two times or when the number is raised to the second power.

square root: The number that, when multiplied by itself, gives you the original number. For example, 5 is the square root of 25. Its symbol is $\sqrt{}$; $\sqrt{25} = 5$.

sum: The result of addition.

tenth: The first decimal place to the right of the decimal point. For example, 0.7 is seven-tenths.

whole number: 0, 1, 2, 3, and so on.

Chapter 2

Algebra

Algebra is an area of mathematics where numbers and quantities, called *variables*, are represented by letters and symbols in algebraic expressions and equations. It is built upon your earlier understandings of arithmetic, and the rules that apply to algebra are basically the same as the rules that apply to arithmetic. As you make the transition from arithmetic to algebra, it is essential to have a solid background of the four basic operations: addition, subtraction, multiplication, and division.

Connecting Algebra and the Common Core Standards

This chapter walks you through multiple approaches to learning algebraic concepts aligned with the Common Core Standards. The topics covered provide a foundation for understanding important conceptual categories that interconnect with algebraic reasoning on the Common Core Standards. These topics introduce critical areas that are part of a conceptually larger set of Common Core ideas that ask you to interpret, explain, prove, and make sense of real-life algebraic scenarios. The following table highlights elements of the Common Core Standards that connect to the domain topics covered in this chapter.

Algebra Common Core Connections

Algebraic Relationships and Functions	Understand algebraic terms, use of variables, properties, order of operations, and the structure of algebraic expressions.
	Apply reasoning to solve algebraic equations.
	Explain the relationship between quantities and algebraic equations.
	Explain exponential relationships with expressions of radicals and rational exponents.
	Build a function that models a relationship between two quantities.
	Analyze functions using different representations.
Equations and Inequalities	Solve equations and inequalities with one variable, including equations from linear and quadratic functions.
	Solve equations and inequalities with two or more variables to represent relationships between quantities.
	Write algebraic expressions in equivalent forms to solve problems.
	Perform arithmetic operations on polynomials.
	Solve systems of equations.
Algebra and Descriptive Statistics	Interpret linear algebraic models.
	Solve equations and inequalities graphically.
	Interpret data from one or two categorical and/or quantitative variables on graphs and tables.
Modeling	Interpret algebraic expressions (terms, factors, and coefficients) in terms of their context.
	Use the structure of an algebraic expression to identify how to rewrite it.
	Construct and compare linear, quadratic, and exponential models to solve problems.

Algebra Diagnostic Test

Questions

1. $\{1, 3, 5\} \cap \{1, 2, 3\} =$

2. $\{2, 5\} \cup \{3, 4, 5\} =$

3. True or false: $\{3, 4, 6\} = \{4, 3, 6\}$

4. True or false: $\{8, 9, 10\} \sim \{a, b, c\}$

5. Express algebraically: five increased by three times x.

Question 6 refers to the following information.

Three students scored goals at Franklin High School's hockey game. Dante scored one-half of the total goals, Julian scored one-third of the total goals, and Daley scored one goal. No other player scored a goal.

6. How many total goals were scored for Franklin High School?

7. If $f(x) = x^2 - 3x - 4$, find $f(5)$.

8. Evaluate $\dfrac{x}{3} - \dfrac{x+2y}{y}$ if $x = 2$ and $y = 6$.

9. Solve for x: $2x - 9 = 21$.

10. Solve for y: $\dfrac{4}{7}y + 6 = 18$.

11. Solve for x: $8x - 8 = 4x + 3$.

12. Solve for x: $wx + r = t$.

13. Solve for m: x is to y as a is to m.

14. The fixed production cost to manufacture one ceramic hair blow-dryer is $107. The cost for material and labor is $2 for each ceramic blow-dryer produced. What is the total cost for manufacturing 5,000 blow-dryers?

15. Solve for y: $\dfrac{8}{y} = \dfrac{3}{7}$.

16. The ratio of a 6-year-old boy's head to his entire body length is $\dfrac{1}{6}$. From head to toe, his body measures 42 inches tall. How many inches is the height of his head?

17. If $f(x) = x^2 - 3$ and $g(x) = -2x^2$, find $f(g(-1))$.

18. Solve this system for x and y: $\begin{array}{l} 8x + 2y = 7 \\ 3x - 4y = 5 \end{array}$.

19. $\dfrac{4xy^2z}{-7xy^2z}$

20. $12x + 4x - 23x - (-3x) =$

21. Teagan has 16 coins in her pocket totaling 52¢. The coins are all pennies and dimes. If she subtracts half the number of pennies from the total amount, how much is left?

22. What are three consecutive odd numbers that total 159?

23. $6x^2y(4xy^2) =$

24. $(2x^3y^4)^3 =$

25. $\dfrac{a^7b^3}{a^2b} =$

26. $\dfrac{-5\left(a^3b^2\right)\left(2a^2b^5\right)}{a^4b^3} =$

27. $(4x - 7z) - (3x - 4z) =$

28. $(4x + 2y)(3x - y) =$

29. $\dfrac{16x^2y + 18xy^3}{2xy} =$

30. $(x^2 + 3x - 18) \div (x + 6) =$

31. Factor completely: $8x^3 - 12x^2$.

32. Factor: $16a^2 - 81$.

33. Factor: $x^2 - 2x - 63$.

34. Factor: $3a^2 - 4a + 1$.

35. Factor: $m^2 - 2mn - 3n^2$.

36. Solve for r: $r^2 - 10r = -24$.

37. Solve for x: $x^2 - 49 = 0$.

38. Reduce: $\dfrac{x^2 - 3x + 2}{3x - 6}$.

39. Where does the graph of $y = x^2 - 6x + 8$ cross the x-axis, and where is its vertex located?

For questions 40–46, do the arithmetic and simplify the answers.

40. $\dfrac{x^3}{2y} \times \dfrac{5y^2}{6x} =$

41. $\dfrac{x - 5}{x} \times \dfrac{x + 2}{x^2 - 2x - 15} =$

42. $\dfrac{6x - 3}{2} \div \dfrac{2x - 1}{x} =$

43. $\dfrac{3x - 2}{x + 1} - \dfrac{2x - 1}{x + 1} =$

44. $\dfrac{5}{x} + \dfrac{7}{y} =$

45. $\dfrac{3}{a^3 b^5} + \dfrac{2}{a^4 b^2} =$

46. $\dfrac{2x}{x - 1} - \dfrac{x}{x + 2} =$

47. Solve for x: $2x + 3 < 11$.

48. Solve for x: $3x + 4 \geq 5x - 8$.

49. Graph: $\{x: 2 \leq x < 9\}$.

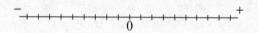

50. Graph: $\{x: -1 < x \leq 6, x \text{ is an integer}\}$.

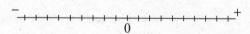

51. $|-5 - 4| =$

52. Solve for x: $|x| = 12$.

53. Solve for x: $|x - 3| = 10$.

54. Give the coordinates represented by points A and B.

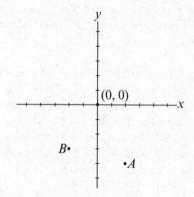

55. Is $x^2 + y = 4$ linear or nonlinear?

56. Graph: $y = x + 2$.

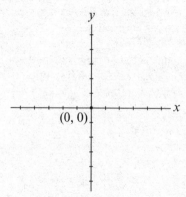

Refer to the answer to Question 56 for the following question.

57. In the graph, if x equals time (t) by the hour and y equals the cost in dollars (d) of electricity for an industrial factory, what would be the electricity cost for a 10-hour work day?

58. Find the slope and y-intercept for the graph of $2x - 3y = 6$.

59. For the equations $6y = jx + 5$ and $-12x + 18y = 5$, find the value of j so that the two lines are parallel.

60. The time (t) it takes to drain a swimming pool varies inversely with the rate (r) of the pump setting. The pump can drain the pool in 2 hours if the pump is programmed to drain at 42 gallons of water per minute. If the rate (r) of the pump is increased to 60 gallons of water per minute, how long will it take to drain the pool?

61. Profits from attendance at the annual school carnival on the first day was $1,523. The total number of people who attended the school carnival on the first day was 203. If adults were charged $10 for admission and children were charged $3.50 for admission, how many children attended the school carnival?

62. Two cars leave the same location and travel in exactly same direction. Car 1 leaves 1 hour before Car 2 and travels at a constant rate (r) of 35 mph, while Car 2 travels at a constant rate (r) of 60 mph. At the time Car 2 overtakes Car 1, how far will each car have traveled?

63. How many gallons of pure alcohol must be added to 3 gallons of 12% alcohol solution to make a 28% alcohol solution?

64. The Vintage Manufacturing Company (VMC) replicates antique lamps. The stained glass lamp is the most popular lamp sold this year, with sales at 1,700 lamps sold per week.

When considering future sales predictions for next year, VMC estimates that stained glass lamp sales will decrease by 30 lamps per week from January through December due to the increased popularity of the Victorian lamp. The sales projection for the new Victorian lamp is 200 per week starting in January, with an additional 20 units to be sold each week from January through December of next year.

In what week of next year will the sales for the antique lamps and Victorian lamps be equal and what is the sales volume for each lamp?

65. Jace deposited $1,000 in a time deposit savings account that will earn 2% interest compounded annually for the next 3 years. How much money will Jace have at the end of 3 years?

66. Simplify: $\sqrt{18 + 2}$.

67. $\sqrt{3} \times \sqrt{12} =$

68. $\sqrt{\dfrac{27}{3}} =$

69. $\sqrt{18} \times \sqrt{2} =$

In questions 70–72, each variable is nonnegative.

70. $\sqrt{36a^2b^8} =$

71. $\sqrt{50a^3b^7} =$

72. $\sqrt{5xy} \times \sqrt{8x^2yz} =$

73. $3\sqrt{2} \times 4\sqrt{5} =$

74. In the binary operation, * is defined for all integers x and y by $x * y = \dfrac{x^2 + y^2}{x^2}$, where $x \neq 0$. What is the value of $3 * -2$?

Answers

Page numbers following each answer refer to the review section applicable to the problem type.

1. $\{1, 3\}$ (p. 86)

2. $\{2, 3, 4, 5\}$ (p. 86)

3. True (p. 86)

4. True (p. 86)

5. $5 + 3x$ (p. 86)

6. 6 (pp. 87–88)

7. $f(5) = 6$ (p. 89)

8. $\dfrac{-10}{6}$ or $\dfrac{-5}{3}$ or $-1\dfrac{2}{3}$ (p. 88)

9. $x = 15$ (p. 90)

10. $y = 21$ (p. 90)

11. $x = \dfrac{11}{4} = 2\dfrac{3}{4}$ (p. 90)

12. $x = \dfrac{t-r}{w}$ (p. 94)

13. $m = \dfrac{ay}{x}$ (p. 96)

14. $545,000 (pp. 87–88)

15. $y = \dfrac{56}{3} = 18\dfrac{2}{3}$ (p. 97)

16. 7 inches (pp. 97–98)

17. 1 (p. 92)

18. $x = 1, y = -\dfrac{1}{2}$ (p. 99)

19. $-3xy^2z$ (p. 112)

20. $-4x$ (p. 112)

21. 46¢ (p. 104)

22. 51, 53, 55 (p. 107)

23. $24x^3y^3$ (p. 113)

24. $8x^9y^{12}$ (p. 113)

25. a^5b^2 (p. 114)

26. $-10ab^4$ (p. 114)

27. $x - 3z$ (p. 115)

28. $12x^2 + 2xy - 2y^2$ (pp. 115–116)

29. $8x + 9y^2$ (p. 117)

30. $x - 3$ (p. 118)

31. $4x^2(2x - 3)$ (p. 122)

32. $(4a - 9)(4a + 9)$ (p. 122)

33. $(x - 9)(x + 7)$ (p. 123)

34. $(3a - 1)(a - 1)$ (p. 123)

35. $(m + n)(m - 3n)$ (p. 123)

36. $\{6, 4\}$ (p. 127)

37. $\{7, -7\}$ (p. 127)

38. $\dfrac{x-1}{3}$ (p. 132)

39. The parabola crosses the x-axis at $(2, 0)$ and $(4, 0)$. The vertex is $(3, -1)$. (p. 147)

40. $\dfrac{5x^2y}{12}$ (p. 133)

41. $\dfrac{x+2}{x(x+3)}$ or $\dfrac{x+2}{x^2+3x}$ (p. 133)

42. $\dfrac{3x}{2}$ (p. 134)

43. $\dfrac{x-1}{x+1}$ (p. 135)

44. $\dfrac{5y+7x}{xy}$ (p. 135)

45. $\dfrac{3a+2b^3}{a^4b^5}$ (p. 135)

46. $\dfrac{x^2+5x}{(x-1)(x+2)}$ (p. 135)

47. $\{x: x < 4\}$ (p. 139)

48. $\{x: x \le 6\}$ (p. 139)

49.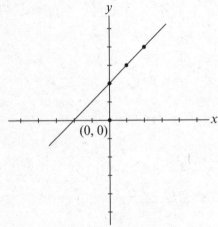

$\cdots$ −2–1 0 1 2 3 4 5 6 7 8 9$\cdots$

  (p. 140)

50.

$\cdots$ −2–1 0 1 2 3 4 5 6 7$\cdots$

  (p. 141)

51. 9 (p. 142)

52. $x = 12$ or $x = -12$ (p. 142)

53. $x - 3 = 10$ or $x - 3 = -10$

    $= 13$ $x = -7$ (p. 142)

54. $A\,(2, -4); B\,(-2, -3)$ (p. 143)

55. Nonlinear (p. 147)

56.

x	y
0	2
1	3
2	4

  (p. 145)

57. \$12 (p. 104)

58. Slope $= \dfrac{2}{3}$; y-intercept is -2 or $(0, -2)$ (p. 154)

59. $j = 4$ (pp. 99, 154)

60. 84 minutes or 1 hour and 24 minutes (p. 104)

61. 78 (p. 99)

62. 84 miles (pp. 104–105)

63. $\dfrac{2}{3}$ gallon (p. 107)

64. 30 weeks and 800 sales for each lamp type (p. 160)

65. \$1,061.21 (p. 108)

66. $\sqrt{20} = 2\sqrt{5}$ (p. 166)

67. $\sqrt{36} = 6$ (p. 163)

68. $\sqrt{9} = 3$ (p. 165)

69. 6 (p. 163)

70. $6ab^4$ (p. 163)

71. $5ab^3\sqrt{2ab}$ (p. 163)

72. $\sqrt{40x^3 y^2 z} = 2xy\sqrt{10xz}$ (p. 167)

73. $12\sqrt{10}$ (p. 167)

74. $\dfrac{13}{9}$ or $1\dfrac{4}{9}$ (pp. 167–168)

Algebra Review

Algebra is essentially arithmetic with some of the numbers replaced by letters. These letters are called *variables*. The variables are merely substitutes for unknown numbers. Initially, algebra referred to equation solving, but now it encompasses the language of algebra and the patterns of reasoning. The rules for algebra are basically the same as the rules for arithmetic.

Some Basic Language

Understood Multiplication

When two or more variables or a number and variable(s) are written next to each other, they are understood to be multiplied. Thus, $8x$ means 8 times x ($x8$ is never written), ab means a times b, and $18ab$ means 18 times a times b.

Parentheses also represent multiplication. Thus, 3(4) means 3 times 4. A raised dot also means multiplication. Thus, $6 \cdot 5$ means 6 times 5.

Caution: Although they may appear in some texts, we recommend that you never use *o*, *e*, or *i* as variables. (Technically, *e* and *i* stand for constants or predetermined numbers, and *o* is too easily confused with zero.) When using *z* or *s*, you may want to write them with a line going through, *z* or *s*, so they are not confused with the numbers 2 or 5, respectively.

Basic Terms in Set Theory

A *set* is a group of objects, numbers, and so on: {1, 2, 3}

An *element* is a member of a set: 3 ∈ {1, 2, 3}. Translation: 3 is an element of the set of 1, 2, 3.

Special Sets

A *subset* is a set within a set: {2, 3} ⊂ {1, 2, 3}. Translation: The set of 2, 3 is a subset of the set of 1, 2, 3.

The *universal set* is the general category set, or the set of all those elements under consideration.

The *empty set,* or *null set,* is a set with no members: or { }

Describing Sets

Rule is a method of naming a set by describing its elements.

> {$x \mid x > 3$, x is a whole number}
> {all students in the class with blue eyes}

Roster is a method of naming a set by listing its members.

> {4, 5, 6 . . . }
> {Fred, Tom, Bob}

Venn diagrams (and Euler circles) are ways of pictorially describing sets:

Types of Sets

Finite sets are countable; they stop: {1, 2, 3, 4}.

Infinite sets are uncountable; they continue forever: {1, 2, 3, . . . }.

Comparing Sets

Equal sets are those that have the exact same members: {1, 2, 3} = {3, 2, 1}.

Equivalent sets are sets that have the same number of members: {1, 2, 3} ~ {a, b, c}.

Operations with Sets

The *union* of two or more sets is all of the members in those sets: {1, 2, 3} ∪ {3, 4, 5} = {1, 2, 3, 4, 5}. Therefore, the union of sets with members 1, 2, 3 and 3, 4, 5 is the set with members 1, 2, 3, 4, 5.

The *intersection* of two or more sets is the set of elements that they share, where they intersect, or overlap: {1, 2, 3} ∩ {3, 4, 5} = {3}. Therefore, the intersection of a set with members 1, 2, 3 and a set with members 3, 4, 5 is a set with only member 3.

Practice: Set Theory

1. True or false: 3 ∈ {prime numbers}

2. True or false: {2, 3, 5} = {3, 2, 5}

3. True or false: {1, 2, 3, 4} ~ {a, b, c, d}

4. True or false: {1, 5} ⊂ {2, 3, 4, 5}

5. {3, 4} ∪ {1, 2, 3} =

6. {6, 7, 8} ∩ {4, 5, 6} =

7. {1, 2, 3} ∩ {4, 5} =

Answers: Set Theory

1. True

2. True

3. True

4. False

5. {1, 2, 3, 4}

6. {6}

7. or { }

Variables and Algebraic Expressions

As noted earlier, a variable is a symbol used to denote any element of a given set. Often a letter is used to stand for a number. Variables are used to change verbal expressions into *algebraic expressions*. For example:

Verbal Expression	Algebraic Expression
the sum of a number and 7	$n + 7$ or $7 + n$
the number diminished by 10	$n - 10$
ten less than a number	$n - 10$ *Note:* Even though the 10 comes first in the word phrase, it comes second in the equation. The phrase "ten less than" or "diminished by" implies that you have to start with a number and then decrease it by 10.
seven times a number	$7n$

Verbal Expression	Algebraic Expression
the product of seven and ten less than a number	$7(n - 10)$ *Note:* When you see the words "the product of . . . and . . .", this may signal the use of parentheses around what follows "and."
x divided by 4	$\dfrac{x}{4}$ or $x \div 4$

Key Words to Look for in Word Problems

The Common Core Standards ask that you conceptualize and interpret mathematical operations in the context of their verbal expressions. Use the list below as a reference for vocabulary that signals a math operation.

Addition

sum	increase
plus	enlarge
more than	rise
greater than	grow
larger than	added to
gain	

Subtraction

difference	decrease
minus	drop
lose	lower
less than	diminish
smaller than	reduce
fewer than	

Multiplication

product	twice
multiplied by	of
times	

Division

quotient	ratio
divided by	half

Practice: Expressing Operations Algebraically

Express each of the following algebraically.

1. a number increased by four

2. five less than a number

3. a number reduced by 12

4. the product of a number and six

5. a number divided by three

6. one-half of a number

7. a number multiplied by 14

8. the ratio of five to a number

9. 12 decreased by four times y

10. the product of five and the sum of x and y

11. five times c, decreased by one-third of b

12. the average of x, y, and z

13. one-third of the difference of a number and five

Answers: Expressing Operations Algebraically

1. $n + 4$ or $4 + n$

2. $n - 5$

3. $n - 12$

4. $6n$

5. $\dfrac{n}{3}$

6. $\left(\dfrac{1}{2}\right)n$ or $\dfrac{n}{2}$

7. $14n$

8. $\dfrac{5}{n}$

9. $12 - 4y$

10. $5(x + y)$ or $(x + y)5$

11. $5c - \dfrac{b}{3}$ or $5c - \left(\dfrac{1}{3}\right)b$

12. $\dfrac{x + y + z}{3}$

13. $\dfrac{1}{3}(x - 5)$

Evaluating Expressions

To evaluate an expression, replace the unknowns with grouping symbols, insert the value for the unknowns, and do the arithmetic.

Examples:

Evaluate $ab + c$ if $a = 5$, $b = 4$, and $c = 3$.
$$(5)(4) + 3 = 20$$
$$= 23$$

Evaluate $2x^2 + 3y + 6$ if $x = 2$ and $y = 9$.
$$2(2)^2 + 3(9) + 6 = 2(4) + 27 + 6$$
$$= 8 + 27 + 6$$
$$= 41$$

Evaluate $-4p^2 + 5q - 7$ if $p = -3$ and $q = -8$.
$$-4(-3)^2 + 5(-8) - 7 = -4(9) + 5(-8) - 7$$
$$= -36 - 40 - 7$$
$$= -76 - 7$$
$$= -83$$

Evaluate $\dfrac{a+c}{5}+\dfrac{a}{b+c}$ if $a = 3$, $b = -2$, and $c = 7$.

$$\frac{(3)+(7)}{5}+\frac{3}{(-2)+(7)}=\frac{10}{5}+\frac{3}{5}$$

$$=\frac{13}{5}$$

$$=2\frac{3}{5}$$

Evaluate $5x^3y^2$ if $x = -2$ and $y = 3$.

$$5(-2)^3(3)^2 = 5(-8)(9)$$

$$=-40(9)$$

$$=-360$$

Use Functions to Evaluate Expressions

Functions are another method to evaluate expressions algebraically, graphically, or in word problems. To solve these types of problems, substitute the function value for x.

Example:

Evaluate $y = x^2 - 2x$ if $x = -2$.

This can also be written as find $f(-2)$ if $f(x) = x^2 - 2x$.

$$f(-2)=(-2)^2-2(-2)$$

$$=4+4$$

$$=8$$

Practice: Evaluating Expressions

1. Evaluate $x^2 + 4x - 7$ if $x = 3$.

2. Evaluate $y^2 - y + 8$ if $y = 5$.

3. Evaluate $7s - 2t^2$ if $s = 3$ and $t = 8$.

4. Evaluate $10m^2 - 5n - 25$ if $m = -6$ and $n = -3$.

5. Evaluate $\dfrac{x}{2}+\dfrac{x+y}{y}$ if $x = 1$ and $y = 4$.

6. Evaluate $3x^2y^3z$ if $x = 2$, $y = 3$, and $z = -1$.

Answers: Evaluating Expressions

1. $(3)^2 + 4(3) - 7 = 9 + 12 - 7$

$$=21-7$$

$$=14$$

2. $(5)^2 - 5 + 8 = 25 - 5 + 8$

$$=20+8$$

$$=28$$

3. $7(3) - 2(8)^2 = 7(3) - 2(64)$

$$=21-128$$

$$=-107$$

4. $10(-6)^2 - 5(-3) - 25 = 10(36) + 15 - 25$

$$=360+15-25$$

$$=375-25$$

$$=350$$

5. $\dfrac{1}{2}+\dfrac{1+4}{4}=\dfrac{2}{4}+\dfrac{5}{4}$ (finding common denominator)

$$=\frac{7}{4}$$

$$=1\frac{3}{4}$$

6. $3(2)^2(3)^3(-1) = 3(4)(27)(-1)$

$$=12(27)(-1)$$

$$=324(-1)$$

$$=-324$$

Equations and Functions

Solving Equations

An *equation* is a mathematical sentence, a relationship between numbers and/or symbols. Remember that an equation is like a balance scale, with the equal sign (=) being the fulcrum or center. Thus, if you do the *same thing to both sides* of the equal sign (say, add 5 to each side), the equation will still be balanced.

Example:

Solve for x: $x - 5 = 23$.

To solve the equation $x - 5 = 23$, you must get x by itself on one side; therefore, add 5 to both sides:

$$\begin{array}{r} x - 5 = 23 \\ \underline{+5 \quad +5} \\ x \quad\;\; = 28 \end{array}$$

In the same manner, you may subtract, multiply, or divide *both* sides of an equation by the same (nonzero) number, and the equation will not change. Sometimes you may have to use more than one step to solve for an unknown.

Examples:

Solve for x: $3x + 4 = 19$.

Subtract 4 from both sides to get the $3x$ by itself on one side:

$$\begin{array}{r} 3x + 4 = 19 \\ \underline{-4 \quad -4} \\ 3x \quad\;\; = 15 \end{array}$$

Then divide both sides by 3 to get x:

$$\frac{3x}{3} = \frac{15}{3}$$
$$x = 5$$

Remember: Solving an equation is using opposite operations until the letter is on a side by itself (for addition, subtract; for multiplication, divide; and so on).

To check, substitute your answer into the original equation.

$$3x + 4 = 19$$
$$3(5) + 4 = 19$$
$$15 + 4 = 19$$
$$19 = 19$$

Solve for x: $\dfrac{x}{5} - 4 = 2$.

Add 4 to both sides:

$$\dfrac{x}{5} - 4 = 2$$
$$\underline{+4 \quad +4}$$
$$\dfrac{x}{5} \quad = 6$$

Multiply both sides by 5 to get x:

$$(5)\dfrac{x}{5} = (5)6$$
$$x = 30$$

Solve for x: $\dfrac{3}{5}x - 6 = 12$.

Add 6 to each side:

$$\dfrac{3}{5}x - 6 = 12$$
$$\underline{+6 \quad +6}$$
$$\dfrac{3}{5}x \quad = 18$$

Multiply each side by $\dfrac{5}{3}$.

$$\left(\dfrac{5}{3}\right)\dfrac{3}{5}x = \left(\dfrac{5}{3}\right)18$$
$$x = \left(\dfrac{5}{\cancel{3}_1}\right)\dfrac{\cancel{18}^{6}}{1}$$
$$x = 30$$

Solve for x: $5x = 2x - 6$.
Add $-2x$ to each side:

$$5x = 2x - 6$$
$$\underline{-2x \quad -2x}$$
$$3x = \quad -6$$

Divide both sides by 3:

$$\dfrac{3x}{3} = \dfrac{-6}{3}$$
$$x = -2$$

Solve for x: $6x + 3 = 4x + 5$.

Add -3 to each side:

$$\begin{array}{r} 6x + 3 = 4x + 5 \\ \underline{-3 \qquad -3} \\ 6x \quad = 4x + 2 \end{array}$$

Add $-4x$ to each side:

$$\begin{array}{r} 6x = 4x + 2 \\ \underline{-4x - 4x} \\ 2x = \quad 2 \end{array}$$

Divide each side by 2:

$$\frac{2x}{2} = \frac{2}{2}$$
$$x = 1$$

Solving Functions

The Common Core Standards call attention to understanding the concept of a function and using function notation. Remember that functions are just another method to interpret algebraic expressions using different representations.

Examples:

Evaluate $f(x) = \dfrac{4^x}{3}$ if $x = 2$.

$$f(2) = \frac{4^2}{3} = \frac{16}{3} \text{ or } 5\frac{1}{3}$$

Evaluate $f(7) - g(-2)$ if $f(x) = 2x$ and $g(x) = 2x^2$.

$$f(7) = 2(7) = 14$$

$$g(-2) = 2(-2)^2 = 2 \times 4 = 8$$

$$f(7) - g(-2) = 14 - 8 = 6$$

Evaluate $f(g(8))$ if $f(x) = 2x$ and $g(x) = 2x^2$.

First, solve for $g(8)$.

Then, insert your answer into the function f and multiply.

$$g(8) = 2(8)^2 = 128$$
$$f(128) = 2(128) = 256$$
$$f(g(8)) = 256$$

Practice: Solving Equations and Functions

For questions 1–8, solve each equation for y.

1. $y + 8 = 19$

2. $y - 9 = 21$

3. $4y + 8 = 32$

4. $-\dfrac{y}{5} = 8$

5. $-\dfrac{2}{3}y + 1 = 13$

6. $4y = 52$

7. $7y = 4y - 12$

8. $5y - 4 = 3y + 4$

9. Find $f(4)$ if $f(x) = \dfrac{x^2 - 2x}{-2}$.

10. Evaluate $g(2) \cdot f[f(-2)]$ for $f(x) = -2x + 3$ and $g(x) = \dfrac{x^3}{2}$.

Answers: Solving Equations and Functions

1.
$$y + 8 = 19$$
$$\underline{-8 \quad -8}$$
$$y \quad = 11$$

2.
$$y - 9 = 21$$
$$\underline{+9 \quad +9}$$
$$y \quad = 30$$

3.
$$4y + 8 = 32$$
$$\underline{-8 \quad -8}$$
$$4y \quad = 24$$
$$\frac{4y}{4} = \frac{24}{4}$$
$$y = 6$$

4.
$$-\frac{y}{5} = 8$$
$$\left(\frac{-\cancel{5}}{1}\right)\left(-\frac{y}{\cancel{5}}\right) = 8(-5)$$
$$y = -40$$

5.
$$-\frac{2}{3}y + 1 = 13$$
$$\underline{-1 \quad -1}$$
$$-\frac{2}{3}y \quad = 12$$
$$\left(-\frac{3}{2}\right)\left(-\frac{2}{3}\right)y = 12\left(-\frac{3}{2}\right)$$
$$y = -18$$

6.
$$\frac{4y}{4} = \frac{52}{4}$$
$$y = 13$$

7.
$$7y = 4y - 12$$
$$\underline{-4y \quad -4y}$$
$$3y = \quad -12$$
$$\frac{3y}{3} = \frac{-12}{3}$$
$$y = -4$$

8.
$$5y - 4 = 3y + 4$$
$$\underline{+4 = \qquad +4}$$
$$5y \quad = 3y + 8$$

$$5y - 4 = 3y + 4$$
$$\underline{-3y \qquad = -3y}$$
$$2y \quad = \quad 8$$

$$\frac{2y}{2} = \frac{8}{2}$$
$$y = 4$$

9. $f(4) = \dfrac{x^2 - 2x}{-2}$

$$f(4) = \frac{(4)^2 - 2(4)}{-2}$$

$$f(4) = \frac{16 - 8}{-2}$$

$$f(4) = \frac{8}{-2}$$

$$f(4) = -4$$

10. First, find $g(x) = \dfrac{x^3}{2}$ when $x = 2$.

$$g(2) = \frac{2^3}{2}$$

$$g(2) = \frac{8}{2}$$

$$g(2) = 4$$

Next, just like other math problem calculations, simplify the innermost parentheses first.

$$f(-2) = -2x + 3$$
$$f(-2) = -2(-2) + 3$$
$$f(-2) = 7$$

Now that the function $f(-2) = 7$ is solved, substitute into $f[f(-2)]$, which becomes $f(7)$.

$$f(7) = -2x + 3$$
$$f(7) = -2(7) + 3$$
$$f(7) = -14 + 3 = -11$$

Now put it all together:

$$g(2) \cdot f[f(-2)] = -4 \cdot (-11) = -44$$

Literal Equations

Literal equations have no numbers, only symbols (letters).

Examples:

Solve for Q: $QP - X = Y$.

First add X to both sides.

$$QP - X = Y$$
$$\underline{+X = \quad +X}$$
$$QP \quad = Y + X$$

Then divide both sides by P:

$$\frac{QP}{P} = \frac{Y + X}{P}$$

$$Q = \frac{Y + X}{P}$$

Operations opposite to those in the original equation were used to isolate Q. To remove the $-X$, we *added* a $+X$ to both sides of the equation; since we had Q times P, we *divided* both sides by P.

Solve for y: $\dfrac{y}{x} = c$.

Multiply both sides by x to get y on one side of the equal sign:

$$(x)\frac{y}{x} = (x)c$$
$$y = xc$$

Solve for x: $\dfrac{b}{x} = \dfrac{p}{q}$.

To solve this equation quickly, you cross multiply. To cross multiply, bring the denominators up next to the opposite side numerators and multiply:

$$\frac{b}{x} = \frac{p}{q}$$
$$bq = px$$

Then divide both sides by p to get x by itself:

$$\frac{bq}{p} = \frac{px}{p}$$
$$\frac{bq}{p} = x \quad \text{or} \quad x = \frac{bq}{p}$$

Cross multiplying can be used only when the format is two fractions separated by an equal sign.

Example:

Solve for c: $\dfrac{g}{m} = \dfrac{k}{c}$.

Cross multiply:

$$gc = mk$$

Divide both sides by g:

$$\frac{gc}{g} = \frac{mk}{g}$$

Thus,

$$c = \frac{mk}{g}$$

Be aware that cross multiplying is most effective only when the letter you are solving for is on the bottom (the *denominator*) of a fraction. If it is on top (the *numerator*), it's easier simply to clear the denominator under the unknown you're solving for.

Example:

Solve for x: $\dfrac{x}{k} = \dfrac{p}{q}$.

Multiply both sides by k:

$$(k)\dfrac{x}{k} = (k)\dfrac{p}{q}$$

$$x = \dfrac{kp}{q}$$

In the previous problem, there was no need to cross multiply.

Practice: Literal Equations

1. Solve for z: $\dfrac{b}{z} = \dfrac{d}{e}$.

2. Solve for q: $\dfrac{m}{n} = \dfrac{r}{q}$.

3. Solve for c: $\dfrac{a}{b} = \dfrac{c}{d}$.

4. Solve for c: $\dfrac{d}{x} = \dfrac{y}{c}$.

Answers: Literal Equations

1. $\dfrac{b}{z} = \dfrac{d}{e}$

$be = dz$

$\dfrac{be}{d} = \dfrac{dz}{d}$

$\dfrac{be}{d} = z$

2. $\dfrac{m}{n} = \dfrac{r}{q}$

$mq = nr$

$\dfrac{mq}{m} = \dfrac{nr}{m}$

$q = \dfrac{nr}{m}$

3. $\dfrac{a}{b} = \dfrac{c}{d}$

$(d)\dfrac{a}{b} = (d)\dfrac{c}{d}$

$\dfrac{ad}{b} = c$

4. $\dfrac{d}{x} = \dfrac{y}{c}$

$dc = yx$

$\dfrac{dc}{d} = \dfrac{yx}{d}$

$c = \dfrac{yx}{d}$

Ratios and Proportions

A *ratio* is a method of comparing two or more numbers or variables. Ratios are written as $a{:}b$ or in working form as a fraction, $\dfrac{a}{b}$, and are read as "a is to b." Notice that whatever comes after the "to" goes second or at the bottom of the fraction.

Proportions are written as two ratios (fractions) equal to each other: $\dfrac{a}{b} = \dfrac{c}{d}$.

Examples:

Solve this proportion for x: p is to q as x is to y. First, the proportion may be rewritten:

$$\frac{p}{q} = \frac{x}{y}$$

Multiply both sides by y:

$$(y)\frac{p}{q} = (y)\frac{x}{y}$$

$$\frac{yp}{q} = x$$

Solve this proportion for t: s is to t as r is to q. Rewrite:

$$\frac{s}{t} = \frac{r}{q}$$

Cross multiply:

$$sq = rt$$

Divide both sides by r:

$$\frac{sq}{r} = \frac{rt}{r}$$

$$\frac{sq}{r} = t$$

Practice: Ratios and Proportions

1. Solve for p: c is to p as g is to h.

2. Solve for s: t is to q as z is to s.

3. Solve for h: l is to k as h is to d.

4. Solve for b: a is to b as c is to d.

Answers: Ratios and Proportions

1.
$$\frac{c}{p} = \frac{g}{h}$$
$$ch = pg$$
$$\frac{ch}{g} = \frac{pg}{g}$$
$$\frac{ch}{g} = p$$

2.
$$\frac{t}{q} = \frac{z}{s}$$
$$ts = qz$$
$$\frac{ts}{t} = \frac{qz}{t}$$
$$s = \frac{qz}{t}$$

3.
$$\frac{l}{k} = \frac{h}{d}$$
$$(d)\frac{l}{k} = (d)\frac{h}{d}$$
$$\frac{dl}{k} = h$$

4.
$$\frac{a}{b} = \frac{c}{d}$$
$$ad = bc$$
$$\frac{ad}{c} = \frac{bc}{c}$$
$$\frac{ad}{c} = b$$

Solving Proportions for Value

Use the same rules as for ratios. When solving a portion for a value, start by cross multiplying the fraction then solve the remaining equation.

Example:

Solve for x: $\dfrac{4}{x} = \dfrac{2}{5}$.

Cross multiply:

$$(4)(5) = 2x$$
$$20 = 2x$$

Divide both sides by 2:

$$\dfrac{20}{2} = \dfrac{2x}{2}$$
$$10 = x$$

In word problems, the numerator represents one type of unit (as in pages or days) and the denominator represents the other type of unit.

Example:

In a random sample inspection of 630 manufactured cell phones, an average of five cell phones were defective. The cell phone company produces 3,528 cell phones per month. If the rate in the number of manufactured defective cell phones remains constant, how many cell phones are expected to be defective per month?

$$\dfrac{\text{defective cell phones}}{\text{total manufactured cell phones}}$$

$$\dfrac{5}{630} = \dfrac{x}{3,528}$$

Cross multiply:

$$630x = 17,640$$
$$x = 28$$

Practice: Solving Proportions for Value

Solve for the unknown.

1. $\dfrac{3}{k} = \dfrac{1}{11}$

2. $\dfrac{2}{5} = \dfrac{8}{R}$

3. $\dfrac{14}{5} = \dfrac{7}{t}$

4. $\dfrac{15}{2} = \dfrac{25}{t}$

5. The brightness (luminosity) of a star is proportional to its surface area. The surface area of Star 1 has a ratio to the surface area of Star 2 that equals $\dfrac{1}{3}$. If Star 1 emits 600 photons per minute (photons measure luminosity), how many photons will Star 2 emit per minute?

6. Eric has one dog, Greta, who weighs 31 pounds and eats 3 cups of dog food per day. Eric adopted a second dog, Charley, who weighs 50 pounds. Assuming that both dogs will eat in proportion to their weight, how many combined cups of dog food per day will the dogs eat (rounded to the nearest cup)?

Answers: Solving Proportions for Value

1. $\dfrac{3}{k} = \dfrac{1}{11}$

$33 = 1k$ or $33 = k$

2. $\dfrac{2}{5} = \dfrac{8}{R}$

$2R = 40$

$\dfrac{2R}{2} = \dfrac{40}{2}$

$R = 20$

Note that this problem could have been done intuitively if you noticed that the second ratio (fraction) is four times the first:

Intuitively: $2 \times 4 = 8$

$5 \times 4 = 20$

3. $\dfrac{14}{5} = \dfrac{7}{t}$

$14t = 35$

$\dfrac{14t}{14} = \dfrac{35}{14}$

$t = \dfrac{35}{14} = 2\dfrac{7}{14} = 2\dfrac{1}{2}$

Intuitively: $14 \div 2 = 7$

$5 \div 2 = 2\dfrac{1}{2}$

4. $\dfrac{15}{2} = \dfrac{25}{t}$

$15t = 50$

$\dfrac{15t}{15} = \dfrac{50}{15}$

$t = \dfrac{50}{15} = 3\dfrac{5}{15} = 3\dfrac{1}{3}$

5. Set up the ratio to solve for x.

$$\dfrac{\text{Star 1}}{\text{Star 2}} = \dfrac{1}{3}$$

Star 1 emits 600 photons, which is the numerator, and the unknown variable (x) is the denominator.

Cross multiply:

$$\dfrac{1}{3} = \dfrac{600}{x}$$

$$x = 1{,}800$$

Star 2 will emit 1,800 photons per minute.

6. Write down what is known in a proportion to solve for x.

$$\dfrac{\text{dog's weight}}{\text{amount of dog food (cups)}}$$

$\text{Greta} = \dfrac{31 \text{ pounds}}{3 \text{ cups}}$ and $\text{Charley} = \dfrac{50 \text{ pounds}}{x}$

Cross multiply:

$$\dfrac{31}{3} = \dfrac{50}{x}$$

$$150 = 31x$$

$$x \approx 4.8$$

Charley eats 4.8 cups of dog food per day, but you must perform one more step to solve the question "how many *combined cups* of dog food per day will the dogs eat?" Round 4.8 to 5 cups.

Greta = 3 cups per day

Charley = 5 cups per day

The combined amount of dog food per day is $3 + 5 = 8$ cups.

Solving Systems of Equations for Two Unknowns

If you solve two equations with the same two unknowns in each, you can solve for both unknowns. One method is as follows:

1. Multiply one or both equations by some number to make the number in front of one of the letters (unknowns) the same in each equation.

2. Add or subtract the two equations to eliminate one letter.

3. Solve for the other unknown.

4. Insert the value of the first unknown into one of the original equations to solve for the second unknown.

When working with a system of linear equations, there are three possible types (*system* just means two or more equations [or lines]):

- **One solution.** Solving the equations will yield an intersecting *point* (a value for x and a value for y). If you graphically plot the equations instead of solving them, this is the point where the two lines cross.

- **Infinitely many solutions.** The point of the intersection is called the *solution*. The solution will provide values equal to each other, such as $3 = 3$ or $-27 = -27$. In this scenario, the lines are the same. By graphing these equations, you can see that there is only one line.

- **No solution.** A false solution is shown graphically as parallel lines. An example is $3 = 15$. The graph for these solutions shows that the lines are parallel and will never intersect.

Example:

Solve for x and y: $\begin{array}{l} 3x + 3y = 24 \\ 2x + y = 13 \end{array}$.

First multiply the bottom equation by 3. Now, the y is preceded by a 3 in each equation:

$$3x + 3y = 24 \qquad 3x + 3y = 24$$
$$3(2x) + 3(y) = 3(13) \quad 6x + 3y = 39$$

Now you can subtract equations, eliminating the y terms, and solve for x:

$$\begin{array}{r} 3x + 3y = 24 \\ -6x + -3y = -39 \\ \hline -3x \qquad = -15 \end{array}$$

$$\frac{-3x}{-3} = \frac{-15}{-3}$$

$$x = 5$$

Insert $x = 5$ into one of the original equations to solve for y:

$$2x + y = 13$$
$$2(5) + y = 13$$

$$10 + y = 13$$
$$\begin{array}{r} -10 \qquad -10 \\ \hline y = \quad 3 \end{array}$$

Answer: $x = 5$, $y = 3$

Of course, if the number in front of a letter is already the same in each equation, you don't have to change either equation. Simply add or subtract.

Examples:

Solve for x and y: $\begin{array}{l} x+y=7 \\ x-y=3 \end{array}$.

$$x + y = 7$$
$$\underline{x - y = 3}$$
$$2x \quad\;\; = 10$$

$$\frac{2x}{2} = \frac{10}{2}$$
$$x = 5$$

Now, insert 5 for x in the first equation:

$$5 + y = 7$$
$$\underline{-5 \quad\;\; -5}$$
$$y = 2$$

Answer: $x = 5$, $y = 2$

Solve for p and q: $\begin{array}{l} 3p+4q=9 \\ 2p+2q=6 \end{array}$.

Multiply the second equation by 2:

$$(2)2p + (2)2q = (2)6$$
$$4p + 4q = 12$$

Subtract the equations:

$$3p + 4q = \;\;9$$
$$\underline{(-)4p + 4q = 12}$$
$$-p \quad\;\; = -3$$
$$p \quad\; = \;\;3$$

Now that you know $p = 3$, plug in 3 for p in either of the two original equations to find q.

$$3p + 4q = 9$$
$$3(3) + 4q = 9$$
$$9 + 4q = 9$$
$$4q = 0$$
$$q = 0$$

Answer: $p = 3$, $q = 0$

You should note that this method will not work when the two equations are, in fact, the same equation but written in two different forms, as is shown in the next example.

Example:

Solve for a and b: $\begin{array}{c} 3a + 4b = 2 \\ 6a + 8b = 4 \end{array}$.

The second equation is actually the first equation multiplied by 2. The system does not have a unique solution. Any replacements for a and b that make one of the sentences true will also make the other sentence true. For example, if $a = 2$ and $b = -1$, then each sentence would be true. If $a = 6$ and $b = -4$, then each sentence would be true. The system has infinitely many solutions for a and b.

Sometimes a system is more easily solved by the substitution method.

Examples:

Solve for x and y: $\begin{array}{c} x = y + 8 \\ x + 3y = 48 \end{array}$.

From the first equation, substitute $(y + 8)$ for x in the second equation:

$$(y + 8) + 3y = 48$$

Solve for y by combining the y variables:

$$4y + 8 = 48$$
$$\underline{-8 \quad -8}$$
$$4y \quad = 40$$

$$\frac{4y}{4} = \frac{40}{4}$$
$$y = 10$$

Now, insert $y = 10$ into one of the original equations:

$$x = y + 8$$
$$x = 10 + 8$$
$$x = 18$$

Answer: $y = 10$, $x = 18$

Practice: Systems of Equations

Solve for both unknowns.

1. $6a - 2b = 32$
$\quad\ 3a + 2b = 22$

2. $3a + 3b = 24$
$\quad\ 2a + b = 13$

3. $3x + 2y = 10$
$\quad\ 2x + 3y = 5$

4. $6x + 2y = 24$
$\quad\ x = -y + 5$

Answers: Systems of Equations

1. Add the two equations:

$$6a - 2b = 32$$
$$\underline{(+)3a + 2b = 22}$$
$$9a \quad\ = 54$$

$$\frac{9a}{9} = \frac{54}{9}$$
$$a = 6$$

Now, plug in 6 for a in one of the original equations:

$$3a + 2b = 22$$
$$3(6) + 2b = 22$$
$$18 + 2b = 22$$
$$\underline{-18 \qquad -18}$$
$$2b = 4$$
$$\frac{2b}{2} = \frac{4}{2}$$
$$b = 2$$

Answer: $a = 6$, $b = 2$

2. Multiply the second equation by 3:

$$(3)2a + (3)b = (3)13$$
$$6a + 3b = 39$$

Subtract the first equation from the second:

$$6a + 3b = 39$$
$$\underline{(-)3a + 3b = 24}$$
$$3a = 15$$
$$\frac{3a}{3} = 15$$
$$a = 5$$

Now, plug in 5 for a in one of the original equations:

$$2a + b = 13$$
$$2(5) + b = 13$$
$$10 + b = 13$$
$$\underline{-10 \qquad -10}$$
$$b = 3$$

Answer: $a = 5$, $b = 3$

3. Multiply the first equation by 2:

$$(2)3x + (2)2y = (2)10$$
$$6x + 4y = 20$$

Multiply the second equation by 3:

$$(3)2x + (3)3y = (3)5$$
$$6x + 9y = 15$$

Subtract the second equation from the first:

$$6x + 4y = 20$$
$$\underline{(-)6x + 9y = 15}$$
$$-5y = 5$$
$$\frac{-5y}{-5} = \frac{5}{-5}$$
$$y = -1$$

Now, plug in -1 for y in one of the original equations:

$$3x + 2y = 10$$
$$3x + 2(-1) = 10$$
$$3x - 2 = 10$$
$$\underline{+2 \qquad +2}$$
$$3x = 12$$
$$\frac{3x}{3} = \frac{12}{3}$$
$$x = 4$$

Answer: $y = -1$, $x = 4$

4. Substitute the value of x from the second equation into the first equation:

$$6x + 2y = 24$$
$$6(-y + 5) + 2y = 24$$
$$-6y + 30 + 2y = 24$$
$$-4y + 30 = 24$$
$$\underline{-30 - 30}$$
$$-4y = -6$$
$$\frac{-4y}{-4} = \frac{-6}{-4}$$
$$y = \frac{3}{2} \quad \text{or} \quad 1\frac{1}{2}$$

Now, plug in $1\frac{1}{2}$ for y in one of the original equations:

$$x = -y + 5$$
$$x = -\left(1\frac{1}{2}\right) + 5$$
$$x = 3\frac{1}{2}$$

Answer: $y = 1\frac{1}{2}$, $x = 3\frac{1}{2}$

Solving Word Problems Using Algebraic Equations

This section covers word problems using algebraic equations to solve problems involving money, distance (motion), integers, solution (mixture), and compound interest.

Money

If you are solving a money problem that asks you to determine the number of coins, set up one equation for the quantity of coins and the second equation for the money values.

Example:

James has 10 coins in his pocket that total $1.10. If all of the coins are quarters and nickels, how many quarters does James have in his pocket?

Equation #1: Set up the equation by using the letter Q for the number of quarters and the letter N for the number of nickels.

$$Q + N = 10$$

Equation #2: When solving problems with money, place the value of the money in front of the variable. Doing so makes it easier to multiply the equation by 100 to eliminate the decimals.

$$.25Q + .05N = 1.10$$
$$25Q + 5N = 110$$

Now that you have two equations, it will be easy to solve the equation by using the substitution method. Since Equation #1 has single unit variables, it is easier to use Equation #1 to solve for the variable.

Equation #1:

$$Q + N = 10$$
$$\underline{-N = \quad -N}$$
$$Q \quad = 10 - N$$

Replace this equation for Q in the second equation.

Equation #2:

$$25Q + 5N = 110$$
$$25(10 - N) + 5N = 110$$
$$250 - 25N + 5N = 110$$
$$250 - 20N = 110$$
$$\underline{+20N \qquad +20N}$$
$$250 = 110 + 20N$$
$$\underline{-110 = -110}$$
$$140 = 20N$$
$$7 = N$$

James has 7 nickels. He has 10 coins total, so he has $10 - 7 = 3$ quarters.

Distance (Motion)

Distance (motion) problems use the following basic formula:

$$\text{Total distance} = \text{average rate} \times \text{total time, or } d = r \times t$$

Distance problems commonly appear in two forms: (1) traveling the same direction or (2) traveling different directions. Since the Common Core Standards emphasize visual illustrations to conceptualize equations, it is helpful to create a chart to organize information. Notice that the setup is slightly different in the two types of problems. The first problem asks you to calculate the time it will take for two vehicles to travel at two different rates of speed. The second problem asks you to calculate the time it will take for two boats to be a certain distance apart.

Examples:

Vehicle 1 travels south on the interstate at 50 mph. Vehicle 2 is also traveling south on the interstate at 65 mph, but leaves 15 minutes after Vehicle 1. How long, in minutes, will it take before the Vehicle 2 reaches Vehicle 1?

First, convert 15 minutes into hours. There are 60 minutes in 1 hour, so 15 minutes $= \dfrac{15}{60} = \dfrac{1}{4}$ hour.

Since Vehicle 2 leaves 15 minutes after Vehicle 1, Vehicle 1 has traveled $\dfrac{1}{4}$-hour longer than Vehicle 2 when they meet. If t represents the amount of time Vehicle 2 has traveled, then $t + \dfrac{1}{4}$ represents the amount of time Vehicle 1 has traveled.

	Distance (d) miles	=	Rate (r) mph	×	Time (t) hours
Vehicle 1	d	=	50	×	$t + \dfrac{1}{4}$
Vehicle 2	d	=	65	×	t

Equation #1: $d = 50\left(t + \dfrac{1}{4}\right)$; Equation #2: $d = 65t$

Since the distances are the same, set the equations equal to each other and solve.

$$50\left(t + \frac{1}{4}\right) = 65t$$

$$50t + \frac{50}{4} = 65t$$

$$\underline{-50t \qquad\qquad -50t}$$

$$\frac{50}{4} = 15t$$

$$\frac{50}{4} \div 15 = t$$

$$\frac{50}{4} \times \frac{1}{15} = t$$

$$\frac{50}{60} = t$$

$$\frac{5}{6} = t$$

It will take $\dfrac{5}{6}$ hour or 50 minutes for Vehicle 2 to reach Vehicle 1. **Note:** To convert $\dfrac{5}{6}$ of an hour to minutes, multiply by 60.

$$\frac{5}{6} \times 60 =$$

$$\frac{5}{6^1} \times \frac{60^{10}}{1} =$$

$$5 \times 10 = 50 \text{ minutes}$$

Two boats (a sailboat and a powerboat) leave the harbor at exactly the same time. The sailboat heads north at 10 mph. The powerboat heads south at 15 mph. How long will it be, in hours, before the two boats are 50 miles apart? Let t represent the amount of time that each boat traveled.

	Distance (d) miles	=	Rate (r) mph	×	Time (t) hours
Sailboat	distance of sailboat	=	10	×	t
Powerboat	distance of powerboat	=	15	×	t

The two distances together must total 50; therefore, add the distances:

$$\text{Distance of the sailboat} + \text{distance of the powerboat} = 50$$

$$10t + 15t = 50$$

$$25t = 50$$

$$t = 2 \text{ hours}$$

It will take 2 hours for the boats to be 50 miles apart.

A bicyclist is traveling on a flat road with a tailwind of 15 mph. It takes the bicyclist 2 hours to travel to his destination and 5 hours to return in the same windy conditions. What is the bicyclist's speed if there is no wind? Let r represent the bicyclist's speed with no wind.

	Distance (d) miles	=	Rate (r) mph	×	Time (t) hours
To location	d	=	$r + 15$	×	2
Return	d	=	$r - 15$	×	5

$$(r+15)2 = (r-15)5$$

$$2r + 30 = 5r - 75$$

$$\underline{-2r \qquad = -2r}$$

$$30 = 3r - 75$$

$$\underline{+75 = \qquad +75}$$

$$105 = 3r$$

$$35 = r$$

The bicyclist is traveling at 35 mph.

Integers

When working with a set of integers that are given an interval apart, name the variable of your first unknown integer: x. If the integers are consecutive, write x, $x + 1$, $x + 2$, and so on.

The illustration below shows consecutive odd numbers that are spaced two units apart.

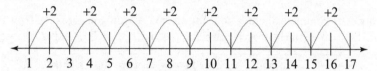

The illustration below shows consecutive even integers that are spaced two units apart.

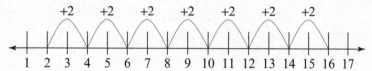

Examples:

Three consecutive integers added together total 96. What are the integers?

$$x + (x + 1) + (x + 2) = 96$$
$$3x + 3 = 96$$
$$3x = 93$$
$$x = 31$$

The three integers are 31, 32, and 33.

Three consecutive even integers added together total 96. What are the integers?

$$x + (x + 2) + (x + 4) = 96$$
$$3x + 6 = 96$$
$$-6 = -6$$
$$3x = 90$$
$$x = 30$$

The three even integers are 30, 32, and 34.

Mixture (Solution)

Create a chart to organize data for a mixture (solution) word problem.

	Amount	×	% or Amount of Additive	=	Total
Solution 1	A_1	×	A_2	=	A_3
	+		+		+
Solution 2	B_1	×	B_2	=	B_3
	=		=		=
Totals	C_1 (amount of Solution 1 + amount of Solution 2)	×	C_2 (amount of the final % that you want)	=	C_3

The previous chart assigns cell labels (A_1, A_2, A_3, B_1, B_2, B_3, C_1, C_2, C_3) to organize information from the solution word problem that will help you construct an equation. Notice that the rows are multiplied across horizontally and the columns are added together vertically. Using math intuition, you can see that the sum of the parts is going to equal the total amount. The equation is $A_3 + B_3 = C_3$.

Example:

Mariah has 6 ounces of commercial grade concentrated 35% hydrogen peroxide. How much water does Mariah need to add to dilute the hydrogen peroxide to equal a 3% hydrogen peroxide solution?

	Amount	% of Hydrogen Peroxide	Total
Solution	6	.35	2.1
Water	x	0	0
Totals	$6 + x$	.03	$.03(6 + x)$

$2.1 + 0 = .03(6 + x)$. This can be written as $.03(6 + x) = 2.0 + 0$.

$$.03(6 + x) = 2.1 + 0$$
$$.18 + .03x = 2.1$$
$$\underline{-.18 \qquad\quad -\ .18}$$
$$.03x = 1.92$$
$$x = 64 \text{ ounces}$$

Mariah will need to add 64 ounces of water to make a solution of 3% hydrogen peroxide.

Compound Interest

In solving problems with compound interest, use the following formula:

$$A = P\left(1 + \frac{r}{n}\right)^{nt}$$

A	Amount (or final amount)
P	Principal (or original amount)
r	Rate of interest (change to a decimal)
n	Number of periods (per year)
t	Time (in years)

The following examples make use of a scientific or graphing calculator.

Examples:

Jeff invests $5,000 in a fixed investment that earns daily compounded interest at a rate of 5%. How much will Jeff have at the end of 5 years?

$$A = 5,000 \left(1 + \frac{.05}{365}\right)^{365 \cdot 5}$$

$$A = 5,000 \left(1 + \frac{.05}{365}\right)^{1,825}$$

$$A \approx 5,000(1.000136986)^{1,825}$$

$$A \approx 5,000 \cdot 1.284003432)$$

$$A \approx 6,420.02$$

At the end of 5 years, Jeff will have $6,420.02.

Nia has $3,791.49 after investing for 2 years at a rate of 4% interest compounded daily. How much money did she originally invest?

This problem combines what you have learned about isolating a variable and using the compound interest formula. Use the formula to replace each value.

$$A = P \left(1 + \frac{r}{n}\right)^{nt}$$

$$3,791.49 = P \left(1 + \frac{.04}{365}\right)^{730}$$

$$3,791.49 \approx P(1 + .000109589)^{730}$$

$$3,791.49 \approx P(1.083282319)$$

$$\frac{3,791.49}{1.083282319} \approx P \frac{(1.083282319)}{1.083282319}$$

$$3,500 \approx P$$

Nia's original principal investment was $3,500.

Practice: Solving Word Problems Using Algebraic Equations

1. For a chemistry experiment, students were asked to remove certain bacteria from 1 gallon of water using .2% chlorine bleach. The chemistry lab only has household bleach, which contains 5.25% chlorine. How many ounces of the 5.25% chlorine bleach should the students add to the 1 gallon of water to complete this experiment? (Round to the nearest tenth of an ounce.)

2. A plane flies 9 hours to get to the destination with a tailwind of 50 mph and 11 hours on the return flight with a headwind of 50 mph. If there was no wind, what would have been the plane's rate of speed? How far did the plane travel in one direction?

3. William and John are arguing about the fastest route to the airport—surface streets or the freeway. William argues it is faster to drive on surface streets because it is a shorter distance to the freeway, 35 miles. The average rate of speed on surface streets is 40 mph. Even though the freeway route is 50 miles, John is convinced that the freeway is the fastest route because the average rate of speed on the freeway is 60 mph (including the surface streets on the route). Who is correct, William or John?

4. A coin-operated washing machine takes quarters and dollar coins. If 50 coins totaling $23.75 are collected at the end of the day, how many quarters and dollar coins were in the machine?

5. Three consecutive odd numbers total 339. What is the middle number?

109

Answers: Solving Word Problems Using Algebraic Equations

1. Create a chart to organize the information. *Note:* One gallon is equivalen to 128 ounces.

	Amount	% of Chlorine	Total
Water	128	0	0
Chlorine	x	.0525	.0525x
Totals	128 + x	.002	.002(128+x)

$$0.002(128+x) = 0.0525x + 0$$
$$.256 + 0.002x = 0.0525x$$
$$\underline{-0.002x = -0.002x}$$
$$\frac{.256}{0.0505} = \frac{0.0505x}{0.0505x}$$
$$5.1\,\text{oz} \approx x \text{ (when rounded to the nearest tenth of an ounce)}$$

2. Create a chart to organize the information.

	Distance	Rate	Time	Totals
Travel destination	d	$r + 50$	9	9(r + 50)
Return	d	$r - 50$	11	11(r − 50)

$$9(r + 50) = 11(r - 50)$$
$$9r + 450 = 11r - 550$$
$$\underline{+\ 550 = \quad +550}$$
$$9r + 1{,}000 = 11r$$
$$\underline{-9r \qquad = -9r}$$
$$1{,}000 = 2r$$
$$500 = r$$

The plane speed without wind would have been 500 mph.

To determine the distance, substitute 500 for r in either equation.

$$9(r + 50) =$$
$$9r + 450 =$$
$$9(500) + 450 =$$
$$4{,}500 + 450 = 4{,}950$$

The plane traveled 4,950 miles in one direction.

3. Create a chart to organize the information. Let t_1 and t_2 represent the amount of time William and John will need, respectively.

	Distance	Rate	Time
William	35	40	t_1
John	50	60	t_2

Setting up the two equations, we have $35 = 40t_1$ and $50 = 60t_2$.

$$\text{William's time:} \frac{35}{40} = \frac{40}{40}t \qquad \text{John's time:} \frac{50}{60} = \frac{60t}{60}t$$

$$0.875 = t \qquad\qquad\qquad 0.833 = t$$

John is correct; his travel time is slightly less than William's time.

4. If q and d represent the number of quarters and dimes, respectively, the two equations are:

$$q + d = 50$$
$$.25q + 1d = 23.75$$

Solving for d in the first equation, your equation is now $d = 50 - q$.

Substituting this equation into the second equation, you have:

$$.25q + 1(50 - q) = 23.75$$
$$.25q + 50 - q = 23.75$$
$$-.75q + 50 = 23.75$$
$$\underline{-50 = -50.00}$$
$$-.75q \quad = -26.25 \quad \text{Divide both sides by } -.75$$
$$q = 35$$

Now, substitute 35 for q into either equation to find how many dollar coins were in the machine.

$$q + d = 50$$
$$35 + d = 50$$
$$\underline{-35 \quad = -35}$$
$$d = 15$$

There are 35 quarters and 15 dollar coins.

5. Let x be the first odd number; therefore, $x + 2$ is the second odd number, and $x + 4$ is the third odd number. Solve for x.

$$x + (x + 2) + (x + 4) = 339$$
$$3x + 6 = 339$$
$$\underline{-6 = -6}$$
$$3x = 333$$
$$x = 111$$

The middle number is 113. Since $x = 111$, which is the first number, the second (or middle) number is $x + 2$, which is 113.

Monomials and Polynomials

A *monomial* is an algebraic expression that consists of only one term. (A *term* is a numerical or literal expression where all numbers and variables are multiplied together.) For example, $9x$, $4a^2$, and $3mpxz^2$ are all monomials.

A *binomial* is a polynomial that consists of exactly two terms. For example, $x + y$ is a binomial.

A *trinomial* is a polynomial that consists of exactly three terms. For example, $y^2 + 9y + 8$ is a trinomial.

A *polynomial* consists of two or more terms. For example, $x + y$, $y^2 - x^2$, and $x^2 + 3x + 5y^2$ are all polynomials.

The number in front of the variable is called the *coefficient*. In $9y$, 9 is the coefficient.

Polynomials are usually arranged in one of two ways:

- *Ascending order* is basically when the power of a term increases for each succeeding term. For example, $x + x^2 + x^3$ and $5x + 2x^2 - 3x^3 + x^5$ are arranged in ascending order.
- *Descending order* is basically when the power of a term decreases for each succeeding term. For example, $x^3 + x^2 + x$ and $2x^4 + 3x^2 + 7x$ are arranged in descending order. Descending order is more commonly used.

Adding and Subtracting Monomials

To add or subtract monomials, follow the same rules as with signed numbers (pp. 17–18), provided that the terms are alike. Notice that you add or subtract the coefficients only and leave the variables the same.

Examples:

$$15x^2yz$$
$$-18x^2yz$$
$$-3x^2yz$$

$$3x + 2x = 5x$$

$$9y$$
$$-3y$$
$$6y$$

$$17q + 8q - 3q - (-4q) =$$
$$22q - (-4q) =$$
$$22q + 4q = 26q$$

Remember that the rules for signed numbers apply to monomials as well.

Practice: Adding and Subtracting Monomials

Perform the indicated operation.

1. $-9m^2s + 5m^2s =$

2. $7qt^2 - 3qt^2 + 20qt^2 =$

3. $\quad 18pc$
$\quad (-)7pc$

4. $\quad -7x^2y$
$\quad (-) - 3x^2y$

Answers: Adding and Subtracting Monomials

1. $-4m^2s$

2. $24qt^2$

3. $11pc$

4. $-4x^2y$

Multiplying Monomials

Reminder: The rules and definitions for powers and exponents introduced in arithmetic (pp. 57–59) also apply in algebra. For example, $5 \cdot 5 = 5^2$ and $x \cdot x = x^2$. Similarly, $a \cdot a \cdot a \cdot b \cdot b = a^3b^2$.

To multiply monomials, add the exponents of the same bases.

Examples:

$(x^3)(x^4) = x^7$

$(x^2y)(x^3y^2) = x^5y^3$

$(6k^5)(5k^2) = 30k^7$

$-4(m^2n)(-3m^4n^3) = 12m^6n^4$

$(c^2)(c^3)(c^4) = c^9$

$(3a^2b^3c)(b^2c^2d) = 3a^2b^5c^3d$

Note that in the fourth example above, the product of -4 and -3 is $+12$, the product of m^2 and m^4 is m^6, and the product of n and n^3 is n^4, because any monomial having no exponent indicated is assumed to have an exponent of 1.

When monomials are being raised to a power, the answer is obtained by multiplying the exponents of each part of the monomial by the power to which it is being raised.

Examples:

$(a^7)^3 = a^{21}$

$(x^3y^2)^4 = x^{12}y^8$

$(2x^2y^3)^3 = 2^3x^6y^9 = 8x^6y^9$

Practice: Multiplying Monomials

1. $(m^3)(m^{10}) =$

2. $(a^5b^6)(a^4b^2) =$

3. $(5k^2)(8k^4) =$

4. $-2(x^2y^3)(6xy^4) =$

5. $(2x^2)(-4x)(x^3y) =$

6. $(d^4)^5 =$

7. $(c^3d^2)^5 =$

8. $(3a^2bc^3)^2 =$

Answers: Multiplying Monomials

1. m^{13}

2. a^9b^8

3. $40k^6$

4. $-12x^3y^7$

5. $-8x^6y$

6. d^{20}

7. $c^{15}d^{10}$

8. $9a^4b^2c^6$

Dividing Monomials

To divide monomials, subtract the exponent of the divisor (denominator) from the exponent of the dividend (numerator) of the same base.

Examples:

$$\frac{y^{15}}{y^4} = y^{11} \text{ or } y^{15} \div y^4 = y^{11}$$

$$\frac{x^5 y^2}{x^3 y} = x^2 y$$

$$\frac{36a^4 b^6}{-9ab} = -4a^3 b^5 \text{ (divide the coefficients)}$$

$$\frac{fg^{15}}{g^3} = fg^{12}$$

$$\frac{x^5}{x^8} = \frac{1}{x^3} \text{ (may also be expressed } x^{-3})$$

$$\frac{-3(xy)(xy^2)}{xy}$$

You can simplify the numerator first:

$$\frac{-3(xy)(xy^2)}{xy} = \frac{-3(x^2 y^3)}{xy} = -3xy^2$$

Or, since the numerator is all multiplication, you can cancel:

$$\frac{-3(\cancel{xy})(xy^2)}{\cancel{xy}} = -3xy^2$$

Practice: Dividing Monomials

1. $\dfrac{x^8}{x^3} =$

2. $a^9 \div a^6 =$

3. $\dfrac{m^5 n^4}{m^2 n^3} =$

4. $\dfrac{-10x^4 z^9}{5x^3 z^4} =$

5. $\dfrac{x^8 y^3}{x^5} =$

6. $(3p^5 q^3) \div (12p^4 q^9) =$

7. $\dfrac{s^4 t^6}{s^7 t^3} =$

8. $\dfrac{2(x^2 y)(3x^2 y^3)}{x^2 y^2} =$

Answers: Dividing Monomials

1. x^5

2. a^3

3. $m^3 n$

4. $-2xz^5$

5. $x^3 y^3$

6. $\dfrac{\cancel{3} p^{\cancel{5}^{1}} q^{\cancel{3}}}{\cancel{12} \, p^{\cancel{4}} q^{\cancel{9}^{6}}}_{4} = \dfrac{1p}{4q^6} = \dfrac{p}{4q^6}$ or $0.25pq^{-6}$

7. $\dfrac{t^3}{s^3}$ or $s^{-3} t^3$

8. $\dfrac{2(x^2 y)(3x^2 y^3)}{x^2 y^2} = \dfrac{6x^4 y^4}{x^2 y^2} = 6x^2 y^2$ or

$$\dfrac{2(\cancel{x^2} y)(3x^2 y^{\cancel{3}^{1}})}{\cancel{x^2} \, \cancel{y^2}} = 6x^2 y^2$$

Adding and Subtracting Polynomials

To add or subtract polynomials, just arrange *like terms* in columns and then add or subtract. (Or simply add or subtract like terms when rearrangement is not necessary.)

Examples:

Add:

$$a^2 + ab + b^2$$
$$\underline{3a^2 + 4ab - 2b^2}$$
$$4a^2 + 5ab - b^2$$

$(5y - 3x) + (9y + 4x) =$

$(5y - 3x) + (9y + 4x) = 14y + x \text{ or } x + 14y$

$3a^2bc + 2ab^2c + 4a^2bc + 5ab^2c =$

$$3a^2bc + 2ab^2c$$
$$\underline{+4a^2bc + 5ab^2c}$$
$$7a^2bc + 7ab^2c$$

or

$3a^2bc + 2ab^2c + 4a^2bc + 5ab^2c = 7a^2bc + 7ab^2c$

Subtract:

$$a^2 + b^2$$
$$\underline{-(2a^2 - b^2)}$$

Change to an addition problem:

$$a^2 + b^2$$
$$\underline{(+) - 2a^2 + b^2}$$
$$-a^2 + 2b^2$$

$(3cd - 6mt) - (2cd - 4mt) =$

$(3cd - 6mt) + (-2cd + 4mt) =$

$(3cd - 6mt) + (-2cd + 4mt) = cd - 2mt$

Practice: Adding and Subtracting Polynomials

Perform the indicated operations and simplify.

1. $5x^2y^2 - 4ab$
   $-6x^2y^2 + 3ab$
   $\underline{-2x^2y^2 - ab}$

2. $(7gr - 3nt) + (5gr - 2nt) =$

3. $(9kb^2 + 6ht - 3ab) - (4kb^2 - 6ht + 2ab) =$

4. $7xyz^2 + 8x^2yz + 9xy^2z + 8xyz^2 + 3xy^2z - 3x^2yz =$

Answers: Adding and Subtracting Polynomials

1. $-3x^2y^2 - 2ab$

2. $12gr - 5nt$

3. $5kb^2 + 12ht - 5ab$

4. $15xyz^2 + 5x^2yz + 12xy^2z$

Multiplying Polynomials

To multiply polynomials, multiply each term in one polynomial by each term in the other polynomial. Then simplify if necessary.

Example:

$$
\begin{array}{r}
2x - 2a \\
\times\ 3x + a \\
\hline
+\ 2ax - 2a^2 \\
6x^2 - 6ax \\
\hline
6x^2 - 4ax - 2a^2
\end{array}
$$

similar to

$$
\begin{array}{r}
21 \\
\times\ 23 \\
\hline
63 \\
42 \\
\hline
483
\end{array}
$$

Or you may wish to use the "F.O.I.L." method with *binomials*. F.O.I.L. stands for "first terms, outside terms, inside terms, last terms." Then simplify if necessary.

Examples:

$(3x + a)(2x - 2a) =$

Multiply *first* terms from each quantity.

$(3x + a)\ (2x - 2a) = 6x^2$ _____

Now the *outside* terms.

$(3x + a)\ (2x - 2a) = 6x^2 - 6ax$ _____

Now the *inside* terms.

$(3x + a)\ (2x - 2a) = 6x^2 - 6ax + 2ax$ _____

Now the *last* terms.

$(3x + a)\ (2x - 2a) = 6x^2 - 6ax + 2ax - 2a^2$

Now simplify.

$6x^2 - 6ax + 2ax - 2a^2 = 6x^2 - 4ax - 2a^2$

$(x + y)(x + y + z) =$

$$
\begin{array}{r}
x + y + z \\
\times\ x + y \\
\hline
xy + y^2 + yz \\
x^2 + xz + xy \\
\hline
x^2 + xz + 2xy + y^2 + yz
\end{array}
$$

Practice: Multiplying Polynomials

1. $(2x + y)(3x + 5y) =$

2. $(7a + b)(2a - 3b) =$

3. $(9x + 5)(3x - 2) =$

4. $(-6y + z^2)(2y - 3z) =$

Answers: Multiplying Polynomials

1.

$$
\begin{array}{r}
2x + y \\
\times\ 3x + 5y \\
\hline
+10xy + 5y^2 \\
+\ 6x^2 + 3xy \\
\hline
6x^2 + 13xy + 5y^2
\end{array}
$$

3.

$$
\begin{array}{r}
9x + 5 \\
\times\ 3x - 2 \\
\hline
-18x - 10 \\
+\ 27x^2 + 15x \\
\hline
27x^2 - 3x - 10
\end{array}
$$

2.

$$
\begin{array}{r}
7a + b \\
\times\ 2a - 3b \\
\hline
-21ab - 3b^2 \\
+\ 14a^2 + 2ab \\
\hline
14a^2 - 19ab - 3b^2
\end{array}
$$

4.

$$
\begin{array}{r}
-6y + z^2 \\
\times\ 2y - 3z \\
\hline
+18yz - 3z^3 \\
-12y^2 + 2yz^2 \\
\hline
-12y^2 + 2yz^2 + 18yz - 3z^3
\end{array}
$$

or

$$-12y^2 + 18yz + 2yz^2 - 3z^3$$

Dividing Polynomials by Monomials

To divide a polynomial by a monomial, just divide each term in the polynomial by the monomial.

Examples:

$$(6x^2 + 2x) \div (2x) = \frac{6x^2 + 2x}{2x} = \frac{6x^2}{2x} + \frac{2x}{2x} = 3x + 1$$

$$(16a^7 - 12a^5) \div (4a^2) = \frac{16a^7 - 12a^5}{4a^2} = \frac{16a^7}{4a^2} - \frac{12a^5}{4a^2} = 4a^5 - 3a^3$$

Practice: Dividing Polynomials by Monomials

1. $(3x - 9) \div 3 =$

3. $(14a^2b - 8ab + 4a) \div (2a) =$

2. $(16x^3 + 4x^2 + 8x) \div (2x) =$

4. $(84c^2d - 38cd + 18cd^3) \div (2cd) =$

Answers: Dividing Polynomials by Monomials

1. $(3x - 9) \div 3 = \dfrac{3x - 9}{3} = \dfrac{3x}{3} - \dfrac{9}{3} = x - 3$

2. $(16x^3 + 4x^2 + 8x) \div (2x) = \dfrac{16x^3 + 4x^2 + 8x}{2x}$

$$= \frac{16x^3}{2x} + \frac{4x^2}{2x} + \frac{8x}{2x}$$

$$= 8x^2 + 2x + 4$$

3. $(14a^2b - 8ab + 4a) \div (2a) = \dfrac{14a^2b - 8ab + 4a}{2a}$

$$= \frac{14a^2b}{2a} - \frac{8ab}{2a} + \frac{4a}{2a}$$

$$= 7ab - 4b + 2$$

4. $(84c^2d - 38cd + 18cd^3) \div (2cd) = \dfrac{84c^2d - 38cd + 18cd^3}{2cd}$

$$= \frac{84c^2d}{2cd} - \frac{38cd}{2cd} + \frac{18cd^3}{2cd}$$

$$= 42c - 19 + 9d^2$$

Dividing Polynomials by Polynomials

To divide a polynomial by a polynomial, make sure both are in descending order, and then use long division. (*Remember:* Divide by the first term, multiply, subtract, and bring down.)

Examples:

Divide $4a^2 + 18a + 8$ by $a + 4$.

First, divide a into $4a^2$:

$$\begin{array}{r} 4a \\ a+4\overline{)4a^2 + 18a + 8} \end{array}$$

Now multiply $4a$ times $(a + 4)$:

$$\begin{array}{r} 4a \\ a+4\overline{)4a^2 + 18a + 8} \\ 4a^2 + 16a \end{array}$$

Now subtract:

$$\begin{array}{r} 4a \\ a+4\overline{)4a^2 + 18a + 8} \\ (-)4a^2 + 16a \\ \hline 2a \end{array}$$

Now bring down the +8:

$$\begin{array}{r} 4a \\ a+4\overline{)4a^2 + 18a + 8} \\ (-)4a^2 + 16a \\ \hline 2a + 8 \end{array}$$

Now divide a into $2a$:

$$a+4\overline{)4a^2+18a+8}^{\;4a+2}$$

$$\underline{(-)4a^2+16a+8}$$

$$2a+8$$

Now multiply 2 times $(a + 4)$:

$$a+4\overline{)4a^2+18a+8}^{\;4a+2}$$

$$\underline{(-)4a^2+16a+8}$$

$$2a+8$$

$$\underline{2a+8}$$

Now subtract:

$$a+4\overline{)4a^2+18a+8}^{\;4a+2}$$

$$\underline{(-)4a^2+16a+8}$$

$$2a+8$$

$$\underline{(-)2a+8}$$

$$0$$

Therefore, the final answer is:

$$\frac{4a^2+18a+8}{a+4}=4a+2$$

$$a+4\overline{)4a^2+18a+8}^{\;4a+2}$$
$$\underline{(-)4a^2+16a+8}$$
$$2a+8$$
$$\underline{(-)2a+8}$$
$$0$$

similar to

$$53\overline{)1219}^{\;23}$$
$$\underline{(-)106}$$
$$159$$
$$\underline{(-)159}$$
$$0$$

$(3x^2 + 4x+ 1) \div (x + 1) =$

$$x+1\overline{)3x^2+4x+1}^{\;3x+1}$$

$$\underline{(-)3x^2+3x}$$

$$x+1$$

$$\underline{(-)x+1}$$

$$0$$

$(2x + 1 + x^2) \div (x + 1) =$

First, change to descending order: $x^2 + 2x + 1$

Then divide:

$$
\begin{array}{r}
x+1 \\
x+1 \overline{)\, x^2 + 2x + 1} \\
(-)x^2 + 1x \\
\hline
x+1 \\
(-)x+1 \\
\hline
0
\end{array}
$$

$(m^3 - m) \div (m + 1) =$

Note: When terms are missing, be sure to leave proper room between terms.

$$
\begin{array}{r}
m^2 - m \\
m+1 \overline{)\, m^3 + 0m^2 - m} \\
(-)m^3 + m^2 \\
\hline
-m^2 - m \\
(-)-m^2 - m \\
\hline
0
\end{array}
$$

$(10a^2 - 29a - 21) \div (2a - 7) =$

$$
\begin{array}{r}
5a + 3 \\
2a-7 \overline{)\, 10a^2 - 29a - 21} \\
(-)10a^2 - 35a \\
\hline
6a - 21 \\
(-)6a - 21 \\
\hline
0
\end{array}
$$

Note that remainders are possible.

Example:

$(x^2 + 2x + 4) \div (x + 1) =$

$$
\begin{array}{r}
x+1 \text{ (with remainder 3)} \\
x+1 \overline{)\, x^2 + 2x + 4} \\
(-)x^2 + x \\
\hline
x + 4 \\
(-)x + 1 \\
\hline
3
\end{array}
$$

This answer can be rewritten with the remainder written over the divisor as a fraction: $(x+1) + \dfrac{3}{(x+1)}$.

Practice: Dividing Polynomials by Polynomials

1. $(x^2 + 18x + 45) \div (x + 3) =$

2. $(21t + 5 + 4t^2) \div (t + 5) =$

3. $(z^3 - 1) \div (z - 1) =$

4. $(t^2 + 4t - 6) \div (t + 2) =$

5. $(14x^2 + 11x + 2) \div (2x + 1) =$

Answers: Dividing Polynomials by Polynomials

1.
$$\begin{array}{r} x+15 \\ x+3\overline{)x^2+18x+45} \\ \underline{(-)x^2+3x} \\ 15x+45 \\ \underline{(-)15x+45} \\ 0 \end{array}$$

2. Put in descending order: $4t^2 + 21t + 5$

$$\begin{array}{r} 4t+1 \\ t+5\overline{)4t^2+21t+5} \\ \underline{(-)4t^2+20t} \\ t+5 \\ \underline{(-)t+5} \\ 0 \end{array}$$

3.
$$\begin{array}{r} z^2+z+1 \\ z-1\overline{)z^3+0\,z^2+0z\,-1} \\ \underline{(-)z^3-z^2} \\ z^2\,+0z \\ \underline{(-)z^2-z} \\ z-1 \\ \underline{(-)z-1} \\ 0 \end{array}$$

4. $t + 2$ (with remainder -10) or $(t+2) - \dfrac{10}{t+2}$

$$\begin{array}{r} t+2\overline{)t^2+4t-6} \\ \underline{(-)t^2+2t} \\ 2t-6 \\ \underline{(-)2t+4} \\ -10 \end{array}$$

5.
$$\begin{array}{r} 7x+2 \\ 2x+1\overline{)14x^2+11x+2} \\ \underline{(-)14x^2+7x} \\ 4x+2 \\ \underline{(-)4x+2} \\ 0 \end{array}$$

121

Factoring

To *factor* means to find two or more quantities whose product equals the original quantity. Factoring is the opposite of distributing.

Factoring: $4x + 8 = 4(x + 2)$

Distributing: $4(x + 2) = 4x + 8$

Factoring Out a Common Factor

To factor out a common factor, take the following steps:

1. Find the largest common monomial factor of each term.
2. Divide the original polynomial by this factor to obtain the second factor. The second factor will be a polynomial.

Examples:

$5x^2 + 4x = x(5x + 4)$

$2y^3 - 6y = 2y(y^2 - 3)$

$x^5 - 4x^3 + x^2 = x^2(x^3 - 4x + 1)$

Practice: Factoring Out a Common Factor

Factor the following completely.

1. $a^2 + 26a =$

2. $t^2 - 35t =$

3. $3m^3 + 6m^2 + 9m =$

4. $12p^3 + 24p^2 =$

Answers: Factoring Out a Common Factor

1. $a(a + 26)$

2. $t(t - 35)$

3. $3m(m^2 + 2m + 3)$

4. $12p^2(p + 2)$

Factoring the Difference Between Two Squares

To factor the difference between two squares, take the following steps:

1. Find the square root of the first term and the square root of the second term.
2. Express your answer as the product of the sum of the quantities from Step 1, times the difference of those quantities.

Examples:

$x^2 - 144 = (x + 12)(x - 12)$ ***Note:*** $x^2 + 144$ is *not* factorable.

$a^2 - b^2 = (a + b)(a - b)$

$9y^2 - 1 = (3y + 1)(3y - 1)$

Practice: Factoring the Difference Between Two Squares

Factor the following.

1. $x^2 - 25 =$

2. $p^2 - q^2 =$

3. $144 - h^2 =$

4. $x^2y^2 - z^2 =$

5. $4a^2 - 9 =$

6. $2t^2 - 50 =$

Answers: Factoring the Difference Between Two Squares

1. $(x + 5)(x - 5)$

2. $(p + q)(p - q)$

3. $(12 + h)(12 - h)$

4. $(xy + z)(xy - z)$

5. $(2a + 3)(2a - 3)$

6. $2(t^2 - 25) = 2(t + 5)(t - 5)$. First, factor out the greatest common factor of 2, and then recognize the difference of squares ($t^2 - 25$).

Factoring Polynomials Having Three Terms of the Form $Ax^2 + Bx + C$

To factor polynomials having three terms of the form $Ax^2 + Bx + C$, take the following steps:

1. Check to see if you can *monomial factor* (factor out common terms). Then if $A = 1$ (that is, the first term is simply x^2), use double parentheses and factor the first term. Place these factors in the left sides of the parentheses. For example, $(x \quad)(x \quad)$.
2. Factor the last term, and then place the factors in the right sides of the parentheses.

To decide on the signs of the numbers, do the following:

If the sign of the last term is negative:

1. Find two numbers whose product is the last term and whose *difference* is the *coefficient* (number in front) of the middle term.
2. Give the larger of these two numbers the sign of the middle term and the opposite sign to the other factor.

If the sign of the last term is positive:

1. Find two numbers whose product is the last term and whose *sum* is the coefficient of the middle term.
2. Give both factors the sign of the middle term.

Examples:

Factor $x^2 - 3x - 10$.

First, check to see if you can monomial factor (factor out common terms). Since this is not possible, use double parentheses and factor the first term as follows: $(x)(x)$. Next, factor the last term, 10, into 2 times 5 (using Step 2 above, 5 must take the negative sign and 2 must take the positive sign, because they will then total the coefficient of the middle term, which is -3) and add the proper signs, leaving $(x - 5)(x + 2)$.

Multiply *means* (inner terms) and *extremes* (outer terms) to check.

$$(x - 5)\ (x + 2)$$
$$-5x$$
$$+2x$$
$$\overline{}$$
$$-3x \text{ (which is the middle term)}$$

To completely check, multiply the factors together:

$$
\begin{array}{r}
x - 5 \\
\times\ x + 2 \\
\hline
(+)2x - 10 \\
x^2 - 5x \\
\hline
x^2 - 3x - 10
\end{array}
$$

Factor $x^2 + 8x + 15$.

Using the F.O.I.L. method, you get $(x + 3)(x + 5)$. Notice that $3 \times 5 = 15$ and $3 + 5 = 8$, the coefficient of the middle term. Also, note that the signs of both factors are +, the sign of the middle term. Check:

$$(x + 3)\ (x + 5)$$
$$+3x$$
$$+5x$$
$$\overline{}$$
$$+8x \text{ (the middle term)}$$

Factor $x^2 - 5x - 14$.

Using the F.O.I.L. method, you get $(x - 7)(x + 2)$. Notice that $7 \times 2 = 14$ and $7 - 2 = 5$, the coefficient of the middle term. Also, note that the sign of the larger factor, 7, is $-$, while the other factor, 2, has a + sign. Check:

$$(x - 7)\ (x + 2)$$
$$-7x$$
$$+2x$$
$$\overline{}$$
$$-5x \text{ (the middle term)}$$

If, however, $A \neq 1$ (the first term has a coefficient other than 1), then additional trial and error will be necessary. The next example is this type of problem.

Examples:

Factor $4x^2 + 5x + 1$.

At first glance, $(2x + \quad)(2x + \quad)$ works for the first term. But when 1's are used as factors to get the last term $(2x + 1)(2x + 1)$, the middle term comes out as $4x$ instead of $5x$.

$$
\begin{array}{c}
(2x + 1)\,(2x + 1) \\
\underline{+2x} \\
+2x \\
\hline
+4x
\end{array}
$$

Therefore, try $(4x + \quad)(x + \quad)$. Now using 1's as factors to get the last terms gives $(4x + 1)(x + 1)$. Checking for the middle term:

$$
\begin{array}{c}
(4x + 1)\,(x + 1) \\
\underline{+1x} \\
+4x \\
\hline
+5x
\end{array}
$$

Therefore, $4x^2 + 5x + 1 = (4x + 1)(x + 1)$.

Factor $4a^2 + 6a + 2$.

Factoring out a 2 leaves $2(2a^2 + 3a + 1)$.

Now factor as usual, giving $2(2a + 1)(a + 1)$.

Check:

$$
\begin{array}{c}
(2a + 1)\,(a + 1) \\
\underline{+1a} \\
+2a \\
\hline
\end{array}
$$

$+3a$ (the middle term after 2 was factored out)

Factor $5x^3 + 6x^2 + x$.

Factoring out an x leaves $x(5x^2 + 6x + 1)$.

Now factor as usual, giving $x(5x + 1)(x + 1)$.

Check:

$$
\begin{array}{c}
(5x + 1)\,(x + 1) \\
\underline{+1x} \\
+5x \\
\hline
\end{array}
$$

$+6x$ (the middle term after x was factored out)

125

Factor $5 + 7b + 2b^2$ (a slight twist).

This is a slight twist because of the squared variable in the last position, instead of how we usually see it in the first position. Work the problem in the exact same way. Start by arranging your equation as (+ 2b) (+ b), then work on numbers in the first position of each parentheses. That will correct the middle term.

$$(5 + 2b)(1 + b)$$

Check:

$$(5 + 2b)(1 + b)$$
$$+2b$$
$$+5b$$
$$+7b \text{ (the middle term)}$$

Note that $(5 + b)(1 + 2b)$ is incorrect because it gives the wrong middle term.

Factor $x^2 + 2xy + y^2$.

Since there are squared terms in the first position and the last position of the polynomial, there will be an x in the first position of each set of parentheses and a y in the last position of each parentheses: $(x + \_y)(x + \_y)$.

$$(x + y)(x + y)$$

Check:

$$(x + y)(x + y)$$
$$+xy$$
$$+xy$$
$$+2xy \text{ (the middle term)}$$

In the answer above, the coefficient in front of each y is 1, and therefore does not needed to be stated.

There are polynomials that are not factorable, such as $x^2 + 12x + 5$. Since 5 is a prime number, the only possible way to achieve 5 by multiplication is 5×1. There is no possible way to obtain a middle term of 12 with this problem.

Example:

Factor $5x^2 + 3x + 7$.

$$(5x + 7)(x + 1) \qquad (5x + 1)(x + 7)$$
$$+7x \qquad\qquad +1x$$
$$+5x \qquad\qquad +35x$$
$$\overline{12x} \qquad\qquad \overline{+36x}$$
$$(\text{not } 3x) \qquad\qquad (\text{not } 3x)$$

This cannot be factored.

Practice: Factoring Polynomials

Factor the following.

1. $x^2 + 8x + 15 =$

2. $x^2 + 2x - 24 =$

3. $r^3 + 14r^2 + 45r =$

4. $x^2 - 16x + 48 =$

5. $1 + 2x + x^2 =$

6. $c^2 - 2cd + d^2 =$

7. $3y^2 + 4yz + z^2 =$

8. $7a^2 - 20a - 3 =$

Answers: Factoring Polynomials

1. $(x + 3)(x + 5)$

2. $(x + 6)(x - 4)$

3. $r(r + 9)(r + 5)$

4. $(x - 4)(x - 12)$

5. $(1 + x)(1 + x)$

6. $(c - d)(c - d)$

7. $(3y + z)(y + z)$

8. $(7a + 1)(a - 3)$

Solving Quadratic Equations

A *quadratic equation* is an equation that can be written as $Ax^2 + Bx + C = 0$ with $A \neq 0$. To solve a quadratic equation using factoring, take the following steps:

1. Put all terms on one side of the equal sign, leaving zero on the other side.
2. Factor.
3. Set each factor equal to zero.
4. Solve each of these equations. (The solutions are also called the *roots*.)
5. Check by inserting your solutions in the original equation.

Examples:

Solve for x: $x^2 - 6x = 16$.

Following the steps, put all terms on one side of the equal sign. Therefore, $x^2 - 6x = 16$ becomes $x^2 - 6x - 16 = 0$.

Factor:

$$(x - 8)(x + 2) = 0$$

Set each factor equal to 0 and solve:

$$x - 8 = 0 \text{ or } x + 2 = 0$$
$$x = 8 \qquad x = -2$$

Check:

$$8^2 - 6(8) = 16 \text{ or } (-2)^2 - 6(-2) = 16$$
$$64 - 48 = 16 \qquad 4 + 12 = 16$$
$$16 = 16 \qquad 16 = 16$$

Both values, 8 and −2, are solutions to the original equation.

Solve for y: $y^2 = -6y - 5$.

Put all terms on one side of the equal sign:

$$y^2 + 6y + 5 = 0$$

Factor:

$$(y + 5)(y + 1) = 0$$

Set each factor equal to 0 and solve:

$$y + 5 = 0 \text{ or } y + 1 = 0$$
$$y = -5 \qquad y = -1$$

Check:

$$(-5)^2 = -6(-5) - 5 \text{ or } (-1)^2 = -6(-1) - 5$$
$$25 = 30 - 5 \qquad\qquad 1 = 6 - 5$$
$$25 = 25 \qquad\qquad 1 = 1$$

A quadratic missing either or both the constant term and/or the term raised to the first power is called an *incomplete quadratic equation*.

Examples:

Solve for x: $x^2 - 16 = 0$.

Factor:

$$(x + 4)(x - 4) = 0$$
$$x + 4 = 0 \text{ or } x - 4 = 0$$
$$x = -4 \qquad x = 4$$

Check:

$$(-4)^2 - 16 = 0 \text{ or } (4)^2 - 16 = 0$$
$$16 - 16 = 0 \qquad 16 - 16 = 0$$
$$0 = 0 \qquad\qquad 0 = 0$$

Solve for x: $x^2 + 6x = 0$.

Factor:

$$x(x+6) = 0$$
$$x = 0 \text{ or } x + 6 = 0$$
$$x = -6$$

Check:

$$(0)^2 + 6(0) = 0 \text{ or } (-6)^2 + 6(-6) = 0$$
$$0 + 0 = 0 \qquad 36 + (-36) = 0$$
$$0 = 0 \qquad\qquad 0 = 0$$

Solve for x: $2x^2 + 2x - 1 = x^2 + 6x - 5$.

First, simplify by putting all terms on one side and combining like terms:

$$
\begin{aligned}
2x^2 + 2x - 1 &= x^2 + 6x - 5 \\
\underline{-x^2 - 6x + 5} \quad &\ \underline{-x^2 - 6x + 5} \\
x^2 - 4x + 4 &= 0
\end{aligned}
$$

Now factor:

$$(x-2)(x-2) = 0$$
$$x - 2 = 0$$
$$x = 2$$

Since both factors equal the same number, the solution $x = 2$ is a double root.

Check:

$$2(2)^2 + 2(2) - 1 = (2)^2 + 6(2) - 5$$
$$8 + 4 - 1 = 4 + 12 - 5$$
$$11 = 11$$

Practice: Solving Quadratic Equations

1. $x^2 + 7x = -10$

2. $y^2 - 18y = -45$

3. $x^2 - 25 = 0$

4. $3t^2 + 4t + 1 = 0$

5. $2b^2 - b = 0$

6. $3n^2 - 2n = -1 + 2n^2$

Answers: Solving Quadratic Equations

1.
$$x^2 + 7x = -10$$
$$x^2 + 7x + 10 = 0$$
$$(x+2)(x+5) = 0$$
$$x + 2 = 0 \quad \text{or } x + 5 = 0$$
$$x = -2 \qquad x = -5$$

2.
$$y^2 - 18y = -45$$
$$y^2 - 18y + 45 = 0$$
$$(y-15)(y-3) = 0$$
$$y - 15 = 0 \qquad \text{or } y - 3 = 0$$
$$y = 15 \qquad\qquad y = 3$$

3. $x^2 - 25 = 0$

$(x + 5)(x - 5) = 0$

$x + 5 = 0 \quad \text{or} \quad x - 5 = 0$

$x = -5 \qquad x = 5$

4. $3t^2 + 4t + 1 = 0$

$(3t + 1)(t + 1) = 0$

$3t + 1 = 0$

$3t = -1 \quad \text{or} \quad t + 1 = 0$

$t = -\dfrac{1}{3} \qquad t = -1$

5. $2b^2 - b = 0$

$b(2b - 1) = 0$

$b = 0 \quad \text{or} \quad 2b - 1 = 0$

$2b = 1$

$b = \dfrac{1}{2}$

6. $3n^2 - 2n = -1 + 2n^2$

$\underline{-2n^2 \qquad\qquad - 2n^2}$

$n^2 - 2n = -1$

$n^2 - 2n + 1 = 0$

$(n - 1)(n - 1) = 0$

$n - 1 = 0$

$n = 1$

Using the Quadratic Formula

If the problem is not easily solved by factoring, use the quadratic formula: $x = \dfrac{-b \pm \sqrt{b^2 - 4ac}}{2a}$.

To use this formula, set the equation equal to zero. For example, in problem 1 under "Practice: Solving Quadratic Equations," $x^2 + 7x = -10$, after adding 10 to each side of the equal sign you have the equation $x^2 + 7x + 10 = 0$. The values for a, b, and c are the coefficients: $ax^2 + bx + c = 0$. Therefore, for practice problem 1, $a = 1$, $b = 7$, and $c = 10$. There was no number in front of the x^2; therefore, it is the implied 1.

Substituting these values into the formula, we have:

$$\frac{-7 \pm \sqrt{7^2 - 4(1)(10)}}{2(1)} =$$

$$\frac{-7 \pm \sqrt{49 - 40}}{2} =$$

$$\frac{-7 \pm \sqrt{9}}{2} =$$

$$\frac{-7 + 3}{2} \quad \text{or} \quad \frac{-7 - 3}{2} =$$

$$\frac{-4}{2} \quad \text{or} \quad \frac{-10}{2} =$$

$$-2 \quad \text{or} \quad -5$$

Practice: Using the Quadratic Formula

Solve for x.

1. $8x^2 - 8x - 6 = 0$

2. $4x^2 + 10x + 4 = 0$

3. $3x^2 - 10x + 3 = 0$

Answers: Using the Quadratic Formula

1. $8x^2 - 8x - 6 = 0$; $a = 8$, $b = -8$, $c = -6$

$$\frac{-(-8) \pm \sqrt{(-8)^2 - 4(8)(-6)}}{2(8)} =$$

$$\frac{8 \pm \sqrt{64 + 192}}{16} =$$

$$\frac{8 \pm \sqrt{256}}{16} =$$

$$\frac{8 \pm 16}{16} =$$

$$\frac{8 + 16}{16} \quad \text{or} \quad \frac{8 - 16}{16}$$

$$\frac{3}{2} \quad \text{or} \quad -\frac{1}{2}$$

2. $4x^2 + 10x + 4 = 0$; $a = 4$, $b = 10$, $c = 4$

$$\frac{-10 \pm \sqrt{10^2 - 4(4)(4)}}{2(4)} =$$

$$\frac{-10 \pm \sqrt{100 - 64}}{8} =$$

$$\frac{-10 \pm \sqrt{36}}{8} =$$

$$\frac{-10 \pm 6}{8} =$$

$$\frac{-10 + 6}{8} \quad \text{or} \quad \frac{-10 - 6}{8} =$$

$$-\frac{1}{2} \quad \text{or} \quad -2$$

3. $3x^2 - 10x + 3 = 0$; $a = 3$, $b = -10$, $c = 3$

$$\frac{-(-10) \pm \sqrt{(-10)^2 - 4(3)(3)}}{2(3)} =$$

$$\frac{+10 \pm \sqrt{100 - 36}}{6} =$$

$$\frac{10 \pm \sqrt{64}}{6} =$$

$$\frac{10 \pm 8}{6} =$$

$$\frac{10 + 8}{6} \quad \text{or} \quad \frac{10 - 8}{6} =$$

$$3 \quad \text{or} \quad \frac{1}{3}$$

Graphing quadratic equations is explained in the "Analytic Geometry" section on pp. 145–147.

Algebraic Fractions

Algebraic fractions are fractions using a variable in the numerator and/or denominator, such as $\dfrac{3}{x}$. Since division by 0 is impossible, variables in the denominator have certain restrictions. The denominator can *never* equal zero; therefore, the following are true:

In $\dfrac{5}{x}$, x cannot equal 0 ($x \neq 0$).

In $\dfrac{2}{x-3}$, x cannot equal 3 ($x \neq 3$).

In $\dfrac{3}{a-b}$, $a - b$ cannot equal 0 ($a - b \neq 0$), so a cannot equal b ($a \neq b$).

In $\dfrac{4}{a^2 b}$, a cannot equal 0 and b cannot equal 0 ($a \neq 0$ and $b \neq 0$).

Be aware of these types of restrictions.

Reducing Algebraic Fractions

The ability to use multiple skills across math problems is a foundation for career readiness, according to the Common Core Standards. When performing operations on algebraic fractions, multiple skills come into play to solve problems (e.g., rules of exponents, simplifying fractions, and math number theory). To reduce an algebraic fraction to the lowest terms, first factor the numerator and the denominator, and then cancel (or divide out) common factors.

Examples:

Reduce: $\dfrac{4x^3}{8x^2}$.

$\dfrac{\overset{1}{4}x^{\overset{1}{3}}}{\underset{2}{8}x^{2}} = \dfrac{1}{2}x \text{ or } \dfrac{x}{2}$

Reduce: $\dfrac{x^2 + 2x + 1}{(3x + 3)}$.

$\dfrac{x^2 + 2x + 1}{(3x + 3)} = \dfrac{(x+1)(x+1)}{3(x+1)} = \dfrac{(x+1)(x+1)}{3(x+1)} = \dfrac{(x+1)}{3}$

Reduce: $\dfrac{(3x - 3)}{(4x - 4)}$.

$\dfrac{(3x - 3)}{(4x - 4)} = \dfrac{3(x - 1)}{4(x - 1)} = \dfrac{3(x-1)}{4(x-1)} = \dfrac{3}{4}$

Warning: Do *not* cancel through an addition or subtraction sign. For example:

$$\dfrac{x+1}{x+2} \neq \dfrac{x+1}{x+2} \neq \dfrac{1}{2} \text{ or } \dfrac{x-6}{6} \neq \dfrac{x-6}{6} \neq x$$

Practice: Reducing Algebraic Fractions

Reduce the following.

1. $\dfrac{8a^2b}{12a^3b}$

2. $\dfrac{5xy^3}{10x^3y}$

3. $\dfrac{10x+5}{8x+4}$

4. $\dfrac{x^2-y^2}{x+y}$

5. $\dfrac{a^2+a}{2a^2+4a+2}$

Answers: Reducing Algebraic Fractions

1. $\dfrac{8a^2b}{12a^3b}=\dfrac{\overset{2}{\cancel{8}}\,\cancel{a^2}\,\cancel{b}}{\underset{3}{\cancel{12}}\,a^{\cancel{3}}\,\cancel{b}}=\dfrac{2}{3a}$

2. $\dfrac{5xy^3}{10x^3y}=\dfrac{\overset{1}{\cancel{5}}\,\cancel{x}\,y^{\overset{2}{\cancel{3}}}}{\underset{2}{\cancel{10}}\,x^{\cancel{3}}\,y}=\dfrac{1y^2}{2x^2}=\dfrac{y^2}{2x^2}$

3. $\dfrac{10x+5}{8x+4}=\dfrac{5(2x+1)}{4(2x+1)}=\dfrac{5\cancel{(2x+1)}}{4\cancel{(2x+1)}}=\dfrac{5}{4}=1\dfrac{1}{4}$

4. $\dfrac{x^2-y^2}{x+y}=\dfrac{(x-y)(x+y)}{x+y}=\dfrac{(x-y)\cancel{(x+y)}}{\cancel{x+y}}=\dfrac{(x-y)}{1}=x-y$

5. $\dfrac{a^2+a}{2a^2+4a+2}=\dfrac{a(a+1)}{2(a^2+2a+1)}=\dfrac{a(a+1)}{2(a+1)(a+1)}=\dfrac{a\cancel{(a+1)}}{2(a+1)\cancel{(a+1)}}=\dfrac{a}{2(a+1)}$

Multiplying Algebraic Fractions

To multiply algebraic fractions, first factor the numerators and denominators that are polynomials, and then cancel where possible. Multiply the remaining numerators together and the remaining denominators together. (If you've canceled properly, your answer will be in reduced form.)

Examples:

$$\dfrac{2x}{3}\times\dfrac{y}{5}=\dfrac{2xy}{15}$$

$$\dfrac{x^2}{3y}\times\dfrac{2y}{3x}=\dfrac{x^{\overset{1}{\cancel{2}}}}{3\cancel{y}}\times\dfrac{2\cancel{y}}{3\cancel{x}}=\dfrac{2x}{9}$$

$$\dfrac{x+1}{5y+10}\times\dfrac{y+2}{x^2+2x+1}=\dfrac{x+1}{5(y+2)}\times\dfrac{y+2}{(x+1)(x+1)}=\dfrac{\overset{1}{\cancel{x+1}}}{5\cancel{(y+2)}}\times\dfrac{\overset{1}{\cancel{y+2}}}{\cancel{(x+1)}(x+1)}=\dfrac{1}{5(x+1)}$$

Practice: Multiplying Algebraic Fractions

1. $\dfrac{6x}{11} \times \dfrac{2}{5y} =$

2. $\dfrac{3a^2}{5b} \times \dfrac{2b}{9a} =$

3. $\dfrac{5}{x+1} \times \dfrac{3x+3}{6} =$

4. $\dfrac{x^2-4}{6} \times \dfrac{3y}{2x+4} =$

5. $\dfrac{x^2+4x+4}{x-3} \times \dfrac{5}{3x+6} =$

Answers: Multiplying Algebraic Fractions

1. $\dfrac{6x}{11} \times \dfrac{2}{5y} = \dfrac{12x}{55y}$

2. $\dfrac{3a^2}{5b} \times \dfrac{2b}{9a} = \dfrac{\cancel{3}\,\overset{1}{a^{\cancel{2}}}\,^a}{5\cancel{b}} \times \dfrac{2\cancel{b}}{\underset{3}{\cancel{9}}\,\cancel{a}} = \dfrac{2a}{15}$

3. $\dfrac{5}{x+1} \times \dfrac{3x+3}{6} = \dfrac{5}{x+1} \times \dfrac{3(x+1)}{6} = \dfrac{5}{\cancel{x+1}} \times \dfrac{\overset{1}{\cancel{3}}\,\cancel{(x+1)}}{\underset{2}{\cancel{6}}} = \dfrac{5}{2} = 2\dfrac{1}{2}$

4. $\dfrac{x^2-4}{6} \times \dfrac{3y}{2x+4} = \dfrac{(x+2)(x-2)}{6} \times \dfrac{3y}{2(x+2)} = \dfrac{\cancel{(x+2)}(x-2)}{\cancel{6}} \times \dfrac{\overset{1}{\cancel{3}}\,y}{2\,\cancel{(x+2)}} = \dfrac{(x-2)y}{4}$

5. $\dfrac{x^2+4x+4}{x-3} \times \dfrac{5}{3x+6} = \dfrac{(x+2)(x+2)}{x-3} \times \dfrac{5}{3(x+2)} = \dfrac{(x+2)\,\cancel{(x+2)}}{x-3} \times \dfrac{5}{3\,\cancel{(x+2)}} = \dfrac{5(x+2)}{3(x-3)}$

Dividing Algebraic Fractions

To divide algebraic fractions, invert the fraction doing the dividing and multiply. ***Remember:*** You can cancel only *after* you invert.

Examples:

$$\frac{3x^2}{5} \div \frac{2x}{y} = \frac{3x^2}{5} \times \frac{y}{2x} = \frac{3x^{\overset{1}{\cancel{2}}}}{5} \times \frac{y}{2\cancel{x}} = \frac{3xy}{10}$$

$$\frac{4x-8}{6} \div \frac{x-2}{3} = \frac{4x-8}{6} \times \frac{3}{x-2} = \frac{4(x-2)}{6} \times \frac{3}{x-2} = \frac{4\,\overset{1}{\cancel{(x-2)}}}{\underset{2}{\cancel{6}}} \times \frac{\cancel{3}}{\underset{1}{\cancel{x-2}}} = \frac{4}{2} = 2$$

Practice: Dividing Algebraic Fractions

1. $\dfrac{8x^3}{15} \div \dfrac{6x^2}{3} =$

2. $\dfrac{y^2}{5} \div y^2 =$

3. $\dfrac{2x+6}{5} \div \dfrac{x+3}{10} =$

4. $\dfrac{x^2}{x^2+5x+6} \div \dfrac{x}{x+3} =$

Answers: Dividing Algebraic Fractions

1. $\dfrac{8x^3}{15} \div \dfrac{6x^2}{3} = \dfrac{8x^3}{15} \times \dfrac{3}{6x^2} = \dfrac{\overset{4}{\cancel{8}}\,\overset{1}{\cancel{x^3}}}{\underset{5}{\cancel{15}}} \times \dfrac{\overset{1}{\cancel{3}}}{\underset{3}{\cancel{6}}\,\cancel{x^2}} = \dfrac{4x}{15}$

2. $\dfrac{y^2}{5} \div y^2 = \dfrac{y^2}{5} \div \dfrac{y^2}{1} = \dfrac{y^2}{5} \times \dfrac{1}{y^2} = \dfrac{\overset{1}{\cancel{y^2}}}{5} \times \dfrac{1}{\underset{1}{\cancel{y^2}}} = \dfrac{1}{5}$

3. $\dfrac{2x+6}{5} \div \dfrac{x+3}{10} = \dfrac{2x+6}{5} \times \dfrac{10}{x+3} = \dfrac{2(x+3)}{5} \times \dfrac{10}{x+3} = \dfrac{2\,\overset{}{\cancel{(x+3)}}}{\underset{1}{\cancel{5}}} \times \dfrac{\overset{2}{\cancel{10}}}{\underset{1}{\cancel{x+3}}} = \dfrac{4}{1} = 4$

4. $\dfrac{x^2}{x^2+5x+6} \div \dfrac{x}{x+3} = \dfrac{x^2}{x^2+5x+6} \times \dfrac{x+3}{x} = \dfrac{\overset{1}{\cancel{x^2}}\,x}{\cancel{(x+3)}(x+2)} \times \dfrac{\overset{1}{\cancel{x+3}}}{\underset{1}{\cancel{x}}} = \dfrac{x}{x+2}$

Adding or Subtracting Algebraic Fractions

To add or subtract algebraic fractions that have a common denominator, simply keep the denominator and combine (add or subtract) the numerators. Reduce if necessary.

Examples:

$$\frac{4}{x} + \frac{5}{x} = \frac{4+5}{x} = \frac{9}{x}$$

$$\frac{x-4}{x+1} + \frac{3}{x+1} = \frac{x-4+3}{x+1} = \frac{x-1}{x+1}$$

$$\frac{3x}{y} - \frac{2x-1}{y} = \frac{3x-(2x-1)}{y} = \frac{3x-2x+1}{y} = \frac{x+1}{y}$$

Practice: Adding or Subtracting Algebraic Fractions

1. $\dfrac{3}{x} + \dfrac{2}{x} =$

2. $\dfrac{x-1}{y} + \dfrac{3x+2}{y} =$

3. $\dfrac{4x-3}{x} - \dfrac{3x-3}{x} =$

4. $\dfrac{6x-3}{x-4} - \dfrac{x+2}{x-4} =$

Answers: Adding or Subtracting Algebraic Fractions

1. $\dfrac{3}{x}+\dfrac{2}{x}=\dfrac{3+2}{x}=\dfrac{5}{x}$

2. $\dfrac{x-1}{y}+\dfrac{3x+2}{y}=\dfrac{x-1+3x+2}{y}=\dfrac{4x+1}{y}$

3. $\dfrac{4x-3}{x}-\dfrac{3x-3}{x}=\dfrac{4x-3-(3x-3)}{x}=\dfrac{4x-3-3x+3}{x}=\dfrac{x}{x}=1$

4. $\dfrac{6x-3}{x-4}-\dfrac{x+2}{x-4}=\dfrac{6x-3-(x+2)}{x-4}=\dfrac{6x-3-x-2}{x-4}=\dfrac{5x-5}{x-4}=\dfrac{5(x-1)}{x-4}$

To add or subtract algebraic fractions having different denominators, first find a lowest common denominator (LCD), change each fraction to an equivalent fraction with the common denominator, then combine each numerator. Reduce if necessary.

Examples:

$\dfrac{2}{x}+\dfrac{3}{y}=$

LCD = xy

$\dfrac{2}{x}\times\dfrac{y}{y}+\dfrac{3}{y}\times\dfrac{x}{x}=\dfrac{2y}{xy}+\dfrac{3x}{xy}=\dfrac{2y+3x}{xy}$

$\dfrac{x+2}{3x}+\dfrac{x-3}{6x}=$

LCD = $6x$

$\dfrac{x+2}{3x}\times\dfrac{2}{2}+\dfrac{x-3}{6x}=\dfrac{2x+4}{6x}+\dfrac{x-3}{6x}=\dfrac{2x+4+x-3}{6x}=\dfrac{3x+1}{6x}$

If there is a common variable factor with more than one exponent, use its greatest exponent.

Examples:

$\dfrac{2}{y^2}-\dfrac{3}{y}=$

LCD = y^2

$\dfrac{2}{y^2}-\dfrac{3}{y}\times\dfrac{y}{y}=\dfrac{2}{y^2}-\dfrac{3y}{y^2}=\dfrac{2-3y}{y^2}$

$\dfrac{4}{x^3y}+\dfrac{3}{xy^2}=$

LCD = x^3y^2

$\dfrac{4}{x^3y}\times\dfrac{y}{y}+\dfrac{3}{xy^2}\times\dfrac{x^2}{x^2}=\dfrac{4y}{x^3y^2}+\dfrac{3x^2}{x^3y^2}=\dfrac{4y+3x^2}{x^3y^2}$

$$\frac{x}{x+1} - \frac{2x}{x+2} =$$

LCD $= (x + 1)(x + 2)$

$$\frac{x}{x+1} \times \frac{(x+2)}{(x+2)} - \frac{2x}{x+2} \times \frac{(x+1)}{(x+1)} = \frac{x^2+2x}{(x+1)(x+2)} - \frac{2x^2+2x}{(x+1)(x+2)}$$

$$= \frac{x^2+2x-2x^2-2x}{(x+1)(x+2)} = \frac{-x^2}{(x+1)(x+2)}$$

To find the lowest common denominator, it is often necessary to factor the denominators and proceed as follows.

Example:

$$\frac{2x}{x^2-9} - \frac{5}{x^2+4x+3} = \frac{2x}{(x+3)(x-3)} - \frac{5}{(x+3)(x+1)} =$$

LCD $= (x + 3)(x - 3)(x + 1)$

$$\frac{2x}{(x+3)(x-3)} \times \frac{(x+1)}{(x+1)} - \frac{5}{(x+3)(x+1)} \times \frac{(x-3)}{(x-3)} = \frac{2x^2+2x}{(x+3)(x-3)(x+1)} - \frac{(5x-15)}{(x+3)(x-3)(x+1)}$$

$$= \frac{2x^2+2x-(5x-15)}{(x+3)(x-3)(x+1)}$$

$$= \frac{2x^2+2x-5x+15}{(x+3)(x-3)(x+1)}$$

$$= \frac{2x^2-3x+15}{(x+3)(x-3)(x+1)}$$

Since $2x^2 - 3x + 15$ is not factorable, this is the reduced answer.

Practice: Adding or Subtracting Algebraic Fractions

1. $\dfrac{5}{x} + \dfrac{2}{y} =$

2. $\dfrac{x}{4} - \dfrac{y}{3} =$

3. $\dfrac{y+5}{2y} + \dfrac{y-2}{8y} =$

4. $\dfrac{7}{x} + \dfrac{3}{x^3} =$

5. $\dfrac{3x}{x^2y} + \dfrac{2x}{xy^2} =$

6. $\dfrac{x}{3x+3} + \dfrac{2x}{x+1} =$

7. $\dfrac{3}{x^2-4} - \dfrac{2x}{x^2+4x+4} =$

8. $\dfrac{1}{x} + \dfrac{1}{y} + \dfrac{1}{z} =$

Answers: Adding or Subtracting Algebraic Fractions

1. LCD $= xy$

$$\frac{5}{x} \times \frac{y}{y} + \frac{2}{y} \times \frac{x}{x} = \frac{5y}{xy} + \frac{2x}{xy} = \frac{5y+2x}{xy}$$

2. LCD $= 12$

$$\frac{x}{4} \times \frac{3}{3} - \frac{y}{3} \times \frac{4}{4} = \frac{3x}{12} - \frac{4y}{12} = \frac{3x-4y}{12}$$

3. LCD = $8y$

$$\frac{y+5}{2y} \times \frac{4}{4} + \frac{y-2}{8y} = \frac{4y+20}{8y} + \frac{y-2}{8y} =$$

$$\frac{4y+20+y-2}{8y} = \frac{5y+18}{8y}$$

4. LCD = x^3

$$\frac{7}{x} \times \frac{x^2}{x^2} + \frac{3}{x^3} = \frac{7x^2}{x^3} + \frac{3}{x^3} = \frac{7x^2+3}{x^3}$$

5. LCD = $x^2 y^2$

$$\frac{3x}{x^2} \times \frac{y}{y} + \frac{2x}{xy^2} \times \frac{x}{x} = \frac{3xy}{x^2 y^2} + \frac{2x^2}{x^2 y^2} = \frac{3xy+2x^2}{x^2 y^2} = \frac{\overset{1}{\cancel{x}}(3y+2x)}{\underset{x^1}{\cancel{x^2}} y^2} = \frac{3y+2x}{xy^2} = \frac{2x+3y}{xy^2}$$

6. $\dfrac{x}{3x+3} + \dfrac{2x}{x+1} = \dfrac{x}{3(x+1)} + \dfrac{2x}{x+1}$

LCD = $3(x + 1)$

$$\frac{x}{3(x+1)} + \frac{2x}{x+1} \times \frac{3}{3} = \frac{x}{3(x+1)} + \frac{6x}{3(x+1)}$$

$$\frac{x+6x}{3(x+1)} = \frac{7x}{3(x+1)}$$

7. $\dfrac{3}{x^2-4} - \dfrac{2x}{x^2+4x+4} = \dfrac{3}{(x+2)(x-2)} - \dfrac{2x}{(x+2)(x+2)}$

LCD = $(x + 2)(x - 2)(x + 2)$

$$\frac{3}{(x+2)(x-2)} \times \frac{(x+2)}{(x+2)} - \frac{2x}{(x+2)(x+2)} \times \frac{(x-2)}{(x-2)} = \frac{3x+6}{(x+2)(x-2)(x+2)} - \frac{2x^2-4x}{(x+2)(x+2)(x-2)}$$

$$= \frac{3x+6-(2x^2-4x)}{(x+2)(x-2)(x+2)}$$

$$= \frac{3x+6-2x^2+4x}{(x+2)(x-2)(x+2)}$$

$$= \frac{-2x^2+7x+6}{(x+2)(x-2)(x+2)}$$

Since $-2x^2 + 7x + 6$ is not factorable, this is the reduced answer.

8. LCD = xyz

$$\frac{1}{x} \times \frac{yz}{yz} + \frac{1}{y} \times \frac{xz}{xz} + \frac{1}{z} \times \frac{xy}{xy} = \frac{yz}{xyz} + \frac{xz}{xyz} + \frac{xy}{xyz} = \frac{yz+xz+xy}{xyz}$$

Inequalities

The ability to represent and solve inequalities is often referenced in the Common Core Standards. An *inequality* is a statement in which the relationships are not equal. Instead of using an equal sign (=) as in an equation, inequalities use > (greater than) and < (less than), or ≥ (greater than or equal to) and ≤ (less than or equal to), or ≠ (not equal to).

Solving Inequalities

When working with inequalities, treat them exactly like equations with one exception: If you multiply or divide both sides by a negative number, you must *reverse* the direction of the inequality.

Example:

Solve for x: $2x + 4 > 6$.

$$2x + 4 > 6$$
$$\underline{\quad -4 - 4 \quad}$$
$$2x \quad\;\; > 2$$
$$\frac{2x}{2} > \frac{2}{2}$$
$$x > 1$$

Answers are sometimes written in set builder notation $\{x: x > 1\}$, which is read "all x such that x is greater than 1."

Examples:

Solve for x: $-7x > 14$.

Divide by -7 and reverse the inequality:

$$\frac{-7x}{-7} < \frac{14}{-7}$$
$$x < -2$$

Solve for x: $3x + 2 \geq 5x - 10$.

$$3x + 2 \geq 5x - 10$$
$$\underline{\quad -2 \qquad\;\; -2 \quad}$$
$$3x \quad \geq 5x - 12$$
$$\underline{-5x \quad\; -5x \quad}$$
$$-2x \quad\;\; \geq \;\; -12$$

Notice opposite operations are used: Divide both sides by -2 and reverse the inequality:

$$\frac{-2x}{-2} \leq \frac{-12}{-2}$$
$$x \leq 6$$

In set builder notation: $\{x: x \leq 6\}$.

Practice: Solving Inequalities

Solve for x.

1. $7x + 4 > 32$

3. $3 - 2x > 7$

2. $\dfrac{2}{3}x + 5 \leq 17$

4. $5x + 6 > 2x + 21$

Answers: Solving Inequalities

1. $7x + 4 > 32$

$$\dfrac{-4 \quad -4}{7x \quad\quad > 28}$$

$$\dfrac{7x}{7} > \dfrac{28}{7}$$

$x > 4$ or $\{x: x > 4\}$

2. $\dfrac{2}{3}x + 5 \leq 17$

$$\dfrac{\quad -5 \; -5}{\dfrac{2}{3}x \quad\;\; \leq 12}$$

$$\dfrac{3}{2} \times \dfrac{2}{3}x \leq \dfrac{\overset{6}{\cancel{12}}}{1} \times \dfrac{3}{\underset{1}{\cancel{2}}}$$

$x \leq 18$ or $\{x: x \leq 18\}$

3. $3 - 2x > 7$

$$\dfrac{-3 \quad\quad -3}{-2x > 4}$$

$$\dfrac{-2x}{-2} < \dfrac{4}{-2}$$

$x < -2$ or $\{x: x < -2\}$

4. $5x + 6 > 2x + 21$

$$\dfrac{-2x - 6 \; -2x - 6}{3x \quad\; > \quad\; 15}$$

$$\dfrac{3x}{3} > \dfrac{15}{3}$$

$x > 5$ $\{x: x > 5\}$

Graphing on a Number Line

Integers and real numbers can be represented on a *number line*. The point on this line associated with each number is called the *graph* of the number. Notice that number lines are equally (or proportionately) spaced.

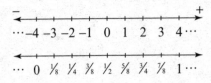

Graphing Inequalities

When graphing inequalities involving only integers, dots are used.

Example:

Graph the set of x such that $1 \leq x \leq 4$ and x is an integer. $\{x: 1 \leq x \leq 4, x \text{ is an integer}\}$

When graphing inequalities involving real numbers, lines, rays, and dots are used. A *dot* is used if the number is included. A *hollow dot* is used if the number is not included.

140

Examples:

Graph the set of x such that $x \geq 1$. $\{x: x \geq 1\}$

···−2 −1 0 1 2 3 4 5 6···

Graph the set of x such that $x > 1$. $\{x: x > 1\}$

···−3 −2 −1 0 1 2 3 4···

Graph the set of x such that $x < 4$. $\{x: x < 4\}$

···−3 −2 −1 0 1 2 3 4···

Note: A ray with a hollow dot is often called an *open ray* or an *open half line*. The hollow dot distinguishes an open ray from a ray.

Intervals

An *interval* consists of all the numbers that lie within two certain boundaries (or endpoints). If the two boundaries, or fixed numbers, are included, the interval is called a *closed interval*. If the fixed numbers are not included, the interval is called an *open interval*. If the interval includes only one of the boundaries, it is called a *half-open interval*.

Examples:

Closed interval: $\{x: -1 \leq x \leq 2\}$

···−2 −1 0 1 2 3 4···

Half-open interval: $\{x: -1 < x \leq 2\}$

···−2 −1 0 1 2 3 4···

Open interval: $\{x: -1 < x < 2\}$

···−2 −1 0 1 2 3···

Practice: Graphing Inequalities

Graph each of the following.

1. $\{x: 2 \leq x \leq 6, x \text{ is an integer}\}$

2. $\{x: -3 < x < 5, x \text{ is an integer}\}$

3. $\{x: x \geq -2\}$

4. $\{x: x < 3\}$

5. $\{x: x \leq -1\}$

Answers: Graphing Inequalities

1.

4.

2.

5.

3.

Absolute Value

The numerical value when direction or sign is not considered is called the *absolute value*. The absolute value of x is written $|x|$. The absolute value of a number is always positive except when the number is 0.

$$|0| = 0$$
$$|x| > 0, \text{ when } x \neq 0$$
$$|-x| > 0, \text{ when } x \neq 0$$

Examples:

$|4| = 4$

$|6| = 6$

$|7 - 9| = |-2| = 2$

$3 - |-6| = 3 - 6 = -3$ (Note that absolute value is calculated first.)

Solve for x: $|x| = 8$.
$x = 8$ or $x = -8$

Solve for x: $|2x - 1| = 7$.
$2x - 1 = 7$ or $2x - 1 = -7$
$2x = 8$ or $2x = -6$
$x = 4$ $x = -3$

Solve for x: $|x| = -3$.

There is no solution because the absolute value of any number is never negative.

$|2x - 1| \geq 0$

The answer is all real numbers, because the absolute value of any number is always positive or zero.

Practice: Absolute Value

1. $|-9| =$

2. $|6| =$

3. $|-3 + 2| =$

4. $|-6 - 6| =$

5. $|4 - 8| =$

6. $|-5| + 3 =$

7. $9 + |-5| =$

8. $-6 - |-8| =$

9. $|x| = 10$

10. $|3x - 6| = 12$

11. $|2x + 3| < 0$

12. $|x - 4| > 0$

Answers: Absolute Value

1. 9

2. 6

3. $|-3 + 2| = |-1| = 1$

4. $|-6 - 6| = |-12| = 12$

5. $|4 - 8| = |-4| = 4$

6. $|-5| + 3 = 5 + 3 = 8$

7. $9 + |-5| = 9 + 5 = 14$

8. $-6 - |-8| = -6 - 8 = -14$

9. $x = 10$ or $x = -10$

10. $|3x - 6| = 12$

$$3x - 6 = 12 \text{ or } 3x - 6 = -12$$
$$3x = 18 \text{ or } \quad 3x = -6$$
$$x = 6 \text{ or } \quad x = -2$$

11. No solution

12. Any real number except 4

Analytic Geometry

Coordinate Graphs

Each point on a number line is assigned a number. In the same way, each point in a plane is assigned a pair of numbers. These numbers represent the placement of the point relative to two intersecting lines, which allows for the visual representation of numbers, a Common Core Standards component. In *coordinate graphs,* two perpendicular number lines are used and are called *coordinate axes.* One axis is horizontal and is called the *x-axis.* The other is vertical and is called the *y-axis.* The point of intersection of the two number lines is called the *origin* and is represented by the coordinates (0, 0).

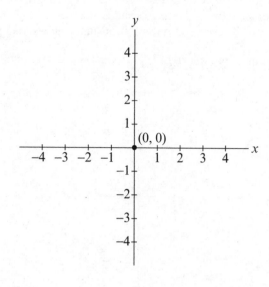

Each point on a plane is located by a unique ordered pair of numbers called the *coordinates*. Some coordinates are noted below.

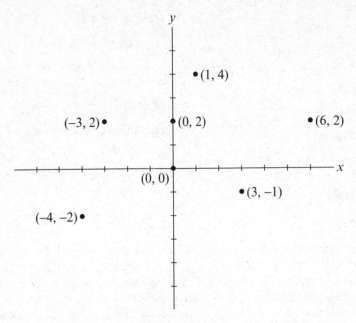

Notice that on the *x*-axis, numbers to the right of 0 are positive and to the left of 0 are negative. On the *y*-axis, numbers above 0 are positive and below 0 are negative. Also, note that the first number in the ordered pair is called the *x-coordinate,* or *abscissa,* while the second number is the *y-coordinate,* or *ordinate.* The *x*-coordinate shows the right or left direction, and the *y*-coordinate shows the up or down direction.

The coordinate graph is divided into four quarters called *quadrants.* These quadrants are labeled below.

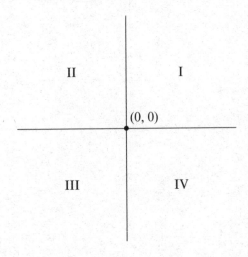

Notice the following:

- In quadrant I, *x* is always positive and *y* is always positive.
- In quadrant II, *x* is always negative and *y* is always positive.

- In quadrant III, x and y are both always negative.
- In quadrant IV, x is always positive and y is always negative.

Practice: Coordinate Graphs

Identify the points (A, B, C, D, E, and F) on the coordinate graph below.

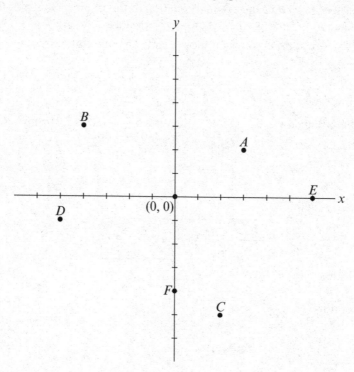

Answers: Coordinate Graphs

A (3, 2) D (−5, −1)

B (−4, 3) E (6, 0)

C (2, −5) F (0, −4)

Graphing Equations on the Coordinate Plane

To graph an equation on the coordinate plane, find the solutions by giving a value to one variable and solve the resulting equation for the other value. Repeat this process to find other solutions. (When giving a value for one variable, start with 0, then try 1, and so on.) Then graph the solutions.

Quadratic equations can be easily graphed following these steps:

1. Solve the discriminant $\sqrt{b^2 - 4ac}$ (which is part of the quadratic formula). If the discriminant is a positive number, there are two places where the parabola crosses the x-axis; if the discriminant is a zero, it touches the x-axis, but it does not cross it; if the discriminant is a negative number, it does not cross the x-axis. If the discriminant is positive or zero, then continue to graph the equation using steps 2 through 5. If the discriminant is negative, create an xy-chart to graph.

2. Solve the quadratic equation. This shows you the point where the parabola crosses the x-axis. If your discriminant is zero, steps 3 and 4 will provide you with where it touches the x-axis. Continue to Step 5 to find more points for graphing.

3. Find the x value of the *vertex* (highest or lowest point) of the parabola using the formula $-\dfrac{b}{2a}$.

4. Insert your answer for Step 3 into the original equation to the y value. Now plot that point. This gives you the vertex point and the points where it crosses the x-axis.

5. Add other values for x to solve if you want more points on your graph.

Example:

Graph the equation $x + y = 6$.

If x is 0, then y is 6.   If x is 1, then y is 5.   If x is 2, then y is 4.

$$(0) + y = 6$$
$$y = 6$$

$$(1) + y = 6$$
$$\underline{-1 \qquad -1}$$
$$y = 5$$

$$(2) + y = 6$$
$$\underline{-2 \qquad -2}$$
$$y = 4$$

Using a simple chart is helpful.

x	y
0	6
1	5
2	4

Now plot these coordinates.

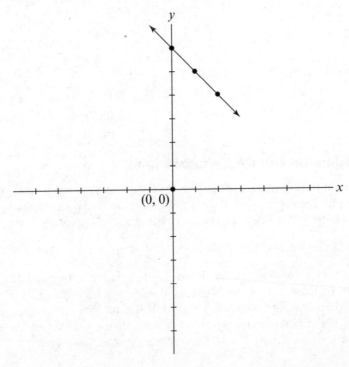

Notice that the solutions for the example problem above, when plotted, form a straight line. Equations whose solution sets form a straight line are called *linear equations*. Equations that have a variable raised to a power, show division by a variable, involve variables with square roots, or have variables multiplied together will not form a straight line when their solutions are graphed. These are called *nonlinear equations*.

Example:

Graph the equation $y = x^2 + 4$.

If x is 0, then y is 4.   If x is 1 or -1, then y is 5.   If x is 2 or -2, then y is 8.

$$y = (0)^2 + 4 \qquad\qquad y = (1)^2 + 4 \qquad y = (-1)^2 + 4 \qquad y = (2)^2 + 4 \qquad y = (-2)^2 + 4$$

$$y = 0 + 4 \qquad\qquad\quad y = 1 + 4 \qquad\quad y = 1 + 4 \qquad\qquad y = 4 + 4 \qquad\quad y = 4 + 4$$

$$y = 4 \qquad\qquad\qquad\; y = 5 \qquad\qquad y = 5 \qquad\qquad\quad y = 8 \qquad\qquad y = 8$$

Use a simple chart.

x	y
-2	8
-1	5
0	4
1	5
2	8

Now plot these coordinates.

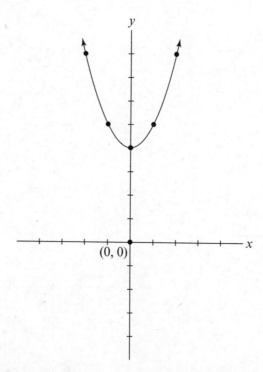

Notice that these solutions, when plotted, give a U-shaped curve (nonlinear). The graph is called a parabola. The more points plotted, the easier it is to see and describe the solution set.

Practice: Graphing Equations on the Coordinate Plane

State whether the following equations are linear or nonlinear.

1. $x - y = 5$

2. $x + 5 = y$

3. $x^2 + y = 3$

4. $xy = 1$

5. $x + \dfrac{5}{y} = 0$

6. $y = x + 7$

Graph the following equations.

7. $x - y = 3$

8. $y = x + 2$

9. $y = x^2 + 1$

10. $3x + y = 12$

11. $x + 4 = y + 2x - 3$

12. $y = 4$

13. $y = x^2 - 6x + 8$

14. $y = 4x^2 + 4x + 1$

15. $y = x^2 + 12x + 32$

Answers: Graphing Equations on the Coordinate Plane

1. Linear

2. Linear

3. Nonlinear

4. Nonlinear

5. Nonlinear

6. Linear

7.

x	y
3	0
4	1
5	2

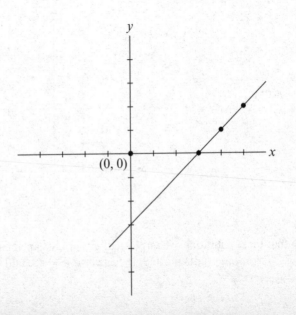

8.

x	y
0	2
1	3
2	4

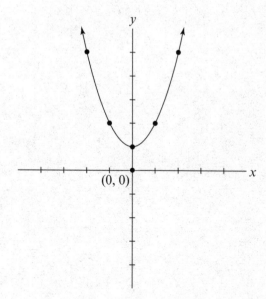

9. If $x = 0$: If $x = 1$: If $x = 2$: If $x = -1$: If $x = -2$:

$y = (0)^2 + 1$ $y = (1)^2 + 1$ $y = (2)^2 + 1$ $y = (-1)^2 + 1$ $y = (-2)^2 + 1$

$y = 0 + 1$ $y = 1 + 1$ $y = 4 + 1$ $y = 1 + 1$ $y = 4 + 1$

$y = 1$ $y = 2$ $y = 5$ $y = 2$ $y = 5$

x	y
-2	5
-1	2
0	1
1	2
2	5

10.

If $x = 0$:	If $x = 1$:	If $x = 2$:
$3(0) + y = 12$	$3(1) + y = 12$	$3(2) + y = 12$
$0 + y = 12$	$3 + y = 12$	$6 + y = 12$
$y = 12$	$\underline{-3 \qquad -3}$	$\underline{-6 \qquad -6}$
	$y = 9$	$y = 6$

x	y
0	12
1	9
2	6

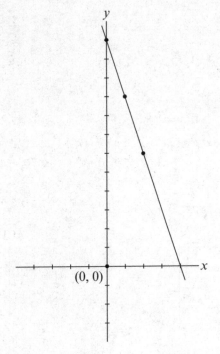

11. First, simplify by combining like terms:

$$x + 4 = y + 2x - 3$$
$$\underline{-2x \qquad\qquad -2x}$$
$$-x + 4 = y - 3$$
$$\underline{+3 \qquad\quad +3}$$
$$-x + 7 = y \qquad \text{or } 7 = x + y$$

x	y
0	7
1	6
2	5

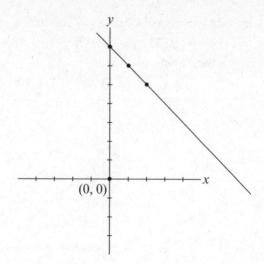

12.

x	y
0	4
1	4
2	4

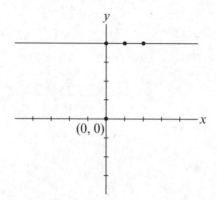

13. Step 1. The discriminant is $(-6)^2 - 4(1)(8) = 4$, a positive number; therefore, the graph crosses the x-axis in two places.

Step 2. Use the quadratic formula.

$$x = \frac{-(-6) \pm \sqrt{(-6)^2 - 4(1)(8)}}{2(1)} = \frac{6 \pm \sqrt{36 - 32}}{2}$$

$$= \frac{6 \pm \sqrt{4}}{2}$$

$$= \frac{6 \pm 2}{2}$$

$$= \frac{6 + 2}{2} \text{ and } \frac{6 - 2}{2}$$

$$= 4 \text{ and } 2$$

Step 3. The x-coordinate at the vertex is $\dfrac{-b}{2a} = \dfrac{-(-6)}{2(1)} = 3$.

Step 4. Insert 3 into the original equation to find the y-coordinate for the vertex.

Step 5. $(3)^2 - 6(3) + 8 = -1$. The vertex is $(3, -1)$.

Plot the points on the graph.

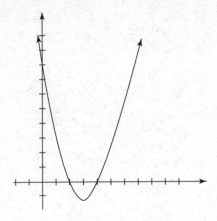

14. Step 1. The discriminant $b^2 - 4ac = (4)^2 - 4(4)(1) = 0$; therefore, it touches but does not cross the x-axis.

Step 2. Use the quadratic formula.

$$x = \frac{-4 \pm \sqrt{4^2 - 4(4)(1)}}{2(4)} = \frac{-4 \pm \sqrt{16 - 16}}{2(4)}$$

$$= \frac{-4 \pm \sqrt{0}}{2(4)}$$

$$= \frac{-4 \pm 0}{8}$$

$$= -\frac{1}{2}$$

Step 3. The x-coordinate for the vertex is $\dfrac{-b}{2a} = \dfrac{-4}{2(4)} = -\dfrac{1}{2}$.

Step 4. It only touches the x-axis at one point and that point was solved above. The point is $\left(-\dfrac{1}{2}, 0\right)$.

Step 5. Since we only have one point, make an xy-chart to find other points.

$4x^2 + 4x + 1$

x		y
0	$4(0)^2 + 4(0) + 1 = 1$	1
1	$4(1)^2 + 4(1) + 1 = 9$	9
−2	$4(−2)^2 + 4(−2) + 1 = 9$	9

Step 6. Graph the points.

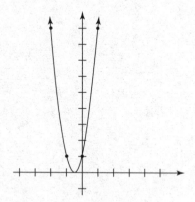

15. Step 1. The discriminant is $b^2 - 4ac$; $a = 1$, $b = 12$, $c = 32$.

$$(12)^2 - 4(1)(32) = 16$$

The discriminant is a positive number and crosses the x-axis in two places.

Step 2. Solve using the quadratic formula.

$$x = \frac{-12 \pm \sqrt{(12)^2 - 4(1)(32)}}{2(1)}$$

$$= \frac{-12 \pm \sqrt{16}}{2}$$

$$= \frac{-12 + 4}{2} \text{ and } \frac{-12 - 4}{2}$$

$$= -4 \quad \text{and} \quad -8$$

The x-intercepts are at $(-4, 0)$ and $(-8, 0)$.

Step 3. Find the x-coordinate of the vertex.

$$\frac{-b}{2a} = \frac{-12}{2(1)} = -6$$

Step 4. Input the value for x of the vertex into the equation to find the y value.

$$(-6)^2 + 12(-6) + 32 = -4$$

The vertex is $(-6, -4)$.

Step 5. Graph the points found—$(-8, 0)$, $(-4, 0)$, and $(-6, -4)$—and use them to sketch the graph.

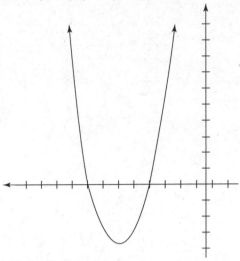

Slope and Intercept of Linear Equations

There are two relationships between the graph of a linear equation and the equation itself that need pointing out. One involves the *slope of the line,* and the other involves the point of intersection of the line with the y-axis, known as the *y-intercept*. When a linear equation is written in the $y =$ form, or the $y = mx + b$ form, the m value becomes the slope value for the line, and the b value is the location where the line intercepts the y-axis. Thus, the $y = mx + b$ form is called the *slope-intercept form* for the equation of a line.

Examples:

Rewrite each of the following linear equations in slope-intercept form and identify the slope value and the y-intercept. Also, graph each linear equation.

(a) $x - y = 3$

(b) $y = -2x + 1$

(c) $x - 2y = 4$

(a) $x - y = 3$

$$-y = -x + 3$$
$$y = x - 3$$

Slope $= 1$, y-intercept $= -3$ or y-intercept location $= (0, -3)$

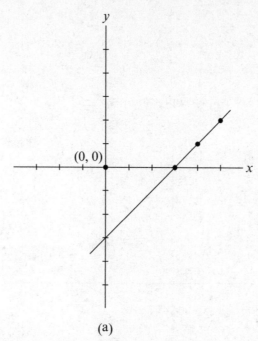

(0, 0)

(a)

(b) The equation $y = -2x + 1$ is already in slope-intercept form.

Slope $= -2$, y-intercept $= 1$ or y-intercept location $= (0, 1)$

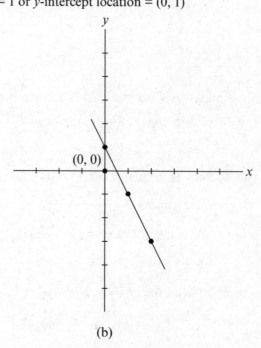

(0, 0)

(b)

(c) $x - 2y = 4$

$-2y = -x + 4$

$y = \dfrac{1}{2}x - 2$

Slope $= \dfrac{1}{2}$, y-intercept $= -2$ or y-intercept location $= (0, -2)$

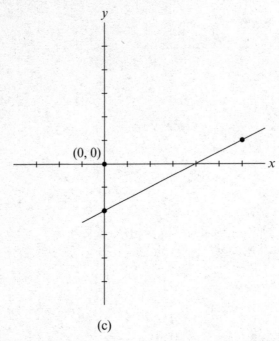

(c)

If you know the ordered pairs of two points on a line, you can evaluate the slope of the line. If (x_1, y_1) and (x_2, y_2) represent any two points on a line, then slope $= \dfrac{y_2 - y_1}{x_2 - x_1}$; that is, $m = \dfrac{y_2 - y_1}{x_2 - x_1}$.

Example:

Find the slope of the line passing through the points $(-2, 6)$ and $(3, 5)$.

Let $(x_1, y_1) = (-2, 6)$ and $(x_2, y_2) = (3, 5)$; then $m = \dfrac{5 - 6}{3 - (-2)} = \dfrac{-1}{5} = -\dfrac{1}{5}$.

If the order of the points is reversed—that is, if $(x_1, y_1) = (3, 5)$ and $(x_2, y_2) = (-2, 6)$—then

$m = \dfrac{6 - 5}{-2 - 3} = \dfrac{1}{-5} = -\dfrac{1}{5}$.

Therefore, it doesn't matter to which point you give which label when evaluating the slope of the line.

Graphing Linear Equations Using Slope and Intercept

To graph linear equations using slope and intercept, take the following steps:

1. Write the equation in slope-intercept form.
2. Locate the y-intercept on the graph. (This is one point on the line.)
3. Write the slope as a ratio (fraction) to use to locate other points on the line.
4. Draw the line through the points.

Examples:

Graph the equation $2x - y = -4$ using slope and y-intercept.

$$2x - y = -4 \qquad \text{(Rewrite in slope-intercept form.)}$$
$$-y = -2x - 4$$
$$y = 2x + 4 \qquad \text{(Slope} = 2 \text{ and } y\text{-intercept} = 4)$$

Locate the point $(0, 4)$ on the y-axis and, from this point, count as shown in the figure.

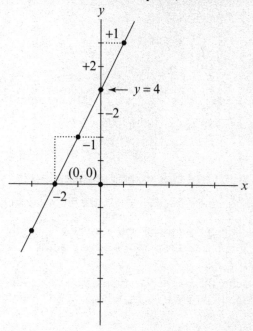

Slope $= 2$. Rewritten as a ratio, slope $= \dfrac{2}{1}$ (for every 2 up, go 1 to the right) or slope $= \dfrac{-2}{-1}$ (for every 2 down, go 1 to the left).

Graph the equation $x + 3y = 0$.

$$x + 3y = 0 \qquad \text{(Rewrite in slope-intercept form.)}$$
$$3y = -x + 0$$
$$y = -\frac{1}{3}x + 0 \quad \left(\text{Slope} = -\frac{1}{3} \text{ and } y\text{-intercept} = 0\right)$$

Locate the point $(0, 0)$ on the y-axis and, from this point, count as shown in the figure.

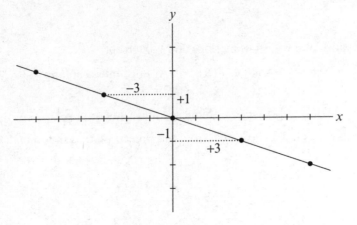

$\text{Slope} = -\frac{1}{3}$, $\text{slope} = \frac{-1}{3}$ (for every 1 down, go 3 to the right), or $\text{slope} = \frac{1}{-3}$ (for every 1 up, go 3 to the left).

Graphing Linear Equations Using the *x*- and *y*-intercepts

To graph linear equations using the x- and y-intercepts, take the following steps:

1. Find the x-intercept by replacing the y-variable with the value 0, and then solve for x. (The *x-intercept* of a graph occurs when the graph is on the x-axis. When a point is on the x-axis, its y-coordinate there is 0.)

2. Find the y-intercept by replacing the x-variable with the value 0, and then solve for y. (The *y-intercept* of a graph occurs when the graph is on the y-axis. When a point is on the y-axis, its x-coordinate there is 0.)

3. Draw a line passing through the x- and y-intercepts.

Example:

Graph the linear equation $2x + 3y = 6$ using the x-intercept and the y-intercept.

Find the x-intercept by replacing y with 0, and then solve for x.

$$2x + 3(0) = 6$$
$$2x = 6$$
$$x = 3$$

The x-intercept is located at (3, 0).

Find the y-intercept by replacing x with 0, and then solve for y.

$$2(0) + 3y = 6$$
$$3y = 6$$
$$y = 2$$

The y-intercept is at (0, 2).

Draw the line passing through the x- and y-intercepts.

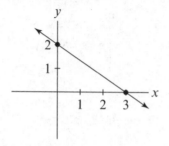

Finding an Equation of a Line

To find an equation of a line when working with ordered pairs, slopes, or intercepts, use the following approach:

1. Find the slope, m (either it is given or you need to calculate it from two given points).
2. Find the y-intercept, b (either it is given or you need to use the equation $y = mx + b$ and substitute the slope value you found in Step 1 and the x- and y-coordinates of any given point).
3. Write the equation of the line in the $y = mx + b$ slope-intercept form using the values found in steps 1 and 2.

Examples:

Find an equation of the line with a slope of -4 and a y-intercept of 3.

You are given that $m = -4$ and that $b = 3$; therefore, an equation for this line is $y = -4x + 3$.

159

Find an equation for the line passing through (6, 4) with a slope of −3.

You are given that $m = -3$. Use the equation $y = mx + b$. Substitute −3 for m and use the point (6, 4) to substitute 6 for x and 4 for y in order to find b.

$$4 = -3(6) + b$$
$$4 = -18 + b$$
$$22 = b$$

Therefore, an equation for this line is $y = -3x + 22$.

Find an equation for a line that passes through the points (5, −4) and (3, −2).

Find the slope using the two points.

$$m = \frac{-2 - (-4)}{3 - 5} = \frac{2}{-2} = -1$$

Use the equation $y = mx + b$. Substitute −1 for m and use one of the two points. You can use either (5, −4) or (3, −2). For this example, use (5, −4). Substitute 5 for x and −4 for y in order to find b.

$$-4 = -1(5) + b$$
$$-4 = -5 + b$$
$$1 = b$$

Therefore, an equation for this line is $y = -x + 1$.

Using the point (3, −2) and $m = -1$ in the equation $y = mx + b$, substitute 3 for x and −2 for y in order to find b.

$$3 = -1(-2) + b$$
$$3 = 2 + b$$
$$1 = b$$

It doesn't matter which of the two points is used in the substitution in order to find b.

Systems of Equations Word Problems

The Common Core Standards include word problems with systems of equations. To set up linear word problems, translate the words into equations and then put the equations into the following format (slope-intercept form) to solve.

$$y = mx + b$$

Carefully read what the question is asking before solving the equation. Equations can be solved by using various methods learned for systems of equations, such as substitution, graphing, and addition methods. It is important to remember that when you are solving these equations, you are finding the point on a graph where the two lines would intersect. Each problem requires a careful review to determine the easiest way to solve it.

Examples:

The sum of two numbers is 28 and their difference is 6. What are the two numbers?

Write the equation for the two unknown variables.

$$x + y = 28 \text{ and } x - y = 6$$

The easiest way to solve this problem is through systems of equations using an addition method.

Note: The addition method is helpful when you add the two equations together and one of the variables is solved.

$$
\begin{array}{r}
x + y = 28 \\
\underline{x - y = \ 6} \\
2x \quad\ = 34 \\
x = 17
\end{array}
$$

Now, input the value of x into either equation and solve for y.

$$17 + y = 28$$
$$y = 11$$

The substitution method requires solving for one equation and then substituting it into the other equation.

$$x + y = 28$$
$$x = 28 - y$$

Next, put the value for x into the second equation.

$$x - y = 6$$
$$(28 - y) - y = 6$$
$$28 - 2y = 6$$
$$-2y = -22$$
$$y = 11$$

Finally, put the value of y into either equation and solve for x.

$$x + y = 28$$
$$x + 11 = 28$$
$$x = 17$$

Use the following information to answer the next two example questions (a) and (b).

Carissa has been offered two sales positions. The first job offer has a base salary of $1,000 per month, plus a commission of 2% on her sales. The second job offer includes a base of $750 per month, plus a commission of 6% on her sales.

(a) If Carissa works for only one month, how much money in sales would she have to make in order for her income to be the same for either job?

For this part of the problem, only consider one month. Therefore, only represent how much in sales Carissa makes and how much she will earn for those sales.

Let x = the dollar amount of sales Carissa makes for each job, and let y = the amount earned at that job for one month.

For the 2% job: $y = 0.02x + 1,000$. For the 6% job: $y = 0.06x + 750$.

Since we are trying to get equal incomes, set the two "y" expressions equal to one another and solve for x.

$$0.02x + 1,000 = 0.06x + 750$$
$$1,000 = 0.04x + 750$$
$$250 = 0.04x$$
$$6,250 = x$$

Clarissa would have to sell $6,250 worth of products in her first month in order for the total earnings to be the same.

(b) If Clarissa's sales are $10,000 for her first month, which job would pay her more?

Let y = total income for the first month.

For the 2% job: $y = 0.02(\$10,000) + \$1,000 = \$1,200$. For the 6% job: $y = 0.06(\$10,000) + \$750 = \$1,350$.

Thus, the 6% job would pay more for a month's work.

The fixed overhead costs for a company are $500 per month. If sales of its product yield $22 per unit, how much, to the nearest unit, would the company have to sell to be profitable?

Set up an equation for the fixed costs of $500 per month. It should have a horizontal line: $y = 500$.

The second equation is $y = 22x$.

$$22x = 500$$
$$x = 22.\overline{72}$$

In order to be profitable, the company would have to sell 23 units because you cannot sell a partial unit.

Practice: Systems of Equations Word Problems

1. Ajay is deciding between two cell phone plans to use while out of the country on vacation. The first plan is $20 per month and 99¢ a minute with unlimited text messages. The second plan is $45 dollars a month and 50¢ a minute. The second plan also has unlimited text messages. For approximately how many minutes will the two plans have the same cost?

Answer: Systems of Equations Word Problems

1. Let x = number of minutes used. Let y = total cost.

   First plan: $y = 0.99x + 20$

   Second plan: $y = 0.50x + 45$

   Since the cost must be equal, set the two equations equal to one another.

$$0.99x + 20 = 0.50x + 45$$
$$-0.50x - 20 = -0.50x - 20$$
$$0.49x = 25$$
$$x \approx 51$$

   The two plans have equal cost for approximately 51 minutes of use.

Roots and Radicals

Note: This subject is introduced in the Arithmetic Review.

The symbol $\sqrt{\ }$ is called a *radical sign* and is used to designate *square root*. To designate *cube root,* a small three is placed above the radical sign: $\sqrt[3]{\ }$. When two radical signs are next to each other, they automatically mean that the two are multiplied. The multiplication sign may be omitted. Note that the square root of a negative number is not possible within the real number system. A completely different system of imaginary numbers is used for roots of negative numbers. Typical standardized exams use only the real number system as a general practice. The (so-called) imaginary numbers are multiples of the imaginary unit i: $\sqrt{-1} = i$, $\sqrt{-4} = 2i$, $\sqrt{-9} = 3i$, and so on. The ACT and some college placement exams deal with simple imaginary numbers and their operations.

Simplifying Square Roots

A square root with no sign indicated to its left represents a positive value. A square root with a negative to its left represents a negative value.

Examples:

$$\sqrt{9} = 3$$

$$-\sqrt{9} = -3$$

$$\sqrt{18} = \sqrt{9 \cdot 2} = \sqrt{9} \cdot \sqrt{2} = 3\sqrt{2}$$

If each variable is nonnegative (not a negative number), $\sqrt{x^2} = x$.

If each variable is nonnegative, $\sqrt{x^4} = x^2$.

If each variable is nonnegative, $\sqrt{x^6 y^8} = \sqrt{x^6}\sqrt{y^8} = x^3 y^4$.

If each variable is nonnegative, $\sqrt{25a^4 b^6} = \sqrt{25}\sqrt{a^4}\sqrt{b^6} = 5a^2 b^3$.

If x is nonnegative, $\sqrt{x^7} = \sqrt{x^6(x)} = \sqrt{x^6}\sqrt{x} = x^3\sqrt{x}$.

If x is nonnegative, $\sqrt{x^9 y^8} = \sqrt{x^9}\sqrt{y^8} = \sqrt{x^8(x)}\sqrt{y^8} = x^4\sqrt{x} \cdot y^4 = x^4 y^4 \sqrt{x}$.

If each variable is nonnegative, $\sqrt{16x^5} = \sqrt{16}\sqrt{x^5} = \sqrt{16}\sqrt{x^4(x)} = 4x^2\sqrt{x}$.

Practice: Simplifying Square Roots

Simplify the following. All variables are nonnegative.

1. $\sqrt{36} =$

2. $-\sqrt{49} =$

3. $\sqrt{121} =$

4. $\sqrt{50} =$

5. $\sqrt{72} =$

6. $\sqrt{y^6} =$

7. $\sqrt{x^6 y^{10}} =$

8. $\sqrt{36a^2 b^8} =$

9. $\sqrt{a^9} =$

10. $\sqrt{49a^5 b^4} =$

Answers: Simplifying Square Roots

1. 6

2. -7

3. 11

4. $\sqrt{50} = \sqrt{25 \cdot 2} = \sqrt{25} \cdot \sqrt{2} = 5\sqrt{2}$

5. $\sqrt{72} = \sqrt{36 \cdot 2} = \sqrt{36} \cdot \sqrt{2} = 6\sqrt{2}$

6. y^3

7. $\sqrt{x^6 y^{10}} = \sqrt{x^6}\sqrt{y^{10}} = x^3 y^5$

8. $\sqrt{36a^2 b^8} = \sqrt{36}\sqrt{a^2}\sqrt{b^8} = 6ab^4$

9. $\sqrt{a^9} = \sqrt{a^8(a)} = a^4\sqrt{a}$

10. $\sqrt{49a^5 b^4} = \sqrt{49}\sqrt{a^5}\sqrt{b^4}$
$$= \sqrt{49}\sqrt{a^4(a)}\sqrt{b^4}$$
$$= 7a^2\sqrt{a}(b^2)$$
$$= 7a^2 b^2 \sqrt{a}$$

Operations with Square Roots

You may perform operations under a single radical sign.

Examples:

$$\sqrt{(5)(20)} = \sqrt{100} = 10$$

$$\sqrt{30 + 6} = \sqrt{36} = 6$$

$$\sqrt{\frac{32}{2}} = \sqrt{16} = 4 \ (\textit{Note: } \sqrt{\frac{32}{2}} = \frac{\sqrt{32}}{\sqrt{2}}.)$$

$$\sqrt{30 - 5} = \sqrt{25} = 5$$

$$\sqrt{2 + 5} = \sqrt{7}$$

You can add or subtract square roots themselves only if the values under the radical sign are equal. Simply add or subtract the coefficients (numbers in front of the radical sign) and keep the original number in the radical sign.

Examples:

$$2\sqrt{3} + 3\sqrt{3} = (2 + 3)\sqrt{3} = 5\sqrt{3}$$

$$4\sqrt{6} - 2\sqrt{6} = (4 - 2)\sqrt{6} = 2\sqrt{6}$$

$$5\sqrt{2} + \sqrt{2} = 5\sqrt{2} + 1\sqrt{2} = (5 + 1)\sqrt{2} = 6\sqrt{2}$$

Note that 1 is understood in $\sqrt{2}$ (in other words, $1\sqrt{2}$).

You may not add or subtract different square roots.

Examples:

$$\sqrt{28} - \sqrt{3} \neq \sqrt{25}$$

$$\sqrt{16} + \sqrt{9} \neq \sqrt{25}$$

Practice: Operations Under the Radical and Adding and Subtracting Square Roots

1. $\sqrt{(18)(2)} =$

2. $\sqrt{\dfrac{200}{8}} =$

3. $\sqrt{17 + 32} =$

4. $\sqrt{31 - 16} =$

5. $4\sqrt{3} + 2\sqrt{3} =$

6. $12\sqrt{7} - 6\sqrt{7} =$

7. $8\sqrt{11} - \sqrt{11} =$

8. $3\sqrt{5} - 7\sqrt{5} =$

Answers: Operations Under the Radical and Adding and Subtracting Square Roots

1. $\sqrt{(18)(2)} = \sqrt{36} = 6$

2. $\sqrt{\dfrac{200}{8}} = \sqrt{25} = 5$

3. $\sqrt{17 + 32} = \sqrt{49} = 7$

4. $\sqrt{31 - 16} = \sqrt{15}$

5. $6\sqrt{3}$

6. $6\sqrt{7}$

7. $7\sqrt{11}$ (derived from $8\sqrt{11} - 1\sqrt{11}$)

8. $-4\sqrt{5}$ (derived from $3\sqrt{5} - 7\sqrt{5} = (3 - 7)\sqrt{5} = -4\sqrt{5}$)

Addition and Subtraction of Square Roots After Simplifying

Sometimes after simplifying the square root(s), addition or subtraction becomes possible. Always simplify if possible.

Examples:

$\sqrt{50} + 3\sqrt{2} =$

These cannot be added until $\sqrt{50}$ is simplified: $\sqrt{50} = \sqrt{25 \cdot 2} = \sqrt{25} \cdot \sqrt{2} = 5\sqrt{2}$.

Now, since both are alike under the radical sign: $5\sqrt{2} + 3\sqrt{2} = (5 + 3)\sqrt{2} = 8\sqrt{2}$.

$\sqrt{300} + \sqrt{12} =$

Try to simplify each one:

$\sqrt{300} = \sqrt{100 \cdot 3} = \sqrt{100} \cdot \sqrt{3} = 10\sqrt{3}$

$\sqrt{12} = \sqrt{4 \cdot 3} = \sqrt{4} \cdot \sqrt{3} = 2\sqrt{3}$

Now, since both are alike under the radical sign: $10\sqrt{3} + 2\sqrt{3} = (10 + 2)\sqrt{3} = 12\sqrt{3}$.

Practice: Addition and Subtraction of Square Roots After Simplifying

1. $4\sqrt{5} - \sqrt{20} =$

2. $\sqrt{18} + \sqrt{32} =$

3. $9\sqrt{7} - \sqrt{28} =$

4. $\sqrt{40} + \sqrt{27} =$

Answers: Addition and Subtraction of Square Roots After Simplifying

1. $4\sqrt{5} - \sqrt{20} =$

    Simplify: $\sqrt{20} = \sqrt{4 \cdot 5} = \sqrt{4} \cdot \sqrt{5} = 2\sqrt{5}$

    Now subtract: $4\sqrt{5} - 2\sqrt{5} = 2\sqrt{5}$

2. $\sqrt{18} + \sqrt{32} =$

    Simplify: $\sqrt{18} = \sqrt{9 \cdot 2} = \sqrt{9} \cdot \sqrt{2} = 3\sqrt{2}$

    Simplify: $\sqrt{32} = \sqrt{16 \cdot 2} = \sqrt{16} \cdot \sqrt{2} = 4\sqrt{2}$

    Now add: $3\sqrt{2} + 4\sqrt{2} = 7\sqrt{2}$

3. $9\sqrt{7} - \sqrt{28} =$

    Simplify: $\sqrt{28} = \sqrt{4 \cdot 7} = \sqrt{4} \cdot \sqrt{7} = 2\sqrt{7}$

    Now subtract: $9\sqrt{7} - 2\sqrt{7} = 7\sqrt{7}$

4. $\sqrt{40} + \sqrt{27} =$

    Simplify: $\sqrt{40} = \sqrt{4 \cdot 10} = \sqrt{4} \cdot \sqrt{10} = 2\sqrt{10}$

    Simplify: $\sqrt{27} = \sqrt{9 \cdot 3} = \sqrt{9} \cdot \sqrt{3} = 3\sqrt{3}$

    Now add: $2\sqrt{10} + 3\sqrt{3}$ (cannot be combined)

Products of Nonnegative Roots

Remember that in multiplication of roots, the multiplication sign may be omitted. Always simplify the answer when possible.

Examples:

$$\sqrt{2} \cdot \sqrt{8} = \sqrt{16} = 4$$

If x is nonnegative, $\sqrt{x^3} \cdot \sqrt{x^5} = \sqrt{x^8} = x^4$.

If each variable is nonnegative, $\sqrt{ab} \cdot \sqrt{ab^3c} = \sqrt{a^2b^4c} = \sqrt{a^2}\sqrt{b^4}\sqrt{c} = ab^2\sqrt{c}$.

If each variable is nonnegative, $\sqrt{3x} \cdot \sqrt{6xy^2} \cdot \sqrt{2xy} = \sqrt{36x^3y^3} = \sqrt{36}\sqrt{x^3}\sqrt{y^3}$ and $\sqrt{36}\sqrt{x^2(x)}\sqrt{y^2(y)} = 6xy\sqrt{xy}$.

$$2\sqrt{5} \cdot 7\sqrt{3} = (2 \cdot 7)\sqrt{5 \cdot 3} = 14\sqrt{15}$$

Practice: Products of Nonnegative Roots

In the following, all variables are nonnegative.

1. $\sqrt{12} \cdot \sqrt{3} =$

2. $\sqrt{6} \cdot \sqrt{8} =$

3. $\sqrt{y^5} \cdot \sqrt{y^7} =$

4. $\sqrt{x^2y} \cdot \sqrt{xy^2} =$

5. $\sqrt{abc} \cdot \sqrt{bc} \cdot \sqrt{ac^2} =$

6. $\sqrt{5a^2} \cdot \sqrt{2ab} \cdot \sqrt{10b^2}$

7. $3\sqrt{2} \cdot 2\sqrt{5} =$

8. $4\sqrt{2} \cdot 5\sqrt{8} =$

Answers: Products of Nonnegative Roots

1. $\sqrt{12} \cdot \sqrt{3} = \sqrt{36} = 6$

2. $\sqrt{6} \cdot \sqrt{8} = \sqrt{48} = \sqrt{16 \cdot 3} = \sqrt{16}\sqrt{3} = 4\sqrt{3}$

3. $\sqrt{y^5} \cdot \sqrt{y^7} = \sqrt{y^{12}} = y^6$

4. $\sqrt{x^2y} \cdot \sqrt{xy^2} = \sqrt{x^3y^3} = \sqrt{x^2(x)y^2(y)} = xy\sqrt{xy}$
   or $\sqrt{x^2y} \cdot \sqrt{xy^2} = x\sqrt{y} \cdot y\sqrt{x} = xy\sqrt{xy}$

5. $\sqrt{abc} \cdot \sqrt{bc} \cdot \sqrt{ac^2} = \sqrt{a^2b^2c^4} = abc^2$

6. $\sqrt{5a^2} \cdot \sqrt{2ab} \cdot \sqrt{10b^2} = \sqrt{100a^3b^3}$
   $= \sqrt{100}\sqrt{a^3}\sqrt{b^3}$
   $= \sqrt{100}\sqrt{a^2(a)}\sqrt{b^2(b)}$
   $= 10ab\sqrt{ab}$

7. $3\sqrt{2} \cdot 2\sqrt{5} = (3 \cdot 2)\sqrt{2 \cdot 5} = 6\sqrt{10}$

8. $4\sqrt{2} \cdot 5\sqrt{8} = (4 \cdot 5)\sqrt{2 \cdot 8} = 20\sqrt{16} = 20(4) = 80$

"False" Operations

Many standardized exams include a question or two using operations created uniquely for that particular problem. The operation may be represented by unusual symbols (such as @ , *, or #) that are then defined with standard operations of $+$, $-$, $\times$, $\div$, and so on. Don't let these new or different symbols alarm you.

Example:

If $x @ y = \dfrac{x}{y}$ and $y \neq 0$, then what is $4 @ 2$?

This operation shows that the first value is divided by the second value; therefore, $4 @ 2 = \dfrac{4}{2} = 2$.

The key to understanding these types of problems is simply understanding the definition of the operation—how to replace, or plug in, values. Notice that the definitions are given in terms of standard operations with which you are familiar.

Examples:

If $x \$ y = x^2 + y^2$, then $2 \$ 5 = ?$

$2 \$ 5 = (2)^2 + (5)^2 = 4 + 25 = 29$

If $a \# b = \dfrac{a+b}{2}$, $3 \# 5 = ?$

$3 \# 5 = \dfrac{3+5}{2} = \dfrac{8}{2} = 4$

Practice: "False" Operations

1. For all integers a and b, the binary operation $\#$ is defined by $a \# b = ab + b$. What is the value of $5 \# 7$?

2. $x @ y = \dfrac{x^2 + y^2}{xy}$ for all real numbers x and y such that $xy \neq 0$. What is the value of $2 @ 6$?

3. The operation $\not{c}$ is defined for all nonzero numbers x and y by the equation $x \not{c} y = (x - y)(x + y)(x)$. What is the value of $5 \not{c} 6$?

4. If $a * b$ means that a^2 is greater than b^2, then which of the following relationships must be true?

   I. $a = 0$

   II. $a > b$

   III. $a \neq 0$

5. $[(x)(y)(z)]^{\#} = x^2 + yz$ for all real numbers x, y, and z. What is the value of $[(3)(4)(5)]^{\#}$?

6. The operation $\$$ is defined on ordered pairs of numbers as follows: $(x, y) \$ (w, z) = (xw, yz)$. What is the value of $(3, 5) \$ (4, 6)$?

7. If $x @ y = xy$ for all positive integers x and y, what is the value of a if $b @ a = b$?

8. If $x \star y = \dfrac{x+y}{5}$, then which of the following must always be true?

   I. $a \star b = b \star a$

   II. $a \star b = a \star a$

   III. $a \star b = b \star b$

Answers: "False" Operations

1. $a \# b = ab + b$

   $5 \# 7 = (5)(7) + 7$

   $\quad\;\; = 35 + 7$

   $\quad\;\; = 42$

   Note that *binary operation* simply means an operation between two values or variables.

2. $x @ y = \dfrac{x^2 + y^2}{xy}$

   $2 @ 6 = \dfrac{(2)^2 + (6)^2}{(2)(6)}$

   $\quad\;\; = \dfrac{4 + 36}{12}$

   $\quad\;\; = \dfrac{40}{12} = \dfrac{10}{3} = 3\dfrac{1}{3}$

3. $x \; ¢ \; y = (x - y)(x + y)(x)$

   $5 \; ¢ \; 6 = (5 - 6)(5 + 6)(5)$

   $\quad\;\;\; = (-1)(11)(5)$

   $\quad\;\;\; = -55$

4. Note that if a^2 is to be greater than b^2, then a^2 must be a positive number, as the smallest value for b^2 is 0. Therefore, statement I is false. Statement II is not necessarily true, since a could be -3 and b could be $+2$, yet $a^2 > b^2$. Statement III is true because if $a \neq 0$, a^2 will always be positive.

5. $[(x)(y)(z)]^{\#} = x^2 + yz$

   $[(3)(4)(5)]^{\#} = (3)^2 + (4)(5)$

   $\quad\qquad\quad = 9 + 20$

   $\quad\qquad\quad = 29$

6. $(x, \, y) \, \$ \, (w, \, z) = (xw, \, yz)$

   $(3, \, 5) \, \$ \, (4, \, 6) = (3 \cdot 4, \, 5 \cdot 6)$

   $\quad\qquad\qquad\;\; = (12, \, 30)$

7. $x @ y = xy$

   $b @ a = b$

   If $b @ a = b$, then

   $\quad ba = b$ (divide each side by b)

   $\quad\; a = 1$

   Therefore, the value of a is 1.

8. Only statement I is always true. The sum of $x + y$ equals the sum of $y + x$; therefore, the original placement of a and b is irrelevant since $\dfrac{a+b}{5} = \dfrac{b+a}{5}$. Statements II and III are not always true. They are true only if $a = b$.

Algebra Review Test

Questions

1. A set within a set is called a _____.

2. A set with no members is called the _____ or _____.

3. Naming a set by describing its elements is called the _____ method.

4. A method of naming a set by listing its members is called _____.

5. Sets that are countable or stop are called _____.

6. Sets that continue forever are uncountable and are called _____.

7. True or false: {1, 2, 3, 4} = {a, b, c, d}

8. True or false: {2, 4, 6} ~ {1, 3, 5}

9. {2, 7, 8} ∩ {1, 3, 8} =

10. {4, 5, 6} ∪ {1, 3, 5} =

11. Express each of the following algebraically.

    (a) four more than twice a number

    (b) a number decreased by six

    (c) a number increased by ten

    (d) a number x decreased by four times y

12. Evaluate $p^2 + 7p - 5$ if $p = 6$.

13. Evaluate $4x^2y^3z^2$ if $x = 2$, $y = 3$, and $z = 4$.

14. Evaluate $\dfrac{xy}{4} - \dfrac{x + yz}{z}$ if $x = 3$, $y = 4$, and $z = 6$.

15. If $f(x) = x^2 - \dfrac{1}{3}x$ and $g(x) = x^2 - x + 1$, find $f(9) - g(8)$.

16. Evaluate $\dfrac{f(2)}{g(3)}$ for $f(x) = \dfrac{x^3}{2x}$ and $g(x) = \dfrac{3x - 1}{2}$.

17. Solve for x: $x + 18 = 64$.

18. Solve for x: $4x - 8 = 32$.

19. Solve for y: $\dfrac{y}{8} - 3 = 9$.

20. Solve for z: $\dfrac{2}{5}z + 4 = 13$.

21. Solve for x: $7x = 4x - 9$.

22. Solve for n: $5n + 7 = 3n - 9$.

23. Solve for y: $\dfrac{-y}{6} = 14$.

24. Solve for y: $my - n = x$.

25. Solve for m: $\dfrac{m}{n} = a$.

26. Solve for x: $\dfrac{r}{x} = \dfrac{s}{t}$.

27. Solve for x: x is to y as z is to a.

28. Solve for x: $\dfrac{x}{6} = \dfrac{1}{2}$.

29. Solve for c: $\dfrac{7}{2} = \dfrac{12}{c}$.

30. According to the city, shopping centers should have 3 square feet of parking for every square foot of shopping. The new proposed shopping center has 650,000 square feet of shopping. How many square feet of parking is needed to be approved by the city?

31. Referencing question 30 above, if the average parking space is 250 square feet, how many parking spaces will the shopping center have?

32. Solve this system for x and y: $\begin{array}{l} x - 2y = 8 \\ 3x + 2y = 4 \end{array}$

33. Solve this system for a and b: $\begin{array}{l} 3a + 2b = 1 \\ 2a - 3b = -8 \end{array}$

34. Solve this system for x and y: $\begin{array}{l} y = x + 3 \\ 2x + y = 8 \end{array}$

Use the information below to answer questions 35–37.

Makala is deciding whether she should purchase a new car with better gas mileage. Her current car costs an average of $75 per month to operate (repairs and maintenance) and, at current gas prices, costs her $0.26 per mile in gas. If she purchases a new car with better gas mileage with a cost $300 per month to operate (for maintenance and car payment), the cost per mile in gasoline will drop to $0.17.

35. If Makala drives for only one month, how many miles would she have to drive so the total cost would be the same?

36. If Makala drives only 1,500 miles during her first month, which car would have the lesser cost?

37. If Makala drives only 1,500 miles during her first month of driving, what would be the difference in costs between the two cars?

38. There are four consecutive even numbers that total 92. What is the product of these numbers?

39. $12xy$

$-15xy$

40. $6qt^2 - 2qt^2 + 6qt^2 =$

41. Simplify: $a \cdot a \cdot a \cdot x \cdot x \cdot y$.

42. Simplify: $3(x)(y)(2)(z)$.

43. $(y^3)(y^5) =$

44. $(a^2b)(a^3b^4) =$

45. $(-2x^2y)(3x^3y^4) =$

46. $-3(m^3n^3)(-2m^4n^2) =$

47. $(4a^2b^3c^3)(b^3c^2d) =$

48. $(x^7)^4 =$

49. $(a^2b^3)^3 =$

50. $(3x^3y^5)^2 =$

51. $x^5 \div x^2 =$

52. $\dfrac{a^6b^2}{a^4b} =$

53. $\dfrac{14x^6y^4}{2xy} =$

54. $(3p^6q^4) \div (15p^4q^8) =$

55. $x^2 + \ xy + 2y^2$

$+ 3x^2 + 5xy + 3y^2$

56. $(3x + 7y) + (6x - 2y) =$

57. $(3s^2 + 4st + 13t^2) - (2s^2 + 2st + 3t^2) =$

58. $2a^2b + 3ab^2 + 7a^2b - 5ab^2 =$

59. $(2x + 4)(3x - 1) =$

60. $(a + 3ab + 4)(2a + b) =$

61. $(12a^8 - 8a^7) \div (2a^3) =$

62. $\dfrac{-3(x^2y^3)(-4xy^4)}{2xy^2} =$

63. $(x^2 + 2x + 1) \div (x + 1) =$

64. $(5x^2 + 6x + 1) \div (x + 1) =$

65. $(a^3 - 27) \div (a - 3) =$

66. Factor: $9a - 6$.

67. Factor completely: $5x^3 + 10x^2$.

68. Factor: $n^2 - 9$.

69. Factor: $36a^2 - b^2$.

70. Factor completely: $2a^2 - 32$.

71. Factor: $x^2 + 3x + 2$.

72. Factor: $x^2 - 5x - 6$.

73. Factor: $3x^2 - 20x - 7$.

74. Factor completely: $x^3 - 4x^2 + 3x$.

75. Factor: $24 - 10r + r^2$.

76. Factor: $x^2 - 2xy + y^2$.

77. Solve for y: $y^2 = 5y - 4$.

78. Solve for x: $x^2 - 25 = 0$.

79. Solve for x: $x^2 - 5x = 0$.

80. Solve for t: $3t^2 + 21t = 2t^2 - 3t + 81$.

81. Reduce: $\dfrac{9x^5}{12x^3}$.

82. Reduce: $\dfrac{5x - 15}{4x - 12}$.

83. Reduce: $\dfrac{x^2 - 9x + 20}{x^2 - x - 12}$.

84. $\dfrac{8x^5}{9y^2} \cdot \dfrac{3y^4}{2x^3} =$

85. $\dfrac{x - 1}{x} \cdot \dfrac{x + 3}{x^2 - 7x + 6} =$

86. $\dfrac{4x^3}{7} \div \dfrac{2x}{9} =$

87. $\dfrac{10y + 5}{4} \div \dfrac{2y + 1}{2} =$

88. $\dfrac{y + 3}{y} + \dfrac{2y + 5}{y} =$

89. $\dfrac{4x - 5}{x - 1} - \dfrac{3x + 6}{x - 1} =$

90. $\dfrac{7}{x} - \dfrac{6}{y} =$

91. $\dfrac{x - 3}{2x} + \dfrac{x + 1}{4x} =$

92. $\dfrac{7x}{x^4y^7} + \dfrac{3}{x^6y^2} =$

93. $\dfrac{3x}{x-3} - \dfrac{2x}{x+1} =$

94. $\dfrac{x}{x^2-16} + \dfrac{4x}{x^2+5x+4} =$

95. Solve for x: $5x + 2 > 17$.

96. Solve for y: $-4y - 8 \le 12$.

97. Solve for x: $5x + 6 \ge 2x + 2$.

98. Graph: $\{x: 5 \ge x \ge 3\}$.

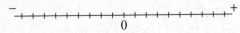

99. Graph: $\{x: -2 \le x < 8, x \text{ is an integer}\}$.

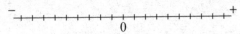

100. Graph: $\{x: x > 1\}$.

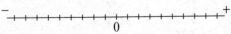

101. Graph: $\{x: x \le -2\}$.

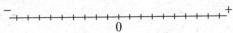

102. $|-6| =$

103. $|3 - 7| =$

104. $5 - |-3| =$

105. Solve for x: $|2x - 7| = 9$.

106. Give the coordinates represented by points A, B, C, and D.

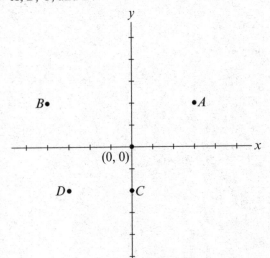

107. Is $x + \dfrac{3}{y} = 5$ linear or nonlinear?

108. Graph: $x + y = 9$.

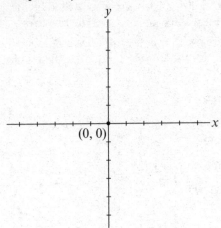

109. Rewrite the equation $3x + 4y = 12$ in slope-intercept form. Then identify the slope and y-intercept values.

110. For the equation $3x + 4y = 12$, find the x-intercept.

111. Graph: $y = x^2 + 3$.

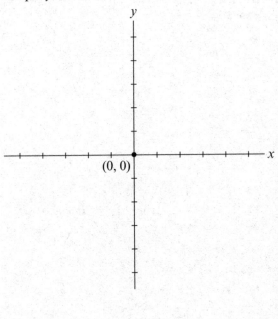

112. A phone company charges a monthly rate of $20 plus $0.02 per minute. If x = the number of minutes used, and y = total cost, write an equation to represent the given information, and graph it with minutes from 0 to 200 in intervals of 20 minutes.

113. A benefit concert sold 12,584 tickets (11,616 adult tickets; 968 child tickets) totaling $268,378. Adult tickets cost $22.50 each, and child tickets cost $7.25 each. What is the difference in the total ticket proceeds between the adult and children's tickets sold?

114. Lauren is deciding which rental car company to use. Company A offers a daily rate of $30 plus $0.15 per mile; Company B is having a special of $33 a day with unlimited miles. In how many miles would the cost be the same if you only use the car for one day?

115. Two cars leave from the same location in opposite directions. One car travels at 45 mph, while the other car travels at 60 mph. How long (to the nearest tenth of an hour) will it take for the cars to be 300 miles apart?

116. A helicopter leaves the airport traveling at 120 mph. One hour later, a small plane leaves the airport traveling in the same direction parallel to the helicopter at 250 mph. How long will it take (to the nearest minute) until the airplane and the helicopter are the same distance from the airport?

117. If you have 64 ounces of a solution that is 30% acid, how much water would you need to add to have a solution that's 12% acid?

118. A vegetable garden grows best with a fertilizer that has 15% single superphosphate. You have one fertilizer that is 18% single superphosphate and another that is 14% single superphosphate. If you want 128 ounces of 15% single superphosphate, how much of each of your current fertilizers do you need to add?

119. $-\sqrt{64} =$

120. $\sqrt{144} =$

121. Simplify: $\sqrt{75} =$

In questions 122–136, each variable is nonnegative.

122. $\sqrt{x^8} =$

123. $\sqrt{x^2 y^8} =$

124. $\sqrt{9x^6 y^{10}} =$

125. $\sqrt{y^9} =$

126. $\sqrt{a^3 b^3} =$

127. $\sqrt{27 a^3 b^6} =$

128. $\sqrt{(18)(2)} =$

129. $\sqrt{25 + 4} =$

130. $7\sqrt{5} + 3\sqrt{5} =$

131. $\sqrt{60} + 2\sqrt{15} =$

132. $\sqrt{27} + \sqrt{48} =$

133. $\sqrt{6} \cdot \sqrt{10} =$

134. $\sqrt{x^3 y} \cdot \sqrt{x^2 yz} =$

135. $\sqrt{2xy} \cdot \sqrt{32 x^3 y^2} =$

136. $6\sqrt{6} \cdot 2\sqrt{3} =$

137. If $a @ b = (a + b)^2$ for all real numbers a and b, what is the value of 5 @ 4?

138. Simplify $x^5 - x^4 - 12x^3 + 20x^2 - 7x + 3$ divided by $x - 3$.

139. Simplify $-x^4 + 6x^3 - 3x^2 - 9x + 1$ divided by $x + 1$.

Answers

Page numbers following each answer refer to the review section applicable to the problem type.

1. subset (p. 85)

2. empty; null set (p. 85)

3. rule (p. 85)

4. roster (p. 85)

5. finite (p. 85)

6. infinite (p. 85)

7. false (p. 86)

8. true (p. 86)

9. {8} (p. 86)

10. {1, 3, 4, 5, 6} (p. 86)

11. (a) $2x + 4$ (p. 86)

    (b) $x - 6$ (p. 86)

    (c) $x + 10$ (p. 86)

    (d) $x - 4y$ (p. 86)

12. 73 (p. 88)

13. 6,912 (p. 88)

14. $-\dfrac{3}{2}$ or $-1\dfrac{1}{2}$ (p. 89)

15. 21 (p. 89)

16. $\dfrac{1}{2}$ (p. 89)

17. $x = 46$ (p. 90)

18. $x = 10$ (p. 90)

19. $y = 96$ (p. 90)

20. $z = \dfrac{45}{2}$ or $22\dfrac{1}{2}$ (p. 91)

21. $x = -3$ (p. 91)

22. $n = -8$ (p. 91)

23. $y = -84$ (p. 91)

24. $y = \dfrac{x+n}{m}$ (p. 94)

25. $m = an$ (p. 94)

26. $x = \dfrac{rt}{s}$ (p. 94)

27. $x = \dfrac{zy}{a}$ (pp. 96–97)

28. $x = 3$ (pp. 97–98)

29. $c = \dfrac{24}{7}$ or $3\dfrac{3}{7}$ (p. 98)

30. 1,950,000 square feet (p. 97)

31. 7,800 (p. 97)

32. $x = 3,\ y = \dfrac{-5}{2}$ or $-2\dfrac{1}{2}$ (pp. 99–100)

33. $a = -1,\ b = 2$ (pp. 99–100)

34. $x = \dfrac{5}{3}$ or $1\dfrac{2}{3},\ y = \dfrac{14}{3}$ or $4\dfrac{2}{3}$ (p. 99)

35. 2,500 (pp. 99, 160)

36. Her current car is less expensive to drive each month. (p. 160)

37. $90 per month (p. 160)

38. The four consecutive even numbers are 20, 22, 24, and 26. Their product is 274,560. (p. 107)

39. $-3xy$ (p. 112)

40. $10qt^2$ (p. 112)

41. a^3x^2y (p. 113)

42. $6xyz$ (p. 113)

43. y^8 (p. 113)

44. a^5b^5 (p. 113)

45. $-6x^5y^5$ (p. 113)

46. $6m^7n^5$ (p. 113)

47. $4a^2b^6c^5d$ (p. 113)

48. x^{28} (p. 113)

49. a^6b^9 (p. 113)

50. $9x^6y^{10}$ (p. 113)

51. x^3 (p. 114)

52. a^2b (p. 114)

53. $7x^5y^3$ (p. 114)

54. $\dfrac{p^2}{5q^4}$ or $0.2p^2q^{-4}$ (p. 114)

55. $4x^2 + 6xy + 5y^2$ (p. 115)

56. $9x + 5y$ (p. 115)

57. $s^2 + 2st + 10t^2$ (p. 115)

58. $9a^2b - 2ab^2$ (p. 115)

59. $6x^2 + 10x - 4$ (pp. 115–116)

60. $2a^2 + 6a^2b + 8a + ab + 3ab^2 + 4b$ (p. 116)

61. $6a^5 - 4a^4$ (p. 117)

62. $6x^2y^5$ (p. 117)

63. $x + 1$ (p. 118)

64. $5x + 1$ (p. 118)

65. $a^2 + 3a + 9$ (p. 118)

66. $3(3a - 2)$ (p. 122)

67. $5x^2(x + 2)$ (p. 122)

68. $(n - 3)(n + 3)$ (p. 122)

69. $(6a - b)(6a + b)$ (p. 122)

70. $2(a - 4)(a + 4)$ (p. 122)

71. $(x + 1)(x + 2)$ (p. 123)

72. $(x - 6)(x + 1)$ (p. 123)

73. $(3x + 1)(x - 7)$ (p. 123)

74. $x(x - 3)(x - 1)$ (p. 123)

75. $(6 - r)(4 - r)$ (p. 123)

76. $(x - y)(x - y)$ (p. 123)

77. $y = 1$ or $y = 4$ (p. 127)

78. $x = 5$ or $x = -5$ (p. 127)

79. $x = 0$ or $x = 5$ (p. 127)

80. $t = 3$ or $t = -27$ (p. 127)

81. $\dfrac{3x^2}{4}$ (p. 132)

82. $\dfrac{5}{4}$ or $1\dfrac{1}{4}$ (p. 132)

83. $\dfrac{x - 5}{x + 3}$ (p. 132)

84. $\dfrac{4x^2y^2}{3}$ (p. 133)

85. $\dfrac{x + 3}{x(x - 6)}$ or $\dfrac{x + 3}{x^2 - 6x}$ (p. 133)

86. $\dfrac{18x^2}{7}$ (p. 134)

87. $\dfrac{5}{2}$ or $2\dfrac{1}{2}$ (p. 134)

88. $\dfrac{3y + 8}{y}$ (pp. 135–136)

89. $\dfrac{x - 11}{x - 1}$ (pp. 135–136)

90. $\dfrac{7y - 6x}{xy}$ (pp. 135–136)

91. $\dfrac{3x - 5}{4x}$ (pp. 135–136)

92. $\dfrac{7x^3 + 3y^5}{x^6y^7}$ (pp. 135–136)

93. $\dfrac{x^2 + 9x}{(x - 3)(x + 1)}$ (pp. 135–136)

94. $\dfrac{5x^2 - 15x}{(x + 4)(x - 4)(x + 1)}$ (pp. 135–136)

95. $\{x: x > 3\}$ (p. 139)

96. $\{y: y \geq -5\}$ (p. 139)

97. $\left\{x: x \geq -\dfrac{4}{3}\right\}$ (p. 139)

98.

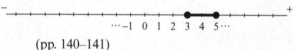

(pp. 140–141)

99.

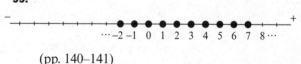

(pp. 140–141)

100.

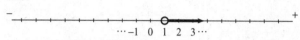

(pp. 140–141)

101.

(pp. 140–141)

102. 6 (p. 142)

103. 4 (p. 142)

104. 2 (p. 142)

105. $x = 8$ or $x = -1$ (p. 142)

106. A (3, 2), B (−4, 2), C (0, −2), and D (−3, −2) (p. 143)

107. nonlinear (p. 147)

108. (p. 145)

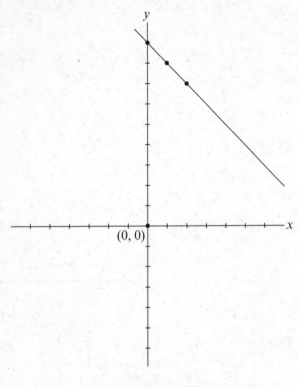

x	y
0	9
1	8
2	7

109. $y = -\dfrac{3}{4}x + 3$, slope $= -\dfrac{3}{4}$, y-intercept $= 3$ or (0, 3) (p. 154)

110. 4 or the location (4, 0) (pp. 145, 158)

111. (pp. 145–146)

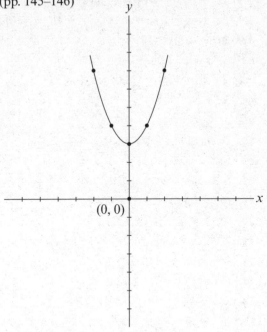

x	y
−2	7
−1	4
0	3
1	4
2	7

112. $y = .02x + 20$ (pp. 104, 154)

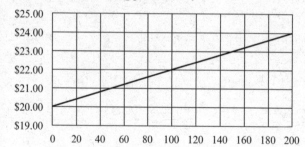

113. $11,616 \ (22.50) = \$261,360$

$- \ 968 \quad (7.25) = \ -7,018$

$ \$254,342$

(pp. 104, 160)

114. 20 miles (p. 104)

115. 2.9 hours (p. 104)

116. $t \approx 55$ minutes (p. 104)

117. 96 ounces (p. 107)

118. 32 ounces of the 18% single superphosphate and 96 ounces of the 14% single superphosphate (p. 107)

119. -8 (p. 163)

120. 12 (p. 163)

121. $5\sqrt{3}$ (p. 163)

122. x^4 (pp. 163–164)

123. xy^4 (pp. 163–164)

124. $3x^3 y^5$ (pp. 163–164)

125. $y^4 \sqrt{y}$ (pp. 163–164)

126. $ab\sqrt{ab}$ (pp. 163–164)

127. $3ab^3 \sqrt{3a}$ (pp. 163–164)

128. 6 (pp. 163–164)

129. $\sqrt{29}$ (p. 165)

130. $10\sqrt{5}$ (p. 165)

131. $4\sqrt{15}$ (p. 166)

132. $7\sqrt{3}$ (p. 166)

133. $2\sqrt{15}$ (p. 167)

134. $x^2 y\sqrt{xz}$ (p. 167)

135. $8x^2 y\sqrt{y}$ (p. 167)

136. $12\sqrt{18} = 36\sqrt{2}$ (p. 167)

137. 81 (pp. 167–168)

138. $x^4 + 2x^3 - 6x^2 + 2x - 1$ (p. 118)

139. $-x^3 + 7x^2 - 10x + 1$ (p. 118)

Algebra Glossary of Terms

abscissa: The x-coordinate of a point. In the point (3, 2), the abscissa is 3.

absolute value: The numerical value when direction or sign is not considered.

algebra: Arithmetic operations using letters and/or symbols in place of numbers.

algebraic fractions: Fractions using a variable in the numerator and/or denominator.

ascending order: Basically, when the power of a term increases for each succeeding term.

binary operation: An operation that combines two numbers or variables.

binomial: An algebraic expression consisting of exactly two terms.

closed interval: An interval that includes both endpoints or fixed boundaries.

coefficient: The number in front of a variable. For example, in $9x$, 9 is the coefficient.

coordinate axes: Two perpendicular number lines used in a coordinate graph.

coordinate graph: Two perpendicular number lines, the x-axis and the y-axis, creating a plane on which each point is assigned a pair of numbers.

coordinates: An ordered pair of numbers that denote a location on a plane. For example, the x and y values for points on a graph.

cube: The result when a number is multiplied by itself thrice. Designated by the exponent 3, as in x^3.

cube root: The number that when multiplied by itself thrice gives you the original number. For example, 5 is the cube root of 125. Its symbol is $\sqrt[3]{}$. For example, $\sqrt[3]{125} = 5$.

denominator: Everything below the fraction bar in a fraction.

descending order: Basically, when the power of a term decreases for each succeeding term.

discriminant: The value inside the radical sign in the quadratic formula $\sqrt{b^2 - 4ac}$, where $b^2 - 4ac$ is the discriminant. The discriminant is used to determine where (if at all) the parabola meets or crosses the x-axis.

double root: When solving a quadratic equation by factoring, you get two factors that produce the same answer. For example, $x^2 - 10x + 25 = 0$ factors into $(x - 5)(x - 5) = 0$. Then $x - 5 = 0$ gives $x = 5$, and $x - 5 = 0$ gives $x = 5$. $x = 5$ is called a double root.

element: A member of a set.

empty set: A set with no members. Null set.

equal sets: Sets that have exactly the same members.

equation: A balanced relationship between numbers and/or symbols. A mathematical sentence with an equal sign.

equivalent sets: Sets that have the same number of members.

evaluate: To determine the value or numerical amount.

exponent: A numeral used to indicate the power of a number.

extremes: The outer terms of a proportion. In $\dfrac{a}{b} = \dfrac{c}{d}$, the a and d are the extremes.

factor: As a verb, factor means to find two or more quantities whose product equals the original quantity.

finite: Countable. Having a definite ending.

F.O.I.L. method: A method of multiplying binomials in which first terms, outside terms, inside terms, and last terms are multiplied.

half-open interval: An interval that includes one endpoint or boundary.

imaginary numbers: Square roots of negative numbers. The imaginary unit is i.

incomplete quadratic equation: A quadratic equation missing the constant term and/or the term with the variable raised to the first power.

inequality: A statement in which the relationships are not equal. A mathematical sentence that uses $<$, $\leq$, $>$, $\geq$, or $\neq$.

infinite: Uncountable. Continues forever.

intercepts: The x-intercept of a graph occurs when the graph is on the x-axis. When a point is on the x-axis, its y-coordinate there is 0. The y-intercept of a graph occurs when the graph is on the y-axis. When a point is on the y-axis, its x-coordinate there is 0.

intersection of sets: The set formed by only using the common elements found in each set (the place[s] where the sets overlap).

interval: All the numbers that lie within two certain boundaries or endpoints.

linear equation: An equation whose solution set forms a straight line when plotted on a coordinate graph.

literal equation: An equation having mostly variables.

means: The inner terms of the proportion. In $\dfrac{a}{b} = \dfrac{c}{d}$, the b and c are the means.

monomial: An algebraic expression consisting of only one term.

nonlinear equation: An equation whose solution set does not form a straight line when plotted on a coordinate graph.

null set: A set with no members. Empty set.

number line: A graphic representation of integers and other real numbers. The point on this line associated with each number is called the graph of the number.

numerator: Everything above the fraction bar in a fraction.

open interval: An interval that does not include endpoints or fixed boundaries.

open ray: A ray that does not include its endpoint (an open half line).

ordered pair: Any pair of elements (x, y) having a first element x and a second element y. Used to identify or plot points on a coordinate grid.

ordinate: The y-coordinate of a point. In the point (3, 2), the ordinate is 2.

origin: The point of intersection of the two number lines on a coordinate graph, which is represented by the coordinates (0, 0).

parabola: In a quadratic graph, a parabola is a graph of the equation in the form $y = ax^2 + bx + c$ or $x = ay^2 + by + c$ (where $a \neq 0$); it is a U-shaped curve. The graph of an equation of the form $y = ax^2 + bx + c$ will be a parabola opening upward if $a > 0$, or a parabola opening downward if $a < 0$. Similarly, the graph of an equation in the form $x = ay^2 + by + c$ will be a parabola opening to the right if $a > 0$, or a parabola opening to the left if $a < 0$.

polynomial: An algebraic expression consisting of two or more terms.

proportion: Two ratios equal to each other. For example, a is to c as b is to d. Also written as $\dfrac{a}{c} = \dfrac{b}{d}$.

quadrants: Four quarters or divisions of a coordinate graph.

quadratic equation: An equation that can be written $Ax^2 + Bx + C = 0$ with $A \neq 0$.

quadratic formula: $x = \dfrac{-b \pm \sqrt{b^2 - 4ac}}{2a}$.

radical sign: The symbol used to indicate a root. For example, $\sqrt{}$ indicates square root, $\sqrt[3]{}$ indicates cube root.

ratio: A method of comparing two or more numbers. For example, $a{:}b$. Often written as a fraction.

ray: A half line that includes its endpoint.

real numbers: The set consisting of all rational and irrational numbers.

root: The solution(s) of both linear equations and quadratic equations. These are the points on a straight line where the parabola will meet or cross the x-axis.

roster: A method of naming a set by listing its members.

rule: A method of naming a set by describing its elements.

set: A group of objects, numbers, and so on.

set builder notation: A formal method of describing a set. Often used for inequalities. For example, $\{x{:}\ x > 1\}$, which is read "x such that all x is greater than 1."

simplify: To combine several or many terms into fewer terms.

slope: A value that describes the steepness and direction of a line. If a line has a positive slope, it slants upward toward the right. If a line has a negative slope, it slants downward toward the right. If (x_1, y_1) and (x_2, y_2) represent any two points on a line, then slope $= \dfrac{y_2 - y_1}{x_2 - x_1}$; that is, $m = \dfrac{y_2 - y_1}{x_2 - x_1}$.

slope-intercept form: A way to write an equation of a line in order to recognize its slope and y-intercept. When a linear equation is written in $y = mx + b$ form, the m value becomes the slope value for the line, and the b value is the location on the y-axis where the line intercepts the y-axis.

solution set or solution: All the answers that satisfy a mathematical sentence.

square: The result when a number is multiplied by itself. Designated by the exponent 2. For example, x^2.

square root: The number that, when multiplied by itself, gives you the original number. For example, 5 is the square root of 25. Its symbol is $\sqrt{}$. For example, $\sqrt{25} = 5$.

subset: A set within a set.

system of equations: Simultaneous equations.

term: A numerical or literal expression with its own sign.

trinomial: An algebraic expression consisting of exactly three terms.

union of sets: The set formed by combining all the elements found in the sets (the place[s] that have elements from either set).

universal set: The general category set, or the set of all those elements under consideration.

unknown: A letter or symbol whose value is not known.

value: Numerical amount.

variable: A letter or symbol used to stand for a number.

Venn diagram: A pictorial description of sets.

vertex: The highest or lowest point of a parabola. It is the turning point on the graph of a parabola. The parabola can turn up or down, and either left or right depending on the quadratic equation.

x-axis: The horizontal axis in a coordinate graph.

x-coordinate: The first number in the ordered pair. Refers to the distance on the x-axis or abscissa.

x-intercept: The point(s) where a line, parabola, or other shape crosses the x-axis.

y-axis: The vertical axis in a coordinate graph.

y-coordinate: The second number in the ordered pair. Refers to the distance on the y-axis or ordinate.

y-intercept: The point(s) where a line, parabola, or other shape crosses the y-axis.

Chapter 3

Statistics and Probability

The Common Core Standards ask that you look beyond step-by-step mathematical procedures and be able to organize, describe, and analyze numerical data. The Common Core statistics and probability domain draws upon numerical data to understand the relationships of numbers, make inferences, and link the conclusions to real-world scenarios.

Connecting Statistics and Probability to the Common Core Standards

This chapter is organized by statistics and probability topics that are part of a conceptually larger set of Common Core ideas. The following table highlights elements of the Common Core Standards that connect to the domain topics covered in this chapter.

Statistics and Probability Common Core Connections

Data Collection and Analysis	Use statistics to shape the measures of central tendency and spread (mean, median, mode, range, and standard deviation) of two or more data sets of real-world scenarios.
	Summarize and represent data on a single count or measurement variable.
	Understand that statistics is a method for making inferences about a population based on the sample collected.
Representing and Interpreting Data	Summarize categorical data in two-way frequency tables.
	Construct, plot, and interpret data graphically to show the distribution of data on line graphs, bar graphs, and scatter plots.
	Interpret trends in data and understand the differences in extreme data points.
	Understand the process of making predictions based upon data collection.
	Interpret the slope of a linear model in the context of the data.
	Use technology to interpret data.
Probability	Understand the probability of independent, dependent, and mutually exclusive events.
	Interpret theoretical and experimental probabilities for compound events.
	Understand the conditional probability of a given event.
	Use probability to analyze the outcome of decisions.

Statistics and Probability Diagnostic Test

Questions

1. What is the probability of rolling two dice so they total 9?

2. How many ways can the letters in the word *team* be arranged?

3. If the last letter of a word must remain *m*, how many ways can the word *team* be arranged?

4. A scientist is trying to select three members for her research team from six possible applicants. How many possible sets of three are there, assuming all applicants are qualified?

5. Three names are randomly drawn from a bag containing 12 student council member names to determine the president, vice-president, and secretary. How many possible arrangements are there if the first draw is president, the second draw is vice-president, and the third draw is secretary?

Questions 6 and 7 refer to the following data set of numbers.

$$6, 4, 4, 2, 5, 9$$

6. Find the arithmetic mean, mode, median, and range of the group of numbers.

7. If the value 8 is added to the group of numbers, name all of the following that change in value.

   Ⓐ mean
   Ⓑ mode
   Ⓒ median
   Ⓓ range

8. Find the next number in the sequence: 2, 5, 11, 23, 47, ___.

9. What is the interquartile range for the following data set?

$$7, 3, 8, 22, 19, 5, 34, 10, 25$$

Questions 10 and 11 refer to the following frequency table.

x	f
2	1
3	1
4	2
5	1
6	1
9	1
11	2
15	1

10. Find the standard deviation (to the nearest tenth) for the set of data given in the frequency table.

11. How many standard deviations above or below the mean is 5?

12. What is the 3rd quartile for the following set of numbers?

$$2, 2, 3, 4, 5, 7, 9, 12, 14, 15, 18, 20$$

Question 13 refers to the following information and table.

Healthy Snack Company (HSC) has conducted a demographic survey for a new product launch. To maximize their marketing efforts, the survey questions were focused on two population demographics:

   a. age—children under 12 years old or adolescents between 12 and 18 years old
   b. sex—boys or girls

The table below shows the results from the survey.

	Children Under 12	Adolescents 12–18	Total
Boys	75	100	175
Girls	100	125	225
	175	225	400

13. What is the relative frequency of girls between 12 and 18 years old (to the nearest hundredth of a percent)?

Answers

Page numbers following each answer refer to the review section applicable to this problem type.

1. $\frac{4}{36} = \frac{1}{9}$ (pp. 199–200)

2. 24 (p. 204)

3. 6 (p. 204)

4. 20 (p. 204)

5. 1,320 (p. 204)

6. mean = 5, mode = 4, median = $4\frac{1}{2}$ or 4.5, range = 7 (pp. 187–189)

7. **A, C.** The mean would increase (choice A), the mode is unchanged (choice B), the median would increase (choice C), and the range would remain unchanged (choice D). (pp. 187–189)

8. 95 (p. 29)

9. $17\frac{1}{2}$ or 17.5 (p. 193)

10. $\sqrt{16.4} \approx 4.0$ (p. 191)

11. $\frac{1}{2}$ of a standard deviation below the mean (p. 191)

12. $14\frac{1}{2}$ or 14.5 (p. 193)

13. 55.56% (p. 195)

Statistics and Probability Review

The Common Core Standards draw upon your knowledge of descriptive statistics, probability, factorials, combinations, and permutations.

Statistics

Descriptive statistics organize data with numbers and graphics to describe, inform, and summarize information about populations and phenomena. Drawing conclusions from samples of a population help to make general and specific statements about people, events, and situations.

In descriptive statistics, data can be described as *discrete* or *continuous*. A simple way to consider these terms is to remember that discrete data "counts" the number of data, while continuous data "measures" data. For example, discrete data counts the number of students in a classroom, the number of pets in a household, or the number of registered voters in a city. Continuous data can be measured and described for any value within a range. For example, the time it takes to drive to work in the morning or the time it takes to run and finish a 5k race.

Graphic Displays

The method of collecting, organizing, and displaying data impacts your understanding and interpretation of the data. This is why the Common Core Standards highlight the use of graphic representations to analyze and compare statistical data. When data is collected, there are many ways to show the data visually.

Frequency Distribution Table

A *frequency distribution* table is used to organize data so that you can make sense of the data collected. Generally, there is a column on the left (the data values) and a column on the right (the frequency), which indicates how many of each data value are in the data set.

For example, the data below represents class math scores for the semester. The first and third columns show the score, and the second and fourth columns show the frequency (the number of times during the semester) that the score was given on math assignments.

Distribution of Student's Math Scores

Score	Frequency (f)	Score	Frequency (f)
60	2	85	9
65	1	86	1
68	4	88	12
70	4	90	10
72	2	92	8
74	5	94	6
76	1	96	2
79	3	98	4
80	8	100	2
82	5		

Stem-and-Leaf Plot

The *stem-and-leaf plot* is another useful visual representation to show the range of data. The stem-and-leaf plot takes the first number (digit) as the *stem* and uses the remaining digits as the *leaf*. For example, in the score of 60, the number 6 is the stem and the number 0 is the leaf. Using the scores from the frequency distribution table above, the stem-and-leaf plot would look like the graphic display below. The scores in the first row across read 60, 60, 65, 68, 68 68, 68.

Stem	Leaf
6	0, 0, 5, 8, 8, 8, 8
7	0, 0, 0, 0, 2, 2, 4, 4, 4, 4, 4, 6, 9, 9, 9
8	0, 0, 0, 0, 0, 0, 0, 0, 2, 2, 2, 2, 2, 5, 5, 5, 5, 5, 5, 5, 5, 5, 6, 8, 8, 8, 8, 8, 8, 8, 8, 8, 8, 8, 8
9	0, 0, 0, 0, 0, 0, 0, 0, 0, 0, 2, 2, 2, 2, 2, 2, 2, 2, 4, 4, 4, 4, 4, 4, 6, 6, 8, 8, 8, 8
10	0, 0

Bar Graph and Line Graph

Distribution tables are useful to gather and organize data. However, for a good visual analysis, and to quickly see what the data actually means, data from distribution tables are often transferred and presented pictorially in a graph such as a bar graph or a line graph.

Notice that the bar graph and line graph below help you to quickly see that a score of 88 occurred more times than any other score in the class.

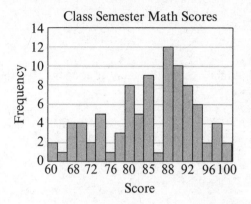

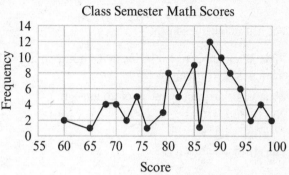

Measuring and Interpreting Data

Before interpreting data, it must be measured and described. The Common Core Standards recognize that a measure of the center for a data set summarizes all of its values. A measure of central tendency helps to describe any number in the middle of the data set. It indicates the "center of a distribution."

Measures of Central Tendencies

Any measure indicating a center of a distribution is called a *measure of central tendency*. The three basic measures of central tendency are

- mean (or arithmetic mean)
- median
- mode

Mean

The *mean* (or arithmetic mean) is what is usually called the *average*. The arithmetic mean is the most frequently used measure of central tendency. It is generally reliable, is easy to use, and is more stable than the median. To determine the arithmetic mean, simply total the items and then divide by the number of items.

Examples:

What is the arithmetic mean of 0, 12, 18, 20, 31, and 45?

$0 + 12 + 18 + 20 + 31 + 45 = 126$

$126 \div 6 = 21$

The arithmetic mean is 21.

What is the arithmetic mean of 25, 27, 27, and 27?

$$25 + 27 + 27 + 27 = 106$$

$$106 \div 4 = 26\frac{1}{2}$$

The arithmetic mean is $26\frac{1}{2}$.

Note: What happens to the mean if another number is added? Unless the number added is $26\frac{1}{2}$, the mean will increase or decrease.

What is the arithmetic mean of 20 and –10?

$$20 + (-10) = +10$$

$$10 \div 2 = 5$$

The arithmetic mean is 5.

Practice: Arithmetic Mean

1. Find the arithmetic mean of 3, 6, and 12.

2. If the numbers 7 and 5 are added to the numbers above, will the mean increase or decrease?

3. Find the arithmetic mean of 26, 28, 36, and 40.

4. Find the arithmetic mean of 3, 7, –5, and –13.

Answers: Arithmetic Mean

1. $21 \div 3 = 7$

2. The mean will decrease because the mean of the additional numbers is less than the current mean (the actual new mean is $33 \div 5 = 6.6$).

3. $130 \div 4 = 32\frac{1}{2}$

4. $-8 \div 4 = -2$

Median

The *median* of a set of numbers arranged in ascending or descending order is the middle number (*if* there is an odd number of items in the set). If there is an even number of items in the set, the median is the arithmetic mean of the middle two numbers. The median is easy to calculate and is not influenced by extreme measurements.

Examples:

Find the median of 3, 4, 6, 9, 21, 24, 56.

Since there are seven values, 9 is the median.

Find the median of 5, 4, 10, 6.

These values need to be rearranged in either ascending or descending order. Since there are four values, the median is the average of the second and third terms. $5\frac{1}{2}$ is the median.

Practice: Median

Find the median of each group of numbers.

1. 9, 3, 5

2. 18, 16, 0, 7, 12

3. 100, 101, 102, 20

4. 71, –5, –3, –100

Answers: Median

1. 5   3, $\boxed{5}$, 9 (the middle term)

2. 12   0, 7, $\boxed{12}$, 16, 18 (the middle term)

3. 100.5   20, $\overset{100.5}{\overline{100,\ 101}}$, 102 (the average of the two middle terms)

4. −4   −100, $\overset{-4}{\overline{-5,\ -3}}$, 71 (the average of the two middle terms)

Mode

The set, class, or classes that appear most or whose frequency is the greatest is the *mode* or modal class. In order to have a mode, there must be a repetition of a data value. Mode is not greatly influenced by extreme cases, but it is probably the least important or least used of the types of central tendency measures. *Note:* There can be more than one mode in a set.

Example:

Find the mode of 3, 4, 8, 9, 9, 2, 6, 11

The mode is 9 because it appears more often than any other number.

Practice: Mode

Find the mode of each group of numbers.

1. 2, 2, 3

2. 8, 4, 3, 5, 4, 6

3. 7, 8, 4, −3, 2, −3

4. 100, 101, 100, 102, 100, 101

5. 72, 85, 72, 61, 85, 90

Answers: Mode

1. 2

2. 4

3. −3

4. 100

5. 72 and 85

Range

For a set of numbers, the *range* is the difference between the largest and the smallest number. It provides limited information about the spread of the numbers. For example, the following two data sets will have the same range, but the data are quite different.

Examples:

Set 1: 3, 4, 5, 5, 5, 23

Range: 23 − 3 = 20

Set 2: 20, 22, 24, 26, 28, 30, 32, 34, 36, 38, 40

Range: 40 − 20 = 20

An *outlier* is a number that is significantly different from the other numbers and can have a great impact on the spread of numbers. The outlier for Set 1 in the range examples above is 23 because it is extremely divergent from the other numbers in the data set.

Example:

Find the range of 3, 5, 7, 3, 2.

$7 - 2 = 5$

The range is 5.

Tip: Remember to first arrange the values in a set to be in ascending order before determining the range.

Practice: Range

1. Find the range of 2, 45, 106, 99

2. Find the range of 6, 101, 152, –5

Answers: Range

1. $106 - 2 = 104$

2. $152 - (-5) = 157$

Practice: Measures of Central Tendencies

Find the mean, mode, median, and range of each of the sets.

1. 7, 8, 8, 14, 18

2. 9, 10, 106, 120, 120

3. –3, –1, 0, 2, 2, 3

4. $\dfrac{1}{2}, \dfrac{2}{3}, \dfrac{1}{4}, \dfrac{5}{6}, \dfrac{3}{4}$

Answers: Measure of Central Tendencies

1. Mean = 11

$55 \div 5 = 11$

Mode = 8
Median = 8

Range = 11
$18 - 7 = 11$

2. Mean = 73
$365 \div 5 = 73$

Mode = 120
Median = 106

Range = 111
$120 - 9 = 111$

3. Mean = 0.5
$3 \div 6 = 0.5$

Mode = 2
Median = 1
average of 0 and 2

Range = 6
$3 - (-3) = 6$

4. Mean = $\dfrac{3}{5}$

The lowest common denominator is 12. Rewrite the fractions $\dfrac{6}{12}, \dfrac{8}{12}, \dfrac{3}{12}, \dfrac{10}{12}, \dfrac{9}{12}$.

Now, add them together, which equals $\dfrac{36}{12}$ and reduces to 3. Then divide 3 by 5 (the number of fractions) to get the mean of $\dfrac{3}{5}$.

Mode = none

Median = $\dfrac{2}{3}$

Arrange the fractions in order from least to greatest: $\dfrac{3}{12}, \dfrac{6}{12}, \dfrac{8}{12}, \dfrac{9}{12}, \dfrac{10}{12}$. The median is $\dfrac{8}{12}$, which reduces to $\dfrac{2}{3}$.

Range = $\dfrac{7}{12}$

$\dfrac{10}{12} - \dfrac{3}{12} = \dfrac{7}{12}$

Standard Deviation

The *standard deviation* of a set of data is a measure of how far data values of a population are from the mean value of the population. A small standard deviation indicates that the data values tend to be very close to the mean value. A large standard deviation indicates that the data values are "spread out" from the mean value.

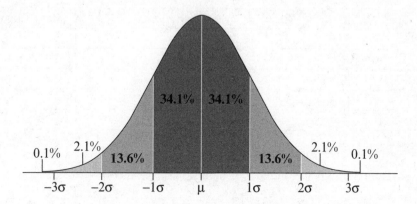

The diagram above represents a set of data that has a normal distribution. This shape is also referred to as a *bell curve*. In it, μ represents the mean value of the set of data. Each shaded band has a width of one standard deviation. For normally distributed data, you will find approximately 68% of all the data values within one standard deviation from the mean. You will find approximately 95.5% of all the data values within two standard deviations from the mean. At three standard deviations from the mean, approximately 99.8% of all the data values are found.

The basic method for calculating the standard deviation for a *population* is lengthy and time consuming. It involves five steps:

1. Find the mean value for the set of data.
2. For each data value, find the difference between it and the mean value, and then square that difference.
3. Find the sum of the squares found in Step 2.
4. Divide the sum found in Step 3 by the number of data values.
5. Find the square root of the value found in Step 4.

The result found in Step 4 is referred to as the *variance*. The square root of the variance is the standard deviation.

Example:

Find the variance and standard deviation for the following set of data: $\{3, 7, 7, 8, 10\}$.

1. Find the mean value: $\dfrac{3+7+7+8+10}{5} = \dfrac{35}{5} = 7$.

2. Find the squares of the differences between the data values and the mean.

Data Value	Mean	Data Value – Mean	(Data Value – Mean)^2
3	7	−4	16
7	7	0	0
7	7	0	0
8	7	1	1
10	7	3	9

3. Find the sum of the squares from Step 2: $16 + 1 + 9 = 26$.

4. Divide the sum from Step 3 by the number of data values: variance $= \dfrac{26}{5} = 5.2$.

5. Find the square root of the value found in Step 4: standard deviation $= \sqrt{5.2} \approx 2.28$.

Note: If the instructions list a sample population, Step 4 above changes. The denominator becomes the number of data values − 1. The answer for the sample population for the data above would be:

$$\text{variance} = \frac{26}{4} = 6.5 \qquad \text{standard deviation} = \sqrt{6.5} \approx 2.55$$

If each data value in the example above were increased by the same amount, certain statistical values would be affected while others would not. The statistical values that would be affected are the mean, median, and mode. The statistical values that would not be affected are the range, variance, and standard deviation. The mean, median, and mode would each increase by the amount that each data value was increased.

Example:

A scientist discovered that the instrument used for an experiment was off by 2 milligrams. If each weight in his experiment needed to be increased by 2 milligrams, then which of the following statistical measures would not be affected?

   I.   mean
  II.   median
 III.   mode
 IV.   range
  V.   standard deviation

  Ⓐ   I and II only
  Ⓑ   II and III only
  Ⓒ   III and IV only
  Ⓓ   IV and V only

The answer is choice D (IV and V only). Only range and standard deviation would not be affected.

192

Data Quartiles

Quartiles are the values of a set of data that separate the numbers into groups after the data has been arranged in ascending order. Quartiles are labeled Q_1, Q_2, and Q_3.

- Q_1 can be described as the first quartile in the 25th percentile. It indicates that approximately 25% of the data values are to the left in the list of data values.

- Q_2 can be described as the second quartile in the 50th percentile. Therefore, it is the middle of all measures (median).

- Q_3 can be described as the third quartile in the 75th percentile. It indicates that approximately 75% of the data values are to the left in the list of data values.

Let's review two data sets of numbers to determine the quartiles. Find the first, second, and third quartile values for the following data set:

$$\{12, 22, 18, 19, 17, 25, 27\}$$

To find the first, second, and third quartile values, first find Q_2 (the median).

Step 1: First find Q_2 (the median). Start by putting the numbers in ascending order and divide in half to find the median $\{12, 17, 18, \underline{19}, 22, 25, 27\}$. $Q_2 = 19$ (approximately 50% of the data values are to the left of 19). Now your data is divided into two groups. Set A is the data set left of Q_2. Set B is the data set to the right of Q_2. The median of Set A is Q_1, and the median of Set B is Q_3.

Step 2: Find Q_1 (first quartile). The median of the data set $\{12, 17, 18\}$ to the left of $Q_2 = 17$ (approximately 25% of the data values are to the left of 17).

Step 3: Find Q_3 (third quartile). The median of the data set $\{22, 25, 27\}$ to the right of $Q_2 = 25$ (approximately 75% of the data values are to the left of 25).

Interquartile Range

The *interquartile range* is a way to look at how numbers are distributed between upper and lower quartiles. It is the difference between the highest and lowest values. Are they close or far apart? To find the interquartile range in a data set of quartile values, find the difference between the third and first quartile values. Using the above example, the interquartile range is the difference between 25 and 17, or 8.

Box-and-Whisker Plot

Now, let's try finding the interquartile range using a box-and-whisker plot. A box-and-whisker plot is a visual way of displaying the data set on a line. The values are proportionally spaced along the line.

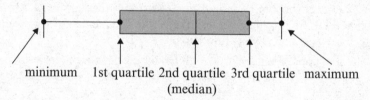

minimum   1st quartile 2nd quartile 3rd quartile maximum
(median)

Draw a box-and-whisker plot for the following data set:

$$\{5, 7, 2, 6, 9, 10, 2, 4, 5, 9, 7, 12, 4, 8, 8, 7, 15, 10, 11, 3\}$$

193

First, rearrange the data values in ascending order

$$\{2, 2, 3, 4, 4, 5, 5, 6, 7, 7, 7, 8, 8, 9, 9, 10, 10, 11, 12, 15\}$$

and find Q_2.

Since there are 20 data values, the median will be the average of the 10th and 11th terms. The 10th and 11th terms are both 7, so $Q_2 = 7$ (technically, it is located between the second and third "7"). The data set to the left of Q_2 is $\{2, 2, 3, 4, 4, 5, 5, 6, 7, 7\}$. Now, find the median of this data set to find Q_1. Since there are 10 terms in the set, the median will be the average of the 5th and 6th terms. The 5th term is 4 and the 6th term is 5; thus, $Q_1 = 4.5$. The data set to the right of Q_2 is $\{7, 8, 8, 9, 9, 10, 10, 11, 12, 15\}$. Lastly, find the median of this data set to find Q_3. Since the data set has 10 terms, the median will be the average of the 5th and 6th terms. The 5th term is 9 and the 6th term is 10, or $Q_3 = 9.5$. Therefore, the interquartile range of the data set is $9.5 - 4.5 = 5$.

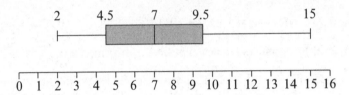

Practice: Data Quartiles

1. In the data set below, what is the value of Q_3?

   $\{5, 7, 2, 6, 9, 10, 2, 4, 5, 9, 7, 12, 4, 8, 8, 7, 15, 10, 11\}$

2. What does Q_3 represent?

Questions 3 and 4 refer to the following box-and-whisker plot.

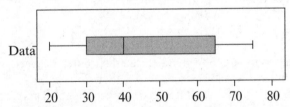

3. What is the median score of the data based on the box-and-whisker plot?

4. The box between the 30 and 40 is smaller than the box between the 40 and 65. What does this infer?

Answers: Data Quartiles

1. $Q_3 = 10$. List the data in ascending order: $\{2, 2, 4, 4, 5, 5, 6, 7, 7, 7, 8, 8, 9, 9, 10, 10, 11, 12, 15\}$. First, find the value of Q_2. Since there are 19 data values, Q_2 is the 10th value, or $Q_2 = 7$ (technically the third 7). Notice that there are nine data values to its right. The median of these nine data values will be the 5th term, which is 10 (technically the first 10), or $Q_3 = 10$.

2. Q_3 is the data value that approximately 75% of all the data values are to its left.

3. The median score of the data is 40. The median score of the data is the one represented by the vertical line separating the second and third quartile scores.

4. The smaller box shows that there are fewer data values between 30 and 40 than there are between 40 and 65.

Bivariate Data

The term *bivariate* shows the relationship between two variables (numbers and categories). In statistics, bivariate relationships of two variables are explained by showing correlation in scatter plots when pairs of points are graphed on a plane.

In the previous section, we used numbers that could be placed on a number line (one variable), but to display bivariate data, you need to place the data in a table or on a coordinate plane. Tables compare the raw data, and scatter plots compare the data on a coordinate graph.

Two-Way Frequency Table

Use a *two-way frequency table* to show bivariate data in a table. For example, a local theater conducts a survey to determine the popular genres of movies to show. The two-way frequency table below shows the results of the survey.

Cinema Movie Preferences

	Comedies	Dramas	Totals
Men	55	45	100
Women	45	30	75
Totals	100	75	175

By reviewing this bivariate table, the theater owner should be able to answer the following questions to make a decision about which films to show.

1. What is the total sample population?

   175

2. Did the men who were surveyed prefer drama films?

   No. According to the 100 men surveyed, 55 men preferred comedies, while only 45 men preferred dramas.

Two-Way Relative Frequency Table

Use a *two-way relative frequency table* to show percentages. To help the theater owner answer questions about percentages, the data can be displayed as a two-way relative frequency table. Using the same data from the survey, construct the table by dividing each cell by the total population sample of 175.

	Comedies	Dramas	Totals
Men	$\frac{55}{175} \approx 31\%$	$\frac{45}{175} \approx 26\%$	$\frac{100}{175} \approx 57\%$
Women	$\frac{45}{175} \approx 26\%$	$\frac{30}{175} \approx 17\%$	$\frac{75}{175} \approx 43\%$
Totals	$\frac{100}{175} \approx 57\%$	$\frac{75}{175} \approx 43\%$	$\frac{175}{175} = 100\%$

A two-way relative frequency table allows the theater owner to easily answer questions about a *part* of the total sample population surveyed.

195

Examples:

What percentage of the people surveyed were female?
About 43%

What is the relative frequency of the men surveyed who preferred dramatic movies?
About 26%

What is the relative frequency of women surveyed who preferred dramatic movies?
About 17%

What percentage of the total sample population surveyed preferred comedies?
About 57%

Bivariate Correlation Trends

Using a scatter plot is another way to display results to look for correlation of bivariate data. *Scatter plots* can show if unusual patterns exist, such as outliers. Scatter plots are particularly helpful if you are trying to find a trend or strong linearity in the two variables. The three possible trends are no correlation, positive correlation, and negative correlation.

No Correlation

If the patterns of the points have no correlation, no trend line can be seen:

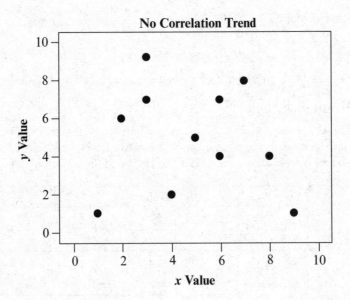

Positive Correlation

If the patterns of the points are positively correlated, a trend line can be plotted on the points. Points appear to be plotted upward. A relationship is positive if one variable increases in value as the other variable increases in value. In the scatter plot below, notice that with a positve trend, the values are rising from left to right.

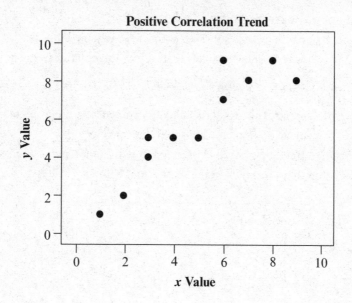

Negative Correlation

If the patterns of the points are negatively correlated, a trend line can be plotted on the points. Points trend in a downward direction. A relationship is negative if one variable decreases in value as the other variable increases in value. In the scatter plot below, notice that with a negative trend, the larger the x value, the smaller the y value.

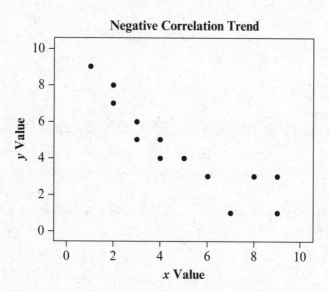

Practice: Bivariate Data

1. Create a two-way frequency table from a sample survey of 85 men and 175 women. The results from the survey show that 40 men and 90 women prefer diet soda rather than regular soda.

With the results of this two-way frequency table from question 1, answer questions 2–4.

2. Do both men and women prefer diet soda?
3. What is the total number of the people surveyed who prefer regular soda?
4. From the data in the two-way frequency table, create a two-way relative frequency table.

With the results of this two-way relative frequency table from question 4, answer questions 5 and 6.

5. What is the relative percentage of the total of men and women who prefer regular soda?
6. What is the relative percentage of women who prefer diet soda?
7. What type of correlation trend line would exist in a population that increases over time?
8. What type of correlation trend is shown in the scatter plot below?

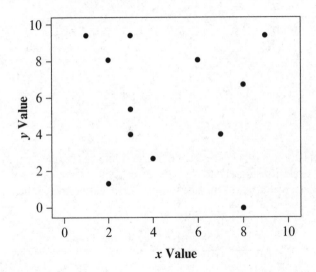

Answers: Bivariate Data

1.

	Diet Soda	Regular Soda	Total
Men	40	45	85
Women	90	85	175
Total	130	130	260

2. No, men in this sample survey prefer regular soda over diet soda. The women surveyed like diet soda better than regular soda.

3. 130

4.

	Diet Soda	Regular Soda	Total
Men	$\dfrac{40}{260} \approx 15\%$	$\dfrac{45}{260} \approx 17\%$	$\dfrac{85}{260} \approx 33\%$
Women	$\dfrac{90}{260} \approx 35\%$	$\dfrac{85}{260} \approx 33\%$	$\dfrac{175}{260} \approx 67\%$
Total	$\dfrac{130}{260} = 50\%$	$\dfrac{130}{260} = 50\%$	$\dfrac{260}{260} = 100\%$

5. 50% of the men and women in this survey prefer regular soda. This is the same percentage as those who prefer diet soda.

6. The relative percentage of women who prefer diet soda is 35%.

7. A positive correlation trend

8. No correlation

Probability

Probability is the numerical measure of the chance of an outcome or event occurring. Statistical research is more than just describing numerical data. Researchers must use statistical methods to draw probable conclusions with a high level of confidence about events, people, or other phenomena being investigated.

Random sampling states that each member of a group (population) has an equal chance of being selected. Random sampling applies the laws of probability to the collected data. Thus, the results of a random sampling are representative of the entire population being studied without bias in the selection process.

The probability of a *chance* occurrence shows a fair and equal advantage of something being selected. For instance, even when a coin toss is repeated over and over again, there is an equal chance that the coin will be either heads or tails.

In the Common Core Standards, both experimental and theoretical probability are used to make predictions about future events. Probability theory states that *all outcomes have an equal chance of occurring.* This is determined by the ratio of the number of favorable outcomes (or "successes") to the total number of outcomes. The probability of the occurrence of a given outcome can be found by using the following formula:

$$\text{probability} = \frac{\text{number of favorable outcomes}}{\text{number of possible outcomes}}$$

Examples:

Using the equally spaced spinner below, what is the probability of spinning a 6 in one spin?

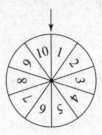

Since there is only *one* 6 on the spinner out of *ten* numbers and all the numbers are equally spaced, the probability is $\frac{1}{10}$.

Using the equally spaced spinner above, what is the probability of spinning either a 3 or a 5 in one spin? Since there are *two favorable outcomes* out of *ten possible outcomes,* the probability is $\frac{2}{10}$, or $\frac{1}{5}$.

Independent Probability

When two events are *independent* of each other, multiply their individual probabilities to find their combined probability: $P(A \text{ and } B) = P(A) \times P(B)$.

Examples:

What is the probability that both equally spaced spinners below will stop on a 3 on the first spin?

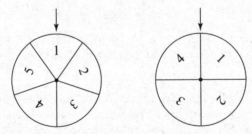

Since the probability that the first spinner will stop on the number 3 is $\frac{1}{5}$ and the probability that the second spinner will stop on the number 3 is $\frac{1}{4}$, and since each event is independent of the other, simply multiply: $\frac{1}{5} \times \frac{1}{4} = \frac{1}{20}$.

What is the probability that on two consecutive rolls of a die the numbers will be 2 and then 3? Since the probability of getting a 2 on the first roll is $\frac{1}{6}$ and the probability of getting a 3 on the second roll is $\frac{1}{6}$, and since the rolls are independent of each other, simply multiply: $\frac{1}{6} \times \frac{1}{6} = \frac{1}{36}$.

What is the probability of tossing heads three consecutive times with a two-sided fair coin?

Since each toss is *independent* and the probability is $\frac{1}{2}$ for each toss, the probability would be $\frac{1}{2} \times \frac{1}{2} \times \frac{1}{2} = \frac{1}{8}$.

What is the probability of rolling two dice in one toss so that they total 5?

Since there are six possible outcomes on each die, the total possible outcomes for two dice is $6 \times 6 = 36$. The favorable outcomes are $(1 + 4)$, $(4 + 1)$, $(2 + 3)$, and $(3 + 2)$. These are all the ways of tossing a total of 5 on two dice. Therefore, there are four favorable outcomes, which gives the probability of throwing a total of 5 as $\frac{4}{36} = \frac{1}{9}$.

Three green marbles, two blue marbles, and five yellow marbles are placed in a jar. What is the probability of selecting at random a green marble on the first draw?

Since there are ten marbles (total possible outcomes) and three green marbles (favorable outcomes), the probability is $\frac{3}{10}$.

Costa Coffee's billboard ad claims that 7 out of 10 consumers prefer its cappuccino over other coffeehouse chains. If Costa Coffee surveyed approximately 2,400 people, how many people would they expect to *not* prefer Costa Coffee's cappuccino?

If 70% of the surveyed population prefer Costa Coffee cappuccino over other coffeehouse chain cappuccinos, this means that 30% of the population do not prefer Costa Coffee's cappuccino. $30\% \times 2,400 = 720$ people would be expected to not prefer Costa Coffee's cappuccino.

If Costa Coffee surveys 300 more people, how many more people would they expect to prefer Costa Coffee's cappuccino?

$70\% \times 300 = 210$. Therefore, 210 of the additional 300 people surveyed would be expected to prefer Costa Coffee's cappuccino.

Dependent Probability

Dependent probability explains how the outcome of the first event affects the outcome of the second event. Two events are dependent if the outcome of the first event affects the outcome of the second event.

Example:

What is the probability of drawing a jack from a well-shuffled standard deck of 52 playing cards without putting it back into the deck, and then drawing an ace from the deck of cards?

Since there are four jacks in a standard deck of 52 playing cards, the probability of this event is $\frac{4}{52}$.

The probability of drawing an ace in the next event is $\frac{4}{51}$. The first event changed the second event (the reduction in the number of cards from the deck). Therefore, the outcome of the second event is dependent on the first event. Multiply them together to find the probability: $\frac{4}{52} \times \frac{4}{51} = \frac{16}{2,652} = \frac{4}{663}$.

Conditional Probability

Conditional probability explains the relationship between two events: the probability that Event B will happen after Event A has already happened. If the probabilities are *independent,* the area of intersection is $P(A) \times P(B)$.

If the events are *dependent,* the formula is $P(A \cap B) = P(A) \times P(B|A)$, which can also be written as

$P(A|B) = \dfrac{P(A \cap B)}{P(B)}$. A Venn diagram helps illustrate this formula.

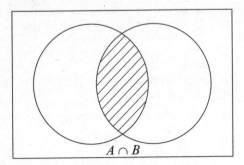

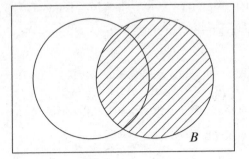

$A \cap B$ is the numerator and B is the denominator for solving these problems.

Example:

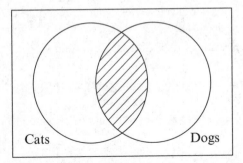

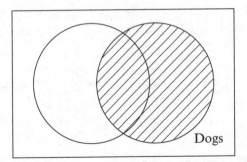

A high school survey found that 38% of students have a dog as a pet and that 20% of the students have both a dog and a cat as a pets. What is the probability that a student owns a cat, given that the student also owns a dog (rounded to the nearest percentage)?

The intersection of $A \cap B$ (the students who have both a cat and a dog as pets) = 20% or 0.2 and the percentage of dog owners is 0.38.

$$\frac{P(A \cap B)}{P(B)} = \frac{0.2}{0.38} \approx 53\%$$

Practice: Probability

Use the following equally spaced spinner to answer questions 1 and 2.

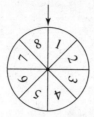

1. What is the probability of spinning a 4 or greater in one spin?
2. What is the probability of spinning either a 2 or a 5 on one spin?
3. What is the probability of rolling two dice in one toss so that they total 7?
4. What is the probability of tossing tails four consecutive times with a two-sided fair coin?

Use the following equally spaced spinners to answer question 5.

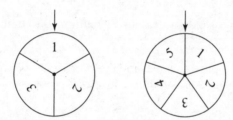

5. What is the probability that each spinner will stop on a 2 on its first spin?
6. In a well-shuffled standard deck of 52 playing cards, what is the probability of drawing a heart on the first draw? (There are 13 hearts in a standard deck.)

Answers: Probability

1. Since there are five numbers out of the eight numbers that are 4 or greater and all the numbers are equally spaced, the probability is $\frac{5}{8}$.

2. Since there are two favorable outcomes out of eight possible outcomes, the probability is $\frac{2}{8}$, or $\frac{1}{4}$.

3. There are six ways to total 7 on two dice—(1 + 6), (6 + 1), (2 + 5), (5 + 2), (3 + 4), (4 + 3)—out of a possible 36 outcomes (6 × 6), so the probability is $\frac{6}{36}$, or $\frac{1}{6}$.

4. Each toss is independent, and the probability is $\frac{1}{2}$ for each toss; therefore, the probability would be $\frac{1}{2} \times \frac{1}{2} \times \frac{1}{2} \times \frac{1}{2} = \frac{1}{16}$.

5. The probability that the first spinner will stop on the number 2 is $\frac{1}{3}$, and the probability that the second spinner will stop on the number 2 is $\frac{1}{5}$. Since each event is independent of the other, simply multiply: $\frac{1}{3} \times \frac{1}{5} = \frac{1}{15}$.

6. There are 13 favorable outcomes out of 52 possible outcomes, so the probability is $\frac{13}{52}$, or $\frac{1}{4}$.

Combinations and Permutations

If there are a *number of successive choices* to make and the choices are *independent of each other* (order makes no difference), then *combinations* are involved. The total number of possible choices is the product of each of the choices at each stage.

Example:

How many possible choices of shirts and ties are there if there are five different color shirts and three different color ties?

To find the total number of possible choices, simply multiply the number of shirts times the number of ties: $5 \times 3 = 15$.

If there are a *number of successive choices* to make and the choices are *affected by the previous choice or choices* (dependent upon order), then *permutations* are involved.

Examples:

How many ways can you arrange the letters S, T, O, P in a row?

number of choices for the first letter		number of choices for the second letter		number of choices for the third letter		number of choices for the fourth letter
4	×	3	×	2	×	1

$$4! = 4 \times 3 \times 2 \times 1 = 24$$

The product $4 \times 3 \times 2 \times 1$ can be written 4! (read *4 factorial* or *factorial 4*). Thus, there are 24 different ways to arrange the four different letters.

How many ways can you arrange the letters Y, I, E, L, D in a row?

You could arrange the letters in 5! ways or $5 \times 4 \times 3 \times 2 \times 1 = 120$ different ways.

How many ways can you arrange the letters Y, I, E, L, D in a row, if the first and last letters must be vowels?

There are only two vowels in the above letters. Therefore, the arrangement can start with I and end with E, or start with E and end with I (two possibilities). With the first and last letters accounted for, the remaining letters can be arranged in 3!, or 6 different ways. This needs to be multiplied by the two possibilities for the vowels. Therefore, the answer is $6 \times 2 = 12$ different ways.

In how many ways can four out of seven books be arranged on a shelf?

Notice that the order in which the books are displayed makes a difference. The symbol to denote this is $P(n, r)$, which is read as the permutations of n things taken r at a time. The formula used is $P(n,r) = \dfrac{n!}{(n-r)!}$.

Since $n = 7$ and $r = 4$ (seven taken four at a time), the equation is as follows:

$$\frac{7!}{(7-4)!} = \frac{7!}{3!} = \frac{7 \times 6 \times 5 \times 4 \times 3 \times 2 \times 1}{3 \times 2 \times 1} = 7 \times 6 \times 5 \times 4 = 840$$

If, from among five people, three executives are to be selected, how many possible combinations of executives are there? (Notice that the order of selection makes no difference.) The symbol used to denote this situation is $C(n, r)$, which is read as the number of combinations of n things taken r at a time. The formula used is $C(n,r) = \dfrac{n!}{r!(n-r)!}$.

Since $n = 5$ and $r = 3$ (five people taken three at a time), the equation is as follows:

$$\frac{5!}{3!(5-3)!} = \frac{5 \times \overset{2}{\cancel{4}} \times \cancel{3} \times \cancel{2} \times 1}{\cancel{3} \times \cancel{2} \times 1 \times \cancel{2} \times 1} = 10$$

Tip: If the problem involves very few possibilities, you may want to actually list the possible choices.

Practice: Combinations and Permutations

1. How many possible outfits could Tim wear if he has three different color shirts, four different types of slacks, and two pairs of shoes?

Use the following information to answer questions 2 and 3.

The personal identification number (PIN) is a security feature that requires the user to create a three-digit PIN using a combination of numbers from 0 to 9.

2. How many three-digit PINs can be created?
3. How many different possible PINs exist if the middle number is 2?
4. How many different ways are there to arrange three jars in a row on a shelf?
5. There are nine horses in a race. How many different first-, second-, and third-place finishes are possible?
6. A coach is selecting a starting lineup for her basketball team. She must select from among nine players to get her starting lineup of five. How many possible starting lineups could she have?
7. How many possible arrangements of a, b, c, and d taken two at a time are there?

Answers: Combinations and Permutations

1. To find the total number of possible arrangements, simply multiply the numbers together.

$$3 \times 4 \times 2 = 24$$

2. Note that each position in the PIN is independent of the others; thus, since each has a possible of ten numbers, $10 \times 10 \times 10 = 1{,}000$ possible PINs.

3. Because one position is taken away from the three digits, there are only two remaining digits (the first and last possible combinations of the numbers 0 to 9), $10 \times 10 = 100$ possible PINs.

4. Since the order of the items is affected by the previous choice(s), the number of different ways equals 3! or $3 \times 2 \times 1 = 6$ different ways.

5. The order in which a horse finishes makes a difference, so use the permutations formula with $n = 9$ and $r = 3$.

$$\frac{9!}{(9-3)!} = \frac{9!}{6!} = \frac{9 \times 8 \times 7 \times 6 \times 5 \times 4 \times 3 \times 2 \times 1}{6 \times 5 \times 4 \times 3 \times 2 \times 1} = 9 \times 8 \times 7 = 504$$

6. The order in which players is selected does not matter; thus, use the combinations formula with $n = 9$ and $r = 5$ (nine players taken five at a time):

$$\frac{9!}{5!(9-5)!} = \frac{9 \times 8 \times 7 \times 6 \times 5 \times 4 \times 3 \times 2 \times 1}{5 \times 4 \times 3 \times 2 \times 1(4)!} = \frac{9 \times \overset{2}{8} \times 7 \times \overset{\overset{1}{2}}{6} \times 5 \times 4 \times 3 \times 2 \times 1}{5 \times 4 \times 3 \times 2 \times 1 \times 4 \times 3 \times 2 \times 1} = 126$$

7. Since $n = 4$ and $r = 2$ (four letters taken two at a time), the equation is as follows:

$$\frac{4!}{2!(4-2)!} = \frac{4!}{2!(2)!} = \frac{\overset{2}{4} \times 3 \times 2 \times 1}{2 \times 1 \times 2 \times 1} = 6$$

You might simply have listed the possible combinations as *ab*, *ac*, *ad*, *bc*, *bd*, and *cd*.

Statistics and Probability Review Test

Questions

1. Elijah scores a goal in a soccer game 20% of the time. What is the probability that Elijah will score a goal in three consecutive games?

Use the following two equally spaced spinners to answer question 2.

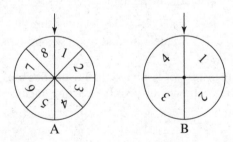

A   B

2. What is the probability that spinner A will stop on 5 and spinner B will stop on 2 if each spinner is given one spin?

3. What is the probability of rolling two dice on one toss so that their sum is 6?

4. What is the probability of tossing tails five consecutive times with a two-sided fair coin?

5. How many different ways are there to arrange four books in a row on a shelf?

6. If among five people, two game-show contestants must be chosen, how many possible ways are there to select the two contestants?

7. Find the arithmetic mean, mode, median, and range of the following set of numbers: 7, 4, 3, 9, 6, 8, 9.

8. Find the next number in the sequence: 4, 6, 9, 13, 18, _____.

9. Dante measured the height of everyone in his class and placed them in a stem-and-leaf plot, as shown below. What is the positive difference between the range and the median?

Stem	Leaf
5	8, 8, 9
6	0, 0, 0, 0, 0, 2, 2, 4, 4, 4, 4, 6, 9, 9, 9
7	0, 0, 1, 1, 2, 3

10. In how many different ways can six of nine books be arranged on a shelf?

Answers

Page numbers following each answer refer to the review section applicable to the problem type.

1. $\frac{1}{125}$ or 0.8% (p. 199)

2. $\frac{1}{32}$ (p. 200)

3. $\frac{5}{36}$ (p. 200)

4. $\frac{1}{32}$ (p. 202)

5. 24 ways (p. 204)

6. 10 possible combinations (p. 204)

7. mean $= 6\frac{4}{7}$, mode $= 9$, median $= 7$, range $= 6$ (pp. 187–189)

8. 24 (p. 29)

9. 49 (pp. 186, 188–189)

10. 60,480 permutations (p. 204)

Statistics and Probability Glossary of Terms

bell curve: A symmetrical, single-peaked frequency distribution. Also called a *normal curve*.

bivariate data: A data set that has two variables.

conditional probability: The probability that one event will happen after another event has happened. The events may be conditional or dependent.

correlation: When two or more quantities change together in a consistent manner. Thus, if the value of one variable is known, the other can be immediately determined from their relationship.

data: Numerical information about variables. The measurements or observations to be analyzed with statistical methods.

dependent probability: When the outcome of one event has a bearing or effect on the outcome of another event.

dependent variable: A variable that is caused or influenced by another.

discrete variable: A variable that can be measured only by means of whole numbers or one which assumes only a certain set of definite values and no others.

distribution: A collection of measurements. How scores tend to be dispersed about a measurement scale.

frequency distribution: The frequency of occurrence of the values of a variable. For each possible value of the variable, there is an associated frequency.

independent events: When the outcome of one event has no bearing or effect on the outcome of another event.

interquartile range: The difference between the third and the first quartile values of a set of data.

lower quartile (Q_1): The value in the data set so that approximately 25% of the data values are to its left when data values are written in ascending order.

mean (arithmetic): The average of a number of items in a group (total the items and divide by the number of items).

measures of central tendency: Descriptive measures that indicate the center of a set of values (mean, median, and mode).

median: The middle item in an ordered group. If the group has an even number of items, the median is the average of the two middle terms.

mode: The number appearing most frequently in a group.

mutually exclusive: Events such that the occurrence of one precludes the occurrence of the other.

normal distribution: A symmetrical bell-shaped curve.

outlier: In a given data set, an outlier is a number that is significantly different from the other numbers. It is usually much higher or lower and substantially changes the range of the data set.

population: A group of phenomena that have something in common. The population is the larger group, whose properties are estimated by taking a smaller sample from within the population.

positive relationship: A relationship between two variables such that when one increases, the other increases or when one decreases, the other decreases.

probability: The numerical measure of the chance of an outcome or event occurring.

quartiles: Quartiles show data in ascending order. Each of the parts are called a quartile and are labeled (Q_1, Q_2, and Q_3).

random: An event for which there is no way to know, before it occurs, what the outcome will be. Instead, only the probabilities of each possible outcome can be stated.

range: The difference between the largest and the smallest number in a set of numbers.

sample: A group of members of a population selected to represent that population. The sample applied should be randomly drawn from the population.

scatter plot: A graphic display used to illustrate degree of correlation between two variables.

standard deviation: The standard deviation of a population is a measure of the deviation of scores from the mean score. It is calculated by taking the positive square root of the variance.

statistic: A statistic is an estimate of the population parameter. For larger samples, the statistic is a better estimate of the parameter.

stem-and-leaf plot: A graphic display that shows actual scores as well as distribution of classes.

trend: The trend of bivariate data can be a positive correlation, a negative correlation, or no correlation. With a positive correlation, the y values generally increase as the x values increase. A negative correlation will have y values decrease as x values increase. No correlation means that no visible correlation is on a coordinate plane.

two-way frequency table: In a two-way frequency table, each category is divided by the total of that category to get the corresponding percentages.

two-way relative frequency table: A table that shows bivariate data in percentages of the total data.

upper quartile (Q_3): Tha value in the data set so that 75% of the data values are to its left when the data values are written in ascending order.

value: A measurement or classification of a variable.

variance: The variance of a population of scores is a measure of the deviation of scores from the mean score. The variance of a population is calculated by taking each data value, subtracting it from the mean, squaring each difference, adding these squares together, and then dividing the sum by the number of data values.

Chapter 4

Geometry

Geometry is a branch of mathematics that explores the position, relationship, measurement, and transformation of points, lines, angles, and objects. Although different types of geometry exist, the Common Core Standards primarily use *plane Euclidean geometry* (with coordinates and without coordinates) and *trigonometry*.

Connecting Geometry and the Common Core Standards

The topics covered in this chapter provide important conceptual categories that interconnect geometric reasoning to the Common Core Standards. As you study the geometric shapes, angles, and other configurations, always use math logic and reasoning before solving problems.

The following table highlights elements of the Common Core Standards that connect to the domain topics covered in this chapter. These topics introduce critical areas that are part of a conceptually larger set of Common Core Standards that ask you to interpret, explain, and provide proof to make sense of real-life geometric scenarios.

Geometry Common Core Connections

Proof and Reasoning	Identify geometric diagrams, angles, and other shapes (terms, definitions, properties, and formulas).
	Use logic and deductive reasoning to solve geometric problems.
	Apply multiple methods to solve real-world spatial problems.
	Prove important theorems pertaining to lines, right triangles, circles, sines, and cosines.
	Understand properties of special triangles and quadrilaterals.
	Use both trigonometric ratios and the Pythagorean theorem to solve problems with right triangles.
Measurement	Identify important elements of geometric measurements (angle measure, length, area, perimeter, volume, circumference).
	Use geometric measures to describe and model objects.
Two- and Three-Dimensional Objects	Use visualization to picture and solve real-life reasoning problems with two- and three-dimensional objects composed of angles, perimeter, area, surface area, and volume.
Circles	Understand theorems about circles.
	Find arc lengths and areas of sectors of circles.
	Translate between the geometric description and the equation for a conic section.

(Continued)

Geometry Common Core Connections (*continued*)

Transformations and Similarity	Understand the concept of two objects being congruent, similar, or symmetrical.
	Understand the function of rigid motions (i.e., translations, rotations, and reflections).
	Prove theorems involving similarity.
	Identify criteria for similarity of triangles to solve right triangle trigonometry problems.
Coordinate Geometry	Apply coordinates to prove simple geometric theorems algebraically.
	Apply the Pythagorean theorem to a coordinate plane.
	Explain transformations by using geometric coordinates.
Applications of Probability	Interpret geometric probabilities to make informed decisions about real-life events.
	Use the rules of probability to compute probabilities of compound events.

As you approach geometry problems in this chapter, keep in mind that the visual illustrations of geometric figures are *not* necessarily drawn to scale. However, lines shown in the figures are straight, and points on the line are in the order shown. Some shapes may appear larger, while others may appear smaller.

Geometry Diagnostic Test

Questions

1. Name any angle of the following triangle three different ways.

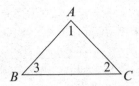

2. A(n) _____ angle measures less than 90°.

3. A(n) _____ angle measures 90°.

4. A(n) _____ angle measures more than 90° but less than 180°.

5. A(n) _____ angle measures 180°.

6. Two angles are complementary when the sum of their measures is _____.

7. Two angles are supplementary when the sum of their measures is _____.

8. In the following diagram, find the measure of $\angle a$, $\angle b$, and $\angle c$.

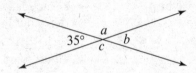

9. In the following diagram, find the measure of all remaining angles. *Note:* $l \parallel m$.

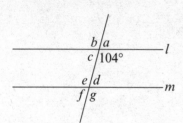

10. Lines that stay the same distance apart and never meet are called _____ lines.

11. Lines that meet to form right angles are called _____ lines.

12. A(n) _____ triangle has three equal sides; therefore, each interior angle measures _____.

13. In $\triangle ABC$ below,

   (a) segment BD is a(n) _____.
   (b) segment BE is a(n) _____.
   (c) segment BF is a(n) _____.

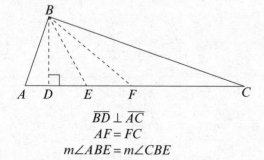

$$\overline{BD} \perp \overline{AC}$$
$$AF = FC$$
$$m\angle ABE = m\angle CBE$$

14. In the following diagram, ABC is an isosceles triangle: $AB = AC$. Find the measure of $\angle A$ and $\angle C$.

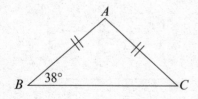

Questions 15 and 16 are based on the following triangle.

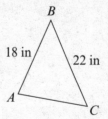

15. In the triangle above, AC must be less than _____ inches.

16. In the triangle above, which angle is smaller, $\angle A$ or $\angle C$?

17. In the following triangle, what is the measure of $\angle ACD$?

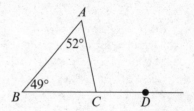

18. In the following triangle, what is the length of $\overline{AC}$?

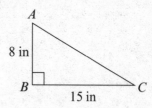

19. In the following triangle, what is the length of $\overline{BC}$?

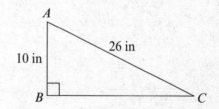

20. In the following triangle, what is the value of x?

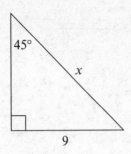

21. In the following triangle, what is the value of a?

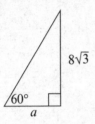

22. In the following triangle, what is the value of x (to the nearest tenth of a centimeter)?

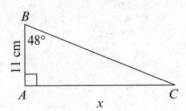

23. Name each of the following polygons.

(a)
$$AB = BC = AC$$
$$m\angle A = m\angle B = m\angle C = 60°$$

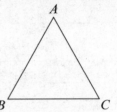

(b)
$$AB = BC = CD = AD$$
$$m\angle A = m\angle B = m\angle C = m\angle D = 90°$$

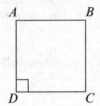

(c)
$$\overline{AB} \parallel \overline{DC}$$
$$\underline{AB} = \underline{DC}$$
$$\overline{AD} \parallel \overline{BC}$$
$$AD = BC$$

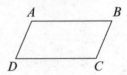

(d)
$$AB = DC$$
$$AD = BC$$
$$m\angle A = m\angle B = m\angle C = m\angle D = 90°$$

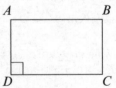

(e) $AB \parallel DC$

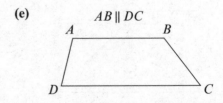

24. For which of the following quadrilaterals *must* the following be true? Check all that apply.

Property	Square	Rectangle	Rhombus	Parallelogram	Trapezoid
Diagonals are equal					
Diagonals bisect each other					
Diagonals are perpendicular					
Diagonals bisect the angles					
All sides are equal in length					
All angles are equal in measure					
Opposite angles are equal in measure					
Opposite sides are equal in length					
At least one pair of opposite sides are parallel					
At least two pairs of consecutive angles are supplementary					

Questions 25 and 26 relate to the following figure.

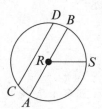

25. Fill in the blanks for circle R.

    (a) $\overline{RS}$ is called a _____.

    (b) $\overline{AB}$ is called a _____.

    (c) $\overline{CD}$ is called a _____.

26. If $m\widehat{BS} = 62°$, what is the measure of $\angle BRS$?

27. In the following circle, if $m\widehat{BS} = 62°$, what is the measure of $\angle BCS$?

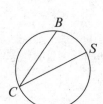

28. Find the area and circumference for the circle O below. (Use $\pi \approx \frac{22}{7}$.)

(a) area = _____
(b) circumference = _____

29. Find the area and perimeter of the following trapezoid.

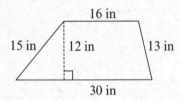

(a) area = _____
(b) perimeter = _____

30. Find the area and perimeter of parallelogram $ABCD$ below.

(a) area = _____
(b) perimeter = _____

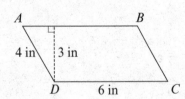

31. The areas of the right triangle and parallelogram below are equal. Find the height of the parallelogram.

32. The figure below is a square with sides of 4 feet. What is the area of the shaded region? (Use 3.14 for π.)

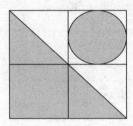

33. Find the volume of the following right circular cylinder. (Use 3.14 for π.)

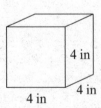

34. What is the surface area and volume of the following cube?

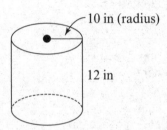

(a) surface area = _____
(b) volume = _____

35. Perform the translation of $(x, y) \rightarrow (x-7, y + 3)$ in the figure below.

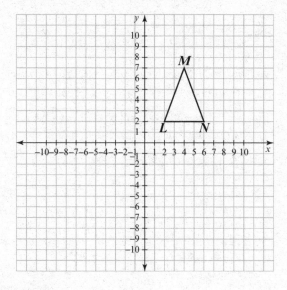

36. Rotate the figure below counterclockwise 270° around the point of origin.

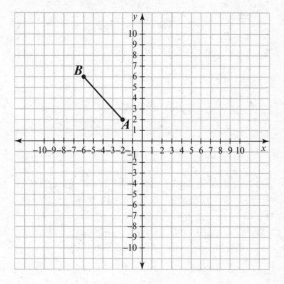

Answers

Page numbers following each answer refer to the review section applicable to the problem type.

1. $\angle 1$, $\angle BAC$, $\angle CAB$, $\angle A$

$\angle 2$, $\angle ACB$, $\angle BCA$, $\angle C$

$\angle 3$, $\angle CBA$, $\angle ABC$, $\angle B$ (p. 220)

2. acute (p. 221)

3. right (p. 221)

4. obtuse (p. 221)

5. straight (p. 221)

6. 90° (p. 223)

7. 180° (p. 223)

8. $m\angle a = 145°$

$m\angle b = 35°$

$m\angle c = 145°$ (p. 222)

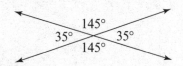

9. $m\angle a, m\angle c, m\angle d, m\angle f = 76°$

$m\angle b, m\angle e, m\angle g = 104°$ (p. 226)

104°	76°
76°	104°
104°	76°
76°	104°

10. parallel (p. 226)

11. perpendicular (p. 225)

12. equilateral; 60° (p. 234)

13. **(a)** altitude
(b) angle bisector
(c) median (pp. 236–237)

14. $38° + 38° + x° = 180°$

$\qquad 76° + x° = 180°$

$\qquad\qquad\quad x° = 104°$

$\qquad\qquad m\angle A = 104°$

$\qquad\qquad m\angle C = 38°$

(p. 238)

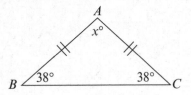

15. 40 inches. Since $AB + BC = 40$ inches, $AC < AB + BC$. Therefore, $AC < 40$ inches. (p. 239)

16. $\angle C$ must be the smaller angle, since it is opposite the shorter side, $\overline{AB}$. (p. 239)

17. $m\angle ACD = 101°$ (p. 239)

18. $AC = 17$ inches (p. 242)

19. $BC = 24$ inches. Since 5, 12, 13 is a Pythagorean triple, doubled is 10, 24, 26. (p. 242)

20. $x = 9\sqrt{2}$. Since this is an isosceles right triangle, the ratio of the sides is $x, x, x\sqrt{2}$. (p. 244)

21. $a = 8$. Since this is a 30°-60°-90° right triangle, the ratio of the sides is $x, x\sqrt{3}, 2x$. (p. 245)

22. $x = 12.2$ cm (p. 249)

23. **(a)** equilateral triangle or equiangular triangle (p. 238)

(b) square (p. 251)

(c) parallelogram (p. 252)

(d) rectangle (p. 251)

(e) trapezoid (p. 252)

24. (pp. 251–252)

Property	Square	Rectangle	Rhombus	Parallelogram	Trapezoid
Diagonals are equal	✓	✓			
Diagonals bisect each other	✓	✓	✓	✓	
Diagonals are perpendicular	✓		✓		
Diagonals bisect the angles	✓		✓		
All sides are equal in length	✓		✓		
All angles are equal in measure	✓	✓			
Opposite angles are equal in measure	✓	✓	✓	✓	
Opposite sides are equal in length	✓	✓	✓	✓	
At least one pair of opposite sides are parallel	✓	✓	✓	✓	✓
At least two pairs of consecutive angles are supplementary	✓	✓	✓	✓	✓

25. **(a)** radius (p. 261)

(b) diameter (p. 261)

(c) chord (p. 261)

26. 62° (p. 265)

27. 31° (p. 265)

28. **(a)** area $= \pi r^2$

$$= \pi \left(7^2\right)$$

$$= \frac{22}{7}(7)(7)$$

$$= 154 \text{ square inches}$$

(p. 263)

(b) $d = 14$ inches, since $r = 7$ inches.

circumference $= \pi d$

$$= \pi (14)$$

$$= \frac{22}{7}(14)$$

$$= 44 \text{ inches}$$

(p. 262)

29. **(a)** area $= \frac{1}{2}(a+b)h$

$$= \frac{1}{2}(16+30)12$$

$$= \frac{1}{2}(46)12$$

$$= 23(12)$$

$$= 276 \text{ square inches}$$

(pp. 256–257)

(b) perimeter $= 16 + 13 + 30 + 15 = 74$ inches

(pp. 256–257)

30. **(a)** area $= bh$

$$= 6(3)$$

$$= 18 \text{ square inches}$$

(pp. 256–257)

(b) perimeter $= 6 + 4 + 6 + 4 = 20$ inches

(pp. 256–257)

31. 2 cm (pp. 256–257)

32. Notice that the entire square has been cut in half with a diagonal that goes from the upper left corner to the lower right corner. Thus, the shaded region located in the lower left of the square would be half of the area of the entire square. The square has a side of 4 feet. Therefore, the area is 4 × 4 or 16 sq ft, and the lower shaded area is 8 sq ft. The circle has a diameter of 2 feet, therefore, the radius is 1 foot. The area of the circle is $\pi r^2 = (3.14)(1)^2 = 3.14$ sq ft. Hence, the entire shaded region has an area of $8 + 3.14 = 11.14$ sq ft. (pp. 256–257)

33. Volume $= $ (area of base)(height)

$$= (\pi r^2)h$$

$$= (\pi \times 10^2)(12)$$

$$\approx 3.14(100)(12)$$

$$\approx 314(12)$$

$$\approx 3{,}768 \text{ cubic inches}$$

(p. 267)

34. **(a)** All six surfaces have an area of 4 in × 4 in, or 16 square inches, since each surface is a square. Therefore, 16(6) = 96 square inches for the surface area. (p. 269)

(b) Volume $=$ side × side × side or $4^3 = 4 \times 4 \times 4 = 64$ cubic inches. (p. 267)

35.

(pp. 228–229)

36. $A\ (-2, 2) \rightarrow (2, 2)\ B\ (-6, 6) \rightarrow (6, 6)$

(pp. 229–230)

Geometry Review

Plane geometry is the study of shapes and figures in two dimensions (the plane). Plane figures have only length and width.

Solid geometry is the study of shapes and figures in three dimensions (3-D). Solid figures have width, depth, and height.

A *point* is the most fundamental idea in geometry. It is represented by a dot and named by a capital letter.

Angles

The identification of the properties of angles is essential to understanding the relationships in triangles and other shapes. This knowledge is the foundation for solving problems and analyzing complex geometric situations with two-dimensional and three-dimensional shapes.

An *angle* is formed by two rays that have the same endpoint. That point is called the *vertex;* the rays are called the *sides* of the angle. An angle is measured in degrees from 0 to 360. The number of degrees indicates the size of the angle or the difference in direction of the two rays.

In the following diagram, the angle is formed by rays $\overrightarrow{AB}$ and $\overrightarrow{AC}$. A is the vertex. $\overrightarrow{AB}$ and $\overrightarrow{AC}$ are the sides of the angle.

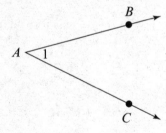

The symbol $\angle$ is used to denote an angle. The symbol $m\angle$ is used to denote the measure of an angle.

An angle can be named in various ways:

- By the letter of the vertex; therefore, the angle above could be named $\angle A$.
- By the number (or small letter) in its interior; therefore, the angle above could be named $\angle 1$.
- By the letters of the three points that form it; therefore, the angle above could be named $\angle BAC$ or $\angle CAB$. The center letter is always the letter of the vertex.

Types of Angles

Right Angle

A *right angle* has a measure of 90°. A small square in the interior of an angle designates the fact that a right angle is formed. In the following diagram, ∠*ABC* is a right angle.

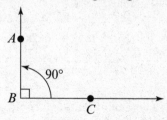

Acute Angle

Any angle whose measure is less than 90° is called an *acute angle.* In the following diagram, ∠*b* is acute.

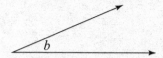

Obtuse Angle

Any angle whose measure is larger than 90° but smaller than 180° is called an *obtuse angle.* In the following diagram, ∠4 is an obtuse angle.

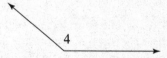

Straight Angle

A *straight angle* has a measure of 180°. In the following diagram, ∠*BAC* is a straight angle (often called a *line*).

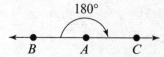

Practice: Types of Angles

For questions 1–4, name the angles.

1.

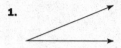

2.

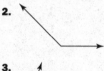

3.

4.

For questions 5–8, indicate what kind of angle is formed between the hands of a clock (measured clockwise) when it is

5. 6 o'clock

6. 2 o'clock

7. 3 o'clock

8. 4 o'clock

221

Answers: Types of Angles

1. acute angle
2. obtuse angle
3. acute angle
4. obtuse angle

5. straight angle
6. acute angle
7. right angle
8. obtuse angle

Pairs of Angles

Adjacent Angles

Adjacent angles are any angles that share a common side and a common vertex but do not share any interior points. In the following diagram, $\angle 1$ and $\angle 2$ are adjacent angles. But $\angle 1$ and $\angle ABC$ are not adjacent angles since they share interior points (for example, point E is in the interior of each angle).

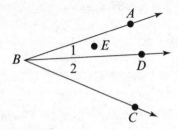

Vertical Angles

If two straight lines intersect, they do so at a point. Four angles are formed. Those angles opposite each other are called *vertical angles.* Those angles sharing a common side and a common vertex are, again, *adjacent angles.* Vertical angles are always equal in measure. In the following diagram, line l and line m intersect at point Q. $\angle 1$, $\angle 2$, $\angle 3$, and $\angle 4$ are formed.

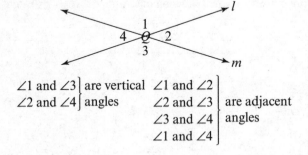

$\angle 1$ and $\angle 3$ ⎫ are vertical $\angle 1$ and $\angle 2$ ⎫
$\angle 2$ and $\angle 4$ ⎭ angles $\angle 2$ and $\angle 3$ ⎬ are adjacent
                          $\angle 3$ and $\angle 4$ ⎪ angles
                          $\angle 1$ and $\angle 4$ ⎭

Therefore,

$$m\angle 1 = m\angle 3$$
$$m\angle 2 = m\angle 4$$

Complementary Angles

Two angles whose sum is 90° are called *complementary angles*. In the following diagram, since $\angle ABC$ is a right triangle, $m\angle 1 + m\angle 2 = 90°$.

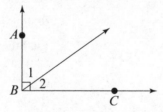

Therefore, $\angle 1$ and $\angle 2$ are complementary angles. If $\angle 1$ has a measure of 55°, its complement, $\angle 2$, would have a measure of 90° − 55° = 35°.

Supplementary Angles

Two angles whose sum is 180° are called *supplementary angles*. Two adjacent angles that form a straight line are supplementary. In the following diagram, since $\angle ABC$ is a straight angle, $m\angle 3 + m\angle 4 = 180°$.

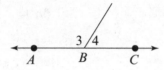

Therefore, $\angle 3$ and $\angle 4$ are supplementary angles. If $\angle 3$ has a measure of 122°, its supplement, $\angle 4$, would have a measure of 180° − 122° = 58°.

Angle Bisector

A ray from the vertex of an angle that divides the angle into two angles of equal measure is called an *angle bisector*. In the following diagram, $\overrightarrow{AB}$ is the angle bisector of $\angle CAD$.

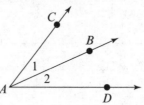

Therefore, $m\angle 1 = m\angle 2$.

Practice: Pairs of Angles

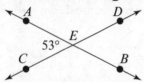

1. In the figure above, if lines AB and CD intersect at E, and if $\angle AEC$ measures 53°, how many degrees are there in $\angle BED$?

2. Find the complement of the following angles.
   (a) 17°
   (b) $t°$

3. Find the supplement of the following angles.

   (a) 124°

   (b) $(x + 9)°$

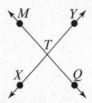

4. In the figure above, $\angle XTM$ and $\angle$_____ are *vertical* angles.

5. Find the complement of an angle whose measure is

   (a) $74\frac{1}{2}°$

   (b) $(q - 5)°$

6. Find the supplement of an angle whose measure is

   (a) 180°

   (b) $(m - 30)°$

Answers: Pairs of Angles

1. Since $\angle AEC$ and $\angle BED$ are vertical angles, $m\angle BED = 53°$.

2. **(a)** $90° - 17° = 73°$

   (b) $(90 - t)°$

3. **(a)** $180° - 124° = 56°$

   (b) $180° - (x + 9)° = 180° - x° - 9° = (171 - x)°$

4. *YTQ*

5. **(a)** $90° - 74\frac{1}{2}° = 15\frac{1}{2}°$

   (b) $90° - (q - 5)° = 90° - q° + 5° = (95 - q)°$

6. **(a)** $180° - 180° = 0°$

   (b) $180° - (m - 30)° = 180° - m° + 30° = (210 - m)°$

Lines

Straight Lines

A *straight line* is often described as the shortest path connecting two points. It continues forever in both directions. A line consists of an infinite number of points and is named by any two points on the line. (When the term *line* is used, it means straight line.) The symbol ⟷ written on top of the two letters is used to denote that line. Line AB, shown below, is written $\overleftrightarrow{AB}$.

A line may also be named by one small letter. The following is line *l*.

Line Segments

A *line segment* is a piece of a line. It has two endpoints and is named by its two *endpoints*. Sometimes the symbol —, written on top of the two letters, is used to denote that line segment. The following is line segment CD. It is written $\overline{CD}$ or segment CD. (Although there is a technical difference, most standardized exams use one form consistently in context.) Note that $\overline{CD}$ is a part of $\overleftrightarrow{AB}$.

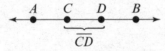

A *midpoint* of a line segment is the halfway point, or the point equidistant, from the endpoints.

Rays

A *ray* has only one endpoint (or origin) and continues forever in one direction. A ray could be thought of as a half-line with an endpoint. It is named by the letter of its endpoint and any other point on the ray. The ray symbol ———→, written on top of the two letters, is used to denote that ray. The following is ray *AB*. It is written $\overrightarrow{AB}$.

When writing a ray, begin with the endpoint, then name another point through which it passes. In the following figure, even though the ray is going to the left, it is written as $\overrightarrow{BC}$.

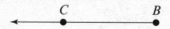

Types of Lines

Intersecting Lines

Two or more lines that meet at a point are called *intersecting lines*. That point would be on each of those lines. In the following diagram, lines *l* and *m* intersect at *Q*.

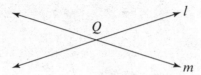

Perpendicular Lines

Two lines that meet to form right angles (90°) are called *perpendicular lines*. The symbol ⊥ is used to denote perpendicular lines. In the following diagram, $l \perp m$.

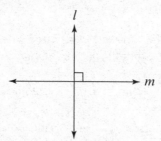

Parallel Lines

Two or more lines that remain the same distance apart at all times are called *parallel lines*. Parallel lines never meet. The symbol ‖ is used to denote parallel lines. In the following diagram, $l \parallel m$.

Parallel Lines Cut by a Transversal

When two parallel lines are both intersected by a third line, it is termed *parallel lines cut by a transversal.* In the diagram below, line *n* is the transversal, and lines *m* and *l* are parallel. Eight angles are formed.

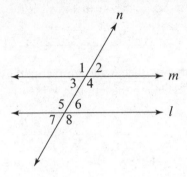

There are many facts and relationships about the angles created when parallel lines are cut by a transversal:

- **Adjacent angles:** Angles 1 and 2 are *adjacent,* and they form a straight line; therefore, they are supplementary or $m\angle1 + m\angle2 = 180°$. Likewise:

  $m\angle2 + m\angle4 = 180°$ $m\angle1 + m\angle3 = 180°$ $m\angle7 + m\angle8 = 180°$

  $m\angle3 + m\angle4 = 180°$ $m\angle5 + m\angle6 = 180°$ $m\angle5 + m\angle7 = 180°$

  $m\angle6 + m\angle8 = 180°$

- **Vertical angles:** Angles 1 and 4 are *vertical angles*; therefore, they are equal or $m\angle1 = m\angle4$. Likewise:

  $m\angle2 = m\angle3$ $m\angle5 = m\angle8$ $m\angle7 = m\angle6$

- **Corresponding angles:** If you could physically pick up line *l* and place it on line *m*, the angles that would coincide with each other would be equal in measure. They are called *corresponding angles.* Therefore:

  $m\angle1 = m\angle5$ $m\angle2 = m\angle6$ $m\angle3 = m\angle7$

  $m\angle4 = m\angle8$

- **Alternate interior and exterior angles:** *Alternate angles* are on the opposite sides of the transversal. *Interior angles* are those contained within the parallel lines. *Exterior angles* are those on the outsides of the parallel lines. Therefore:

  $\angle3$ and $\angle6$ are alternate interior angles and $m\angle3 = m\angle6$. $\angle2$ and $\angle7$ are alternate exterior angles and $m\angle2 = m\angle7$.

  $\angle4$ and $\angle5$ are alternate interior angles and $m\angle4 = m\angle5$. $\angle1$ and $\angle8$ are alternate exterior angles and $m\angle1 = m\angle8$.

- **Consecutive interior angles:** Consecutive interior angles are on the same side of the transversal. Therefore:

  $\angle3$ and $\angle5$ are consecutive interior angles, and $m\angle3 + m\angle5 = 180°$.

  $\angle4$ and $\angle6$ are consecutive interior angles, and $m\angle4 + m\angle6 = 180°$.

  The sum of the measures of each pair of consecutive angles = 180°.

Using all these facts, if you're given the measure of one of the eight angles, the other angle measures can all be determined.

Example:

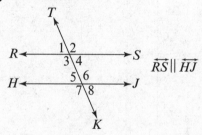

$$m\angle 1 + m\angle 2 = 180°$$

$m\angle 2 = 97°$
$m\angle 3 = 97°$ } vertical angles

$m\angle 4 = 83°$
$m\angle 5 = 83°$ } alternate interior angles

$m\angle 6 = 97°$
$m\angle 7 = 97°$ } vertical angles

$m\angle 8 = 83°$
$m\angle 1 = 83°$ } alternate exterior angles

Note that since the lines are parallel, you can *see* which angles are equal—even if you cannot remember the rules.

Practice: Parallel Lines Cut by a Transversal

1. In the figure above, name all the pairs of the following types of angles.

(a) vertical angles

(b) consecutive interior angles

(c) corresponding angles

(d) alternate interior angles

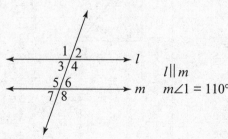

2. In the figure above, find the measure of the angles 2, 3, 4, 5, 6, 7, and 8.

Answers: Parallel Lines Cut by a Transversal

1. **(a)** Vertical angles are 1 and 4, 2 and 3, 5 and 8, 6 and 7.

   (b) Consecutive interior angles are 3 and 5, 4 and 6.

   (c) Corresponding angles are 1 and 5, 3 and 7, 2 and 6, 4 and 8.

   (d) Alternate interior angles are 3 and 6, 4 and 5.

2. Angles 4, 5, and 8 all have measures of 110°.

   Angles 2, 3, 6, and 7 all have measures of 70°.

Translations, Reflections, and Rotations

Translations, reflections, and rotations are the names given when moving two-dimensional figures on a coordinate plane without changing their shapes or sizes. The Common Core Standards frequently reference these types of figures when the location of a figure has been repositioned by sliding, turning, or flipping the original figure. To differentiate the first figure (pre-image) from the second figure (image), insert a slanted single prime ′ symbol after the labeled letter in the image.

Translation

A *translation* is also called a *slide* because the figure moves from one position on a coordinate plane to another.

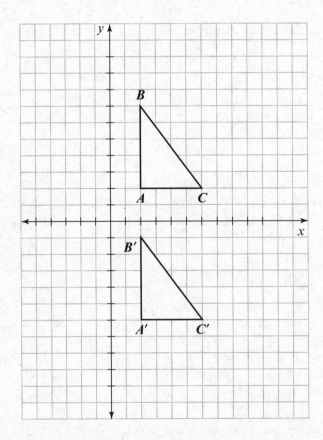

In this example above, point A is (2, 2) and A' (2, –6). Point B is (2, 7) and B' (2, –1). Point C (6, 2) and C' (6, –6). The translation is written as $(x, y) \rightarrow (x, y – 8)$. For A, B, and C, each value of x remains the same. For each point, the value of y is decreased by 8.

Reflection

A *reflection* is a mirror image of the original figure. The figure does not change when reflection takes place, just as a figure does not change when reflected in a mirror. Reflection is called *flipping* a figure.

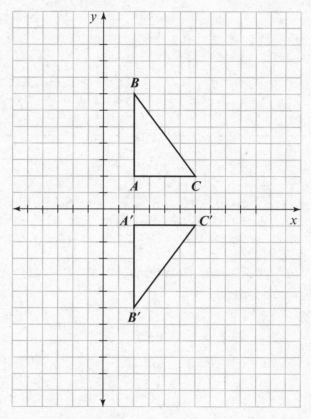

In this example above, the triangle is reflected over the x-axis. It is written as $(x, y) \rightarrow (x, –y)$. If the figure is reflected over the y-axis, it is written as $(x, y) \rightarrow (–x, y)$.

When you work with reflections, think of the same size and shape of a mirror image being flipped. The new shape will be identical to the original shape, but will be flipped over some line. The reflection does not have to be over an axis. It can be on any line. When working on reflection problems, draw the reflection line first and then plot the flipped points.

Rotation

A *rotation* has a central point that stays fixed and everything else rotates around that point in a circle. Rotation is called *turning* a figure.

The point can be on a figure, away from a figure, or inside of a figure. If the figure is rotated 90° counterclockwise around the origin (0, 0), it is written as $(x, y) \rightarrow (-y, x)$. Notice that when rotating 90° around the origin in a counterclockwise direction, the new x-coordinate becomes the opposite of the original y-coordinate, and the new y-coordinate is the same as the original x-coordinate.

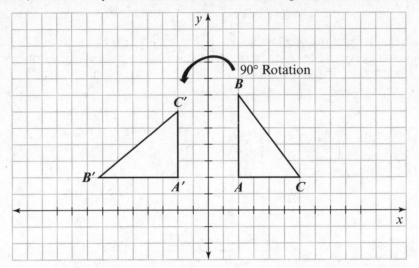

In this example above, point A is (2, 2). After rotation, it is A' (–2, 2). Point B is (2, 6). After rotation, it is B' (–6, 2). Point C is (6, 2). After rotation, it is C' (–2, 6). For a 180° rotation in either a clockwise or counterclockwise direction, $(x, y) \rightarrow (-x, -y)$. For a 270° rotation, $(x, y) \rightarrow (y, -x)$.

Practice: Translations, Reflections, and Rotations

Use the diagram below to answer the questions.

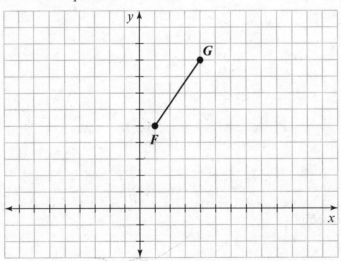

1. Translate $(x, y) \rightarrow (x + 3, y - 2)$.

2. Rotate 270° counterclockwise.

3. Reflect over $y = 2$.

Answers: Translations, Reflections, and Rotations

1. $F(1, 5) \rightarrow (4, 3)$ and $G(4, 9) \rightarrow (7, 7)$

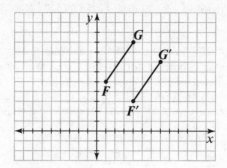

2. $F(1, 5) \rightarrow (5, -1)$ and $G(4, 9) \rightarrow (9, -4)$

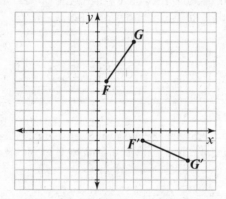

3. $F(1, 5) \rightarrow (1, -1)$ and $G(4, 9) \rightarrow (4, -5)$. The dotted line is $y = 2$.

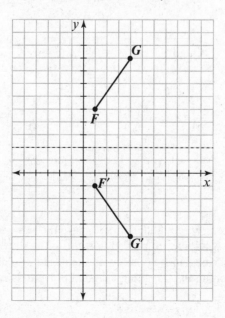

Congruence and Similarity

The Common Core Standards apply previous knowledge of rigid motions (translations, reflections, and rotations) to understand the *congruence* of two shapes. This knowledge is applied to proportional reasoning to help understand *similarity*.

Two plane geometric figures are said to be *congruent* if they are identical in size and shape. Figures are said to be *similar* if they have the same shape, but are not the same size. Similar shapes have corresponding sides in proportion. Thus, if two shapes are identical, they are also similar.

Two triangles are congruent if their corresponding angles and sides have the same measurement.

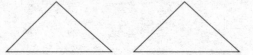

Three squares will always be similar because they have exactly the same shape, have corresponding angles that are equal, and have corresponding sides that are proportional.

Polygons

Closed shapes, or figures in a plane, with three or more sides are called *polygons*. (*Poly* means "many," and *gon* means "sides." Thus, *polygon* means "many sides.") A *plane* is often described as a flat surface.

Examples:

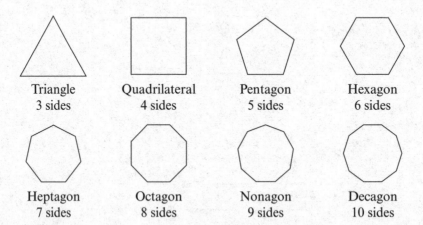

Triangle
3 sides

Quadrilateral
4 sides

Pentagon
5 sides

Hexagon
6 sides

Heptagon
7 sides

Octagon
8 sides

Nonagon
9 sides

Decagon
10 sides

Regular Polygons

Regular means all sides have the same length and all angles have the same measure. A regular three-sided polygon is the equilateral triangle. A regular four-sided polygon is the square. There are no other special names; other polygons are just described as "regular" with their common name. For example, a regular five-sided polygon is called a regular pentagon. A regular six-sided polygon is called a regular hexagon.

Diagonals of Polygons

A *diagonal of a polygon* is a line segment that connects one vertex with another vertex and is not itself a side. In the following figure, $\overline{AD}$ and $\overline{BC}$ are both diagonals.

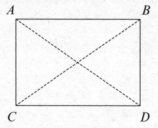

Convex Polygons

A convex polygon has all diagonals within the figure, as shown below. Also, all interior angles are less than 180°.

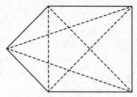

Concave Polygons

A concave (caves in) polygon has at least one diagonal outside the figure, as shown below. Also, at least one interior angle is greater than 180°. ($\overline{AB}$ is the diagonal.)

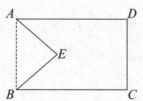

Triangles

This section deals with polygons that have the fewest number of sides or three sides. A *triangle* is a three-sided polygon. It has three angles in its interior. The sum of the measure of these angles is always 180°. The symbol for triangle is Δ. A triangle is named by the three letters of its vertices. ΔABC is shown below.

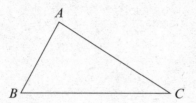

Types of Triangles by Sides

Equilateral Triangles

A triangle having all three sides equal in measure is called an *equilateral triangle*. ***Note:*** By angles, this would be called an *equiangular triangle*—all angles are equal (60° each).

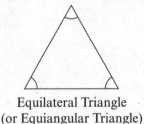

Equilateral Triangle
(or Equiangular Triangle)

Isosceles Triangles

A triangle having at least two equal sides with two equal (congruent) angles, is called an *isosceles triangle*.

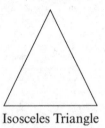

Isosceles Triangle

Scalene Triangles

A triangle having no equal sides, or no equal angles, is called a *scalene triangle*.

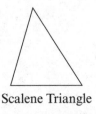

Scalene Triangle

Types of Triangles by Angles

Right Triangles

A triangle containing a right angle (90°) in its interior is called a *right triangle*.

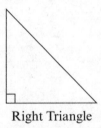

Right Triangle

Obtuse Triangles

A triangle containing an obtuse angle (greater than 90° but less than 180°) in its interior is called an *obtuse triangle.*

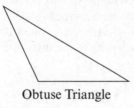

Obtuse Triangle

Acute Triangles

A triangle containing all acute angles (less than 90°) in its interior is called an *acute triangle.*

Acute Equilateral Triangle   Acute Scalene Triangle

Examples:

Two angles of a triangle measure 45° and 85°. How many degrees are there in the third angle?

The angles of a triangle add up to 180°. The sum of 45° and 85° is 130°. Therefore, the remaining angle must be 180° − 130° = 50°.

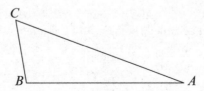

In △ABC above, $m\angle C$ is three times $m\angle A$ and $m\angle B$ is five times $m\angle A$. Find the number of degrees in each angle of the triangle.

Let y equal the number of degrees in $\angle A$. Then $3y$ equals the number of degrees in $\angle C$, and $5y$ equals the number of degrees in $\angle B$. Since the sum of the angles of the triangle is 180°, we can say $y + 3y + 5y = 180$:

$$y + 3y + 5y = 180$$
$$\frac{9y}{9} = \frac{180}{9}$$
$$y = 20° \ (m\angle A)$$
$$3y = 60° \ (m\angle C)$$
$$5y = 100° \ (m\angle B)$$

Notice that 20° + 60° + 100° = 180°.

Facts About Triangles

Base and Height

Any side of a triangle can be called a *base*. With each base, there is an associated *altitude* (or *height*). Each altitude is the *perpendicular* segment from a vertex perpendicular to its opposite side or the extension of the opposite side. To denote that sides of a triangle are equal, small straight lines called *hash marks* (tick marks) are inserted on the corresponding sides. To denote that angles of a triangle are equal, corresponding arcs are inserted on angles.

In the following diagram of $\triangle ABC$, $\overline{BC}$ is the base and $\overline{AE}$ is the height. $\overline{AE} \perp \overline{BC}$.

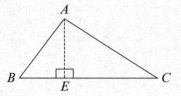

In the following diagram of $\triangle ABC$, $\overline{BC}$ is the base and $\overline{AE}$ is the height. Notice that base $\overline{BC}$ had to be extended in order to be able to draw the height from vertex A.

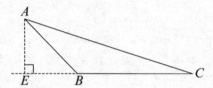

In the following diagram of $\triangle ABC$, $\overline{BC}$ is the base and $\overline{AB}$ is the height. In a right triangle, either of the sides that form the right angle can be called the base and the other side can then be called the height to that base.

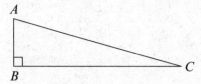

Median

Every triangle has three medians. A *median* is a line segment drawn from a vertex to the midpoint of the opposite side. In the following diagram of $\triangle ABC$, E is the midpoint of $\overline{BC}$; therefore, $BE = EC$ (the hash marks show that $\overline{BE}$ and $\overline{EC}$ are equal line segments). $\overline{AE}$ is a median of $\triangle ABC$.

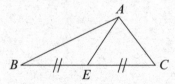

Angle Bisectors

Every triangle has three *angle bisectors.* The angle bisector divides an angle into two smaller angles that are equal in measure. In the following diagram of $\triangle ABC$, segment BD is an angle bisector of $\angle ABC$ because $m\angle ABD = m\angle CBD$ (the arc marks show that $\angle ABD$ and $\angle CBD$ are equal angles).

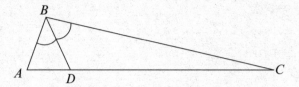

In the diagram of $\triangle QRS$, $\overline{QX}$ is an altitude ($\overline{QX} \perp \overline{RS}$), $\overline{QY}$ is an angle bisector ($m\angle RQY = m\angle SQY$), and $\overline{QZ}$ is a median ($RZ = SZ$). Generally, from one vertex of a triangle, the altitude, angle bisector, and median are different segments.

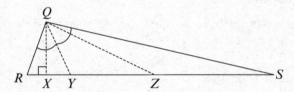

An interesting fact: In any triangle, if one segment is any two of the three special segments in a triangle (altitude, median, or angle bisector), it is automatically the third one, and the triangle is at least isosceles. The vertex from which the segments are drawn becomes the vertex of the isosceles triangle, and it is at the vertex of the isosceles triangle where the equal sides meet.

In the following diagram of $\triangle ABC$, segment BD is an angle bisector and an altitude. This means that segment BD is also a median, hence $AD = CD$. It also means that $\triangle ABC$ is isosceles with the sides AB and BC being the equal sides of the isosceles triangle.

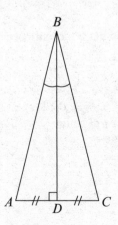

Angles Opposite Equal Sides

Angles that are opposite from equal sides are also equal. In the following diagram of $\triangle ABC$:

$\angle A$ is opposite from side BC.

$\angle B$ is opposite from side AC.

$\angle C$ is opposite from side AB.

Therefore, if $AB = AC$, it follows that $m\angle C = m\angle B$.

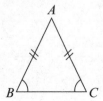

Angles of an Isosceles Triangle

In an isosceles triangle, since two of the sides are equal, the angles opposite those sides are equal. There are always two equal sides in an isosceles triangle.

Angles of an Equilateral Triangle

In an equilateral triangle, because all three sides are equal, all three angles will be equal; they are opposite equal sides. If all three angles are equal, as shown in the following diagram of $\triangle ABC$, and their sum is 180°, the following must be true.

$$x + x + x = 180°$$
$$3x = 180°$$
$$x = 60°$$

Every angle of an equilateral triangle always has a measure of 60°.

Unequal Angles

In any triangle, the longest side is always opposite from the largest angle. Likewise, the shortest side is always opposite from the smallest angle. In a right triangle, the longest side (the *hypotenuse*) will always be opposite from the right angle, because the right angle will be the largest angle in the triangle. In the following diagram of right triangle ABC, $\overline{AC}$ is the longest side.

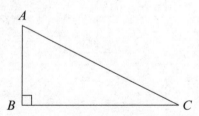

Adding Sides of a Triangle

The sum of the lengths of any two sides of a triangle must be larger than the length of the third side. In the following diagram of $\triangle ABC$, the accompanying equations are true.

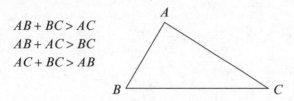

$$AB + BC > AC$$
$$AB + AC > BC$$
$$AC + BC > AB$$

Exterior Angles

If one side of a triangle is extended, the exterior angle formed by that extension is equal to the sum of its remote (farthest away) interior angles. In the following diagram of $\triangle ABC$, side BC is extended to D. $\angle ACD$ is the exterior angle formed.

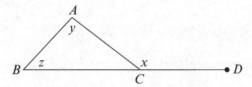

Example:

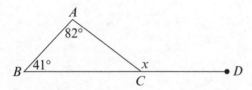

Find x if $y = 82°$ and $z = 41°$.

$$m\angle x = m\angle y + m\angle z$$
$$= 82° + 41°$$
$$= 123°$$

Practice: Triangles

1. Two angles of a triangle measure 50° and 60°. What is the measure of the third angle?

2. One of the angles in a right triangle measures 35°. What is the measure of the other acute angle?

3. In an isosceles triangle, one of the angles opposite an equal side measures 20°. What is the measure of each of the other two angles?

4. In $\triangle ABC$, the measure of $\angle A$ is twice the measure of $\angle B$. The measure of $\angle C$ is three times the measure of $\angle B$. What is the measure of each of the three angles?

5. In the figure below, which side is the largest?

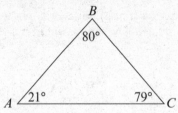

For questions 6 and 7, use the numbers below.

2, 3, 4

2, 2, 5

4, 3, 7

3, 4, 5

3, 3, 6

1, 2, 3

6. Which of the above measurements could be the sides of a triangle?

7. Which of the above measurements could be the sides of an isosceles triangle?

8. In the figure below, what is the value of x, and what is the measure of each angle?

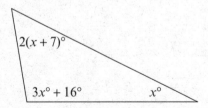

9. What is the measure of the exterior angle of the triangle below?

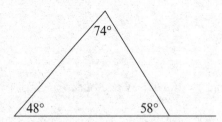

10. In the figure at the top of the next page, identify which segment is a/an

(a) median

(b) altitude (or height)

(c) angle bisector

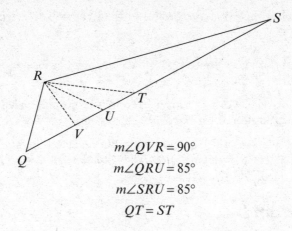

$$m\angle QVR = 90°$$
$$m\angle QRU = 85°$$
$$m\angle SRU = 85°$$
$$QT = ST$$

Answers: Triangles

1. Since the measure of the three angles of a triangle must total 180°, the third angle measures 70°.

2. Since, in a right triangle, one of the angles is 90° and the sum of the three angles in a triangle is 180°, the measure of the remaining acute angle must be 55°.

3. Since equal sides of a triangle have their opposite angles equal, the other two angles measure 20° and 140°.

4. Let the smallest angle equal x. Therefore, the larger angle equals $2x$ and the largest angle equals $3x$. Their total is $6x$, which equals 180°.

   $6x = 180°$
   $x = 30° \ (m\angle B)$
   $2x = 60° \ (m\angle A)$
   $3x = 90° \ (m\angle C)$

5. Side AC is largest, since in any triangle, the largest side is opposite the largest angle.

6. Because the sum of any two sides of a triangle must be greater than its third side, 2, 2, 5; 4, 3, 7; 3, 3, 6; and 1, 2, 3 cannot be sides of a triangle. The two other sets (2, 3, 4 and 3, 4, 5) can.

7. None. To solve this problem, start by working from the answer to question 6. Remember that an isosceles triangle must have two sides of the same length.

8. The interior angles of a triangle total 180°.

$$2(x+7) + x + 3x + 16 = 180°$$
$$2x + 14 + x + 3x + 16 = 180°$$
$$6x + 30 = 180°$$
$$6x = 150°$$
$$x = 25°$$

By replacing the variable in each equation, the angles measure 64°, 25°, and 91°.

9. Considering that an exterior angle of a triangle always equals the sum of its remote two interior angles, the exterior angle measures 122°.

10. (a) $\overline{RT}$ is a median. A median goes from a vertex to the midpoint of the opposite side. Because $QT = ST$, you know that T is the midpoint of $\overline{QS}$.

    (b) $\overline{RV}$ is an altitude (or height). An altitude goes from a vertex and makes a 90° angle with the opposite side or the extension of the opposite side and $m\angle QVR = 90°$.

    (c) $\overline{RU}$ is an angle bisector. An angle bisector divides the angle it is in into two smaller but equal angles. Because $m\angle SRU = 85°$ and $m\angle QRU = 85°$, it follows that $m\angle SRU = m\angle QRU$. Therefore, $\angle QRS$ has been bisected.

Pythagorean Theorem

In any right triangle, the relationship between the lengths of the sides is stated by the *Pythagorean theorem*. The parts of the right triangle shown below are as follows:

- $\angle C$ is the right angle.
- The side opposite the right angle is called the *hypotenuse* (side c). (The hypotenuse will always be the longest side.)
- The other two sides are called the *legs* (sides a and b).

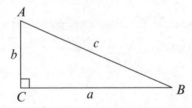

The three lengths a, b, and c will always be numbers such that $a^2 + b^2 = c^2$. If $a = 3$, $b = 4$, and $c = 5$, then

$$a^2 + b^2 = c^2$$
$$3^2 + 4^2 = 5^2$$
$$9 + 16 = 25$$
$$25 = 25$$

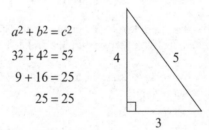

Therefore, 3-4-5 is called a Pythagorean triple. There are other values for a, b, and c that will always work. Some are 5-12-13 and 8-15-17. Any multiple of one of these triples will also work. For example, 6-8-10, 9-12-15, and 15-20-25 will also be Pythagorean triples.

If perfect squares are known, the lengths of these sides can be determined easily. A knowledge of the use of algebraic equations can also be used to determine the lengths of the sides.

Examples:

Solve for x in the following right triangle.

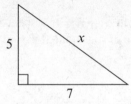

$$a^2 + b^2 = c^2$$
$$5^2 + 7^2 = x^2$$
$$25 + 49 = x^2$$
$$\sqrt{74} = x$$

Solve for x in the following right triangle.

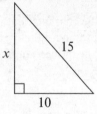

$$a^2 + b^2 = c^2$$
$$x^2 + 10^2 = 15^2$$
$$x^2 + 100 = 225$$
$$x^2 = 125$$
$$x = \sqrt{125}$$
$$x = \sqrt{25} \times \sqrt{5}$$
$$x = 5\sqrt{5}$$

Practice: Pythagorean Theorem

1. Solve for x in the following right triangle.

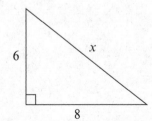

2. Find y in the following right triangle.

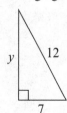

3. If the two legs of a right triangle measure 5 and 9, what is the length of the hypotenuse?

Answers: Pythagorean Theorem

1. $6^2 + 8^2 = x^2$
$36 + 64 = x^2$
$100 = x^2$
$\sqrt{100} = 10 = x$

2. $y^2 + 7^2 = 12^2$
$y^2 + 49 = 144$
$y^2 = 95$
$y = \sqrt{95}$

3. $5^2 + 9^2 = x^2$
$25 + 81 = x^2$
$106 = x^2$
$\sqrt{106} = x$

Special Triangles

Isosceles Right Triangles (45°-45°-90° Right Triangles)

An *isosceles right triangle* has the characteristics of both the isosceles and the right triangles. It will have two equal sides, two equal angles, and one right angle. (The right angle cannot be one of the equal angles or the sum of the angle measures will be more than 180°.)

$\triangle ABC$ below is isosceles.

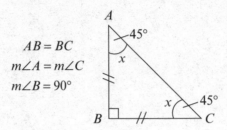

$$AB = BC$$
$$m\angle A = m\angle C$$
$$m\angle B = 90°$$

Therefore, in the diagram the following must always be true:

$$x + x + 90° = 180°$$
$$2x = 90°$$
$$x = 45°$$

The ratio of the sides of an isosceles right triangle is always 1, 1, $\sqrt{2}$ or x, x, $x\sqrt{2}$, as shown in the following diagram.

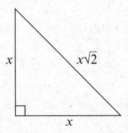

Example:

    If one of the equal sides of an isosceles right triangle is 3, what is the measure of the other two sides? Using the ratio x, x, $x\sqrt{2}$, the measure of the sides must be 3, 3, $3\sqrt{2}$.

Practice: Isosceles Right Triangles

    1. If one of the equal sides of an isosceles right triangle measures 4, what is the measure of the other two sides?

    2. If the longest side of an isosceles right triangle is $5\sqrt{2}$, what is the measure of each of the two equal sides?

3. What is the measure of sides x and y in the triangle below?

Answers: Isosceles Right Triangles

1. The sides of an isosceles right triangle are always in the ratio x, x, $x\sqrt{2}$; therefore, the other two sides are 4 and $4\sqrt{2}$.

2. The two equal sides each equal 5.

3. Since one angle measures 90° and another measures 45°, the third angle must also measure 45°: 180 – (90 + 45) = 45. Therefore, we have an isosceles right triangle with the ratio of sides x, x, $x\sqrt{2}$. Because one equal side is 6, the other must be 6, and the longest side is $6\sqrt{2}$.

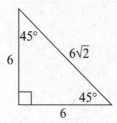

30°-60°-90° Right Triangles

A 30°-60°-90° *right triangle* has a unique ratio of its sides. The ratio of the sides of a 30°-60°-90° right triangle is 1, $\sqrt{3}$, 2 or x, $x\sqrt{3}$, $2x$, placed as follows.

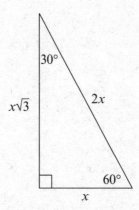

The side opposite 30° is 1 or x. The shortest side will always be across from the smallest angle.

The side opposite 60° is $\sqrt{3}$ or $x\sqrt{3}$.

The side opposite 90° is the longest side (hypotenuse), 2 or $2x$.

Examples:

If the shortest side of a 30°-60°-90° right triangle is 4, what are the measures of the other sides?
Using the ratios x, $x\sqrt{3}$, $2x$, the measures are 4, $4\sqrt{3}$, 8.

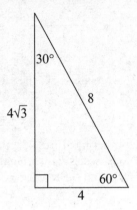

In the triangle below, find the remaining sides.

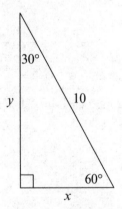

x is half of the hypotenuse, or 5. The side opposite 60° is $x\sqrt{3}$ or $5\sqrt{3}$.

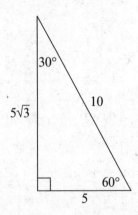

Practice: 30°-60°-90° Right Triangles

1. If the longest side of a 30°-60°-90° right triangle measures 12, what are the measures of the other sides?

2. If one angle of a right triangle measures 30° and the measure of the shortest side is 7, what is the measure of the remaining two sides?

Answers: 30°-60°-90° Right Triangles

1. The ratio of the sides of a 30°-60°-90° right triangle are x, $x\sqrt{3}$, $2x$ and the longest side, $2x$, measures 12. Therefore, the shortest side, x, measures 6, and the third side measures $6\sqrt{3}$.

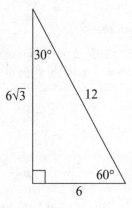

2. If one angle of a right triangle measures 30°, the other angle must be 60°. Hence, you have a 30°-60°-90° right triangle. Using the ratio x, $x\sqrt{3}$, $2x$, with $x = 7$, $2x = 14$, and the third side equals $7\sqrt{3}$.

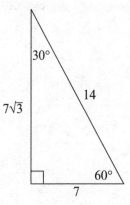

Trigonometry

The Common Core Standards examine trigonometric relationships in special right triangles and the Pythagorean theorem. This understanding includes the ability to use trigonometric ratios in *sine*, *cosine*, and *tangent* functions.

Trigonometry Ratio Theorems

Theorems of sines and cosines state that if two angles of one triangle have the same measure as two angles of another triangle, then the two triangles are similar. Hence, in similar triangles, angle measures and ratios of corresponding sides remain the same. If right triangles that contain another angle of equal measure are similar, the ratio of their corresponding sides must be equal. This means that if the angles of a triangle remain the same, but the sides increase or decrease in length proportionally, these ratios remain the same. Relationships among these angles and sides are considered *trigonometry ratios*.

Note: In trigonometry, lowercase Greek letters are used to name angle measures. The two most commonly used letters are alpha (α) and theta (θ).

Properties of Trigonometry Functions

Sine, cosine and tangent are the three main functions in trigonometry. These functions are often shortened to *sin*, *cos*, and *tan* and are ratios that compare lengths of sides in relation to one of the acute angles of the right triangle.

Sine, Cosine, and Tangent

Sine, cosine and tangent are used to find the missing measure of the side length. Depending on the information specified, you will use one of these three options to solve the problem. An adjacent side is one that meets and includes one side of the angle in the problem, but is not the hypotenuse. A special calculator should be used to compute these functions. The values that your calculator has for sin, cos, and tan are usually lengthy; therefore, it is common to round your answer to the nearest tenth or hundredth.

Note: Sometimes when rounding sin, cos, and tan to the nearest tenth or hundredth, your answer will change slightly if you round off at each step. The preferred method is to wait until the very end to round off your answer to avoid rounding errors.

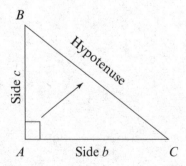

Reminder: The hypotenuse is the longest side and is always opposite the right angle.

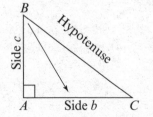
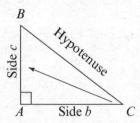

Unless labeled otherwise, the sides of the triangle are labeled by a lowercase italic with the letter of the opposite angle. The hypotenuse is never called a side, it is always referred to as the hypotenuse. To find the length of side b, the degree for angle B, and the hypotenuse, use this formula:

$$\text{sine of } \angle B = \sin \angle B = \frac{b}{h} = \frac{\text{length of side opposite } \angle B}{\text{length of hypotenuse } (h)}$$

$$\text{cosine of } \angle B = \cos \angle B = \frac{c}{h} = \frac{\text{length of side adjacent to } \angle B}{\text{length of hypotenuse } (h)}$$

$$\text{tangent of } \angle B = \tan \angle B = \frac{b}{c} = \frac{\text{length of side opposite } \angle B}{\text{length of side adjacent to } \angle B}$$

Examples:

Look at the data you are given in the problems below. Determine what is necessary in order to solve the problem and then choose the appropriate formula.

The measurement of $\angle B$ is 14°. Find the length of side a.

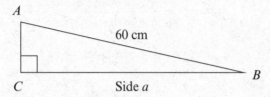

First, always look at the side you are given to determine the length. In this case, the problem includes the hypotenuse and the adjacent sides. Therefore, use cosine to calculate the solution. The calculation for cosine 14 will give you 0.970295726, which rounds to .97. Then, replace 60 with the hypotenuse in the equation and solve using algebra.

$$\cos \angle B = \frac{\text{length of side adjacent } \angle B}{\text{length of hypotenuse}} \qquad \cos (14) = \frac{x}{60}$$

Input cos (14) into your calculator, which rounds to .970295726, or .97:

$$.97 = \frac{x}{60}$$
$$.97 \times 60 = x$$
$$58.2 \approx x$$

The next example question refers to the diagram below.

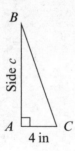

Find the length of side *c* if the measurement of ∠*C* is 42°.

The problem provides us with the measurement of the side adjacent to ∠*C* and asks for the length of the side opposite ∠*C*. Since the problem is working with adjacent and opposite sides, use the tangent function.

$$\tan \angle C = \frac{\text{length of side opposite } \angle C}{\text{length of side adjacent } \angle C}$$

$$\tan 42° = \frac{x}{4}$$

$$.900404044 = \frac{x}{4}$$

$$.900404044 \times 4 = x$$

$$3.6 \approx x$$

Practice: Sine, Cosine, and Tangent

Questions 1 and 2 refer to the following figure. (Round each value to the tenths place.)

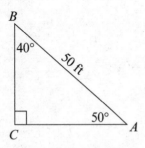

1. Find the length of side *a*.

2. What is the length of side *b*?

3. Given that *m*∠*A* is 90° and *m*∠*C* is 10°, what is the length of the hypotenuse in the diagram below?

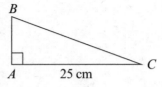

Answers: Sine, Cosine, and Tangent

1. $\sin \angle A = \dfrac{\text{opposite}}{\text{hypotenuse}}$ $.766044443 = \dfrac{x}{50}$

$.766044443 \times 50 = x$

$38.3 \approx x$

3. $\cos \angle C = \dfrac{\text{adjacent}}{\text{hypotenuse}}$ $.984807753 = \dfrac{25}{x}$

$.984807753x = 25$

$25.4 \approx x$

2. $\sin \angle B = \dfrac{\text{opposite}}{\text{hypotenuse}}$ $.64278761 = \dfrac{x}{50}$

$.64278761 \times 50 = x$

$32.1 \approx x$

Quadrilaterals

A polygon having four sides is called a *quadrilateral*. There are four angles in its interior. The sum of the measures of these interior angles will always be 360°. A quadrilateral is named by using the four letters of its vertices named in order either clockwise or counterclockwise.

The following diagram is quadrilateral *ABCD*.

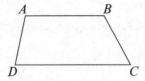

Types of Quadrilaterals

Square

A *square* has four equal sides and four right angles. Its opposite sides are parallel. Diagonals of a square are equal, bisect each other, are perpendicular to each other, and bisect the angles through which they pass.

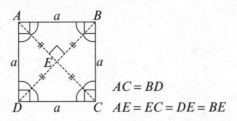

$AC = BD$

$AE = EC = DE = BE$

Rectangle

A *rectangle* has opposite sides equal and parallel and four right angles. Diagonals of a rectangle are equal and bisect each other.

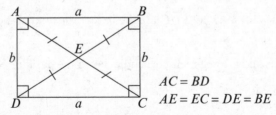

$AC = BD$

$AE = EC = DE = BE$

Parallelogram

A *parallelogram* has opposite sides equal and parallel, opposite angles equal, and consecutive angles supplementary. Diagonals of a parallelogram bisect each other but are not necessarily equal. If the diagonals of a parallelogram are equal, it becomes a rectangle.

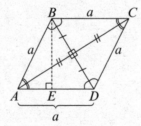

$$m\angle A = m\angle C$$
$$m\angle B = m\angle D$$
$$m\angle A + m\angle B = 180°$$
$$m\angle A + m\angle D = 180°$$
$$m\angle B + m\angle C = 180°$$
$$m\angle C + m\angle D = 180°$$

$\overline{AE}$ is a height (or altitude) in this parallelogram, where $\overline{AE} \perp \overline{CD}$.

Rhombus

A *rhombus* is a parallelogram with four equal sides but not necessarily four equal angles. Diagonals of a rhombus are not necessarily equal, but they do bisect each other, are perpendicular to each other, and bisect the angles through which they pass.

In the following rhombus, $\overline{BE} \perp \overline{AD}$, so $\overline{BE}$ can be considered a height (or altitude) of the rhombus.

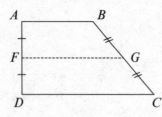

Trapezoid

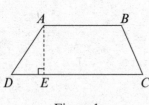

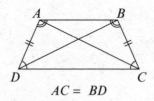

| Figure 1 | Figure 2 | Figure 3 |

The *trapezoid* has only one pair of parallel sides. In Figure 1, $\overline{AB} \parallel \overline{DC}$.

The parallel sides are called the *bases*. $\overline{AB}$ and $\overline{DC}$ are the bases. The nonparallel sides are called the *legs*. $\overline{AD}$ and $\overline{BC}$ are legs.

A height (or altitude) in a trapezoid is a segment perpendicular to the parallel sides. In Figure 1, $\overline{AE}$ is a height of trapezoid *ABCD*.

The *median* of a trapezoid is a line segment that is parallel to the bases and bisects the legs (connects the midpoints of the legs). In Figure 2, $\overline{FG}$ is the median.

Figure 3 is an *isosceles trapezoid* (one in which the legs are equal). The diagonals are equal in length but do not bisect each other. Each pair of angles on the same base are equal in measure.

Comparing Quadrilaterals

- A parallelogram is a quadrilateral with opposite sides and angles equal.
- A rectangle is a parallelogram with right angles.
- A rhombus is a parallelogram with equal sides.
- A square is a rhombus with right angles.
- A trapezoid is a quadrilateral with only one pair of parallel sides.

A Summary of Diagonals, Sides, and Angles of Special Quadrilaterals

The bases of a trapezoid are never equal to each other. The diagonals of a trapezoid do not bisect each other. In all trapezoids, the angles that share the same leg are supplementary.

In isosceles trapezoids, diagonals have the same length and angles that share the same base have equal measures.

$\overline{AB} \parallel \overline{CD}$
$AD = BC$
$AC = BD$
$m\angle ADC = m\angle BCD$
$m\angle DAB = m\angle CBA$

A parallelogram's diagonals bisect each other. Both pairs of opposite sides in a parallelogram are parallel and equal in length. Both pairs of opposite angles in a parallelogram are equal in measure.

$\overline{AB} \parallel \overline{CD}$
$\overline{AD} \parallel \overline{BC}$
$AE = EC$
$DE = EB$
$m\angle DAB = m\angle BCD$
$m\angle ABC = m\angle ADC$

A rectangle's diagonals are equal in measure and bisect each other. The opposite sides of a rectangle are equal in measure and are parallel to one another. All the angles of a rectangle are equal in measure and are each 90°.

$\overline{AB} \parallel \overline{CD}$
$\overline{AD} \parallel \overline{BC}$
$AB = CD$
$AD = BC$
$AC = BD$
$AE = EC = DE = EB$
$m\angle DAB = m\angle ABC = m\angle BCD = m\angle CDA = 90°$

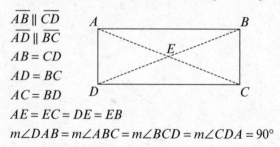

253

A rhombus's diagonals bisect each other and are perpendicular to one another. The diagonals bisect the angles through which they pass. All sides in a rhombus are equal in measure. Opposite sides in a rhombus are parallel to one another. Opposite angles in a rhombus are equal in measure.

$\overline{AB} \parallel \overline{CD}$

$\overline{AD} \parallel \overline{BC}$

$AB = BC = CD = DA$

$\overline{AC} \perp \overline{BD}$

$AE = EC$

$DE = EB$

$m\angle DAB = m\angle BCD$

$m\angle ABC = m\angle ADC$

$m\angle DAC = m\angle BAC = m\angle BCA = m\angle DCA$

$m\angle ABD = m\angle CBD = m\angle CDB = m\angle ADB$

A square has all of the properties of both the rectangle and the rhombus.

$\overline{AB} \parallel \overline{CD}$

$\overline{AD} \parallel \overline{BC}$

$AB = BC = CD = DA$

$AC = BD$

$AE = EC = DE = EB$

$\overline{AC} \perp \overline{BD}$

$m\angle DAB = m\angle BCD = m\angle ABC = m\angle ADC = 90°$

$m\angle DAC = m\angle BAC = m\angle BCA = m\angle DCA = m\angle ABD = m\angle CBD = m\angle CDB = m\angle ADB = 45°$

Practice: Quadrilaterals

Identify the following figures with their special or most descriptive names.

1.

2. A   B

D   C

$\overline{AB} \parallel \overline{DC}$ $\overline{AD} \parallel \overline{BC}$

3.

4.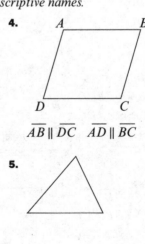

$\overline{AB} \parallel \overline{DC}$ $\overline{AD} \parallel \overline{BC}$

5.

6.

$AB = BC = CD = DA$

7.

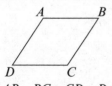

$AB = BC = CD = DA$

8.

9.

10.

 All sides and angles are equal.

True or false:

11. A square must be a parallelogram.

12. A rhombus must be a rectangle.

13. A parallelogram must be a rectangle.

Answers: Quadrilaterals

1. Pentagon

2. Rectangle

3. Hexagon

4. Parallelogram

5. Triangle

6. Square

7. Rhombus

8. Quadrilateral

9. Octagon

10. Regular pentagon

11. True

12. False

13. False

Sum of the Interior Angles of a Polygon

The sum of the interior angles in any polygon can be determined by using this formula: $(n-2)180°$, where n is the number of sides in the polygon.

Examples:

The triangle (3 sides):

$(n-2)180° =$

$(3-2)180° =$

$(1)180° = 180°$

The quadrilateral (4 sides):

$(n-2)180° =$

$(4-2)180° =$

$(2)180° = 360°$

The pentagon (5 sides):

$(n-2)180° =$

$(5-2)180° =$

$(3)180° = 540°$

Practice: Sum of the Interior Angles of a Polygon

1. Find the sum of the interior angles of a hexagon.

2. Find the degree measure of an angle of a regular nonagon.

Answers: Sum of the Interior Angles of a Polygon

1. Since a hexagon has six sides, use $n = 6$.

$$(n-2)180° =$$
$$(6-2)180° =$$
$$(4)180° = 720°$$

2. A regular nonagon has nine equal angles. First find the total degree measure.

$$(n-2)180° =$$
$$(9-2)180° =$$
$$(7)180° = 1,260°$$

Now to find one angle, divide the total by 9 (the number of angles).

$$\frac{1,260°}{9} = 140°$$

Perimeter and Area of Polygons

Perimeter of Polygons

Perimeter means the total distance all the way around the outside of any polygon. The perimeter of any polygon can be determined by adding up the lengths of all the sides. The total distance around will be the sum of all sides of the polygon. No special formulas are really necessary, although these are commonly seen:

Perimeter of a square = $4s$, where s = length of side.

Perimeter of a parallelogram (rectangle and rhombus) = $2l + 2w$ or $2(l + w)$, where l = length and w = width.

Perimeter of a triangle = $a + b + c$, where a, b, and c are the sides of the triangle.

Area of Polygons

Area (A) means the amount of space inside the polygon. The area formulas for each type of polygon are as follows:

Triangle: $A = \frac{1}{2}bh$

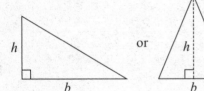

or

Example:

24 in

$$A = \frac{1}{2}bh$$
$$A = \frac{1}{2}(24)(18) = 216 \text{ square inches}$$

Square or rectangle: $A = lw$

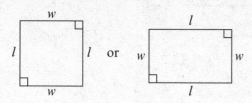

Examples:

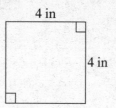

$A = lw = (4)(4) = 16$ square inches

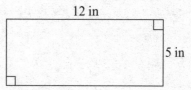

$A = lw = (12)(5) = 60$ square inches

Parallelogram: $A = bh$

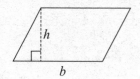

Example:

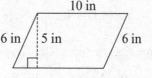

$A = bh = (10)(5) = 50$ square inches

Trapezoid: $A = \dfrac{1}{2}(b_1 + b_2)h$

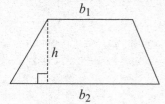

Example:

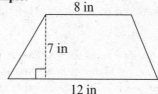

$$A = \frac{1}{2}(b_1 + b_2)h$$
$$= \frac{1}{2}(8 + 12)7$$
$$= \frac{1}{2}(20)7 = 70 \text{ square inches}$$

Area and Perimeter Word Problems

Geometry problems frequently involve situations that ask you to have knowledge about real-life scenario shapes, measures, and properties that combine formulas for area and perimeter. Use the following steps to solve these types of area and perimeter word problems.

1. Carefully read the problem to identify what you are being asked to find.
2. Use the geometric formulas for area and perimeter.

Shape	Area	Perimeter
Square	$A = s^2$	$P = 4s$
Rectangle	$A = bh$	$P = 2(b + h)$
Parallelogram	$A = bh$	$P = 2(b + a)$ where $a + b$ are side measures.
Triangle	$A = \dfrac{1}{2}bh$	$P = x + y + b$

3. Based on the formulas used in Step 2, use deductive reasoning skills to draw conclusions about how the perimeter, area, and angles are related to one another.

Example:

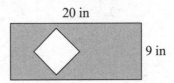

20 in

9 in

The area of the square in the figure above is $\dfrac{1}{5}$ of the area of the rectangle. What is the perimeter of the square?

First, find the area of the rectangle. The area of the rectangle is 180 square inches; therefore, the area of the square is $\dfrac{1}{5}$ of 180 = 36 square inches.

The formula for the area of a square is s^2. The square root of 36 provides the length of one side: $\sqrt{36} = 6$.

The perimeter is found by adding the four sides together: 6 + 6 + 6 + 6 = 24 inches or 4 × 6 = 24 inches.

Real-life geometry word problems do not always provide graphic illustrations. If no illustration is provided, *always* draw the diagram and label the information given in the word problem. Sometimes being able to "see" the facts is more helpful than just reading the words.

Examples:

Umbert is adding a framed 2-inch mat border around the outside edge of a photograph. If the photograph measures 20 in × 30 in, what is the area of the mat?

Sketch and label a diagram to meet the conditions of the word problem. *Note:* The diagram does not need to be to scale.

2 in

30 in

2 in   20 in 2 in

2 in

First, find the diminsensions of the large rectangle in order to find the combined area of the mat and photograph.

Horizontal: 30 + 2 + 2 = 34 inches

Vertical: 20 + 2 + 2 = 24 inches.

Therefore, the total area = 34 × 24 = 816 inches.

Next, find the area of the mat by subtracting the area of the photograph from the total area.

Total area = 816 square inches

Photograph = 30 in × 20 in = 600 square inches

Mat = 816 − 600 = 216 square inches

The ratio of the sides of two regular pentagons is 1:3. If the perimeter of the larger pentagon is 60 inches, what is the perimeter of the smaller pentagon?

Since the shapes are regular pentagons, all sides for each pentagon will be the same length. For the larger pentagon, its perimeter is 60 inches and each side will be 12 inches $(60 \div 5 = 12)$. Now use the given ratio to find the length of each side of the smaller pentagon.

$$\frac{\text{smaller}}{\text{larger}} \quad \frac{1}{3} = \frac{x}{12}$$
$$12 = 3x$$
$$4 = x$$

The perimeter of the smaller pentagon is 4 × 5 = 20 inches.

Practice: Perimeter and Area of Polygons

1. $P =$ ___
$A =$ ___
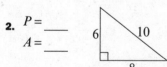

2. $P =$ ___
$A =$ ___

3. $P =$ ___
$A =$ ___

4. $P =$ ___
$A =$ ___
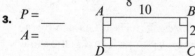
$AB \parallel DC \quad AD \parallel BC$

5. $P =$ ___
$A =$ ___
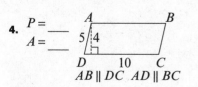

6. $P =$ ___
$A =$ ___
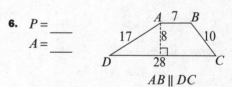
$AB \parallel DC$

7. What is the length of the missing side of the triangle below?
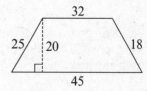

8. Find the area of the shaded region in the figure below.
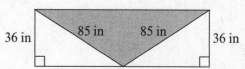

Answers: Perimeter and Area of Polygons

1. $P = 15 + 13 + 14 = 42$

   $A = \dfrac{1}{2}bh = \dfrac{1}{2}(14)(12) = 84$

2. $P = 6 + 8 + 10 = 24$

   $A = \dfrac{1}{2}bh = \dfrac{1}{2}(8)(6) = 24$

3. $P = 2(10) + 2(2) = 24$

   $A = bh = (10)(2) = 20$

4. $P = 2(10) + 2(5) = 30$

   $A = bh = (10)(4) = 40$

5. $P = 4(5) = 20$

   $A = bh = (4)(5) = 20$

6. $P = 17 + 7 + 10 + 28 = 62$

   $A = \dfrac{1}{2}(b_1 + b_2)h = \dfrac{1}{2}(7 + 28)(8) = (4)(35) = 140$

7. Use the Pythagorean theorem to solve this problem and ignore the irrelevant values provided in the diagram.

   $$a^2 + b^2 = c^2$$
   $$20^2 + b^2 = 25^2$$
   $$400 + b^2 = 625$$
   $$b^2 = 225$$
   $$b = 15$$

8. First, find the length of the missing side of the right triangles. Using the Pythagorean theorem,

   $$36^2 + b^2 = 85^2$$
   $$1{,}296 + b^2 = 7{,}225$$
   $$b^2 = 5{,}929$$
   $$b = 77$$

   The missing side length doubled becomes the base of the shaded triangle ($77 \times 2 = 154$).

   Height = 36 inches

   $$A = \dfrac{1}{2}bh$$
   $$A = \dfrac{1}{2}(154)(36)$$
   $$A = 2{,}772 \text{ square inches}$$

Circles

In a plane, the set of all points equidistant from a given point is called a *circle*. Circles are named by the letter of their center point. The following diagram is circle *M*. *M* is the center point, since it is the same distance away from any point on the circle.

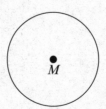

Parts of a Circle

Radius

The *radius* is a line segment whose endpoints lie one at the center of the circle and one on the circle. A radius of a circle can either be the segment that joins the center to any point on the circle or it can be the length of that segment. It is in the context of use that you will know which meaning is being used.

In any circle, all *radii* (plural) are the same length.

$\overline{MA}$ is a radius.

$\overline{MB}$ is a radius.

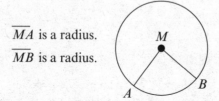

Diameter

A *diameter* of a circle can be either the segment that joins any two points on a circle and passes through the center of the circle or it can be the length of that segment. It is in the context of use that you will know which meaning is being used.

In any circle, all diameters are the same length. Each diameter equals two radii in length.

$\overline{AB}$ is a diameter.

$\overline{CD}$ is a diameter.

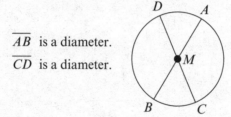

Chord

A *chord* of a circle is a line segment whose endpoints lie on the circle. The diameter is the longest chord in any circle.

$\overline{RS}$ is a chord.

$\overline{UV}$ is a chord.

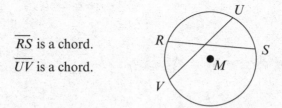

Arc

An *arc* is a portion of a circle between two points on the circle. It can be measured in two ways. One measure is in degrees. The full rotation of a circle is said to have 360°. Another measure is its length. This would be a portion of the circumference of the circle. The symbol ⌢ is used to denote an arc. It is written on top of the two endpoints that form the arc. Usually it is in the context of use that you would know whether the measure is intended to be a degree measure or a length measure. The following diagram shows $\overset{\frown}{EF}$.

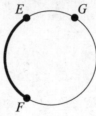

Minor $\overset{\frown}{EF}$ is the shorter arc between E and F.

Major $\overset{\frown}{EGF}$ is the longer arc between E and F. When an arc involves half or more than half of a circle, three letters must be used with the first and third indicating the ends of the arc and the middle letter indicating an additional point through which the arc passes.

When $\overset{\frown}{EF}$ is written, the minor arc is assumed.

Practice: Parts of a Circle

Match the parts of the following circle with center O.

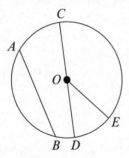

1. Radius

2. Diameter

3. Chord

4. Name of circle

Answers: Parts of a Circle

1. $\overline{OE}$, $\overline{OD}$, and $\overline{OC}$

2. $\overline{CD}$

3. $\overline{AB}$ and $\overline{CD}$

4. O

Circumference and Area of a Circle

Circumference

Circumference is the distance around the circle. Since the circumference of any circle divided by its diameter yields the same value, the Greek letter π (pi) is used to represent that value. In fractional or decimal form, the commonly used approximations of π are $\pi \approx 3.14$ or $\pi \approx \dfrac{22}{7}$. Use either value in your calculations. The formula for circumference is $C = \pi d$ or $C = 2\pi r$.

Example:

What is the circumference of circle M, shown above?

In circle M, $d = 8$, since $r = 4$.

$$C = \pi d$$
$$C = \pi(8)$$
$$C \approx 3.14(8)$$
$$C \approx 25.12 \text{ inches}$$

Area

The *area* of a circle can be determined by $A = \pi r^2$.

Example:

What is the area of circle M, shown above?

In circle M, $r = 5$, since $d = 10$.

$$A = \pi r^2$$
$$A = \pi(5^2)$$
$$A \approx 3.14(25)$$
$$A \approx 78.5 \text{ square inches}$$

Practice: Circumference and Area of a Circle

For questions 1 and 2, find the area and circumference (leave in terms of π) of each circle from the given radius or diameter.

1.

$A = $ _____
$C = $ _____

2.

$A = $ _____
$C = $ _____

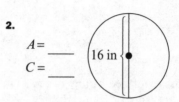

For questions 3 and 4, find the radius.

3. $A = 49\pi$ square inches

4. $C = 60\pi$ inches

5. What is the perimeter of the rectangle below if the four congruent circles each have an area of 9π?

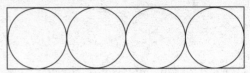

Answers: Circumference and Area of a Circle

1. $A = \pi r^2$

   $= \pi(3)^2$

   $= 9\pi$ square inches

   $C = 2\pi r$

   $= 2\pi(3)$

   $= 6\pi$ square inches

2. $A = \pi r^2$

   $= \pi(8)^2$

   $= 64\pi$ square inches

   $C = 2\pi r$

   $= 2\pi(8)$

   $= 16\pi$ square inches

   or

   $C = 2\pi d$

   $= 16\pi$ square inches

3. $A = \pi r^2$

   $49\pi = \pi r^2$

   $49 = r^2$

   7 inches $= r$

4. $C = 2\pi r$

   $60\pi = 2\pi r$

   $60 = 2r$

   30 inches $= r$

   or

   $C = \pi d$

   $60\pi = \pi d$

   $60 = d$

   30 inches $= r$

5. $A = \pi r^2$

   $= 9\pi$

   Therefore, the radius of each circle is 3; the diameter is 6.

   The length of the rectangle equals 4 times the diameter: $l = 4 \times 6 = 24$.

   The width of the rectangle equals 1 times the diameter: $w = 1 \times 6 = 6$.

   Therefore, the perimeter is $2(l + w)$ or $2(24 + 6) = 60$.

Angles in a Circle

Central Angles

Central angles are angles formed by any two radii in a circle. The vertex is the center of the circle. A central angle is equal to the measure of its intercepted arc.

In the following diagram of circle O, $m\overset{\frown}{AB} = 75°$; therefore, $m\angle AOB = 75°$. ($m\overset{\frown}{AB}$ is sometimes used to denote the measure of arc AB when its answer is meant to be in degrees.)

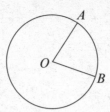

Inscribed Angles

Inscribed angles have their vertex on the circle and have chords as their sides. An inscribed angle is equal to one-half the measure of its intercepted arc.

In the following diagram of circle O, $m\overset{\frown}{CD} = 90°$. Therefore, $m\angle CED = 45°$.

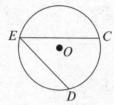

In general as the vertex moves farther away from the arc, the angle measure gets smaller. The closer the vertex is to the arc, the larger the size of the angle.

In the following diagram of circle O, $m\angle ARB$ is less than $m\angle ACB$, which is less than $m\angle AOB$.

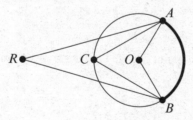

Practice: Angles in a Circle

For questions 1 and 2, use the following diagram of circle A.

1. Find the measure of $\angle x$ in circle A.

2. Find the measure of $\angle y$ in circle A.

For questions 3 and 4, use the following diagram.

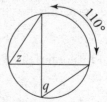

3. Find the measure of $\angle z$.

4. Find the measure of $\angle q$.

nd 6, use the following diagram

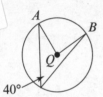

5. Find the measure of $\overparen{AB}$ of circle Q.

6. Find the measure of $\angle AQB$ in circle Q.

Answers: Angles in a Circle

1. Because $\angle x$ is a central angle, it equals the measure of the arc it intercepts, or 60°.

2. Because $\angle y$ is an inscribed angle, it equals one-half the arc it intercepts, or 30°.

3. $\angle z$, an inscribed angle, equals one-half 110°, or 55°.

4. $\angle q$, an inscribed angle, equals one-half 110°, or 55°.

5. $m\overparen{AB}$ is twice the inscribed angle that intercepts $\overparen{AB}$; therefore, $2 \times 40° = 80°$.

6. The measure of central angle AQB equals the measure of the arc it intercepts, or 80°.

Concentric Circles

Circles with the same center are called *concentric circles*.

Tangents to a Circle

A line that touches a circle at only one point is called a *tangent* or tangent line. This line cannot be in the interior of the circle.

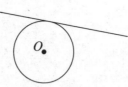

Two tangent segments sharing the same exterior point of a circle with their other endpoints on the circle are

- Equal in length. ($AB = AC$)
- Perpendicular to a radius that meets at that point. ($\overline{AB} \perp \overline{OB}$ and $\overline{AC} \perp \overline{OC}$)

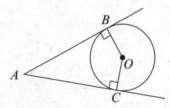

Volumes of Solid Figures

Determining formulas to solve solid figures is an element of the Common Core Standards. Four of the most common solid geometric figures are the cube, the rectangular solid, the cylinder, and the cone. Each of these figures may be thought of as the three-dimensional extensions of three flat two-dimensional figures, namely the square, the rectangle, and the circle.

The *volume* of a solid is the number of cubic units of space the figure contains. Volume is always labeled *cubic* units. The formula for the volume of each shape is different, but in general, it is the area of the base times the height.

Volume of a Cube

The formula for the volume of a cube is $V = s \times s \times s = s^3$.

Volume of a Rectangular Solid

The formula for the volume of a rectangular solid is $V = (lw)(h) = lwh$.

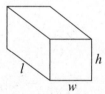

Volume of a Right Circular Cylinder (Circular Bases)

The formula for the volume of a right circular cylinder (circular bases) is $V = (\pi r^2)h = \pi r^2 h$.

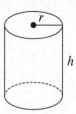

Volume of a Cone

The volume of a cone is $\dfrac{1}{3}$ the base area times the height, or $V = \dfrac{1}{3}\pi r^2 h$.

267

Practice: Volumes of Solid Figures

Find the volumes of the solid figures below whose dimensions are indicated. (Use $\frac{22}{7}$ for π.)

1. Rectangular solid

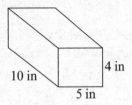

10 in · 5 in · 4 in

2. Cube

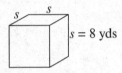

$s = 8$ yds

3. Cylinder

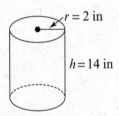

$r = 2$ in · $h = 14$ in

4. Cone

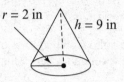

$r = 2$ in · $h = 9$ in

Use 3.14 for π.

5. Dena has a rectangular piece of fabric and needs to cut two triangles from the fabric whose angles are 45°-45°-90°. If the length of the rectangle is 20 inches, what is the area of the remaining fabric after the triangles are cut?

5 in

Answers: Volumes of Solid Figures

1. $V = lwh = (10)(5)(4) = 200$ cubic inches

2. $V = s^3 = 8 \times 8 \times 8 = 512$ cubic yards

3. $V = \pi r^2 h \approx \frac{22}{7} \times \frac{2}{1} \times \frac{2}{1} \times \frac{14}{1} = 22(8)$

≈ 176 cubic inches

4. $V = \frac{1}{3}\pi r^2 h$

$\approx \frac{1}{3}(3.14)(2)^2(9)$

≈ 37.68 cubic inches

5. There are several ways to solve this problem, but here is one solution. The area of the rectangle prior to cutting is 20 in × 5 in = 100 square inches. An isosceles right triangle (45°-45°-90°) has two equal sides, two equal angles, and one right angle. Therefore, the two triangles make a square with an area of 25 square inches:

$$100 - 25 = 75 \text{ square inches}$$

Surface Areas of Solid Figures

Surface Area of a Rectangular Solid

To determine the surface area of a rectangular solid, find the area of each of the three unique sides and then multiply each of these by 2 (since there are two of each side), and then add the three areas together.

Example:

Find the area of the following rectangular solid.

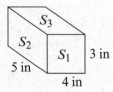

Area of side 1 = 3 × 4 = 12 square inches

Area of side 2 = 5 × 3 = 15 square inches

Area of side 3 = 5 × 4 = 20 square inches

Since there are two of each of these sides:

$$\text{Surface area} = 2(12) + 2(15) + 2(20)$$
$$= 24 + 30 + 40$$
$$= 94 \text{ square inches}$$

Surface Area of a Right Circular Cylinder

To determine the surface area of a right circular cylinder, it is best envisioned "rolled out" onto a flat surface as shown below.

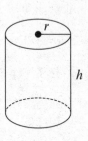

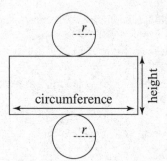

Now find the area of each individual piece. The area of each circle equals πr^2. Note that the length of the rectangle equals the circumference of the circle. The rectangle's area equals circumference times height. Adding the three parts gives the surface area of the cylinder as shown in the next example.

Example:

Find the surface area of a cylinder with radius 5 feet and height 12 feet.

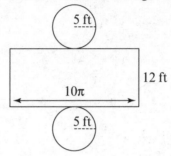

The area of the top circle = $\pi(r^2) = \pi(5^2) = 25\pi$ square feet.

The area of the bottom circle is the same: 25π square feet.

The length of the rectangle is the circumference of the circle: $2\pi r = 2\pi(5) = 10\pi$.

Therefore, the area of the rectangle equals its height times 10π or $12 \times 10\pi = 120\pi$ square feet.

Totaling all the pieces gives $25\pi + 25\pi + 120\pi = 170\pi$ square feet.

Practice: Volumes and Surface Areas of Solids

1. What is the volume of a cube whose side is $5\frac{1}{2}$ inches?

2. If a rectangular solid has a length of 4 inches, a width of 3 inches, and a height of 2 feet, what is its volume?

3. Given that a cylinder's height is 42 inches and its radius is 3 inches, determine its volume. (Use $\frac{22}{7}$ for.)

4. Find the surface area of a rectangular solid that measures 4 inches by 7 inches by 6 inches.

5. Find the surface area of a right circular cylinder that has a height of 20 inches and a radius of 4 inches (in π square inches).

Answers: Volumes and Surface Areas of Solids

1. $166\frac{3}{8}$ cubic inches

   $$V = s^3 = 5\frac{1}{2} \times 5\frac{1}{2} \times 5\frac{1}{2} = \frac{11}{2} \times \frac{11}{2} \times \frac{11}{2} = \frac{1,331}{8} = 166\frac{3}{8} \text{ cubic inches}$$

2. 288 cubic inches

   $$V = l \times w \times h = 4 \times 3 \times 24 = 288 \text{ cubic inches}$$

   Note: The 2 feet had to be converted to 24 inches so that all dimensions would be expressed in the same units.

3. 1,188 cubic inches

$$V = \pi r^2 h = \frac{22}{\cancel{7}} \times \frac{9}{1} \times \frac{\overset{6}{\cancel{42}}}{1} \approx 1{,}188 \text{ cubic inches}$$

4. 188 square inches

Area of side 1 = 4 × 6 = 24 square inches

Area of side 2 = 6 × 7 = 42 square inches

Area of side 3 = 4 × 7 = 28 square inches

$$\begin{aligned} \text{Surface area} &= 2(24) + 2(42) + 2(28) \\ &= 48 + 84 + 56 \\ &= 188 \text{ square inches} \end{aligned}$$

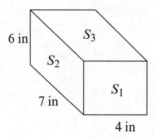

5. 192π square inches

Area of top circle = $\pi r^2 = 16\pi$ square inches

Area of bottom circle = $\pi r^2 = 16\pi$ square inches

$$\begin{aligned} \text{Area of rectangle} &= 20 \times \text{circumference} \\ &= 20 \times 2\pi r \\ &= 20 \times 2\pi(4) \\ &= 20 \times 8\pi \\ &= 160\pi \text{ square inches} \end{aligned}$$

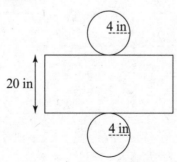

Adding all the pieces, total surface area is $16\pi + 16\pi + 160\pi = 192\pi$ square inches.

Geometry Formulas

The following table lists geometry formulas with which you should be familiar.

Geometry Formulas

Shape	Illustration	Perimeter	Area
Square		$P = 4a$	$A = a^2$
Rectangle		$P = 2b + 2h$ or $P = 2(b + h)$	$A = bh$
Parallelogram		$P = 2a + 2b$ or $P = 2(a + b)$	$A = bh$
Triangle		$P = a + b + c$	$A = \dfrac{bh}{2}$ or $A = \dfrac{1}{2}bh$
Rhombus		$P = 4a$	$A = ah$
Trapezoid		$P = b_1 + b_2 + x + y$	$A = \dfrac{h(b_1 + b_2)}{2}$ or $A = \dfrac{1}{2}h(b_1 + b_2)$
Circle		$C = \pi d$ or $C = 2\pi r$	$A = \pi r^2$

(Continued)

Geometry Formulas (*continued*)

Shape	Illustration	Perimeter	Area
Cube	a	$SA = 6a^2$	$V = a^3$
Rectangular Prism	Base h l w	$SA = 2(lw + lh + wh)$ or $SA = $ (Perimeter of the Base)h + 2(Area of the Base)	$V = lwh$ or $V = $ (Area of the Base)h
Prisms in general	Base h	$SA = $ (Perimeter of the Base)h + 2(Area of the Base)	$V = $ (Area of the Base)h
Cylinder	Base r h	$SA = $ Perimeter of the Base or Circumference)h + 2(Area of the Base) or $SA = 2\pi rh + 2\pi r^2$ or $SA = 2\pi r(h + r)$	$V = $ (Area of the Base) h or $V = \pi r^2 h$
Sphere	r *Label radius as "r"*	$SA = 4\pi r^2$	$V = \dfrac{4}{3}\pi r^3$

Right Triangles

The Pythagorean theorem is specific to right triangles. It states the following: The sum of the squares of the legs of a right triangle equals the square of the hypotenuse ($a^2 + b^2 = c^2$).

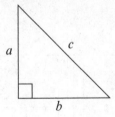

Geometry Review Test

Questions

1. The study of shapes and figures in two dimensions is called _____ geometry.

2. The study of shapes and figures in three dimensions is called _____ geometry.

3. An angle is formed by two rays that have the same endpoint; that endpoint is called the _____.

4. Which of the following name the same angle in the triangle?

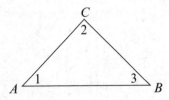

   Ⓐ $\angle A$, $\angle ACB$, and $\angle CAB$
   Ⓑ $\angle ACB$ and $\angle CAB$
   Ⓒ $\angle A$, $\angle 1$, $\angle B$
   Ⓓ $\angle A$, $\angle CAB$, and $\angle 1$
   Ⓔ $\angle ACB$, $\angle 1$, and $\angle B$

5. A right angle measures _____.

6. An acute angle measures _____.

7. An obtuse angle measures _____.

8. A straight angle measures _____.

9. Two angles next to each other, sharing a common side and vertex, are called _____.

10. Based on the diagram below, which of the following is true?

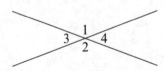

   Ⓐ $m\angle 1 = m\angle 3$
   Ⓑ $m\angle 1 = m\angle 2$ and $m\angle 3 = m\angle 4$
   Ⓒ $m\angle 2 = m\angle 4$ and $m\angle 2 = m\angle 3$
   Ⓓ $m\angle 1 = m\angle 2$ and $m\angle 3 = m\angle 2$
   Ⓔ $m\angle 1 = m\angle 4$ and $m\angle 2 = m\angle 3$

11. Two angles, the sum of whose measures is 90°, are said to be _____ to each other.

12. Two angles, the sum of whose measures is 180°, are said to be _____ to each other.

13. An angle bisector _____.

14. A _____ is often described as the path joining two points; it goes forever in two opposite directions.

15. A part of a line with two endpoints is called a _____.

16. A part of a line that continues in one direction and has only one endpoint is called a _____.

17. If two lines meet at a point they are called _____ lines.

18. Two lines that meet at right angles are _____ to each other.

19. Two or more lines that remain the same distance apart at all times are called _____.

20. In the diagram below, $l \parallel m$, which of the following statements are true?

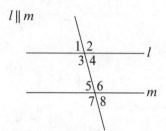

I. $m\angle 1 = m\angle 2 = m\angle 4 = m\angle 5$

II. $m\angle 1 = m\angle 4 = m\angle 5 = m\angle 8$

III. $m\angle 2 = m\angle 3 = m\angle 6 = m\angle 7$

IV. $m\angle 5 = m\angle 8$ only

V. $m\angle 5 = m\angle 6 = m\angle 8$

Ⓐ   I and V
Ⓑ   II
Ⓒ   III
Ⓓ   II and III
Ⓔ   II and IV

For questions 21–28, name the following.

21. A three-sided polygon: _____

22. A four-sided polygon: _____

23. A five-sided polygon: _____

24. A six-sided polygon: _____

25. A seven-sided polygon: _____

26. An eight-sided polygon: _____

27. A nine-sided polygon: _____

28. A ten-sided polygon: _____

29. If all sides and angles have the same measure, the polygon is called _____.

30. In a polygon, a line segment that connects one vertex to another but is not the side of the polygon is called a _____.

31. The polygon below is called a _____ polygon.

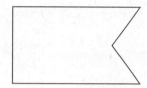

32. The sum of the measures of the interior angles of any triangle is _____.

33. If all sides of a triangle are equal, the triangle is _____.

34. A triangle that has two equal sides is called _____.

35. A triangle whose three sides are of different lengths is called _____.

36. A triangle having a 90° angle is called a(n) _____.

37. A triangle containing an angle greater than 90° is called a(n) _____.

38. If all angles in a triangle are less than 90°, the triangle is called a(n) _____.

39. In a triangle, a line segment drawn from a vertex to the midpoint of the opposite side is called a(n) _____.

40. If two angles of a triangle measure 43° each, what is the measure of the third angle?

41. In $\triangle ABC$ below, the longest side is _____.

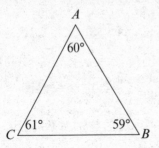

42. A triangle can have sides of length 2, 2, and 5. True or false?

43. Find the measure of $\angle z$ in the triangle below.

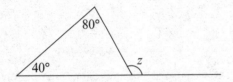

44. Find the length of side c in right triangle ABC below.

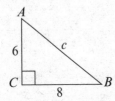

45. Find the length of side r in right $\triangle QRS$ below.

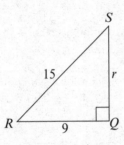

46. Find x, y, and z in the triangle below.

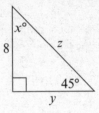

47. Find a, b, and c in the triangle below.

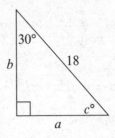

For questions 48–51, name the following figures.

48.

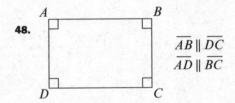

$$\overline{AB} \parallel \overline{DC}$$
$$\overline{AD} \parallel \overline{BC}$$

49.

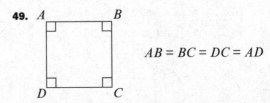

$$AB = BC = DC = AD$$

50.

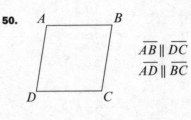

$$\overline{AB} \parallel \overline{DC}$$
$$\overline{AD} \parallel \overline{BC}$$

51.

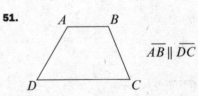

$$\overline{AB} \parallel \overline{DC}$$

52. What is the sum of the measures of the interior angles of a heptagon?

53. Find the area of △*ABC* shown below.

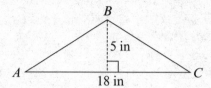

54. Find the area and perimeter of square *ABCD* shown below.

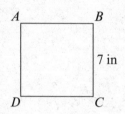

55. Find the area and perimeter of rectangle *ABCD* shown below.

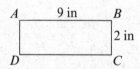

56. Find the area of parallelogram *ABCD* shown below.

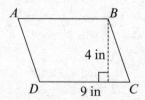

57. Find the area of trapezoid *ABCD* shown below.

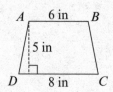

58. Jose plans to pour 3 feet of concrete decking around his rectangular-shaped swimming pool. The length of the pool is 3 times the width, and the length times the width of the pool is 588 sq ft. What is the area of the concrete that will frame the pool?

59. If the two figures below are similar with *ABCD* ~ *QRST*, what is the length of $\overline{BC}$?

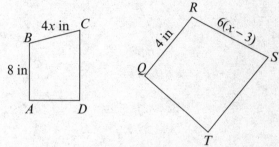

Figures not drawn to scale.

Questions 60–62 refer to the following circle.

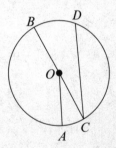

60. $\overline{OA}$ is called a _____ of circle *O*.

61. $\overline{BC}$ is called a _____ of circle *O*.

62. $\overline{DC}$ is called a _____ of circle *O*.

63. Find the area and circumference of circle *A*, shown below, in terms of π.

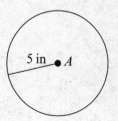

277

64. In the figure *ABCDE* below, the area of isosceles △*ABE* (with the base $\overline{BE}$) is 8 square inches. If the height of this triangle (drawn to $\overline{BE}$) is 4 inches long, what is the numerical difference between the area of the circle inscribed in square *BCDE* and the circumference of the circle?

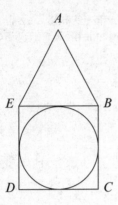

65. In the circle shown below, if $m\overset{\frown}{AB} = 50°$, what is the measure of the central angle *AOB*?

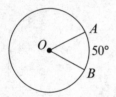

66. In the circle shown below, if $m\overset{\frown}{AB} = 100°$, what is the measure of the inscribed angle *ADB*?

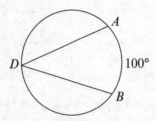

67. Circles with the same center are called _____.

68. A line that touches a circle at one point is called a _____.

69. Polygons that are the same shape but different in size are called _____.

70. Polygons that are exactly the same in shape and size are called _____.

For questions 71–73, find the volumes and surface areas of the figures below.

71.

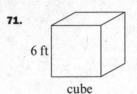

cube

72.

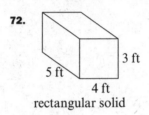

rectangular solid

73.

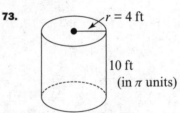

right circular cylinder

74. A machinist at Metal Casting Engineering receives an order to cast a right circular metal cylinder (without a top cover). The cylinder must be able to store a cone inside with the same base and height. The radius of the cylinder must be 24 inches and the height must be 12 inches (use 3.14 for π).

With a cone inserted inside the cylinder, sand is poured into the void space of the cylinder. How many cubic inches of sand are needed to fill the void space?

Answers

Page numbers following each answer refer to the review section applicable to the problem type.

1. plane (p. 220)
2. solid (p. 220)
3. vertex (p. 220)
4. **D.** $\angle A$, $\angle CAB$, $\angle 1$ (p. 220)
5. 90° (p. 221)
6. less than 90° (p. 221)
7. greater than 90° but less than 180° (p. 221)
8. 180° (p. 221)
9. adjacent angles (p. 222)
10. **B.** $m\angle 1 = m\angle 2$ and $m\angle 3 = m\angle 4$ (p. 222)
11. complementary (p. 223)
12. supplementary (p. 223)
13. divides an angle into two angles of equal measure (p. 223)
14. line (p. 224)
15. line segment (p. 224)
16. ray (p. 225)
17. intersecting (p. 225)
18. perpendicular (p. 225)
19. parallel lines (p. 225)
20. **D.** II and III (p. 226)
21. triangle (p. 232)
22. quadrilateral (p. 232)
23. pentagon (p. 232)
24. hexagon (p. 232)
25. heptagon or septagon (p. 232)
26. octagon (p. 232)
27. nonagon (p. 232)
28. decagon (p. 232)
29. regular (p. 232)
30. diagonal (p. 233)
31. concave (p. 233)
32. 180° (p. 233)
33. equilateral (p. 234)
34. isosceles (p. 234)
35. scalene (p. 234)
36. right triangle (p. 234)
37. obtuse triangle (p. 235)
38. acute triangle (p. 235)
39. median (p. 236)
40. 94° (p. 233)
41. $\overline{AB}$ (p. 238)
42. False (p. 239)
43. 120° (p. 239)
44. 10 (p. 242)
45. 12 (p. 242)
46. $x = 45°$, $y = 8$, $z = 8\sqrt{2}$ (p. 244)
47. $a = 9$, $b = 9\sqrt{3}$, $c = 60°$ (p. 245)
48. rectangle (p. 251)
49. square (p. 251)
50. parallelogram (p. 252)
51. trapezoid (p. 252)
52. 900° (p. 255)
53. 45 square inches (p. 256)
54. area = 49 square inches
    perimeter = 28 inches (p. 256)
55. area = 18 square inches
    perimeter = 22 inches (p. 256)
56. 36 square inches (p. 256)
57. 35 square inches (p. 256)

58. Write an equation with the information provided: $l \times w = 588$ feet. Since the length is 3 times the width, written as $l = 3w$, you can substitute this information into an equation.

$$3w \cdot w = 588 \text{ sq ft}$$
$$3w^2 = 588 \text{ sq ft}$$
$$w^2 = 196 \text{ sq ft}$$
$$w = 14 \text{ ft}$$
$$l = 3(14 \text{ ft}) = 42 \text{ ft}$$

Now that you have the dimensions of the pool, draw a diagram that represents the pool and add a 3-foot border to each side. The dimensions are now 20 ft × 48 ft = 960 square feet. Now, subtract the area of the length and width of the pool 960 – 588 = 372 square feet of concrete. (pp. 257–258)

59. For these diagrams $ABCD \sim QRST$; therefore, the corrresponding sides are proportional. Since $AB = 8$ and $QR = 4$, quadrilateral $QRST$ sides are half the lengths of sides of the quadrilateral $ABCD$. Therefore, twice $6(x - 3)$ is equal to $4x$.

$2[6(x - 3)] = 4x$	Multiply side RS by 2
$2[6x - 18)] = 4x$	Distribute the 6 inside
	the parentheses
$12x - 36 = 4x$	Simplify
$+36 = \quad + 36$	

The following steps isolate the variable.

$$12x = 4x + 36$$
$$-4x = -4x$$
$$8x = 36$$
$$x = 4.5 \text{ inches}$$

Therefore, $4x = 18$ inches. (pp. 232, 253–254)

60. radius (p. 261)

61. diameter (could be called a chord) (p. 261)

62. chord (p. 261)

63. area = 25π square inches

circumference = 10π inches (p. 262)

64. The area of the triangle is 8, the height is 4; therefore, the base must also be 4. The problem states that the circle is inscribed inside a square; therefore, the sides of the square are 4. The side of the square is equal to the diameter of the circle. The area for a circle is $\pi r^2 = \pi 2^2$, which is equal to 4π. The circumference is $\pi d = 4\pi$. The area and the circumference are equal, and the answer is 0. (pp. 262–263)

65. 50° (p. 265)

66. 50° (p. 265)

67. concentric circles (p. 266)

68. tangent line (p. 266)

69. similar (p. 232)

70. congruent (p. 232)

71. volume = 216 cubic feet (p. 267)

surface area = 216 square feet (p. 269)

72. volume = 60 cubic feet (p. 267)

surface area = 94 square feet (p. 269)

73. volume = 160π cubic feet (p. 267)

surface area = 112π square feet (p. 269)

74. The difference between the volume of a cylinder and the volume of a cone is $V = 1\pi r^2 h - \frac{1}{3}\pi r^2 h$. Therefore, $V = \frac{2}{3}(3.14)(24)^2 = 14{,}469.12$ cubic inches. (pp. 269–270)

Geometry Glossary of Terms

acute angle: An angle whose measure is less than 90°.

acute triangle: A triangle containing all acute angles.

adjacent angles: Angles that share a common side and a common vertex but do not have any common interior points.

angle: Formed by two rays with a common endpoint.

angle bisector: A line, ray, or segment that divides an angle into two smaller angles equal in measure.

arc: Part of the circle between any two points on the circle.

area: The space within a shape, measured in square units.

bisects: Divides into two equal parts.

central angle: An angle whose vertex is the center of the circle. The measure of a central angle is equal to the measure of its arc.

chord: A chord of a circle is a line segment whose endpoints are any two points that lie on a circle.

circle: In a plane, the set of points all equidistant from a given point.

circumference: The distance around a circle; equals two times π times the radius or π times the diameter ($C = 2\pi r$ or πd).

complementary angles: Two angles whose sum measures 90°.

concave polygon: A polygon that contains at least one diagonal outside the figure and at least one interior angle is greater than 180°.

concentric circles: Circles with the same center.

congruent: Exactly alike. Identical in shape and size.

consecutive: Next to each other.

convex polygon: A polygon in which all diagonals lie within the figure and all interior angles are less than 180°.

corresponding: In the same position. Coinciding.

cosine (cos): A trigonometric function used to find a missing length for a right triangle. The cosine of an acute angle in a right triangle is the length of the adjacent side divided by the length of the hypotenuse.

cube: A six-sided solid. All sides are congruent squares and all edges are equal.

decagon: A plane closed figure with ten sides and ten angles.

degree: A unit of measurement of an angle.

diagonal of a polygon: A line segment that connects one vertex to another vertex and is not a side of the polygon.

diameter: Either a segment that joins any two points on a circle and passes through the center of the circle or the length of that segment. It is in the context of use that you will know which meaning is being used. A diameter is the longest chord in a circle.

equilateral triangle: A triangle in which all three angles are equal in measure and all three sides have the same length.

exterior angle: An angle formed outside the polygon by extending one side. In a triangle, the measure of an exterior angle equals the sum of the measures of the two remote interior angles.

hash marks (tick marks): Small straight lines that are inserted on corresponding sides of a triangle to denote that sides are equal (or congruent).

height (or altitude): A segment drawn from a point and is perpendicular to a base or an extension of a base or a segment drawn that is perpendicular to each of two parallel lines.

heptagon or septagon: A plane closed figure with seven sides and seven angles.

hexagon: A plane closed figure with six sides and six angles.

hypotenuse: In a right triangle, the side opposite the 90° angle.

inscribed angle: An angle with its vertex on a circle and has chords as its sides. The vertex is where the chords intersect. The measure of an inscribed angle is equal to one-half the measure of its intercepted arc.

interior angles: Angles formed inside the shape or within two parallel lines.

intersecting lines: Lines that meet at a point.

isosceles right triangle: A triangle having two equal sides, two equal angles, and one 90° angle. Its sides are always in the ratio $1:1:\sqrt{2}$.

isosceles triangle: A triangle having two equal sides (and thus, two equal angles across from those sides).

legs: In a right triangle, the two sides forming the 90° angle. In a trapezoid, the nonparallel sides.

line: The path joining two points; it goes forever in two opposite directions (also known as a straight angle).

line segment: A part of a line that has two endpoints.

median: In a triangle, a line segment drawn from a vertex to the midpoint of the opposite side. In a trapezoid, a line segment parallel to the bases and bisecting the legs.

midpoint: The halfway point of a line segment, equidistant from each endpoint.

minute: A subdivision of an angle: $\frac{1}{60}$ degree.

nonagon: A plane closed figure with nine sides and nine angles.

obtuse angle: An angle greater than 90° but less than 180°.

obtuse triangle: A triangle containing an obtuse angle.

octagon: A plane closed figure with eight sides and eight angles.

parallel lines: Two or more lines, always the same distance apart. Parallel lines never meet.

parallelogram: A four-sided plane closed figure with opposite sides that are equal and parallel. (Its opposite angles are equal, and its consecutive angles are supplementary.)

pentagon: A five-sided plane closed figure. The sum of its five angles is 540°.

perimeter: The total distance around any figure. In a circle, this is referred to as the *circumference.*

perpendicular lines: Two lines that intersect at right angles.

pi (π): A constant used in determining a circle's area or circumference. Commonly used approximations for π are 3.14 and $\frac{22}{7}$.

plane: Often described as a flat surface, it is determined by three non-collinear points.

plane figure: Any shape that can be drawn on a plane (a two-dimensional figure).

plane geometry: The study of shapes and figures in two dimensions (the plane).

point: A basic element of geometry, a location. If two lines intersect, they do so at a point that is represented by a dot and named by a capital letter.

polygon: A many-sided plane closed figure. Triangle, quadrilateral, pentagon, and so on are examples of polygons.

prism: A three-dimensional shape bounded by congruent parallel bases and a set of parallelograms formed by joining the corresponding vertices of the bases.

Pythagorean theorem: A theorem that applies to right triangles. The sum of the squares of a right triangle's two legs equals the square of the hypotenuse: $a^2 + b^2 = c^2$.

quadrilateral: A four-sided plane closed figure. The sum of its four angles equals 360°.

radii: Plural of *radius.*

radius: Either the segment that joins the center of a circle to any point on the circle or the length of that segment. You will know which meaning is being used by the context.

ray: A half-line that continues forever in one direction and has one endpoint.

rectangle: A four-sided plane closed figure; its opposite sides are equal and parallel, and it has four right angles.

reflection: In transformational geometry, a reflection is the image of an object flipped over a line.

regular polygon: A polygon in which the sides and angles are all equal. For example, a regular pentagon has five equal angles and five equal sides.

rhombus: A parallelogram with four equal sides.

right angle: An angle whose measure is equal to 90°.

right circular cone: A solid having a circular base with each point on the circle the same distance away from a point off the plane of a circle. That point is called the vertex of the cone.

right circular cylinder: A solid shaped like a can whose circular bases meet the remaining side at right angles.

right triangle: A triangle containing a 90° angle.

rotation: Moving a line, line segment, or shape around a given point on a coordinate plane. Rotating an object is also called "turning" an object.

scalene triangle: A triangle having none of its sides equal (or angles equal).

sine (sin): A trigonometric function. The sine of an acute angle in a right triangle is the ratio of the length of the opposite side to that of the hypotenuse.

similar: Having the same shape but not the same size. Similar figures have angles in the same positions equal in measure and sides in the same positions proportional in measure.

solid geometry: The study of shapes and figures in three dimensions: width, depth, and height.

square: A four-sided plane closed figure with equal sides and four right angles. Its opposite sides are parallel.

straight angle: An angle equal to 180°; often referred to as a line.

straight line: The path joining two points; it goes forever in two opposite directions.

supplementary angles: Two angles whose sum measures 180°.

surface area: The sum of the areas of all the surfaces of a three-dimensional figure.

tangent (tan): A trigonometric function of an acute angle of a right triangle. The tangent is the ratio of the side opposite the angle to the side adjacent to the angle.

tangent to a circle: A line, line segment, or ray that touches a circle at one point (cannot go within the circle).

translation: Moving an object or line on a coordinate plane by increasing or decreasing the values of x and y by a constant amount. Also called a "slide."

transversal: A line crossing two or more parallel or nonparallel lines in a plane.

trapezoid: A four-sided plane closed figure with only one pair of parallel sides, called *bases*.

triangle: A three-sided plane closed figure. It contains three angles whose sum measures 180°.

vertex: The point at which two rays meet and form an angle, or the point at which two sides meet in a polygon.

vertical angles: The opposite angles formed by the intersection of two lines. Vertical angles are equal in measure.

vertices: Plural of *vertex*.

volume: Capacity to hold, measured in cubic units. Volume of rectangular prism equals length × width × height.

Chapter 5

Word and Graph Interpretation Problems

To solve word problems on standardized tests, you must be able to translate English words into math equations. By translating word problems into numbers, equations, objects, and diagrams, you are creating math models to solve real-life narratives. To solve graph interpretation problems, you must be able to use reasoning skills to evaluate visual illustrations in graphs, charts, tables, and diagrams. Math modeling is a method for choosing the necessary math operations of arithmetic, algebra, geometry, statistics, and probability to understand quantitative situations represented in word or graph interpretation problems. The goal is to find a mathematical way to organize the problem so that you can work toward a solution.

Connecting Word and Graph Interpretation Problems to the Common Core Standards

Modeling math word and graph interpretation problems is fundamental to the Common Core Standards. Modeling math engages your reasoning and decision-making processes as you draw conclusions and find solutions to narrative or visual illustrations about everyday events. As you study and solve the math problems in this chapter, always keep math logic and reasoning in mind.

Word Problems

The following table highlights important elements of word problems that are covered in the Common Core Standards. In this chapter, we show you how to translate word problems into quantitative scenarios and take you through the steps to solve them. As discussed in Chapter 2, "Algebra," some word problems necessitate the substitution of a variable in place of an unknown quantity.

Common Math Word Problems

Problem Type	Description
Distance (Motion) Problems	Distance problems are known as motion problems. These types of problems calculate the distance, rate of speed (or velocity), and time that it takes to travel from one point to another.
Work Problems	Work problems calculate how much time it takes to complete a given job based on the number of tasks, the amount of time, the rate of speed, and the number of people working together.
Mixture Problems	Mixture problems organize information from different quantities and concentration values that are mixed together. Chemical solutions and liquids are most often used in this type of word problem.
Age Problems	Age problems determine the chronological relationship between the ages of people based on their current ages, past ages, and predicted future ages.

(Continued)

Common Math Word Problems (*continued*)

Problem Type	Description
Number Problems	Number problems involve several types of arithmetic and algebraic operations: integer problems, simple interest, and compound interest.
Percentage Problems	Percentage problems are fundamental word problems. These types of problems ask you to find "some percent" of a given value.
Percent Change Problems	Percent change problems ask you to find how much a quantity has changed by an increase, decrease, gain, loss, mark up, mark down, rise, or fall.
Ratio and Proportion Problems	Ratio and proportion problems ask you to consider "a part" of a value in relation to the whole to compare two values.
Graph Interpretation Problems	Graph interpretation problems (data interpretation) ask you to evaluate information accompanied by data from a diagram to look for patterns and trends, and draw conclusions about the information from the word problem.
Geometry Problems	Geometry problems ask you to find solutions by drawing diagrams to solve problems involving angles, perimeter, area, surface area, and volume.

Word and Graph Interpretation Problems Diagnostic Test

Questions

1. What is the simple interest on $2,500 invested at an annual rate of 8% over 3 years?

2. A map's key shows that 1 inch = 25 miles. How many inches apart on the map will two cities be if they are exactly 12 miles apart? Show your answer to the nearest hundredth.

3. A plane flies from Los Angeles to Denver, a distance of 1,120 miles, at 280 miles per hour. A train from Denver to Los Angeles travels at a rate of 70 miles per hour. Assuming the train also travels 1,120 miles, if a passenger took the plane to Denver and then returned to Los Angeles on the train, how long did the entire trip take?

4. In order to pass an examination, a student must answer exactly 30 questions correctly to obtain the minimum passing grade of 60%. How many questions are on the examination?

5. Last year, Tom's income was $36,000. This year, he was given a new position with the company with a salary of $48,000. What was the percent increase in Tom's salary?

6. If one number is 4 times as large as another number and the smaller number is decreased by 2, the result is 14 less than the larger number. What are the two numbers?

7. Fred is 6 years older than Sylvia. In 2 years, the sum of their ages will be 18. How old is Sylvia now?

8. The length of a rectangle is 3 inches more than the width. If the perimeter of the rectangle is 26 inches, what are the measures of its length and width?

9. Adam can do a job in 5 hours, and Jennifer can do the same job in 6 hours. If they work together, how long will the job take them?

10. Nuts costing 70¢ per pound are mixed with nuts costing 40¢ per pound to produce 20 pounds of mixture worth 50¢ per pound. How many pounds of each type are used?

Answers

Page numbers following each answer refer to the review section applicable to the problem type.

1. $600 (p. 306)

2. 0.48 inches (p. 316)

3. 20 hours (p. 290)

4. 50 questions (p. 311)

5. $33\frac{1}{3}\%$ (p. 314)

6. 4 and 16 (p. 303)

7. 4 years old (p. 300)

8. length = 8 inches; width = 5 inches (p. 323)

9. $2\frac{8}{11}$ hours (p. 293)

10. $6\frac{2}{3}$ pounds of 70¢ nuts

    $13\frac{1}{3}$ pounds of 40¢ nuts (p. 296)

Word and Graph Interpretation Problems Review

An underlying expectation of the Common Core Standards for mathematics is to find meaningful solutions for multi-step real-world events (word problems). Math word problems allow you an opportunity to excel at applying logical reasoning skills to math scenarios. Although problems may initially challenge your critical thinking processes, once you learn key problem-solving strategies, you should be able to approach problems with greater confidence.

How to Approach Math Word Problems

There are many types of word problems involving arithmetic, algebra, geometry, and combinations of each with various twists. It is important to have a systematic technique for approaching, translating, and solving word problems. As you approach word problems, remember to focus on logic and reasoning as you translate words into numbers and mathematical functions. Remember to use a variable for the missing information.

Identify what is being asked. Ask yourself, "What am I ultimately trying to find?" How far a car has traveled? How fast a plane flies? How much data usage is left in a smartphone plan? Whatever it is, identify the main point(s) and then *write it down* or *circle it*. This helps ensure that you're solving for what is being asked.

Look for key words and phrases. Look for words that signal a math operation to give you clues as to how the problem should be solved.

- Words that signal an operation (addition, subtraction, multiplication, division). The next section, "Key Words That Signal a Math Operation," provides common examples of math operational words.
- Words that signal the unit of measurement (length, width, area, volume).
- Headings and labels on a chart or graph (title, headings, values, categories, axes labels).

Determine if all of the given information is necessary to solve the problem. Occasionally, you may be given more than enough information to solve a problem. Choose what you need and don't spend needless energy on irrelevant information. It is often helpful to summarize the word problem into a concise statement in your own words to differentiate relevant from irrelevant information.

Order of operations. Always follow the rules of the *order of operations* when setting up your equation. If multiplication, division, exponents, addition, subtraction, or parenthetical (grouping symbols) are all contained in one problem, the order of operations is as follows:

1. Parentheses (or other grouping symbols)
2. Exponents
3. Multiplication or division in the order it occurs from left to right
4. Addition or subtraction in the order it occurs from left to right

Remember the mnemonic PEMDAS to help you remember the order of operations (see p. 14).

Use visual organizers. If you can, set up an equation with mathematical symbols or some straightforward system with the given information. It is often helpful to draw a diagram or chart to help point you to a relationship or equation.

Example:

Set up a chart from the following word problem.

Warren is 12 years younger than his brother Jesse. Last year, the sum of their ages was 30 years old. What is the average of their ages 5 years from now?

Let x represent Jesse's age, and $x - 12$ is Warren's age.

Person	Current Age	Age 1 Year Ago
Jesse	x	$x - 1$
Warren	$x - 12$	$(x - 12) - 1$

Determine the mathematical operation and carefully solve the problem. When you are not sure which mathematical operation to use, ask yourself, "How should I solve this problem?" Look at the words around any unfamiliar term and decide *the context* of the problem. Be sensitive to what question is being asked. What time? How many? How much? How far? How old? What length? What is the ratio?

Be sure that you're working in the same units. For example, you may have to convert feet to inches, pounds to ounces, and so on, in order to keep everything consistent. Use a calculator for time-consuming problems.

Example:

From the chart on p. 288, it is possible to set up a math equation from the statement, "last year the sum of their ages was 30." This translates into $x - 1 + (x - 12) - 1 = 30$.

$$x - 1 + (x - 12) - 1 = 30$$
$$2x - 14 = 30$$
$$2x = 44$$
$$x = 22$$

Therefore, Jesse is currently 22 years old, and Warren is currently 10 years old ($22 - 12 = 10$).

In 5 years, Jesse will be 27 and Warren will be 15. The average of their ages in 5 years is 21: $\dfrac{27 + 15}{2} = 21$.

Double-check your answer and make sure it is reasonable. Double-check that you have answered "all parts" of the word problem. One of the most common errors in answering word problems is the failure to answer what was actually being asked. The following example shows correct and incorrect methods for setting up a math equation from a word problem. Check to make sure that an error in computation or a mistake in setting up your equation did not give you a wrong answer.

Example:

Set up an equation from the following word statement:

Ben purchased twice as many athletic jerseys as athletic shorts.

Select variables and state what each represents: J = number of jerseys and S = number of shorts.

Correct equation: $J = 2S$ (reads: the total of the jerseys equals two times the number of shorts).

Incorrect equation: $2J = S$ (reads: two times the number of jerseys equals the number of shorts).

This example shows that it is often helpful to restate your answer in a verbal sentence to verify that it logically makes sense and that it is reasonable.

Key Words That Signal a Math Operation

The Common Core Standards and many standardized tests emphasize your ability to interpret concepts from various perspectives, including math terms. Word problems can be misleading unless you carefully organize words into math symbols and numbers. The following is a list of the most common words or phrases:

Add

- **Sum:** *The sum of 2, 4, and 6.*
- **Total:** *The total of the first six payments.*
- **Addition:** *A recipe calls for the addition of 5 pints.*
- **Plus:** *3 liters plus 2 liters.*
- **Exceeds:** *The down payment of $50,000 exceeds the minimum due of $30,000. How much more was paid than was necessary?*
- **Increase:** *Her pay was increased by $15.*

- **More than:** *This week the enrollment was eight more than last week.*
- **Added to:** *If you added $3 to the cost . . .*
- **Successive:** *The total of six successive monthly rent payments without missing any month.* (**Note:** The word *consecutive* may be used in place of *successive* in word problems.)

Subtract

- **Difference:** *What is the difference between . . .*
- **Fewer:** *There were 15 fewer men than women.*
- **Remaining:** *How many are left or what quantity remains?*
- **Less than:** *A number is five less than another number.*
- **Reduced by:** *The budget was reduced by $5,000.*
- **Decreased:** *If he decreased the speed of his car by 10 mph . . .*
- **Minus:** *Some number minus 9 is . . .*

Multiply

- **Product:** *The product of 8 and 5 is . . .*
- **Of:** *One-half of the group.*
- **Times:** *Five times as many girls as boys.*
- **At:** *The cost of 10 yards of material at 70¢ a yard is . . .*
- **Total:** *If you spend $15 a week on gas, what is the total for a 3-week period?*
- **Twice:** *Twice the value of some number.*

Divide

- **Quotient:** *The final quotient is . . .*
- **Divided by:** *Some number divided by 12 is . . .*
- **Divided into:** *The group was divided into . . .*
- **Ratio:** *What is the ratio of . . .?*
- **Half:** *Half the profits are . . .*

As you work a variety of word problems, you will discover more key words.

Distance Problems

Distance (motion) problems use the distance formula:

$$d = r \times t \text{ (total distance = average rate} \times \text{total time)}$$

To help you set up the equation, use a visual illustration like the chart below. Just fill in the information from the word problem to help you organize the given information.

	Distance (d)	=	Rate (r)	×	Time (t)
Vehicle A		=		×	
Vehicle B		=		×	

Three common types of distance problems are as follows:

- **Basic distance problems.** This type of problem is expressed in a straightforward statement. It asks you to solve for time (t). For example, if a vehicle is traveling at 60 mph, how long will it take to travel 150 miles?

$$150 = 60 \times t$$

Another version of this problem will show that two vehicles leave from the same starting point, but travel in opposite directions. This version asks you to solve for the time (t) that it takes for two vehicles to be a certain distance apart.

- **Distance (two vehicles leave at different times).** This type of problem shows that two or more vehicles are traveling in the same direction from the same starting point, but leave at different times.

  In these distance problems, you will be adding time to the vehicle that started first (t + time). Ask yourself, "How much time has elapsed when the two vehicles are at the same point?"

- **Distance (a tailwind or headwind that forces the rate of speed to increase or decrease).** This type of question often shows an airplane, ship, bicycle, or other vehicle starting and ending at the same point (round-trip that encounters the force of a tailwind or headwind). Since this problem involves a force on the vehicle, the rate (r) of speed at which the vehicle travels is affected; therefore, you will need to adjust the rate in the equation. If the force is pushing the vehicle (tailwind), you will add this to the rate. If the force is hindering the vehicle (headwind), you will subtract this from the rate.

Sometimes, a distance problem may ask you what the rate of speed of the vehicle would be if there were no forces influencing the speed. When the influencing force is the same in both directions, the answer is the mean (average) of the two rates.

Example:

An airplane is flying to a destination at a rate of speed of 175 mph with a tailwind of 25 mph. On the return trip, the airplane has a rate of speed of 125 mph with a headwind of 25 mph. What would the rate of speed of the airplane be if there is no wind factor?

$$\frac{175 + 125}{2} = 150 \, \text{mph}$$

Practice: Distance Problems

1. How many miles will a speedboat travel going 80 mph for $2\frac{1}{2}$ hours?

2. How long will it take a car averaging 55 mph to travel a distance of 594 miles?

3. What is the average speed of a train (in miles per hour) if it takes 3 complete days to travel 3,600 miles?

4. A plane flies from New York to Chicago (a distance of 1,600 miles) at 400 mph. Returning from Chicago to New York, it flies into a headwind and averages only 320 mph. How many hours total was the plane in the air for the entire trip?

5. Frank rows a boat at 5 mph but travels a distance of only 7 miles in 2 hours. How fast was the current moving against him?

6. How long will it take a bus traveling 72 km/hr to travel 36 kilometers?

Answers: Distance Problems

1. First, circle what you must find: *how many miles (distance)*. Now, using the information given in the problem, plug into the equation:

$$d = rt$$
$$d = 80 \times 2.5$$
$$d = 200 \text{ miles}$$

Thus, the speedboat will travel 200 miles.

2. First, circle what you must find: *how long will it take (time)*. Now, using the information given in the problem, plug into the equation:

$$d = rt$$
$$594 = 55 \times t$$
$$\frac{594}{55} = \frac{55 \times t}{55}$$
$$10.8 = t$$

Therefore, it will take 10.8 hours, or 10 hours and 48 minutes.

3. First, circle what you must find: *average speed (rate)*. Note that the time is given to you in days, but because you're looking for an answer in terms of miles per hour, you need to convert those 3 days to hours. With 24 hours in a day, 3 days equal 72 hours. Now, using the information given in the problem, plug into the equation.

$$d = rt$$
$$3,600 = r \times 72$$
$$\frac{3,600}{72} = \frac{r \times 72}{72}$$
$$50 = r$$

The average speed of the train is 50 mph.

4. First, circle what you must find: *how many hours was the plane in the air (time) round-trip*. Note that this is a two-part question, because the time each way will be different. First, to find the time going to Chicago (t_1) and returning to New York (t_2), set up a visual chart.

	Distance (*d*)	=	Rate (*r*)	×	Time (*t*)
To Chicago	1,600	=	400	×	t_1
Return to New York	1,600	=	320	×	t_2

$$1,600 = 400t_1$$
$$1,600 = 320t_2$$

Solve for t in each equation and add them together.

$$d = rt$$
$$1,600 = 400 \times t_1$$
$$\frac{1,600}{400} = \frac{400 \times t_1}{400}$$
$$4 = t_1$$

Thus, it took 4 hours to fly from New York to Chicago. Now, returning to New York:

$$d = rt$$
$$\frac{1,600}{320} = \frac{320 \times t_2}{320}$$
$$5 = t_2$$

Because returning took 5 hours of flying time, the total time in the air was 4 hours + 5 hours = 9 hours.

5. First, circle what you must find: *how fast was the current moving against him (rate)*. Using the information given in the problem, plug into the equation. Note that Frank traveled 7 miles in 2 hours.

$$d = rt$$
$$7 = r \times 2$$
$$3.5 = r$$

Therefore, Frank's actual speed in the water was $3\frac{1}{2}$ mph. If Frank rows at 5 mph, to find the current against him simply subtract:

$$\text{Frank's speed} - \text{actual speed in water} = \text{speed of the current}$$
$$5 \text{ mph} - 3.5 \text{ mph} = 1.5 \text{ mph}$$

The current was going 1.5 mph against him.

6. First, circle what you must find: *how long will it take (time)*. Now, using the information given in the problem, plug into the equation:

$$d = rt$$
$$36 = 72t$$
$$\frac{36}{72} = \frac{72t}{72}$$
$$\frac{1}{2} = t$$

Therefore, it will take $\frac{1}{2}$ hour (or 30 minutes) for the bus to travel 36 kilometers at 72 km/hr.

Work Problems

Work problems are another version of distance/rate/time problems, but in place of "distance," substitute the word "work." Work problems involve how much time it takes to complete a job, the number of tasks completed in a certain amount of time, the number of products produced in a certain amount of time, or the time it takes for two or more people to "work together" on the same job. These types of problems can be easily calculated by using this formula:

$$\text{total work accomplished } (w) = \text{average rate } (r) \times \text{total time } (t)$$

To find the time it would take for two people working together, take the product of the two times and divide by the sum of the two times.

$$\frac{1}{\text{first's person's time}} + \frac{1}{\text{second's person's time}} = \frac{1}{\text{time together}}$$

Example:

Ernie can plow a field alone in 4 hours. It takes Sid 5 hours to plow the same field alone. If they work together (and each has a plow), how long should it take to plow the field?

First, circle what you must find: *how long . . . together.* Now, using the information given in the problem, plug into the equation:

$$\frac{1}{\text{Ernie's time}} + \frac{1}{\text{Sid's time}} = \frac{1}{\text{time together}}$$

$$\frac{1}{4} + \frac{1}{5} = \frac{1}{t}$$

Find a common denominator:

$$\frac{5}{20} + \frac{4}{20} = \frac{1}{t}$$

$$\frac{9}{20} = \frac{1}{t}$$

Cross multiply:

$$9t = 20$$

$$\frac{9t}{9} = \frac{20}{9} = 2\frac{2}{9} \text{ hours}$$

Therefore, it will take Ernie and Sid $2\frac{2}{9}$ hours working together to plow the field.

Practice: Work Problems

1. Tom can mow Harry's lawn in exactly 3 hours. Bill can mow Harry's lawn in exactly 6 hours. If Harry hires Bill and Tom to work together using two lawn mowers, how long should it take to mow the lawn working together?

2. Tom can paint a house in 8 hours. Dick can paint the same house in 6 hours. Harry can also paint the same house in 6 hours. How long should it take to paint the house if they all work together?

3. Working alone, Bill can do a job in 4 hours. With Fred's help, it takes only $2\frac{2}{9}$ hours. How long should it take Fred working alone to do the job?

4. A tank is being filled at a rate of 10 gallons per hour. However, a hole in the tank allows water to run off at a rate of 2 gallons per hour. How long should it take to fill an empty 50-gallon tank?

5. Sue, Maria, and Lucy decide to type Lucy's term paper. Sue can type three pages per hour, Lucy can type five pages per hour, and Maria can type six pages per hour. If Lucy's paper consists of 30 pages, how long should it take them working together to type the entire paper?

Answers: Work Problems

1. First, circle what you must find: *how long . . . together.* Now, using the information given in the problem, plug into the equation:

$$\frac{1}{\text{Tom's time}} + \frac{1}{\text{Bill's time}} = \frac{1}{\text{time together}}$$

$$\frac{1}{3} + \frac{1}{6} = \frac{1}{t}$$

$$\frac{2}{6} + \frac{1}{6} = \frac{1}{t}$$

$$\frac{3}{6} = \frac{1}{t}$$

$$\frac{1}{2} = \frac{1}{t}$$

Cross multiply:

$$t = 2$$

It should take Tom and Bill 2 hours working together to mow Harry's lawn.

2. First, circle what you must find: *how long . . . together.* Now, using the information given in the problem, plug into the equation:

$$\frac{1}{\text{Tom's time}} + \frac{1}{\text{Dick's time}} + \frac{1}{\text{Harry's time}} = \frac{1}{\text{time together}}$$

$$\frac{1}{8} + \frac{1}{6} + \frac{1}{6} = \frac{1}{t}$$

$$\frac{3}{24} + \frac{4}{24} + \frac{4}{24} = \frac{1}{t}$$

$$\frac{11}{24} = \frac{1}{t}$$

Cross multiply:

$$11t = 24$$

$$\frac{11t}{11} = \frac{24}{11}$$

$$t = 2\frac{2}{11} \text{ hours}$$

Therefore, it should take Tom, Dick, and Harry $2\frac{2}{11}$ hours working together to paint the house.

295

3. First, circle what you must find: *how long . . . Fred . . . alone.* Now, using the information given in the problem, plug into the equation:

$$\frac{1}{\text{Bill's time}} + \frac{1}{\text{Fred's time}} = \frac{1}{\text{time together}}$$

$$\frac{1}{4} + \frac{1}{x} = \frac{1}{2\frac{2}{9}}$$

$$\frac{1}{4} + \frac{1}{x} = \frac{1}{\frac{20}{9}}$$

$$\frac{1}{4} + \frac{1}{x} = \frac{9}{20}$$

$$\frac{1}{x} = \frac{9}{20} - \frac{1}{4}$$

$$\frac{1}{x} = \frac{9}{20} - \frac{5}{20}$$

$$\frac{1}{x} = \frac{4}{20}$$

Cross multiply:

$$4x = 20$$

$$x = 5 \text{ hours}$$

Therefore, it should take Fred 5 hours working alone to do the job.

4. First, circle what you must find in the problem: *how long . . . to fill an empty 50-gallon tank.* Note that, because the hole allows water to leave at 2 gallons per hour, the tank is being filled at only $10 - 2 = 8$ gallons per hour. Therefore, a 50-gallon tank will take $\frac{50}{8} = 6\frac{1}{4}$, or 6.25 hours to fill.

5. First, circle what you must find in the problem: *how long . . . working together.* In this type of problem, their combined rate may be found by *adding* their pages typed each hour:

$$3 + 5 + 6 = 14 \text{ pages typed each hour}$$

Now, simply divide 30 by 14 and you get $2\frac{2}{14}$ or $2\frac{1}{7}$ hours.

Therefore, together it should take Sue, Maria, and Lucy $2\frac{1}{7}$ hours to type Lucy's term paper.

Mixture Problems

Mixture problems, like distance problems, can be solved by using a chart to organize the given information. Depending on the type of mixture problem, different organizing charts can be used.

Example:

Coffee worth $1.05 per pound is mixed with coffee worth 85¢ per pound to obtain 20 pounds of a mixture worth 90¢ per pound. How many pounds of each type are used?

First, circle what you must find: *how many pounds of each type.* Now, let the number of pounds of $1.05 coffee be denoted as x. Therefore, the number of pounds of 85¢-per-pound coffee must be the difference between the 20 pounds and the x pounds, or $20 - x$. Make a chart for the cost of each type and the total cost:

	Cost per Pound	Amount in Pounds	Total Cost of Each
$1.05 coffee	$1.05	x	$1.05x$
85¢ coffee	$0.85	$20 - x$	$0.85(20 - x)$
Mixture	$0.90	20	$0.90(20)$

Now, set up the equation:

$$\underbrace{\text{Total cost of one type}}_{\$1.05x} \quad \underbrace{\text{plus}}_{+} \quad \underbrace{\text{total cost of other type}}_{0.85(20-x)} \quad \underbrace{\text{equals}}_{=} \quad \underbrace{\text{total cost of mixture.}}_{0.90(20)}$$

$$1.05x + 17.00 - 0.85x = 18.00$$
$$17.00 + 0.20x = 18.00$$
$$-17.00 + 17.00 + 0.20x = 18.00 - 17.00$$
$$0.20x = 1.00$$
$$\frac{0.20x}{0.20} = \frac{1.00}{0.20}$$
$$x = 5$$

Therefore, 5 pounds of coffee worth $1.05 are used, and $20 - x = 20 - 5 = 15$ pounds of 85¢-per-pound coffee are used.

Practice: Mixture Problems

1. Tea worth 75¢ per pound is mixed with tea worth 90¢ per pound to produce 10 pounds of a mixture worth 85¢ per pound. How much of each type is used?

2. One solution is 75% saltwater and another solution is 50% saltwater. How many gallons of each should be used to make 10 gallons of a solution that is 60% saltwater?

3. Ms. Gomez invests $1,000. She puts part of it in a bank that pays 8% interest and the remainder in a bank that pays 10% interest annually. If her total interest income for 1 year was $94, how much has she invested at each rate?

4. Ellen has collected nickels and dimes worth a total of $6.30. If she has collected 70 coins in all and each is worth face value, how many of each kind does she have?

5. At a game, adult tickets sold for $2.50 and children's tickets sold for $1.50. If 400 tickets were sold and the income was $900, how many of each type were sold?

Answers: Mixture Problems

1. First, circle what you must find: *how much of each type.* Now, let the number of pounds of 75¢ tea be denoted by x. The number of pounds of 90¢ tea is what's left of the total or $10 - x$. Next, set up a chart.

	Cost per Pound	Amount in Pounds	Total Cost of Each
75¢ tea	$0.75	x	0.75x
90¢ tea	$0.90	$(10 - x)$	0.90(10 − x)
Mixture	$0.85	10	10(0.85)

Now, set up the equation:

$$\underbrace{\text{Total cost of one type}}_{0.75x} \quad \underbrace{\text{plus}}_{+} \quad \underbrace{\text{total cost of other type}}_{0.90(10-x)} \quad \underbrace{\text{equals}}_{=} \quad \underbrace{\text{total cost of mixture.}}_{10(0.85)}$$

$$0.75x + 9 - 0.90x = 8.5$$
$$-0.15x + 9 - 9 = 8.5 - 9$$
$$-0.15x = -0.5$$
$$\frac{-0.15x}{-0.15} = \frac{-0.5}{-0.15}$$
$$x = 3\frac{1}{3}$$

Therefore, $3\frac{1}{3}$ pounds of the 75¢ tea are used. The amount of the 90¢ tea used is

$$10 - x = 10 - 3\frac{1}{3} = 6\frac{2}{3} \text{ pounds.}$$

2. First, circle what you must find: *how many gallons of each.* Now, let the number of gallons of 75% saltwater be x. The remainder of the amount of the 50% solution will be what's left from the total of 10 gallons or $10 - x$. Next, set up a chart:

	Rate	Amount of Solution	Amount of Salt
75% solution	0.75	x	0.75x
50% solution	0.50	$(10 - x)$	0.50(10 − x)
Mixture	0.60	10	0.60(10)

Now, set up the equation:

$$\underbrace{\text{Salt in one solution}}_{0.75x} \quad \underbrace{\text{plus}}_{+} \quad \underbrace{\text{salt in other solution}}_{0.50(10-x)} \quad \underbrace{\text{equals}}_{=} \quad \underbrace{\text{salt in mixture.}}_{0.60(10)}$$

$$0.75x + 5 - 0.50x = 6$$
$$0.25x + 5 = 6$$
$$0.25x + 5 - 5 = 6 - 5$$
$$0.25x = 1$$
$$\frac{0.25x}{0.25} = \frac{1}{0.25}$$
$$x = 4$$

Therefore, 4 gallons of the 75% saltwater solution are used and $10 - 4 = 6$ gallons of the 50% saltwater solution are used.

3. First, circle what you must find: *how much . . . invested at each rate.* Now, let the amount invested at 8% be denoted as x. The remainder invested at 10% will be $\$1,000 - x$. Next, set up a chart:

Amount Invested	Interest Rate	Interest Income
x	0.08	$0.08x$
$(1,000 - x)$	0.10	$0.10(1,000 - x)$

Now, set up the equation:

$$\underbrace{\text{Interest income from 8\%}}_{0.08x} \quad \underbrace{\text{plus}}_{+} \quad \underbrace{\text{interest income from 10\%}}_{0.10(1,000 - x)} \quad \underbrace{\text{equals}}_{=} \quad \underbrace{\text{total income}}_{94}$$

$$0.08x + 100 - 0.10x = 94$$
$$-0.02x + 100 = 94$$
$$-0.02x + 100 - 100 = 94 - 100$$
$$-0.02x = -6$$
$$\frac{-0.02x}{-0.02} = \frac{-6}{-0.02}$$
$$x = 300$$

Therefore, the amount invested at 8% was $300, and the remainder of the $1,000, or $700, was invested at 10%.

4. First, circle what you must find: *how many of each kind.* Now, let x denote the number of nickels. The remainder of the coins $(70 - x)$ will be the number of dimes. Next, set up a chart:

Type of Coin	Number of Coins	Value of Each Coin	Total Value
Nickels	x	0.05	$0.05x$
Dimes	$(70 - x)$	0.10	$0.10(70 - x)$

Now, set up the equation:

$$\underbrace{\text{Total value of nickels}}_{0.05x} \quad \underbrace{\text{plus}}_{+} \quad \underbrace{\text{total value of dimes}}_{0.10(70 - x)} \quad \underbrace{\text{equals}}_{=} \quad \underbrace{\text{total worth.}}_{6.30}$$

$$0.05x + 7 - 0.10x = 6.30$$
$$-0.05x + 7 = 6.30$$
$$-0.05x + 7 - 7 = 6.30 - 7$$
$$-0.05x = -0.70$$
$$\frac{-0.05x}{-0.05} = \frac{-0.70}{-0.05}$$
$$x = 14$$

Therefore, Ellen has 14 nickels and $70 - 14 = 56$ dimes.

5. First, circle what you must find: *how many of each type.* Now, let x denote the number of adult tickets sold. The remainder $(400 - x)$ will denote the number of children's tickets sold. Next, set up a chart:

Type of Ticket	Number of Tickets	Cost Per Ticket	Income
Adults	x	2.50	$2.50x$
Children	$(400 - x)$	1.50	$1.50(400 - x)$

Now, set up the equation:

$$\underbrace{\text{Income from adult tickets}}_{2.50x} \quad \underbrace{\text{plus}}_{+} \quad \underbrace{\text{income from children's tickets}}_{1.50(400 - x)} \quad \underbrace{\text{equals}}_{=} \quad \underbrace{\text{total income.}}_{900}$$

$$2.50x + 600 - 1.50x = 900$$
$$x + 600 = 900$$
$$x + 600 - 600 = 900 - 600$$
$$x = 300$$

Therefore, 300 adult tickets were sold and $400 - 300 = 100$ children's tickets were sold.

Age Problems

Age problems ask you to find solutions to the chronological age timelines of people: current ages, ages in the past, or ages in the future. Use a visual illustration like the chart below to keep the information organized.

Examples:

Tom and Phil are brothers. Phil is 35 years old. Three years ago, Phil was four times as old as Tom was then. How old is Tom now?

First, circle what you must find: *Tom's age now.* Let t be Tom's age now, which means Tom's age 3 years ago would be $t - 3$. Four times Tom's age 3 years ago would be $4(t - 3)$. Phil's age 3 years ago would be $35 - 3 = 32$. A simple chart may also be helpful.

	Now	3 Years Ago
Phil	35	32
Tom	t	$t - 3$

Now, use the problem to set up an equation:

$$\underbrace{\text{Three years ago}} \quad \underbrace{\text{Phil}}_{32} \quad \underbrace{\text{was}}_{=} \quad \underbrace{\text{four times}}_{4 \text{ times}} \quad \text{as old as his} \quad \underbrace{\text{brother was then.}}_{(t-3)}$$

$$\frac{32}{4} = \frac{4(t-3)}{4}$$
$$8 = t - 3$$
$$8 + 3 = t - 3 + 3$$
$$11 = t$$

Therefore, Tom is 11 years old now.

Lisa is 16 years younger than Kathy. If the sum of their ages is 30, how old is Lisa?

First, circle what you must find: *Lisa's age*. Let Lisa's age equal x, which means Kathy is $x + 16$ years old. (Note that because Lisa is 16 years *younger* than Kathy, you must *add* 16 years to Lisa's age to denote Kathy's age.) Now, use the problem to set up an equation:

$$\underbrace{\overbrace{\text{If the sum of their ages}}^{\text{Lisa} + \text{Kathy}}}_{} \quad \underbrace{\text{is}}_{=} \quad \underbrace{30}_{30} \; \ldots$$

$$x + (x + 16) = 30$$
$$2x + 16 = 30$$
$$2x + 16 - 16 = 30 - 16$$
$$2x = 14$$
$$\frac{2x}{2} = \frac{14}{2}$$
$$x = 7$$

Therefore, Lisa is 7 years old.

Practice: Age Problems

1. Clyde is four times as old as John. If the difference between their ages is 39 years, how old is Clyde?

2. Sylvia is 20 years older than Jan. If the sum of their ages is 48 years, how old is Jan?

3. Sheila is three times as old as Kim. The sum of their ages is 24 years. How old is Sheila?

4. In 8 years, Joy will be three times as old as she is now. How old is Joy now?

5. Matt is 6 years older than Hector. In 2 years, Matt will be twice as old as Hector. How old is Hector now?

Answers: Age Problems

1. First, circle what you must find: *Clyde's age*. Let John's age (the smaller of the two ages) equal x, which means Clyde's age equals $4x$. Now, use the problem to set up an equation:

$$\underbrace{\overbrace{\text{If the difference between their ages}}^{\text{Clyde} - \text{John}}}_{} \quad \underbrace{\text{is}}_{=} \quad \underbrace{39}_{39} \; \ldots$$

$$4x - x = 39$$
$$3x = 39$$
$$\frac{3x}{3} = \frac{39}{3}$$
$$x = 13$$

Therefore, Clyde's age, $4x$, is $4 \times 13 = 52$ years old.

2. First, circle what you must find *Jan's age*. Let Jan's age (the younger of the two ages) equal x, which means Sylvia's age equals $x + 20$. Now, use the problem to set up an equation:

$$\underbrace{\text{If the sum of their ages}}_{\text{Jan + Sylvia}} \underbrace{\text{ is }}_{=} \underbrace{48}_{48} \ldots$$

$$x + (x + 20) = 48$$
$$2x + 20 = 48$$
$$2x + 20 - 20 = 48 - 20$$
$$2x = 28$$
$$\frac{2x}{2} = \frac{28}{2}$$
$$x = 14$$

Therefore, Jan is 14 years old.

3. First, circle what you must find: *Sheila's age*. Let Kim's age (the younger of the two ages) equal x, which means Sheila's age equals $3x$. Now, use the problem to set up an equation:

$$\underbrace{\text{The sum of their ages}}_{\text{Shelia + Kim}} \underbrace{\text{ is }}_{=} \underbrace{24}_{24} \ldots$$

$$3x + x = 24$$
$$4x = 24$$
$$\frac{4x}{4} = \frac{24}{4}$$
$$x = 6$$

Therefore, Sheila's age, $3x$, is $3 \times 6 = 18$ years old.

4. First, circle what you must find: *Joy's age now*. You may want to set up a chart for this problem.

	Now	In 8 Years
Joy	x	$x + 8$

Let Joy's age now equal x, so Joy's age 8 years from now will be $x + 8$. Now, use the problem to set up an equation:

$$\underbrace{\text{In 8 years, Joy}}_{x+8} \underbrace{\text{ will be }}_{=} \underbrace{\text{three}}_{3} \underbrace{\text{ times }}_{\text{times}} \text{ as } \underbrace{\text{old as she is now.}}_{x}$$

$$x + 8 - x = 3x - x$$
$$8 = 2x$$
$$\frac{8}{2} = \frac{2x}{2}$$
$$4 = x$$

Therefore, Joy is 4 years old now.

5. First, circle what you must find: *Hector's age now.* Let Hector's age now equal x, which means Matt's age now equals $x + 6$. You may want to set up a chart.

	Now	In 2 Years
Hector	x	$x + 2$
Matt	$x + 6$	$x + 8$

Now, use the problem to set up an equation:

$$\underbrace{\text{In 2 years, Matt}}_{x+8} \ \ \underbrace{\text{will be}}_{=} \ \ \underbrace{\text{twice}}_{2 \text{ times}} \text{ as old as } \underbrace{\text{Hector.}}_{x+2}$$

$$x + 8 = 2x + 4$$
$$x + 8 - x = 2x + 4 - x$$
$$8 = x + 4$$
$$8 - 4 = x + 4 - 4$$
$$4 = x$$

Therefore, Hector is 4 years old now.

Number Problems: Integers

Integer problems usually involve consecutive integers, consecutive even integers, or consecutive odd integers. If you let x represent any integer, $x + 1$ would represent the next larger integer, $x + 2$ would be the next larger after that, and then $x + 3$, and so on.

Examples:

One number exceeds another number by 5. If the sum of the two numbers is 39, find the smaller number.

First, circle what you must find: *the smaller number.* Let the smaller number equal x, so the larger number equals $x + 5$. Now, use the problem to set up an equation:

$$\underbrace{\text{If the sum of the two numbers}}_{x+(x+5)} \ \ \underbrace{\text{is}}_{=} \ \ \underbrace{39}_{39} \ \ ...$$

$$2x + 5 = 39$$
$$2x + 5 - 5 = 39 - 5$$
$$2x = 34$$
$$\frac{2x}{2} = \frac{34}{2}$$
$$x = 17$$

Therefore, the smaller number is 17.

If one number is three times as large as another number and the smaller number is increased by 19, the result is 6 less than twice the larger number. What is the larger number?

First, circle what you must find: *the larger number.* Let the smaller number equal x, so the larger number will be $3x$. Now, use the problem to set up an equation:

The $\underbrace{\text{smaller number}}_{x}$ $\underbrace{\text{increased by}}_{+}$ $\underbrace{19}_{19}$ $\underbrace{\text{is}}_{=}$ $\underbrace{\text{6 less than twice the larger number.}}_{2(3x)-6}$

$$x+19=6x-6$$
$$-x+x+19=-x+6x-6$$
$$19=5x-6$$
$$19+6=5x-6+6$$
$$25=5x$$
$$5=x$$

Therefore, the larger number, $3x$, will be $3 \times 5 = 15$.

The sum of three consecutive integers is 306. What is the largest integer?

First, circle what you must find: *the largest integer.* Let the smallest integer equal x; let the next integer equal $x + 1$; let the largest integer equal $x + 2$. Now, use the problem to set up an equation:

$\underbrace{\text{The sum of three consecutive integers}}_{x+(x+1)+(x+2)}$ $\underbrace{\text{is}}_{=}$ $\underbrace{306.}_{306}$

$$3x+3=306$$
$$3x+3-3=306-3$$
$$3x=303$$
$$\frac{3x}{3}=\frac{303}{3}$$
$$x=101$$

Therefore, the largest integer, $x + 2$, will be $101 + 2 = 103$.

Practice: Integer Problems

1. The sum of three consecutive integers is 51. What is the largest integer?

2. The sum of three consecutive even integers is 612. What is the smallest integer?

3. Two integers total 35. One integer is 23 larger than the other. What are the two integers?

4. The difference between $\frac{1}{2}$ of a number and $\frac{1}{3}$ of the same number is 8. What is the number?

5. If one number is twice as large as another number and the smaller number is increased by 8, the result is 4 less than the larger number. What is the larger number?

Answers: Integer Problems

1. First, circle what you must find: *the largest integer.* Let the consecutive integers equal x, $x + 1$, and $x + 2$. Now, use the problem to set up an equation:

$$\underbrace{\text{The sum of three consecutive integers}}_{x+(x+1)+(x+2)} \underbrace{\text{is}}_{=} \underbrace{51.}_{51}$$

$$3x + 3 = 51$$
$$3x + 3 - 3 = 51 - 3$$
$$3x = 48$$
$$\frac{3x}{3} = \frac{48}{3}$$
$$x = 16$$

Therefore, the largest integer, $x + 2$, will be $16 + 2 = 18$.

2. First, circle what you must find: *the smallest integer.* Let the three integers equal x, $x + 2$, and $x + 4$ (because consecutive even numbers increase by 2). Now, use the problem to set up an equation.

$$\underbrace{\text{The sum of three consecutive even integers}}_{x+(x+2)+(x+4)} \underbrace{\text{is}}_{=} \underbrace{612.}_{612}$$

$$3x + 6 = 612$$
$$3x + 6 - 6 = 612 - 6$$
$$3x = 606$$
$$\frac{3x}{3} = \frac{606}{3}$$
$$x = 202$$

Therefore, the smallest integer, x, is 202.

3. First, circle what you must find: *the two integers.* Let the smaller integer equal x, and the larger integer equals $x + 23$. Now, use the problem to set up an equation:

$$\underbrace{\text{Two integers}}_{x+(x+23)} \underbrace{\text{total}}_{=} \underbrace{35.}_{35}$$

$$2x + 23 = 35$$
$$2x + 23 - 23 = 35 - 25$$
$$2x = 12$$
$$\frac{2x}{2} = \frac{12}{2}$$
$$x = 6$$

Therefore, one integer, x, is 6 and the other integer, $x + 23$, is 29.

4. First, circle what you must find: *the number.* Let the number equal x. Now, use the problem to set up an equation:

The difference between $\dfrac{1}{2}$ of a number and $\dfrac{1}{3}$ of the same number $\quad$ is $\quad$ 8.

$$\left(\frac{1}{2}\right)x - \left(\frac{1}{3}\right)x$$

$$\frac{x}{2} - \frac{x}{3} = 8$$

Using a common denominator:

$$\frac{3x}{6} - \frac{2x}{6} = 8$$

$$\frac{x}{6} = 8$$

$$(6)\frac{x}{6} = (6)8$$

$$x = 48$$

The number is 48.

5. First, circle what you must find: *the larger number.* Let x denote the smaller number, which means the larger number will be $2x$ because it is twice as large as x. Now, use the problem to set up an equation:

If the smaller number is increased by 8, $\quad$ the result $\quad$ is 4 less than the larger number.

$$x + 8 \qquad\qquad = \qquad\qquad 2x - 4$$

$$-x + x + 8 = 2x - x - 4$$

$$8 = x - 4$$

$$8 + 4 = x - 4 + 4$$

$$12 = x$$

Therefore, the larger number, $2x$, is 24.

Number Problems: Simple Interest

Simple interest problems ask you to calculate either the interest paid on a loan or the interest earned on an investement over a specific period of time. Use the following formula for simple interest:

Simple interest (I) = principal (p) × rate (r) × time (t)

Examples:

How much simple interest will an account earn in 5 years if $500 is invested at 8% interest per year?

First, circle what you must find: *simple interest.* Use the following simple interest equation:

$$I = prt$$

Simply plug into the equation:

$$I = \$500 \times 0.08 \times 5$$
$$I = \$200$$

Note that both rate and time are in yearly terms (annual rate and years).

What is the simple interest on a $6,000 loan at a 3% semiannual rate over 5 years?

First, circle what you must find: *simple interest.* Note that the 3% rate is a "semiannual rate." Before plugging numbers into the *I = prt* equation, you have to change the rate to an annual rate. Semiannual means "every half-year," so the annual rate is twice 3%, or 6%.

$$I = prt$$
$$I = \$6,000 \times 0.06 \times 5$$
$$I = \$1,800$$

Hence, the simple interest is $1,800.

Practice: Simple Interest Problems

1. What is the simple interest on $5,000 invested at an annual rate of 6% over 4 years?

2. What is the simple interest on a loan of $10,000 at a 6.5% annual rate over 5 years?

3. What is the simple interest on $4,000 at a 4% semiannual rate over 3 years?

4. A woman invests $30,000 in a mutual fund that pays 3% quarterly. What is her simple interest dividend for 9 months?

5. An investment group receives $3,600 simple interest for a 3-year investment of $10,000. If the interest rate has remained stable throughout the investment period, what simple interest rate is the group receiving?

Answers: Simple Interest Problems

1. First, circle what you must find: *simple interest.* Now, using the information given in the problem, plug into the equation:

$$I = prt$$
$$I = \$5,000 \times 0.06 \times 4$$
$$I = \$1,200$$

Therefore, the simple interest is $1,200.

2. First, circle what you must find: *simple interest.* Now, using the information given in the problem, plug into the equation:

$$I = prt$$
$$I = \$10,000 \times 0.065 \times 5$$
$$I = \$3,250$$

Therefore, the simple interest is $3,250.

3. First, circle what you must find: *simple interest.* However, note that the 4% figure is a *semiannual* rate. Before plugging numbers into the $I = prt$ equation, you have to change the rate to an annual rate. Because *semiannual* means "every half-year," the annual rate would be twice 4%, or 8%.

$$I = prt$$
$$I = \$4,000 \times 0.08 \times 3$$
$$I = \$960$$

Therefore, the simple interest is $960.

4. First, circle what you must find: *simple interest dividend for 9 months.* However, note that the 3% rate is a quarterly rate; thus, the annual rate would be 4 × 3% or 12%. Also, note that the time is 9 months, or $\frac{3}{4}$ of a year. Using this information, plug into the equation:

$$I = prt$$
$$I = \$30,000 \times 0.12 \times \frac{3}{4}$$
$$I = \$2,700$$

Therefore, simple interest for 9 months is $2,700.

5. First, circle what you must find: *simple interest rate.* Now, plug into the equation:

$$I = prt$$
$$\$3,600 = \$10,000 \times r \times 3$$
$$\frac{\$3,600}{3} = \frac{\$10,000 \times r \times 3}{3}$$
$$\$1,200 = \$10,000r$$
$$\frac{\$1,200}{\$10,000} = \frac{\$10,000r}{\$10,000}$$
$$0.12 = r$$

Therefore, the simple interest rate is 12%.

Number Problems: Compound Interest

Compound interest is often used instead of simple interest because simple interest is not realistic in everyday scenarios. Compound interest is added to the original principal loan so that the additional interest also earns interest. Use the following formula for compound interest for the total future value:

$$\text{Future Value Amount} = \text{Principal}\left(1 + \frac{\text{interest rate}}{\text{frequency number per year}}\right)^{\text{frequency} \times \text{number of years}}$$

$$A = P\left(1 + \frac{r}{n}\right)^{(n)(t)}$$

To find the value of the interest earned, use the above equation and subtract the principal from the future value amount.

Example:

What will be the final value after 3 years on an original investment of $1,000 if a 12% annual interest rate is compounded yearly?

First, circle what you must find: *final value.* For this problem, $r = 0.12$, $n = 1$, $t = 3$ and $P = 1,000$.

$$A = P\left(1 + \frac{r}{n}\right)^{(n)(t)}$$

$$A = \$1,000\left(1 + \frac{0.12}{1}\right)^{(1)(3)}$$

$$A = \$1,000(1.12)^3$$

$$A = \$1,000(1.404928)$$

$$A = \$1,404.93 \text{ (rounded to the nearest cent)}$$

The final value after 3 years will be $1,404.93.

Practice: Compound Interest Problems

1. Find the total interest on $140 at a 5% annual rate for 2 years if interest is compounded annually.

2. Dana deposited $1,000 in the Great Island Bank for her trip to Tahiti. If interest is compounded annually at 8%, how much will be in her account at the end of 2 years?

3. If the beginning balance of a savings account is $200 and interest is paid semiannually at a 5% semiannual rate, what is the ending balance after 2 years?

4. Arnie invests $5,000 in a stock that pays dividends of 20% annually. Arnie always reinvests his dividends into his stock. How much stock value will Arnie have after 4 years?

5. Stacy invests $3,000 for 3 years at an annual rate of 8%. Find her total after 3 years if the interest is compounded annually.

Answers: Compound Interest Problems

1. First, circle what you must find: *total interest.* Now, use the compound interest formula.

$$A = P\left(1 + \frac{r}{n}\right)^{(n)(t)}$$

$$A = \$140\left(1 + \frac{0.05}{1}\right)^{(1)(2)}$$

$$A = \$140(1.05)^2$$

$$A = \$140(1.1025)$$

$$A = \$154.35$$

The total interest would be the difference between the total amount (A) and the initial investment (P). Hence, $154.35 - $140 = $14.35 total interest.

2. First, circle what you must find: *how much will be in her account after 2 years* (or the total principal after 2 years). Now, use the compound interest formula.

$$A = P\left(1 + \frac{r}{n}\right)^{(n)(t)}$$

$$A = \$1{,}000\left(1 + \frac{0.08}{1}\right)^{(1)(2)}$$

$$A = \$1{,}000(1.08)^2$$

$$A = \$1{,}000(1.1664) = \$1{,}166.40$$

Therefore, there will be \$1,166.40 in the account at the end of 2 years.

3. First, circle what you must find: *the ending balance after 2 years.* Note that interest is paid semiannually. That means that $n = 2$ for this problem, and since r is the annual interest rate, $r = 10\%$. Therefore,

$$A = P\left(1 + \frac{r}{n}\right)^{(n)(t)}$$

$$A = \$200\left(1 + \frac{0.10}{2}\right)^{(2)(2)}$$

$$A = \$200(1.05)^4$$

$$A = \$200(1.215506251)$$

$$A = \$243.10 \ (\text{rounded to the nearest cent})$$

Therefore, the ending balance is \$243.10 after 2 years.

4. First, circle what you must find: *how much stock . . . after 4 years* (total). Arnie will have:

$$A = P\left(1 + \frac{r}{n}\right)^{(n)(t)}$$

$$A = \$5{,}000\left(1 + \frac{0.20}{1}\right)^{(1)(4)}$$

$$A = \$5{,}000(1.2)^4$$

$$A = \$5{,}000(2.0736) = \$10{,}368$$

Therefore, after 4 years, Arnie will have \$10,368 worth of stock.

5. First, circle what you must find: *total after 3 years.* Stacy will have:

$$A = P\left(1 + \frac{r}{n}\right)^{(n)(t)}$$

$$A = \$3{,}000\left(1 + \frac{0.08}{1}\right)^{(1)(3)}$$

$$A = \$3{,}000(1.08)^3$$

$$A = \$3{,}000(1.259712)$$

$$A = \$3{,}779.14 \ (\text{rounded to the nearest cent})$$

Therefore, Stacy will have a total of \$3,779.14 after 3 years.

Number Problems: Percentage

Percentage word problems are one of the most common types of real-world scenario problems on standardized tests. This type of question will test your ability to analyze situations as you find the percentage of a given number. As you use the following formula for percentage problems, keep in mind that the word "of" simply means to multiply.

1. Use x to replace the unknown value.
2. Replace *is* with an *equal sign* (=) and replace *of* with *multiplication.*

$$\frac{\%\text{-number}}{100} = \frac{\text{``is''-number}}{\text{``of''-number}}$$

Example:

Thirty students are awarded doctoral degrees at a graduate school, and this number comprises 40% of the total graduate student body. How many graduate students were enrolled?

First, circle what you must find: *how many graduate students.* The percentage equation is as follows:

$$\frac{\text{is}}{\text{of}} = \%$$

Try rephrasing the question into a simple sentence. For example, in this case 30 is 40% of what total?

Before attempting to solve a percentage problem, change the percent to a fraction or decimal, depending upon what seems appropriate.

Note that the 30 sits next to the word *is;* therefore, 30 is the "is" number; the percent is 40. Notice that *what total* sits next to the word *of.* Using this information, plug into the equation

$$\frac{\text{is}}{\text{of}} = \%$$

$$\frac{30}{x} = \frac{40}{100}$$

Cross multiply:

$$40x = 3,000$$

$$\frac{40x}{40} = \frac{3,000}{40}$$

$$x = 75$$

Therefore, 75 graduate students were enrolled.

Practice: Percentage Problems

1. In a school of 300 students, 60 do not sign up for after-school sports. What percent of the students in the school signs up for after-school sports?

2. In order to pass an exam, a student must correctly answer at least nine questions in order to receive the minimum passing grade of 75%. How many questions are on the exam?

3. Seventy million Americans are registered voters. Sixty percent are registered Democrats, and the rest are either uncommitted or are registered as "Other." If 10 percent of the total registered voters are uncommitted, how many registered voters are registered as Other?

4. Fifty-five percent of 800 people polled answered vanilla when asked their favorite ice-cream flavor. What percent of those polled answered chocolate as their favorite?

5. A 200-square-yard playground is to be constructed. Exactly 40% must be grass, 30% must be sand, and the remaining percentage must be asphalt. What are the square-yard specifications for grass, sand, and asphalt?

6. A U.S. postage-stamp collection was offered for sale at a stamp show for $800 but went unsold. Its owner resubmitted the collection for sale at the next stamp show but dropped his asking price 30%. The collection, however, still did not sell, so the owner offered an additional discount of 25% off the new asking price. What was the final price of the postage-stamp collection?

Answers: Percentage Problems

1. First, circle what you must find: *what percent . . . signs up.* Now, using the information given in the problem, plug into the equation. Note that since 60 students do *not* sign up for after-school sports, the number that *does* sign up must be the total number of students minus 60, or 300 − 60 = 240 students. The problem may now be reworded as *240 students is what percent of 300.*

$$\frac{is}{of} = \%$$

$$\frac{240}{300} = \frac{x}{100}$$

Cross multiply:

$$24,000 = 300x$$

$$\frac{24,000}{300} = \frac{300x}{300}$$

$$80 = x$$

Therefore, 80% of the students in the school signs up for after-school sports.

2. First, circle what you must find: *how many questions are on the examination.* To plug into the equation, this problem may be reworded as *nine questions is 75% of how many questions.* Now, plug in the numbers:

$$\frac{is}{of} = \%$$

$$\frac{9}{x} = \frac{75}{100}$$

Cross multiply:

$$900 = 75x$$

$$\frac{900}{75} = \frac{75x}{75}$$

$$12 = x$$

Therefore, there are 12 questions on the test.

3. First, circle what you must find: *how many . . . are registered as Other.* Note that if 60% are Democrats and 10% are uncommitted, then 30% must be registered as Other. Now you may restate the question as *how much is 30% of 70 million voters.* Now, plug into the equation:

$$\frac{\text{is}}{\text{of}} = \%$$

$$\frac{x}{70 \text{ million}} = \frac{30}{100}$$

Cross multiply:

$$100x = 2{,}100 \text{ million}$$

$$x = 21 \text{ million}$$

In this problem, because you're finding 30% of 70 million, you could simply multiply: 0.30×70 million = 21 million. Therefore, there are 21 million voters registered as Other.

4. Be careful. Note here that just because 55% like vanilla, that doesn't mean that *all* the remaining 45% like chocolate. There are many ice-cream flavors to choose from, and the remaining 45% could be divided among chocolate, strawberry, pistachio, and so on. Thus, there is not enough information to determine an answer. This type of question appears occasionally.

5. Note that this "three-part" question may be rephrased as:

   - For the grass, what is 40% of 200?
   - For the sand, what is 30% of 200?
   - For the asphalt, what is 30% of 200? (30% is the remaining percentage for the asphalt.)

   Using the equation, for the grass:

$$\frac{\text{is}}{\text{of}} = \%$$

$$\frac{x}{200} = \frac{40}{100}$$

Cross multiply:

$$100x = 8{,}000$$

$$x = 80 \text{ square yards of grass}$$

For the sand:

$$\frac{x}{200} = \frac{30}{100}$$

Cross multiply:

$$100x = 6{,}000$$

$$x = 60 \text{ square yards of sand}$$

For the asphalt: 60 square yards of asphalt (because the percentage of asphalt is the same as the percentage of sand).

6. The original price was $800. A 30% drop in price is 30% of 800 = 0.30×800 = $240 off, so the new price is $800 – $240 = $560. Because the collection still did not sell (at $560), an additional 25% discount was offered:

$$25\% \text{ of } \$560 = 0.25 \times 560 = \$140 \text{ off}$$

Therefore, the final asking price is $560 – $140 = $420.

Number Problems: Percent Change

Percent change problems show an increase or decrease in values. When percent changes are viewed on a line graph, you can see that a percentage increase is "rising upward" and a percentage decrease is "falling downward."

Percent change (percent increase, percentage rise, percent difference, percent decrease, and so on) is always found by using the following equation:

$$\text{percent change} = \frac{\text{change}}{\text{starting point}}; \text{ then convert to a percent}$$

Example:

Last year, Harold earned $250 a month at his after-school job. This year, his after-school earnings have increased to $300 per month. What is the percent increase in his monthly after-school earnings?

First, circle what you must find: *percent increase.*

Plug the information from the problem into the equation.

$$\text{percent change} = \frac{\text{change}}{\text{starting point}}; \text{ then convert to a percent}$$

$$= \frac{\$300 - \$250}{\$250}$$

$$= \frac{\$50}{\$250}$$

$$= \frac{1}{5} = 0.20, \text{ or } 20\%$$

The percent increase in Harold's after-school salary is 20%.

Practice: Percent Change Problems

1. Last year, Hank's income was $49,000. This year it rose to $56,000. What was the percent increase in Hank's salary? (Round your answer to the nearest tenth of one percent.)

2. A 5-year study showed that the population of Hicksville, New York, fell from 65,000 in 1975 to 48,750 in 1980. What was the percent decrease in population over those 5 years?

3. Last year's Dow Jones Index averaged 13,500. This year's index averaged 16,200. What was the percentage rise in the average Dow Jones Index over those years?

4. Economic indicators predict 12% inflation over the next 12 months. If that's true, how much must a $20,000 salary be increased to keep up with inflation?

5. Due to 5% inflation, a woman's monthly salary was increased $800 to exactly keep up with the economy. What is the woman's new monthly salary? (***Hint:*** First find her initial monthly salary.)

Answers: Percent Change Problems

1. First, circle what you must find: *percent increase.* Now, using the information given in the problem, plug into the equation:

$$\text{percent increase} = \frac{\text{change}}{\text{starting point}}; \text{ then convert to a percent}$$

$$= \frac{\$56,000 - \$49,000}{\$49,000}$$

$$= \frac{\$7,000}{\$49,000}$$

$$= 0.1428, \text{ or } 14.3\% \text{ (rounded to the nearest tenth of one percent)}$$

The percent increase was 14.3%.

2. First, circle what you must find: *percent decrease.* Now, using the information given in the problem, plug into the equation:

$$\text{percent decrease} = \frac{\text{change}}{\text{starting point}}; \text{ then convert to a percent}$$

$$= \frac{65,000 - 48,750}{65,000}$$

$$= \frac{16,250}{65,000}$$

$$= 0.25, \text{ or } 25\%$$

The percent decrease was 25%. Note that the fact that the study was a 5-year study had no bearing on the answer.

3. First, circle what you must find: *percentage rise.* Now, using the information given in the problem, plug into the equation:

$$\text{percentage rise} = \frac{\text{change}}{\text{starting point}}; \text{ then convert to a percent}$$

$$= \frac{16,200 - 13,500}{13,500}$$

$$= \frac{2,700}{13,500}$$

$$= 0.20, \text{ or } 20\%$$

The percentage rise in the average Dow Jones Index was 20%.

4. First, circle what you must find: *how much must a . . . salary be increased.* Now, using the information given in the problem, you could simply multiply: $0.12 \times \$20,000 = \$2,400$. Or, if you want to plug into the standard equation:

$$\text{percent increase} = \frac{\text{change}}{\text{starting point}}; \text{ then convert to a percent}$$

$$12\% = \frac{x}{\$20,000}$$

$$\frac{0.12}{1} = \frac{x}{\$20,000}$$

$$0.12 \times \$20,000 = x$$

$$\$2,400 = x$$

The salary must be increased $2,400 to keep up with inflation.

5. First, circle what you must find: *new monthly salary.* Now, using the information given in the problem, plug into the equation:

$$\text{percent increase} = \frac{\text{change}}{\text{starting point}}; \text{ then convert to a percent}$$

$$5\% = \frac{\$800}{x}$$

$$\frac{0.05}{1} = \frac{\$800}{x}$$

$$0.05x = \$800$$

$$\frac{0.05x}{0.05} = \frac{\$800}{0.05}$$

$$x = \$16,000$$

Thus, $16,000 is her *starting* monthly salary. Adding the change of $800 (increase), her *new* monthly salary is $16,800.

Ratio and Proportion Problems

Ratio and proportional relationship word problems commonly appear on standardized tests and are part of the Common Core Standards. Remember that a *ratio* is a comparison of two quantities and is usually written as a fraction. For example, the ratio of 2 to 3 can be expressed as 2:3 or $\frac{2}{3}$. A *proportion* is an equation that states that two ratios are equal. Because $\frac{5}{10}$ and $\frac{4}{8}$ both have values of $\frac{1}{2}$, it can be stated that $\frac{5}{10} = \frac{4}{8}$ or $\frac{5}{10}$ is proportional to $\frac{4}{8}$.

Example:

If Arnold can type 600 pages of manuscript in 21 days, how many days will it take him to type 230 pages if he works at the same rate?

First, circle what you must find: *how many days.* One simple way to work this problem is to set up a framework (proportion) using the categories given in the equation. For this problem, the categories are pages and days, so a framework may be:

$$\frac{\text{pages}}{\text{days}} = \frac{\text{pages}}{\text{days}}$$

Note that you also may have used:

$$\frac{\text{days}}{\text{pages}} = \frac{\text{days}}{\text{pages}}$$

To use these frameworks, notice that both the numerators and denominators must be consistent. They are either pages or numbers. The first ratio is what you are given in the problem. The second ratio contains only partial information.

The answer will still be the same. Now, simply plug into the equation:

$$\frac{600}{21} = \frac{230}{x}$$

Cross multiply:

$$600x = 21 \times 230$$
$$600x = 4,830$$
$$\frac{600x}{600} = \frac{4,830}{600}$$
$$x = 8\frac{1}{20}$$

Therefore, it will take Arnold 8 days, 1 hour, and 12 minutes $\left(8\dfrac{1}{20} \text{ days}\right)$ to type 230 pages.

Practice: Ratio and Proportion Problems

1. A map's key shows that 1 inch = 35 miles. How many inches apart on the map will two cities be if they are exactly 7 miles apart?

2. If 8 pounds of apples cost 98¢, how much will 12 pounds of apples cost?

3. If a girl can run m miles in h hours, how long will it take her to run k miles at the same rate of speed?

4. It takes q hours to drain a pool containing x gallons of water. If the pool contains y gallons of water, how long will it take to drain the pool?

5. In 6 years, a man was able to build 58 violins. Considering that he works at the same speed, how many complete violins can he build in 11 years?

Answers: Ratio and Proportion Problems

1. First, circle what you must find: *how many inches apart.* Now, using the information given in the problem, construct a framework for a proportion and then plug into the equation:

$$\frac{\text{miles}}{\text{inches}} = \frac{\text{miles}}{\text{inches}}$$

$$\frac{35}{1} = \frac{7}{x}$$

Cross multiply:

$$35x = 7$$

$$\frac{35x}{35} = \frac{7}{35}$$

$$x = \frac{1}{5}$$

The two cities will be $\frac{1}{5}$ of an inch apart.

2. First, circle what you must find: *how much will 12 pounds of apples cost.* Now, using the information given in the problem, set up a framework for a proportion and then plug into the equation:

$$\frac{\text{pounds}}{\text{price}} = \frac{\text{pounds}}{\text{price}}$$

$$\frac{8}{98\cancel{c}} = \frac{12}{x}$$

Cross multiply:

$$8x = 98 \times 12$$

$$\frac{8x}{8} = \frac{1,176}{8}$$

$$x = 147\cancel{c}$$

Twelve pounds of apples will cost 147¢ or $1.47.

3. First, circle what you must find: *how fast will she run k miles* (how many hours). Now, using the information given in the problem, set up a framework for a proportion and then plug into the equation:

$$\frac{\text{miles}}{\text{hours}} = \frac{\text{miles}}{\text{hours}}$$

$$\frac{m}{h} = \frac{k}{x}$$

Cross multiply:

$$mx = kh$$

$$\frac{mx}{m} = \frac{kh}{m}$$

$$x = \frac{kh}{m} \text{ or } \frac{hk}{m}$$

It will take her $\dfrac{kh}{m}$ or $\dfrac{hk}{m}$ hours to run k miles.

4. First, circle what you must find: *how long* (time). Now, using the information given in the problem, set up a proportion and then plug into the equation:

$$\frac{\text{hours}}{\text{gallons}} = \frac{\text{hours}}{\text{gallons}}$$

$$\frac{q}{x} = \frac{?}{y}$$

Cross multiply:

$$qy = x(?)$$

$$\frac{qy}{x} = \frac{x(?)}{x}$$

$$\frac{qy}{x} \text{ or } \frac{yq}{x} = ?$$

It will take $\dfrac{qy}{x}$ or $\dfrac{yq}{x}$ hours to drain y gallons of water.

Careful: Notice that because x was in the problem, we used ? for the unknown quantity.

5. First, circle what you must find: *how many complete violins* (note the word *complete*). Now, using the information given in the problem, set up a proportion and then plug into the equation:

$$\frac{\text{violins}}{\text{years}} = \frac{\text{violins}}{\text{years}}$$

$$\frac{58}{6} = \frac{x}{11}$$

Cross multiply:

$$638 = 6x$$

$$\frac{638}{6} = \frac{6x}{6}$$

$$106.33 \approx x$$

He can build 106 complete violins in 11 years.

Graph Interpretation Problems

Graph interpretation word problems (also called *data interpretation*) draw upon your knowledge of reasoning, arithmetic, and data analysis. Visual illustrations of graphs, charts, tables, and diagrams are commonly used to evaluate the numeric values of real-life problems. Visual pictures help to provide a clear picture about the compiled data in order to show patterns and trends and draw conclusions.

Before answering graph interpretation problems, always read the title, labels, and values (if available). The table below highlights the types of graphs you may encounter on standardized tests.

Types of Graphs	
Circle Graph	Circle graphs (also called pie graphs) show comparisons and are used to show relative proportions (fractions) of a whole circle. They are especially good visual representations of percentage problems. For example, a circle graph shows the relationship between a whole circle (100%) and portions (slices) of a circle called *sectors*. The size of each sector compared to the whole circle represents the ratio of the individual categories to the whole circle.
Bar Graph	A bar graph (also called a *histogram*) is commonly used to quickly compare data or frequencies. The bars (columns) can be either vertical or horizontal and can appear as single bars, a group of bars, or stacked bars. The bars should be labeled to indicate the differences between the various categories.
Line Graph	In a line graph, the line represents increases or decreases in data information as points on a two-dimensional coordinate system. This type of graph provides a good visual picture of changes or trends in data values and can be valuable in hypothesizing predictions over time.
Charts and Tables	A chart or table is often used to organize data in a more readable and organized format. Charts often help to effectively view multiple values of data simultaneously, making it easier to compare and compute *averages* or *ranges*.
Venn Diagrams	A Venn diagram is a useful method to visually represent two or more sets and to illustrate whether or not the sets have any elements in common. Sets are generally represented as circles or ovals, but other geometric figures can be used. Sets that have elements in common will overlap, while sets that have no elements in common are shown disjointed from each other.

Circle Graph

Example:

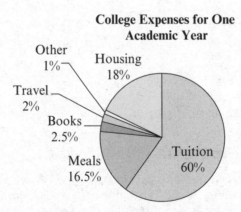

College Expenses for One Academic Year

According to the graph above, what is the ratio of the amount spent on housing to the amount spent on tuition?

The circle graph shows a comparison of a student's college expenses for one academic year. Since housing accounted for 18% of college expenses and tuition accounted for 60%, the ratio of the amount spent on housing to the amount spent on tuition is $\frac{18}{60} = \frac{3}{10}$.

Line Graph

Example:

The graph below shows the average miles per gallon for a hybrid-powered car versus a standard gasoline-powered car at speeds ranging from 0 to 50 mph.

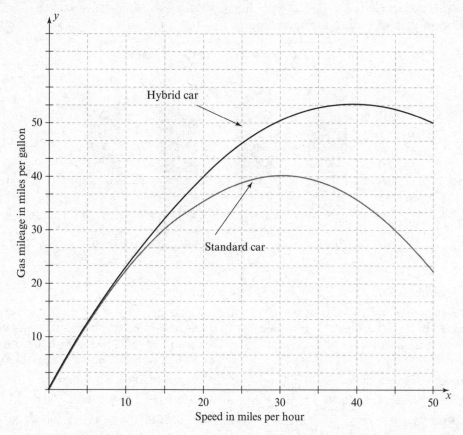

According to the line graph, if each vehicle is driven at a speed of 30 mph for 2 hours, the fuel used by the standard gasoline-powered car is what percent of the fuel used by the hybrid-powered car?

The fuel used by each car is found by dividing the distance in miles it travels by the miles per gallon. At 30 mph, for 2 hours, each car travels 60 miles. The amount of fuel the hybrid uses is $\frac{60 \text{ mi}}{50 \text{ mi/gal}} = 1.2$ gallons. The amount of fuel the standard car uses is $\frac{60 \text{ mi}}{40 \text{ mi/gal}} = 1.5$ gallons.

The question now becomes, 1.5 is what percent of 1.2?

$$\frac{1.5}{1.2} \times 100\% = \frac{\overset{5}{\cancel{1.5}}}{\underset{4}{\cancel{1.2}}} \times 100\% = 125\%$$

A simplified solution is to first notice that because they both travel at the same rate of speed for the same amount of time, their distances are equal. Given equal distance traveled, simply look at the chart and compare the mpg at the 30 mph speed they each traveled: The hybrid's 50 mpg is 125% of the standard's 40 mph.

Bar Graph

Examples:

Four departments in a company, A, B, C, and D, are responsible for sales of the four different products, W, X, Y, and Z, that the company sells. The stacked bar graph that follows shows the sales records of units sold by each of the four departments. During the reporting period represented in the graph, the company sold the same number of units of each of the four products.

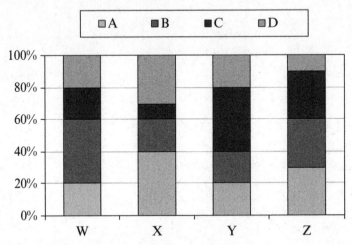

Which department sold 25% of all units sold by the company?

The total number of units sold is not given, but you know that the number of units sold for each product is the same. For ease of computation, assume that 100 units of each product were sold by the company. This gives a total of 400 units for the four products. The number of units sold by each department can be calculated. If the total units sold is 400, the units sold by each department would be the following:

Units sold by Department A: 20% of 100 + 40% of 100 + 20% of 100 + 30% of 100 = 110

Units sold by Department B: 40% of 100 + 20% of 100 + 20% of 100 + 30% of 100 = 110

Units sold by Department C: 20% of 100 + 10% of 100 + 40% of 100 + 30% of 100 = 100

Units sold by Department D: 20% of 100 + 30% of 100 + 20% of 100 + 10% of 100 = 80

The percentage sold by Department C is 25% of 400.

If Department B sold 30 units of product X, how many units of product Z did Department C sell?

Department B sold 20% of the total units of product X. If this is 30 units, the total number of units sold of product X must be 150. Since the total number of units sold of each product is the same, 150 units of product Z were sold by the company. Since Department C sold 30% of the units sold of product Z, Department C sold 45 units of product Z.

Venn Diagram

Example:

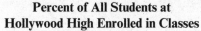

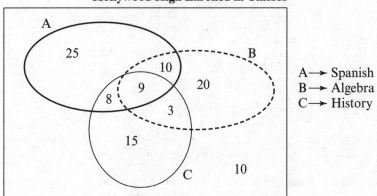

A → Spanish
B → Algebra
C → History

What percent of all the students at Hollywood High are not enrolled in history?

Assumptions: In this Venn diagram, region A represents the percent of the students at Hollywood High who are taking Spanish, region B represents the percent of students at Hollywood High taking algebra, and region C represents the percent of students at Hollywood High taking history.

Only looking at region A and the regions it overlaps, we can draw the following conclusions from the diagram:

- 25% of the students at Hollywood High take Spanish but do not take either algebra or history
- 10% of the students at Hollywood High take Spanish and algebra, but not history
- 9% of the students at Hollywood High take Spanish, algebra, and history
- 8% of the students at Hollywood High take Spanish and history, but not algebra

One approach to help you answer this question is to take the percentage of students who are enrolled in history and subtract it from 100%. Another approach is to add the percentages indicated outside of history and be sure to add in the 10% who are not taking any of the three classes.

According to the diagram, 8% + 9% + 3% + 15% = 35% of the students are taking history; therefore, 100% − 35% = 65% of the students are not taking history.

Geometry Word Problems

Geometry word problems ask you to draw conclusions using math and deductive reasoning skills to measure angles, perimeter, area, surface area, and volume.

Tip: In this section, we show you how to solve geometry word problems algebraically. However, sometimes it is helpful to draw the shapes and label them with the given information.

Example:

If a rectangle's length is twice its width and its area is 200 square inches, find its length and width.

First, circle what you must find: *length and width.* Now, let x denote the rectangle's width; its length will be twice the width or $2x$. Now, set up an equation:

$$\underbrace{\text{Width}}_{(x)} \cdot \underbrace{\text{length}}_{(2x)} \underbrace{\text{equals}}_{=} \underbrace{\text{area.}}_{200}$$

$$2x^2 = 200$$

$$\frac{2x^2}{2} = \frac{200}{2}$$

$$x^2 = 100$$

$$x = 10 \text{ and } 2x = 20$$

Therefore, the width is 10 inches and the length is 20 inches.

Practice: Geometry Word Problems

1. In a triangle, the smallest angle is 20° less than the largest angle. The third angle is 10° more than the smallest angle. What is the measure of each angle?

2. The length of a rectangle is 6 inches less than four times the width. If the perimeter of the rectangle is 28 inches, find its length and width.

3. Each of the equal sides of an isosceles triangle is 5 inches more than twice the third side. If the perimeter of the triangle is 45 inches, find the length of the sides of the triangle.

4. One angle of a triangle is 44°. The second angle is 4° larger than the third angle. How many degrees are in the measure of the other two angles?

5. Find the measure of the sides of a rectangle if the length is 5 inches longer than the width and the perimeter is 50 inches.

Answers: Geometry Word Problems

1. First, circle what you must find: *the measure of each angle.* Let the largest angle be known as x. Therefore, the smallest angle, because it is 20° less than the largest, will be $x - 20$. The third angle is 10° more than the smallest, or $x - 20 + 10$, which equals $x - 10$. ***Remember:*** There are 180° in a triangle. Now, set up the equation:

$$\underbrace{\text{The sum of the degrees in each angle of a triangle}}_{x + (x - 20) + (x - 10)} \underbrace{\text{equals}}_{=} \underbrace{180°.}_{180}$$

$$3x - 30 = 180$$

$$3x - 30 + 30 = 180 + 30$$

$$3x = 210$$

$$\frac{3x}{3} = \frac{210}{3}$$

$$x = 70$$

The largest angle is 70°; the smallest angle is $70 - 20 = 50°$; the third angle is $70 - 10 = 60°$.

2. First, circle what you must find: *length and width.* Now, let x denote the width of the rectangle; its length will be $4x - 6$ (6 less than four times the width). The perimeter of the rectangle equals 28 inches. Now, set up the equation:

$$\underbrace{2\text{ widths}}_{2x} \underbrace{\text{plus}}_{+} \underbrace{2\text{ lengths}}_{2(4x-6)} \underbrace{\text{equals}}_{=} \underbrace{28}_{28} \text{ inches.}$$

$$2x + 8x - 12 = 28$$
$$10x - 12 = 28$$
$$10x - 12 + 12 = 28 + 12$$
$$10x = 40$$
$$\frac{10x}{10} = \frac{40}{10}$$
$$x = 4$$

Therefore, the width of the rectangle is 4 inches; the length of the rectangle, $4x - 6$, is $(4 \times 4) - 6 = 10$ inches.

3. First, circle what you must find: *sides of the triangle.* Now, let x denote the length of the third side. Therefore, each of the equal sides will be $2x + 5$. Now, set up the equation:

$$\underbrace{\text{The sum of the sides of a triangle}}_{x+(2x+5)+(2x+5)} \underbrace{\text{equals}}_{=} \underbrace{\text{the perimeter.}}_{45}$$

$$5x + 10 = 45$$
$$5x + 10 - 10 = 45 - 10$$
$$5x = 35$$
$$\frac{5x}{5} = \frac{35}{5}$$
$$x = 7$$

Therefore, one side is 7 inches, and the other two sides are $2x + 5$ each or $(2 \times 7) + 5 = 19$ inches each.

4. First, circle what you must find: *the other two angles.* Now, let the third angle be denoted as x; the second angle will be $x + 4$. Now, set up the equation:

$$\underbrace{\text{The sum of the angles in a triangle}}_{44+x+(x+4)} \underbrace{\text{equals}}_{=} \underbrace{180°.}_{180}$$

$$2x + 48 = 180$$
$$2x + 48 - 48 = 180 - 48$$
$$2x = 132$$
$$\frac{2x}{2} = \frac{132}{2}$$
$$x = 66$$
$$x + 4 = 70$$

Therefore, the other two angles of the triangle are 66° and 70°.

5. First, circle what you must find: *the measure of the sides.* Let the width be denoted as x; the length will be $x + 5$. Now, set up the equation:

$$\underbrace{2 \text{ widths}}_{2x} \quad \underbrace{\text{plus}}_{+} \quad \underbrace{2 \text{ lengths}}_{2(x+5)} \quad \underbrace{\text{equals}}_{=} \quad \underbrace{\text{the perimeter.}}_{50}$$

$$2x + 2x + 10 = 50$$
$$4x + 10 = 50$$
$$4x + 10 + 10 = 50 - 10$$
$$4x = 40$$
$$\frac{4x}{4} = \frac{40}{4}$$
$$x = 10$$

Therefore, the width is 10 inches and the length is $x + 5 = 15$ inches.

Word and Graph Interpretation Problems Review Test

Questions

1. What is the simple interest on a loan of $5,000 for 8 years at an annual interest rate of 14%?

2. If a woman earns $2,000 simple interest over 4 years on an investment of $5,000, what is the annual interest rate she receives?

3. Mr. Lincoln deposits $4,000 in a savings account that pays 12% annually, but interest is compounded quarterly. What is the total in his account after 1 year? (*Remember:* 3% interest will be paid each quarter.)

4. If Jim can bake 27 pies in 12 days, how many pies can he bake in 20 days?

5. If p pencils cost k cents, at the same price how much will q pencils cost?

6. How long will it take a train traveling at an average speed of 80 miles per hour to travel a distance of 5,600 miles?

7. Two automobiles, A and B, leave at the same time and travel the same route. Automobile A goes at a rate of 55 miles per hour. Automobile B travels at a rate of 40 miles per hour. How many hours after they begin their trip will automobile A be 60 miles ahead of automobile B?

8. Mrs. Baum won $5,600 on a television quiz show. If she has to pay 20% of her winnings to the Internal Revenue Service, how much of her winnings will she have left?

9. A prized Amazon yellow nape parrot is placed on sale for $900 at a bird show. It doesn't sell immediately, so its owner discounts the bird 30%. When the parrot still does not interest any buyers, the owner offers another 20% discount off the new price. What is the final price of the bird?

10. Last year's Los Angeles Dodgers attendance was 2,800,000. This year's attendance was 3,200,000. What was the Dodgers' percent increase in attendance? (Round your answer to the nearest tenth of one percent.)

11. If Arnold's 2016 salary reflects a percent drop of 15% from the previous year, what was his 2016 salary if in 2015 he earned $60,000?

12. Three consecutive odd integers add up to total 33. What is the smallest of the three integers?

13. A green flag costs ten times the price of a blue flag. A red flag costs half the price of a green flag. An orange flag costs $10 less than a red flag. If the four different color flags cost a total of $200, what is the price of an orange flag?

14. Judith is exactly 18 years older than Brad. If today the sum of their ages is 52, how old will Brad be in 1 year?

15. Carol is 7 years older than Lynn. Ann is twice as old as Lynn, and her mother is 65. If the total age of all four persons is 116, how old was Lynn 5 years ago?

16. One angle of a triangle is twice as big as the smallest angle, and the third angle is three times as big as the smallest angle. What are the measures of the three angles of the triangle?

17. If in quadrilateral $ABCD$, side AB is twice side BC, side BC is twice side CD, and side CD is twice side DA, what is the length of side DA if the perimeter of $ABCD$ is 75 inches?

18. Bob can cut a lawn in 4 hours. Bette can cut the same lawn in 3 hours. If they both use lawn mowers and work together, how long should it take them to cut the lawn?

19. Gina can build a house in 12 months alone. Bart can build a house in 6 months alone. How long should it take them to build a house if they work together?

20. A chemistry teacher has 2 quarts of 25% acid solution and 1 quart of 40% acid solution. If she mixes the solutions, what will be the concentration of acid in the final mixture?

21. Programs sell at a baseball game for $2 each, and scorecards sell for 75¢ each. If a total of 200 items was sold (programs *and* scorecards) for a cash income of $250, how many of each were sold?

Answers

Page numbers following each answer refer to the review section applicable to the problem type.

1. $5,600 (p. 306)

2. 10% (p. 306)

3. $4,502.04 (p. 308)

4. 45 pies (p. 316)

5. $\dfrac{qk}{p}$ or $\dfrac{kq}{p}$ (p. 316)

6. 70 hours (p. 290)

7. 4 hours (p. 290)

8. $4,480 (p. 290)

9. $504 (p. 314)

10. approximately 14.3% (p. 314)

11. $51,000 (p. 314)

12. 9 (p. 303)

13. $40 (p. 303)

14. 18 years old (p. 300)

15. 6 years old (p. 300)

16. 30°, 60°, 90° (p. 323)

17. 5 inches (p. 323)

18. $1\dfrac{5}{7}$ hours (p. 293)

19. 4 months (p. 293)

20. 30% acid concentration (p. 296)

21. 80 programs, 120 scorecards (p. 296)

Word and Graph Interpretation Problems Glossary of Terms

annual: Once per year.

average: The arithmetic mean calculated by adding all the numbers in the data set and dividing by how many numbers you added.

balance: Beginning balance is the principal in interest problems. Ending balance is the principal plus interest accrued.

biannual: Twice per year or every 6 months.

compounded: In interest problems, the interest is to be added to the principal at specific intervals and used in the computation of the next interest amount.

consecutive: What comes immediately after. For example, consecutive numbers are 1, 2, 3, 4, and so on. Consecutive odd numbers are 1, 3, 5, 7, 9, and so on.

data interpretation: Evaluating numeric and categorical information found in graphs, charts, and tables. This can include statistical trends and patterns.

dividend: In interest problems, the amount of interest paid.

equation: A number sentence with a balance relationship between numbers or symbols.

evaluate: To determine the value or numerical amount.

percentage change: Expressed also as percent rise, percent difference, percent increase, percent decrease, percent drop, and so on. Found by dividing the actual amount of change by the numerical starting point and then converting to a percent.

principal: The amount of money invested or loaned upon which interest is paid.

quarterly: Four times per year or every 3 months.

range: The difference between the highest and the lowest numbers in a data set.

rate: How fast an object moves (speed). Rate is measured in miles per hour (mph), feet per second (fps), cost per item, and so on.

ratio: A comparison between items. For example, the ratio of 2 to 3 may be written as 2:3 or $\frac{2}{3}$.

semiannual: Twice per year or every 6 months.

simple interest: Interest calculated by multiplying the principal with the interest rate with the length of time of the investment, $I = prt$.

speed: The rate at which an object moves.

value: The numerical amount.

velocity: The speed, or rate, at which an object moves.

Chapter 6

Mathematical Reasoning

Mathematical Reasoning Strategies

Mathematical reasoning problems are a standard question type appearing on many different examinations. Typically, you must answer a question or solve an equation using the information given in the problem and your knowledge of mathematics. Complex computation is usually not required. Common Core math emphasizes multi-procedural problems usually involving real-world circumstances or solving problems that examine the relationships of quantities derived from written narratives. To be successful at solving multi-step problems, break each question up into manageable parts.

Question Types

Mathematical reasoning problems are presented and organized within specific question types for all computer- and paper-administered standardized tests. Most standardized test questions contain four to five answer choices, from which you must choose one answer choice. However, some questions require you to select one or more answer choices from the choices listed. Other questions ask you to type or fill in your answer response. For multiple-answer problems, if you do not mark *all* of the correct answer choices, you will not be given credit for a correct response. There is no partial credit.

Specific instructions about question types are detailed on each test administrator's website. Carefully read and follow the directions related to each question type before answering the question. The importance of understanding the question types cannot be overstated. Research has shown that there is a significant increase in score results when test-takers learn the test format and directions prior to taking the exam.

Common Types of Computer-Based and Paper-Based Questions

Question Type	How Computer-Based Questions May Appear	
Multiple-choice question (select one answer choice)	Ovals	⬭
Multiple-choice question (select one or more answer choices)	Square box	☐
Numeric entry question (fill in your numeric answer)	Rectangular box	▭
Numeric entry question (fill in your fractional answer)	Two stacked boxes	▭ / ▭

Information Provided in the Test Booklet

On many standardized exams (e.g., SAT, PSAT, and CBEST), some basic mathematical formulas and information may be provided. Although this information may appear at the beginning of the test, you should already have a working knowledge of these facts even if you haven't completely committed them to memory.

Data That May Be Used as Reference for the Test

- The area formula for a circle of radius r is $A = \pi r^2$.
- The circumference formula is $C = 2\pi r$.
- A circle is composed of 360°.
- A straight angle measures 180°.

Triangles:

- The sum of the angles of a triangle is 180°.
- If $\angle ADB$ is a right angle, then

    - The area of triangle ABC is $\dfrac{AC \times BD}{2}$
    - $AD^2 + BD^2 = AB^2$

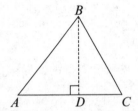

Symbol References

$=$ is equal to

$\neq$ is not equal to

$>$ is greater than

$<$ is less than

$\geq$ is greater than or equal to

$\leq$ is less than or equal to

$\parallel$ is parallel to

$\perp$ is perpendicular to

$\approx$ is approximately equal to

Suggested Approaches with Examples

Here are a number of approaches that can be helpful in attacking many types of mathematics problems. These strategies will not work on *all* problems, but if you become familiar with them, you'll find they'll be helpful in answering quite a few questions.

Mark or Write Down Key Words

Circling, underlining, or writing down key words in each question is an effective test-taking technique. Many times, you may be misled because you overlooked a key word in a problem. By circling or writing down these key words, you'll help yourself focus on what you're being asked to find. ***Remember:*** For paper-based tests, you are allowed to mark and write on your testing booklet. For computer-based tests, you are given a writing board or scratch paper. Take advantage of this feature.

Examples:

In the following number, which digit is in the ten-thousandths place?

$$56,874.12398$$

Ⓐ   5
Ⓑ   7
Ⓒ   2
Ⓓ   3
Ⓔ   9

The key word here is *ten-thousandths.* By circling or writing it down, you'll be paying closer attention to it. This is the kind of question which, under time pressure and testing pressure, may be easily misread as *ten-thousands* place. Your circling or writing down the important words will minimize the possibility of misreading them. Your completed question may look like this after you mark the important words or terms:

Which (digit) is in the (ten-thousandths) place?

56,874.123⑨8

The answer is 9, choice E.

If 6 yards of ribbon cost $3.96, what is the price per foot?
Ⓐ $0.22
Ⓑ $0.66
Ⓒ $1.32
Ⓓ $1.96
Ⓔ $3.96

The key word here is *foot.* Dividing $3.96 by 6 will tell you only the price per *yard*, which is $0.66. (Notice that $0.66 is one of the answer choices, choice B.) However, to answer the question asked, you must still divide by 3 (since there are 3 feet in a yard) to find the cost per foot: $0.66 ÷ 3 = $0.22, which is choice A. As you can see, for this problem, it would be very helpful to circle or write down the words *price per foot.*

If $3x + 1 = 16$, what is the value of $x - 4$?
Ⓐ   −1
Ⓑ   1
Ⓒ   5
Ⓓ   16
Ⓔ   19

331

The key here is to find the value of $x - 4$. Therefore, circle or write down "$x - 4$." Note that solving the original equation will tell only the value of x:

$$3x + 1 = 16$$
$$3x = 15$$
$$x = 5$$

Here again, notice that 5 is one of the answer choices, choice C. But the question asks for the value of $x - 4$, not just x. To continue, replace x with 5 and solve:

$$x - 4 =$$
$$5 - 4 = 1$$

The correct answer is choice B.

Together, a hat and gloves cost \$125. The gloves cost \$25 more than the hat. What is the cost of the gloves?

Ⓐ \$25
Ⓑ \$50
Ⓒ \$75
Ⓓ \$100
Ⓔ \$125

The key words here are *cost of the gloves,* so circle those words. If you solve this algebraically:

$$x = \text{the cost of the hat}$$
$$x + 25 = \text{the cost of the gloves (costs \$25 more than the hat)}$$

Together they cost \$125.

$$(x + 25) + x = 125$$
$$2x + 25 = 125$$
$$2x = 100$$
$$x = 50$$

But this is the cost of the *hat.* Notice that \$50 is one of the answer choices, choice B. Because $x = 50$, $x + 25 = 75$. Therefore, the gloves cost \$75, choice C. *Always answer the question that is being asked.* Circling or writing down the key word or words will help you do that.

Pull Out Information

Pulling information out of a word problem can make the problem more workable for you. Pull out the given facts and identify which of those facts will help you work the problem. Not all facts will always be needed to solve the problem.

Examples:

Bill is 10 years older than his sister. If Bill was 25 years old in 2003, in what year could he have been born?

Ⓐ   1968

Ⓑ   1973

Ⓒ   1978

Ⓓ   1983

Ⓔ   1988

The key words here are *in what year could he have been born.* Thus the solution is simple: $2003 - 25 = 1978$, choice C. Notice that you pulled out the information *25 years old in 2003.* The fact about Bill's age in comparison to his sister's age was not needed to solve the problem and was not pulled out.

Bob is 20 years old. He works for his father for $\frac{3}{4}$ of the year, and he works for his brother for the rest of the year. What is the ratio of the time Bob spends working for his brother to the time he spends working for his father per year?

Ⓐ $\frac{1}{4}$

Ⓑ $\frac{1}{3}$

Ⓒ $\frac{3}{4}$

Ⓓ $\frac{4}{3}$

Ⓔ $\frac{4}{1}$

The key words *rest of the year* point to the answer:

$1 - \frac{3}{4} = \frac{4}{4} - \frac{3}{4} = \frac{1}{4}$ (the part of the year Bob works for his brother)

Also, a key is the way in which the ratio is to be written. The problem becomes that of finding the ratio of $\frac{1}{4}$ to $\frac{3}{4}$:

$$\frac{\frac{1}{4}}{\frac{3}{4}} = \frac{1}{4} \div \frac{3}{4} = \frac{1}{\cancel{4}} \times \frac{\cancel{4}}{3} = \frac{1}{3}$$

Therefore, the answer is choice B. Note that Bob's age is not needed to solve the problem.

Sometimes you may not have sufficient information to solve the problem.

Examples:

The average rainfall for the first few months of 2017 was 4 inches. The next month's average rainfall was 5 inches. What was the average rainfall per month for all those months?

Ⓐ   4 inches

Ⓑ $4\dfrac{1}{4}$ inches

Ⓒ $4\dfrac{1}{2}$ inches

Ⓓ $4\dfrac{3}{4}$ inches

Ⓔ   not enough information

To calculate an average, you must find the total amount and then divide by the number of items. The difficulty here, however, is that *first few months* does not specify exactly *how many* months averaged 4 inches. Does *few* mean two? Or does it mean three? *Few* is not a precise mathematical term. Therefore, there is not enough information to pull out to calculate an average. The answer is choice E.

If gasahol is $\dfrac{2}{9}$ alcohol by volume and $\dfrac{7}{9}$ gasoline by volume, what is the ratio of the volume of gasoline to the volume of alcohol?

Ⓐ $\dfrac{2}{9}$

Ⓑ $\dfrac{2}{7}$

Ⓒ $\dfrac{7}{9}$

Ⓓ $\dfrac{7}{2}$

Ⓔ $\dfrac{9}{2}$

The first bit of information that you should pull out should be what you are looking for, *ratio of the volume of gasoline to the volume of alcohol.* Let G stand for gasoline and A stand for alcohol. Rewrite it as $G{:}A$ and then write it in its mathematical working form, $\dfrac{G}{A}$. Next, you should pull out the volumes of each: $G = \dfrac{7}{9}$ and $A = \dfrac{2}{9}$. Now the answer can be easily figured by inspection or substitution. Using $\dfrac{\frac{7}{9}}{\frac{2}{9}}$, which is the same as $\dfrac{7}{9} \div \dfrac{2}{9}$, invert the second fraction and multiply to get $\dfrac{7}{9} \times \dfrac{9}{2}$. The answer is $\dfrac{7}{2}$ (the ratio of gasoline to alcohol), so the correct answer is choice D.

When pulling out information, actually write out the numbers and/or letters to the side of the problem, putting them into some form and eliminating some of the wording.

Plug in Numbers

When a problem involving *variables* (unknowns or letters) seems difficult and confusing, simply replace those variables with numbers. Simple numbers will make the arithmetic easier for you to do. Usually, problems using numbers are easier to understand. Be sure to make logical substitutions. Use a positive number, a negative number, or zero when applicable to get the full picture.

Examples:

If x is a positive integer in the equation $12x = q$, then q must be

Ⓐ   a positive even integer
Ⓑ   a negative even integer
Ⓒ   zero
Ⓓ   a positive odd integer
Ⓔ   a negative odd integer

At first glance, this problem appears quite complex. But plug in some numbers and see what happens. For example, first plug in 1 (the simplest positive integer) for x:

$$12x = q$$
$$12(1) = q$$
$$12 = q$$

Now try 2:

$$12x = q$$
$$12(2) = q$$
$$24 = q$$

Try it again. No matter what positive integer is plugged in for x, q will always be positive and even. Therefore, the answer is choice A.

If a, b, and c are all positive integers greater than 1 such that $a < b < c$, which of the following is the largest quantity?

Ⓐ $a(b + c)$
Ⓑ $ab + c$
Ⓒ $ac + b$
Ⓓ   they are all equal
Ⓔ   cannot be determined

Substitute 2, 3, and 4 for a, b, and c, respectively:

$a(b+c) =$	$ab+c =$	$ac+b =$
$2(3+4) =$	$2(3)+4 =$	$2(4)+3 =$
$2(7) = 14$	$6+4 = 10$	$8+3 = 11$

Since 2, 3, and 4 meet the conditions stated in the problem and choice A produces the largest numerical value when these numbers are plugged in, choice A will consistently be the largest quantity. Therefore, choice A, $a(b + c)$, is the correct answer. Remember to substitute simple numbers since *you* have to do the work.

If $x > 1$, which of the following decreases as x decreases?

I. $x + x^2$

II. $2x^2 - x$

III. $\dfrac{1}{x+1}$

  Ⓐ   I

  Ⓑ   II

  Ⓒ   III

  Ⓓ   I and II

  Ⓔ   II and III

This problem is most easily solved by substituting simple numbers for x and observing the changes in the values of the different expressions. Recall that you were told that $x > 1$ and it decreases in value.

x	I. $x + x^2$	II. $2x^2 - x$	III. $\dfrac{1}{x+1}$
4	$4 + (4)^2 = 20$	$2(4)^2 - 4 = 28$	$\dfrac{1}{4+1} = \dfrac{1}{5}$
3	$3 + (3)^2 = 12$	$2(3)^2 - 3 = 15$	$\dfrac{1}{3+1} = \dfrac{1}{4}$
2	$2 + (2)^2 = 6$	$2(2)^2 - 2 = 6$	$\dfrac{1}{2+1} = \dfrac{1}{3}$

From the table above, you can observe that, as x decreases, the values for I also decrease, which implies that the final answer must include I. This eliminates choices B, C, and E. As x decreases, the values for II also decrease, which implies that the final answer must include II. Only choice D includes both I and II. Notice that as x decreased, the values for III increased $\left(\dfrac{1}{5} < \dfrac{1}{4} < \dfrac{1}{3}\right)$, which implies the final answer *cannot* contain III, which would have eliminated choices C and E.

Note: This example problem is a multiple-multiple-choice problem. For more on this problem type, see p. 348.

Work from the Answer Choices

Sometimes the solution to a problem will be obvious to you. At other times, it may be helpful to work from the answer choices. This technique is even more efficient when some of the answer choices are easily eliminated.

Examples:

Approximate $\sqrt{1,596}$.

Ⓐ   10
Ⓑ   20
Ⓒ   30
Ⓓ   40
Ⓔ   50

Without the answer choices, this would be a very difficult problem, requiring knowledge of a special procedure to calculate square roots. With the answer choices, however, the problem is easily solvable. How? By working up from the answer choices. Since $\sqrt{1,596}$ means *what number times itself equals 1,596*, you can take any answer choice and multiply it by itself. As soon as you find the answer choice that, when multiplied by itself, approximates 1,596, you've got the correct answer.

But here's another strategy: Start to work up from the middle answer choice. Why? Watch.

Start with choice C, 30. Multiplying it by itself, you get 30 × 30 = 900. Since 900 is too small (you're looking for approximately 1,596), you may eliminate choice C. But notice that you may also eliminate choices A and B because they are also too small.

Working up from the middle choice will often allow you to eliminate more than one answer choice because the answer choices on standardized tests are usually in increasing order. This approach can save you valuable time.

Another way to solve this problem is approximation:

$$\sqrt{1,596} \approx \sqrt{1,600}$$
$$= \sqrt{16}\sqrt{100}$$
$$= 4 \cdot 10$$
$$= 40$$

The correct answer is 40, choice D.

If $\left(\dfrac{x}{4}\right) + 2 = 22$, find x.

Ⓐ   40
Ⓑ   80
Ⓒ   100
Ⓓ   120
Ⓔ   160

If you cannot solve this algebraically, you may use the work from the answer-choices strategy. Again, start with choice C, 100. What if $x = 100$?

$$\left(\frac{x}{4}\right) + 2 = 22$$
$$\left(\frac{100}{4}\right) + 2 \overset{?}{=} 22$$
$$25 + 2 \overset{?}{=} 22$$
$$27 \neq 22$$

Note that since 27 is too large, choices D and E will also be too large. Therefore, try choice A. If choice A is too small, then you know the answer is choice B. If choice A works, the answer is choice A.

$$\left(\frac{x}{4}\right) + 2 = 22$$

$$\left(\frac{40}{4}\right) + 2 \stackrel{?}{=} 22$$

$$10 + 2 \stackrel{?}{=} 22$$

$$12 \neq 22$$

Because choice A is too small, the answer must be choice B.

If Brandon can mow the lawn in 5 hours and Jordan can mow the lawn in 4 hours, how long will it take them to mow the lawn together?

Ⓐ   1 hour

Ⓑ $2\frac{2}{9}$ hours

Ⓒ   4 hours

Ⓓ $4\frac{1}{2}$ hours

Ⓔ   5 hours

Suppose that you aren't familiar with the type of equation for this problem. Try the "reasonable" method. Because Jordan can mow the lawn in 4 hours by himself, you know he'll take less than 4 hours if Brandon helps him. Therefore, choices C, D, and E cannot be correct. Taking this method a little further, suppose that Brandon could also mow the lawn in 4 hours. Then together it would take Brandon and Jordan 2 hours. But, because Brandon is a little slower than Jordan, the total time should be a little more than 2 hours. The correct answer is choice B, $2\frac{2}{9}$ hours. Using the equation for this problem would give the following calculations:

$$\frac{1}{\text{person A's rate}} + \frac{1}{\text{person B's rate}} = \frac{1}{\text{rate together}}$$

$$\frac{1}{4} + \frac{1}{5} = \frac{1}{x}$$

In 1 hour, Brandon could do $\frac{1}{5}$ of the job and in 1 hour Jordan could do $\frac{1}{4}$ of the job; unknown $\left(\frac{1}{x}\right)$ is that part of the job they could do together in 1 hour. Now solving, you calculate as follows:

$$\frac{4}{20} + \frac{5}{20} = \frac{1}{x}$$

$$\frac{9}{20} = \frac{1}{x}$$

Cross multiplying gives $9x = 20$. Therefore, $x = \frac{20}{9}$ or $2\frac{2}{9}$, choice B.

Find the counting number between 11 and 30 that, when divided by 3, has a remainder of 1 but when divided by 4, has a remainder of 2.

Ⓐ 12
Ⓑ 13
Ⓒ 16
Ⓓ 21
Ⓔ 22

By working from the answer choices, you can eliminate wrong answer choices. For example, choices A and C can be immediately eliminated because they are divisible by 4, leaving no remainder. Choices B and D can also be eliminated because they leave a remainder of 1 when divided by 4. Therefore, the correct answer is choice E: 22 leaves a remainder of 1 when divided by 3 and a remainder of 2 when divided by 4.

Approximate

If a problem involves calculations with numbers that seem tedious and time-consuming, scan the answer choices to see if you can round off or approximate those numbers. If so, replace those numbers with numbers that are easier to work with. Find the answer choice closest to your approximated answer.

Examples:

The value for $\dfrac{(0.889 \times 55)}{9.97}$ to the nearest tenth is

Ⓐ 0.5
Ⓑ 4.63
Ⓒ 4.9
Ⓓ 17.7
Ⓔ 49.1

Before starting any computations, take a glance at the answer choices to see how far apart they are. Notice that the only close answer choices are choices B and C, but choice B is not a possible choice because it is to the nearest hundredth, not the nearest tenth. Now, making some quick approximations, $0.889 \approx 1$ and $9.97 \approx 10$, leaving the problem in this form:

$$\frac{1 \times 55}{10} = \frac{55}{10} = 5.5$$

The closest answer choice is choice C; therefore, it is the correct answer. Notice that choices A and E are not reasonable.

The value of $\sqrt{\dfrac{9,986}{194}}$ is approximately

Ⓐ 7
Ⓑ 18
Ⓒ 35
Ⓓ 40
Ⓔ 50

Round off both numbers to the hundreds place. The problem then becomes $\sqrt{\dfrac{10,000}{200}}$. This is much easier to work. By dividing, the problem now becomes $\sqrt{50}$ = slightly more than 7. The closest answer choice is choice A.

Make Comparisons

At times, problems will require you to *compare* the sizes of several decimals or of several fractions. If decimals are being compared, make sure that the numbers being compared have the same number of digits. (*Remember:* Zeros to the far right of a decimal point can be inserted or eliminated without changing the value of the number.)

Examples:

Put these in order from smallest to largest: $0.6, 0.16, 0.66\dfrac{2}{3}, 0.58$.

Ⓐ $0.6, 0.16, 0.66\dfrac{2}{3}, 0.58$

Ⓑ $0.58, 0.16, 0.6, 0.66\dfrac{2}{3}$

Ⓒ $0.16, 0.58, 0.6, 0.66\dfrac{2}{3}$

Ⓓ $0.66\dfrac{2}{3}, 0.6, 0.58, 0.16$

Ⓔ $0.58, 0.6, 0.66\dfrac{2}{3}, 0.16$

Circle *smallest to largest* in the question. Rewrite 0.6 as 0.60 so that all the decimals now have the same number of digits: $0.60, 0.16, 0.66\dfrac{2}{3}, 0.58$. Treating these as though the decimal point were not there (this can be done only when all the numbers have the same number of digits to the right of the decimal), the order is as follows: $0.16, 0.58, 0.60, 0.66\dfrac{2}{3}$. The correct answer is choice C.

Put these in order from smallest to largest: $75\%, \dfrac{2}{3}, \dfrac{5}{8}$.

Ⓐ $\dfrac{2}{3}, 75\%, \dfrac{5}{8}$

Ⓑ $\dfrac{2}{3}, \dfrac{5}{8}, 75\%$

Ⓒ $\dfrac{5}{8}, \dfrac{2}{3}, 75\%$

Ⓓ $75\%, \dfrac{5}{8}, \dfrac{2}{3}$

Ⓔ $75\%, \dfrac{2}{3}, \dfrac{5}{8}$

Using common denominators, you find

$$\frac{2}{3} = \frac{16}{24}$$

$$\frac{5}{8} = \frac{15}{24}$$

$$75\% = \frac{3}{4} = \frac{18}{24}$$

Therefore, the order becomes $\frac{5}{8}, \frac{2}{3}, 75\%$. Using decimal equivalents:

$$\frac{5}{8} = 0.625$$

$$\frac{2}{3} = 0.666\frac{2}{3}$$

$$75\% = 0.750$$

The order again is $\frac{5}{8}, \frac{2}{3}, 75\%$. The answer is choice C.

Draw and Mark Diagrams

When a figure is included with the problem on a paper-based test, mark or write down the given facts on the diagram. For a computer-based test, sketch a simple diagram and write down the given facts. This will help you visualize all the facts that have been given and may tip off a simple solution.

Examples:

If each square in the following figure has a side of length 3, what is the figure's perimeter?

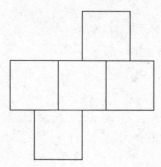

Ⓐ   12
Ⓑ   14
Ⓒ   21
Ⓓ   30
Ⓔ   36

Mark or write down the known facts.

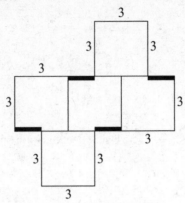

You now have a calculation for the perimeter: 30 *plus* the darkened parts. Now, look carefully at the top two darkened parts. They will add up to 3. (Notice how the top square may slide over to illustrate that fact.)

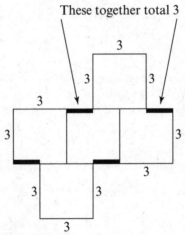

The same is true for the bottom darkened parts. They will add up to 3.

Thus, the total perimeter is 30 + 6 = 36, choice E.

Here's another way to look at things. Since all the squares are identical in size, move the upper square to the left and the lower square to the right to form the figure below:

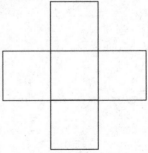

Because each side of each square has a length of 3, the perimeter becomes 12 groups of 3 or 36.

What is the maximum number of pieces of birthday cake of size 4" × 4" that can be cut from the cake shown below?

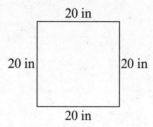

Ⓐ   5
Ⓑ   10
Ⓒ   16
Ⓓ   20
Ⓔ   25

Drawing and marking up the diagram as follows makes this a fairly simple problem.

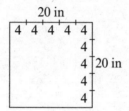

Notice that five pieces of cake will fit along each side; therefore 5 × 5 = 25. The correct answer is choice E. Finding the total area of the cake and dividing it by the area of one of the 4-×-4 pieces would have also given you the correct answer, but be aware of this method because it may not work if the pieces do not fit evenly into the original area.

The perimeter of the following isosceles triangle is 44 inches. The two equal sides are each five times as long as the third side. What are the lengths of each side?

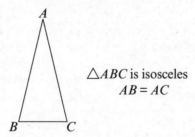

$\triangle ABC$ is isosceles
$AB = AC$

Ⓐ   21, 21, 21
Ⓑ   6, 6, 18
Ⓒ   18, 21, 3
Ⓓ   20, 20, 4
Ⓔ   4, 4, 36

Draw and mark the equal sides on the diagram.

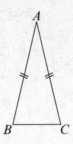

AB and *AC* are each five times as long as *BC*.

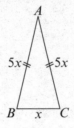

The equation for perimeter is

$$5x + 5x + x = 44$$
$$11x = 44$$
$$x = 4$$

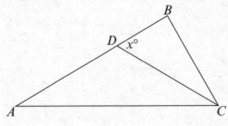

The answer is choice D. ***Note:*** This problem also could have been solved by working from the answer choices.

In the following triangle, $\overline{CD}$ is an angle bisector, $\angle ACD$ is 30°, and $\angle ABC$ is a right angle. What is the measurement of angle x in degrees?

Ⓐ   30°
Ⓑ   45°
Ⓒ   60°
Ⓓ   75°
Ⓔ   180°

You should have read the problem, and then quickly sketched and marked the diagram as follows:

In the following triangle, $\overline{CD}$ is an angle bisector *(Stop and mark in the drawing)*, $\angle ACD$ is 30° *(Stop and mark in the drawing)*, and $\angle ABC$ is a right angle *(Stop and mark in the drawing)*. What is the measurement of angle x in degrees? *(Stop and mark or circle what you are looking for in the drawing.)*

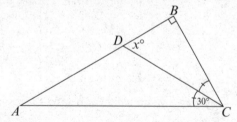

Now with the drawing marked up, it is evident that, given that $\angle ACD$ is 30°, $\angle BCD$ is also 30° because they are formed by an angle bisector (which divides an angle into two equal parts). Given that $\angle ABC$ is 90° (right angle) and $\angle BCD$ is 30°, angle x is 60° because there are 180° in a triangle: $180° - (90 + 30) = 60$. The correct answer is choice C.

Draw Simple Graphic Illustrations

Drawing simple graphic illustrations to meet the conditions set by the word problem can often make the problem easier for you to work. Being able to "see" the facts is more helpful than just reading the words.

Examples:

If all sides of a square are halved, the area of that square

- Ⓐ is halved.
- Ⓑ is divided by 3.
- Ⓒ is divided by 4.
- Ⓓ remains the same.
- Ⓔ not enough information to tell

One way to solve this problem is to draw a square and then halve all of its sides and then compare the two areas.

Your first diagram:

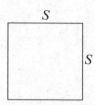

Halving every side:

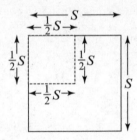

Notice that the total area of the new square will now be one-fourth of the original square. The correct answer is choice C.

A hiking team begins at camp and hikes 5 miles north, then 8 miles west, then 6 miles south, then 9 miles east. In what direction must they now travel in order to return to camp?

Ⓐ   north
Ⓑ   northeast
Ⓒ   northwest
Ⓓ   west
Ⓔ   They already are at camp.

For this question, your diagram would look something like this:

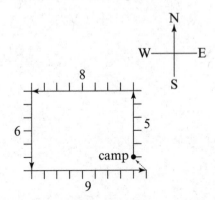

Thus, they must travel northwest (choice C) to return to camp. Note that, in this case, you must draw your diagram very accurately.

Procedure Problems

Some problems (commonly on the Praxis Core, CSET: Multiple Subjects, and CBEST) may not ask you to solve and find a correct numerical answer. Rather, you may be asked how to find the most efficient method to solve the problem.

Examples:

The fastest method to solve $\dfrac{9}{48} \times \dfrac{8}{9}$ would be to

Ⓐ   invert the second fraction and then multiply.

Ⓑ   multiply each column across and then reduce to lowest terms.

Ⓒ   find the common denominator and then multiply across.

Ⓓ   divide 9 into the numerator and denominator, divide 8 into the numerator and denominator, and then multiply across.

Ⓔ   reduce the first fraction to lowest terms and then multiply across.

In this problem, the way to determine the fastest procedure may be to actually work the problem as you would if you were working toward an answer. Then see if that procedure is listed among the answer choices. When comparing your steps to the other methods listed, ask yourself "is one of the other *correct* methods faster than the one I used?" If so, select the fastest.

Procedure problems are not constructed to test your knowledge of *obscure* tricks in solving mathematical equations. Rather, they test your knowledge of common procedures used in standard mathematical equations. Thus, the fastest way to solve this problem would be to first divide 9 into the numerator and denominator.

$$\dfrac{\overset{1}{\cancel{9}}}{48} \times \dfrac{8}{\underset{1}{\cancel{9}}} =$$

Then divide 8 into the numerator and denominator.

$$\dfrac{\overset{1}{\cancel{9}}}{\underset{6}{\cancel{48}}} \times \dfrac{\overset{1}{\cancel{8}}}{\underset{1}{\cancel{9}}} =$$

Multiply across.

$$\dfrac{\overset{1}{\cancel{9}}}{\underset{6}{\cancel{48}}} \times \dfrac{\overset{1}{\cancel{8}}}{\underset{1}{\cancel{9}}} = \dfrac{1}{6}$$

The correct answer is choice D.

A greeting card costs the Key Club $2.00 each. The Key Club sells them for $4.75 each.

Based on the above information, how could Clark determine how many greeting cards must be sold *(Q)* to make a profit of $82.50?

Ⓐ $Q = \$82.50 \div \$2.00$

Ⓑ $Q = \$82.50 - \$2.00$

Ⓒ $Q = \$4.75 - \$2.00$

Ⓓ $Q = \$82.50 \div \$4.75 - \$2.00$

Ⓔ $Q = \$82.50 \div \$2.75$

The correct answer is choice E. Notice that, because the greeting cards are bought for $2.00 each but sold at $4.75 each, the profit on each greeting card is $2.75. Therefore, to determine how many greeting cards equal a profit of $82.50, you need only divide $82.50 by $2.75.

Multiple-Multiple-Choice

Some mathematical reasoning questions use a multiple-multiple-choice format. At first glance, these appear more confusing and more difficult than normal five-choice (A, B, C, D, E) multiple-choice problems. Actually, when you understand multiple-multiple-choice problem types and techniques, they're often easier than a comparable standard multiple-choice question.

Example:

If x is a positive integer, then which of the following *must* be true?

I. $x > 0$

II. $x = 0$

III. $x < 1$

    Ⓐ I only

    Ⓑ II only

    Ⓒ III only

    Ⓓ I and II

    Ⓔ I and III

Since x is a positive integer, it must be a counting number. Note that possible values of x could be 1, or 2, or 3, or 4, and so on. Therefore, statement I, $x > 0$, is always true. So next to I on your question booklet or on your scratch paper, place a T for *true*.

Now realize that the correct final answer choice (A, B, C, D, or E) *must* contain true statement I. This eliminates choices B and C as possible correct answer choices because they do *not* contain true statement I. You should cross out choices B and C on your question booklet or scratch paper.

Statement II is incorrect. If x is positive, x cannot equal zero. Thus, next to II, you should place an F for false.

Knowing that statement II is false allows you to eliminate any answer choices that contain false statement II. Therefore, you should cross out choice D. Only choices A and E are left as possible correct answers. Finally, you realize that statement III is also false because x must be 1 or greater. So you place an F next to statement III, thus eliminating choice E and leaving choice A, I only, as the correct answer.

This technique often saves some precious time and allows you to take a better educated guess should you not be able to complete all parts (I, II, III, IV, and so on) of a multiple-multiple-choice question.

Interpret Data—Graphs, Charts, Tables, and Diagrams

Some math questions are based on interpreting data provided in graphs, charts, and tables. Visual diagrams help to provide a clear picture about the numeric and categorical data. To answer questions, you must accurately read and draw conclusions about information presented in the diagrams before performing calculations.

Spend a few moments studying the title, labels/categories, and numeric values *before* reading the question.

- **Title:** The title always provides an overview of the graph.
- **Labels/categories:** Each category provides information about the whole picture.
- **Numeric values:** The visual illustration of each category quickly distinguishes variations in data (greatest and lowest numerical values).

Examples:

Use the graph below for the next two example questions.

**Grade Distribution of
350 Students Enrolled in
Freshman Mathematics**

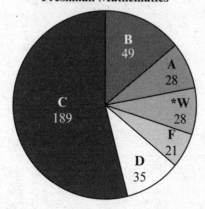

*W = Withdrawn.

If a grade of C or better is required to take the next level mathematics course, what percent of the students qualify?

Ⓐ   54%

Ⓑ   22%

Ⓒ   16%

Ⓓ   76%

Ⓔ   83%

The number of students who received a grade of C or better is 189 + 49 + 28 = 266.

Next you should write 266 over the "total number of students." $\dfrac{266}{350} = 0.76 = 76\%$ of the students qualify to take the next level mathematics course. The correct answer is choice D.

What is the ratio of students who received a grade of B to the total number of students who completed the course?

Ⓐ $\dfrac{7}{50}$

Ⓑ $\dfrac{6}{46}$

Ⓒ $\dfrac{6}{50}$

Ⓓ $\dfrac{49}{350}$

Ⓔ $\dfrac{7}{46}$

Since 28 students withdrew from the class and did not receive a letter grade, 350 − 28 = 322 students completed the course, of which 49 earned a grade of B.

The ratio is:

$$\frac{\text{students who received a B}}{\text{total number of students who completed the course}} \quad \frac{49}{322} = \frac{7}{46}$$

The correct answer is choice E.

Use the graph below for the next two example questions.

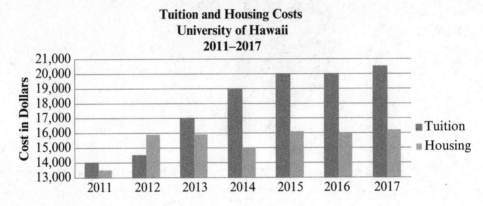

In which year did the largest increase in tuition occur?

Ⓐ   2012

Ⓑ   2013

Ⓒ   2014

Ⓓ   2015

Ⓔ   2016

The largest tuition increase occurred in 2013, which was $17,000 − $14,500 = $2,500. The correct answer is choice B.

In which year was there no change in tuition compared to the previous year?

Ⓐ   2012

Ⓑ   2013

Ⓒ   2015

Ⓓ   2016

Ⓔ   2017

The tuition for both 2015 and 2016 was $20,000. Therefore, there was not a change in tuition in 2016. The correct answer is choice D.

A Patterned Plan of Attack

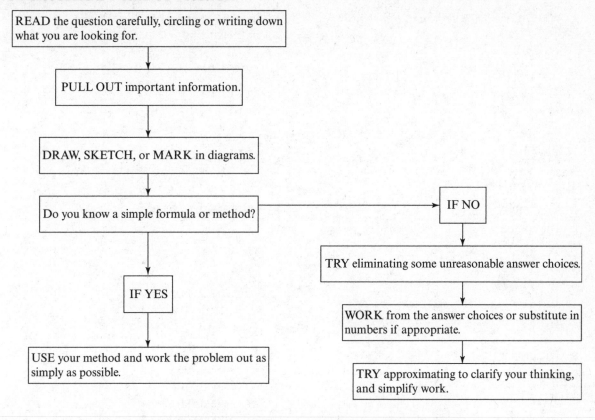

Mathematical Reasoning Practice

General Directions: Questions have several different formats. Answer each question by selecting the correct response from the choices given. Unless otherwise directed, select a single answer choice. For numeric entry questions, follow the instructions below.

Numeric Entry Questions

- Write out your answer choice with numerals.
- Your answer may be an integer, a decimal, or a fraction, and it may be negative.
- If a question asks for a fractional answer, there will be two boxes—one for the numerator and one for the denominator.
- Equivalent forms of the correct answer, such as 4.5 and 4.50, are all correct. Fractions do not need to be reduced to lowest terms.
- Enter the exact answer unless the question asks you to round.

Arithmetic

1. Which of the following pairs are *not* equal?

   Ⓐ $\frac{2}{5}$, 0.4

   Ⓑ $\frac{1}{3}$, $\frac{11}{33}$

   Ⓒ $\frac{5}{4}$, $1\frac{1}{4}$

   Ⓓ $\frac{13}{4}$, $3\frac{1}{4}$

   Ⓔ $\frac{7}{11}$, $\frac{72}{112}$

2. The number 103,233,124 is divisible by

   Ⓐ 3
   Ⓑ 4
   Ⓒ 5
   Ⓓ 6
   Ⓔ 8

3. The product of 1.5 and 0.4 expressed as a fraction is

   Ⓐ $\frac{2}{5}$

   Ⓑ $\frac{1}{2}$

   Ⓒ $\frac{3}{5}$

   Ⓓ $\frac{2}{3}$

   Ⓔ $\frac{4}{5}$

4. The greatest common factor of 32, 48, and 64 is

   Ⓐ 4
   Ⓑ 6
   Ⓒ 8
   Ⓓ 16
   Ⓔ 32

5. Dividing a number by $\frac{8}{2}$ is the same as multiplying by

   Ⓐ 4
   Ⓑ 2
   Ⓒ $\frac{1}{4}$
   Ⓓ $\frac{1}{6}$
   Ⓔ $\frac{1}{8}$

6. What is 0.25% of 2,000?

   Ⓐ 500
   Ⓑ 50
   Ⓒ 5
   Ⓓ 0.5
   Ⓔ 0.05

7. $(9.3 \times 10^7) - (2.1 \times 10^2) =$

   Ⓐ 92,000,790
   Ⓑ 92,999,790
   Ⓒ 93,000,210
   Ⓓ 93,000,790
   Ⓔ 93,999,790

8. The national birth rate of Country A is 72,000 newborn babies each day. Country B has a birth rate of 3 babies per minute. In 1 week, what is the positive difference in births between the two countries?

   Ⓐ 2
   Ⓑ 30,240
   Ⓒ 50,400
   Ⓓ 473,760
   Ⓔ 3,528,000

9. If Data Set A with 50 numbers has an average of 30, and Data Set B with 100 numbers has an average of 25, what is the positive difference of the sum of the data sets?

Ⓐ   1,000
Ⓑ   1,500
Ⓒ   2,500
Ⓓ   3,050
Ⓔ   5,030

10. Which of the following could be the units digit of 73^n, where n is a positive integer?

Select **all** that apply.

Ⓐ   1
Ⓑ   3
Ⓒ   5
Ⓓ   6
Ⓔ   7
Ⓕ   9

11. The number 24 is 20% of what number?

Ⓐ   12
Ⓑ   28
Ⓒ   100
Ⓓ   120
Ⓔ   480

12. If the ratio of males to females at a party is 4 to 5 and the ratio of adults to children at the party is 3 to 2, which of the following could be the number of people at the party?

Ⓐ   18
Ⓑ   25
Ⓒ   35
Ⓓ   45
Ⓔ   60

13. A television regularly selling for $850 is discounted 20%. What is the new selling price of the television?

Ⓐ $650
Ⓑ $670
Ⓒ $680
Ⓓ $700
Ⓔ $750

14. In the table below, the greatest percent increase was between which years?

Dow Jones Average	
2012	13,000
2013	14,500
2014	16,000
2015	17,500
2016	19,000
2017	20,500

Ⓐ   2012 and 2013
Ⓑ   2013 and 2014
Ⓒ   2014 and 2015
Ⓓ   2015 and 2016
Ⓔ   2016 and 2017

15. Find the sum of $\frac{1}{3}$, $\frac{1}{8}$, and $\frac{5}{6}$.

Ⓐ $\frac{13}{24}$

Ⓑ $\frac{15}{24}$

Ⓒ $\frac{31}{24}$

Ⓓ $\frac{33}{24}$

Ⓔ $\frac{35}{24}$

16. Approximate the value for $0.26 \times 0.67 \times 0.5 \times 0.9$.

Ⓐ   0.08
Ⓑ   0.13
Ⓒ   0.8
Ⓓ   0.32
Ⓔ   0.04

17. Given $\sqrt{xz} = 10$ and that x and z are integers, which of the following could be a value of $x + z$?

Select **all** that apply.

Ⓐ   20
Ⓑ   25
Ⓒ   29
Ⓓ   50
Ⓔ   52
Ⓕ   100
Ⓖ   101

18. What is the greatest of four consecutive odd integers if their sum is 512?

Write your answer in the box below.

☐

19. A teacher gave a test to a class. All the boys averaged 82% on the test, while all the girls averaged 85%. If there were 20 boys and 10 girls in the class, what was the average (arithmetic mean) for the entire class?

- Ⓐ $82\frac{1}{2}\%$
- Ⓑ 83%
- Ⓒ $83\frac{1}{2}\%$
- Ⓓ 84%
- Ⓔ 85%

20. If the average (arithmetic mean) of 10, 14, 16, and q is 14, then $q =$

- Ⓐ 10
- Ⓑ 12
- Ⓒ 14
- Ⓓ 16
- Ⓔ 18

21. If the price of apples is decreased from two dozen for $5 to three dozen for $6, how many more apples can be purchased for $30 now than could be purchased before?

- Ⓐ 36
- Ⓑ 48
- Ⓒ 72
- Ⓓ 144
- Ⓔ 180

22. If 28 millimeters is equivalent to 2.8 centimeters, how many millimeters are in 50 centimeters?

- Ⓐ 0.5
- Ⓑ 5
- Ⓒ 50
- Ⓓ 500
- Ⓔ 5,000

23. A fair die is rolled three times. What is the probability that all three rolls resulted in different numbers?

Write your answer in the box below. Round to the nearest one-hundredth.

0.☐

24. Which of the following is (are) equal to $\frac{3}{8}$?

- I. 0.375
- II. $37\frac{1}{2}\%$
- III. $\dfrac{37\frac{1}{2}}{100}$
- IV. $\dfrac{375}{100}$

- Ⓐ I and II
- Ⓑ I, II, and III
- Ⓒ I, II, and IV
- Ⓓ II and III
- Ⓔ IV

25. At a fast food establishment, Jake bought three identical combo meals. The total bill, including the sales tax of 8.75%, was over $15.00, so Jake gave the cashier $20.00. As the cashier was handing Jake his change, Jake said, "Keep the change." Which of the following could be the cost, before added sales tax, of each combo meal?

Select **all** that apply.

- Ⓐ $4.50
- Ⓑ $4.65
- Ⓒ $5.75
- Ⓓ $6.10
- Ⓔ $6.15

26. What is the arithmetic mean of six Tiger players each averaging 0.280 and four Padre players averaging 0.250 each?

Ⓐ   0.268
Ⓑ   0.270
Ⓒ   0.272
Ⓓ   0.274
Ⓔ   0.276

27. Find the simple interest on $3,000 if it is left in an account for 4 months paying a 2% quarterly rate of interest.

Ⓐ $8
Ⓑ $60
Ⓒ $80
Ⓓ $120
Ⓔ $600

28. How many paintings were displayed at the County Museum of Art if 30% of them were by Monet and Monet was represented by 24 paintings?

Ⓐ   48
Ⓑ   50
Ⓒ   60
Ⓓ   76
Ⓔ   80

29. A motorist traveled 120 miles to his destination at the average speed of 60 miles per hour. His return to the starting point took 3 hours. His average speed for the entire trip was

Ⓐ   40 mph
Ⓑ   45 mph
Ⓒ   48 mph
Ⓓ   50 mph
Ⓔ   53 mph

30. A special race is held in which runners may stop to rest. However, if a runner stops, he may then run only half as far as his previous distance between stops, at which point he must stop to rest again. If a runner, Albert, finishes running when stopping for the fifth time, what's the farthest distance Albert can run if he takes his first rest stop after 0.8 kilometers?

Ⓐ   1.5 km
Ⓑ   1.55 km
Ⓒ   1.75 km
Ⓓ   1.80 km
Ⓔ   2.0 km

31. A used bicycle pump, priced originally at $7.00, is discounted 20%. Because it doesn't sell, it is discounted an additional 10%. What is the new sale price?

Ⓐ $4.90
Ⓑ $5.00
Ⓒ $5.04
Ⓓ $5.21
Ⓔ $5.60

32. A student scored 80% on each of two tests. What does he have to score on the third test in order to raise his overall average to 85%?

Ⓐ   90%
Ⓑ   93%
Ⓒ   95%
Ⓓ   98%
Ⓔ   100%

33. Successive discounts of 40% and 20% are equal to a single discount of

Ⓐ   20%
Ⓑ   30%
Ⓒ   52%
Ⓓ   60%
Ⓔ   80%

34. A solution must contain at least 30% orange juice but not more than 20% ginger ale in addition to its other ingredients. If the punch bowl can hold 400 cups of this solution, which of the following are allowable amounts of orange juice and ginger ale?

Ⓐ 120 cups of orange juice, 130 cups of ginger ale

Ⓑ 130 cups of orange juice, 140 cups of ginger ale

Ⓒ 150 cups of orange juice, 70 cups of ginger ale

Ⓓ 20 cups of orange juice, 80 cups of ginger ale

Ⓔ 14 cups of orange juice, 100 cups of ginger ale

35. $\dfrac{1}{2^3}$ is approximately what percent of 2^3?

Ⓐ 0.016%

Ⓑ 0.16%

Ⓒ 1.6%

Ⓓ 16%

Ⓔ 160%

Algebra

1. If $x = -3$ and $y = (x + 5)(x - 5)$, then the value of y is

Ⓐ 64

Ⓑ 16

Ⓒ 9

Ⓓ −9

Ⓔ −16

2. If $9x + 4 = -32$, then what is $x + 1$?

Ⓐ −5

Ⓑ −4

Ⓒ −3

Ⓓ 4

Ⓔ 5

3. If $(4)(4)(4)(4) = \dfrac{(8)(8)}{p}$, then p must equal

Ⓐ $\dfrac{1}{4}$

Ⓑ $\dfrac{1}{2}$

Ⓒ 1

Ⓓ 2

Ⓔ 4

4. Find the value of a^{bc} if $a = 2$, $b = 3$, and $c = 2$.

Ⓐ 8

Ⓑ 16

Ⓒ 32

Ⓓ 64

Ⓔ 128

5. If $*x$ is defined as $x^2 + 4$ and $**x$ is defined as $12x - 2$, then for which positive values of x is $*x > **x$?

Select **all** that apply.

- [A] 8
- [B] 10
- [C] 12
- [D] 14
- [E] none of the numbers apply

6. Solve this system of equations and find the value of $x + y - z$.

$$x + 2y = 10$$
$$x + z = 0$$
$$y - 2z = 11$$

Write your answer in the box below.

7. $\sqrt{(9 - x)^2} = 9 - x$

In the real number system, which of the following cannot be a value for x in the statement above?

- Ⓐ -10
- Ⓑ -9
- Ⓒ 0
- Ⓓ 9
- Ⓔ 10

8. If $\dfrac{1}{t} + \dfrac{1}{p} = \dfrac{1}{2}$, then $t + p =$

- Ⓐ 8
- Ⓑ 2
- Ⓒ 1
- Ⓓ $\dfrac{1}{2}$
- Ⓔ cannot be determined

9. If a and b are positive integers and $a^2 - b^2 = 11$, then $2a + 2b$ must equal

- Ⓐ 11
- Ⓑ 12
- Ⓒ 22
- Ⓓ 26
- Ⓔ 36

10. If $x + 2 = y$, what is the value of $x - 2$ in terms of y?

- Ⓐ $y - 4$
- Ⓑ $y - 2$
- Ⓒ $y + 2$
- Ⓓ $y + 4$
- Ⓔ $y + 6$

11. If $ab = -5$ and $(a + b)^2 = 16$, then $a^2 + b^2 =$

- Ⓐ 11
- Ⓑ 15
- Ⓒ 21
- Ⓓ 25
- Ⓔ 26

12. If x is an even integer, which of the following must also be an even integer?

- Ⓐ $9x + 1$
- Ⓑ $9x - 1$
- Ⓒ $\dfrac{x}{2} + 1$
- Ⓓ $\dfrac{x}{2}$
- Ⓔ $4x + 6$

13. For all m, $m^2 + 11m + 30 = (m + y)(m + z)$. What is the value of yz?

- Ⓐ 5
- Ⓑ 6
- Ⓒ 11
- Ⓓ 30
- Ⓔ cannot be determined

14. If $2x + 5y = 32$, then $4x + 10y =$

Ⓐ   16
Ⓑ   34
Ⓒ   64
Ⓓ   128
Ⓔ   cannot be determined

15. If $25q^2p^2 = 8x$, then $\dfrac{q^2p^2}{4} =$

Ⓐ $16x$
Ⓑ $4x$
Ⓒ $2x$
Ⓓ $\dfrac{2x}{25}$
Ⓔ $\dfrac{x}{25}$

16. If n is a positive integer, then which of the following must be true about (n) and $(n + 1)$?

Ⓐ n is odd and $(n + 1)$ is even.
Ⓑ n is even and $(n + 1)$ is odd.
Ⓒ   The product of the two terms is odd.
Ⓓ   The sum of the two terms is even.
Ⓔ   The product of the two terms is even.

17. On the coordinate grid below, for which point must the product of its x and y coordinates be positive?

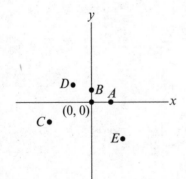

Ⓐ A
Ⓑ B
Ⓒ C
Ⓓ D
Ⓔ E

18. If x, y, and z are all positive integers and $x < y < z$, then which of the following must be true?

Ⓐ $(x + y) > z$
Ⓑ $xy > z$
Ⓒ $(z - y) > x$
Ⓓ $(z - 2) = x$
Ⓔ $z > \dfrac{y}{x}$

19. If $0.002 \le a \le 0.05$ and $0.01 \le b \le 0.50$, then what is the greatest possible value of $\left(\dfrac{a}{b}\right)^2$?

Ⓐ   0.25
Ⓑ   0.5
Ⓒ   1
Ⓓ   5
Ⓔ   25

20. If $\dfrac{x^2yz + xyz^2}{xyz} = x + z$, then a necessary condition for this to be true is

I. $x + z < y$
II. $x^2 > z$
III. $xyz \ne 0$

Ⓐ   I
Ⓑ   I and II
Ⓒ   I and III
Ⓓ   III
Ⓔ   II and III

21. If $\dfrac{1}{5} + \dfrac{1}{2} + \dfrac{1}{x} = 7$, then $x =$

Ⓐ $\dfrac{10}{63}$

Ⓑ $\dfrac{60}{7}$

Ⓒ $\dfrac{63}{10}$

Ⓓ $\dfrac{3}{19}$

Ⓔ $\dfrac{7}{60}$

22. If you flip a fair coin four times, what is the probability of getting at least two heads? Write your answer as a common fraction in the boxes below.

23. The guests at a party each received a thank-you gift from the host. Each guest received either the $12 vase or the $16 plate. If one-fourth of the guests received the $16 plate and the remaining 24 guests received the $12 vase, and some guests might receive an additional plate, then which of the following could be the amount the host spent on thank-you gifts? (solve algebraically)

Select **all** that apply.

Ⓐ $408
Ⓑ $412
Ⓒ $416
Ⓓ $428
Ⓔ $432

24. A fruit drink made from orange juice and water is diluted with more water so that the final solution is one-fourth water. If the original solution was 90% orange juice and 2 liters of water were added, how many liters are in the final solution of fruit drink?

Ⓐ 6
Ⓑ 8
Ⓒ 10
Ⓓ 12
Ⓔ 14

25. Ernie purchased some apples from a grocer for $5.00 and later learned that if he had purchased 20% more apples, he would have been given a 20% discount in price per apple. What would the difference have been in total cost if he had purchased 20% more apples?

Ⓐ 20¢ less
Ⓑ 10¢ less
Ⓒ the same cost
Ⓓ 20¢ more
Ⓔ cannot be determined

26. A college student invests $2,000, part at 7% in a savings account and some at 12% in a special money market account. The annual income from this investment is $200. How much was invested in the money market account?

Ⓐ $400
Ⓑ $600
Ⓒ $1,000
Ⓓ $1,200
Ⓔ $1,350

27. If p pencils cost c cents, n pencils at the same price will cost

Ⓐ $\dfrac{pc}{n}$ cents

Ⓑ $\dfrac{cn}{p}$ cents

Ⓒ npc cents

Ⓓ $\dfrac{np}{c}$ cents

Ⓔ $\dfrac{pc}{np}$ cents

28. A woman bought a set of porch furniture at a 40% reduction sale held late in the summer. The furniture cost her $165. What was the original price of the furniture?

Ⓐ $66
Ⓑ $231
Ⓒ $275
Ⓓ $412.50
Ⓔ $510

29. The midpoint of line segment AB is

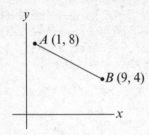

Ⓐ (8, 4)
Ⓑ (3, 6)
Ⓒ (6, 5)
Ⓓ (5, 6)
Ⓔ (4, 8)

30. If a and b are integers, which of the following condition(s) is (are) sufficient for $\dfrac{a^2 - b^2}{a - b} = a + b$ to be true?

Select **all** that apply.

A $a > 0$
B $a < 0$
C $a > b$
D $a < b$
E $b > 0$
F $b < 0$

Geometry

Note: Figures used in the following problems are not necessarily drawn to scale.

1. If, in the figure, l_1 is parallel to l_2, then $x + y$ must equal

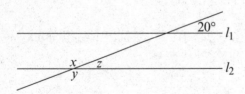

Ⓐ 40°
Ⓑ 120°
Ⓒ 160°
Ⓓ 180°
Ⓔ 320°

2. In the figure, find the degree measure of $\angle y$.

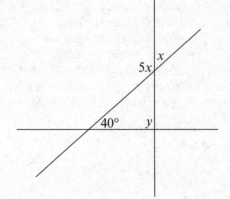

Ⓐ 40°
Ⓑ 50°
Ⓒ 80°
Ⓓ 90°
Ⓔ 110°

3. In the figure, what is the value of p?

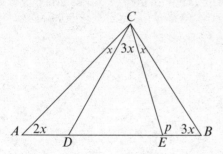

Ⓐ   18
Ⓑ   36
Ⓒ   72
Ⓓ   108
Ⓔ   135

4. In circle O, the measure of arc $AD = 80°$. Find the measure of inscribed angle MDA.

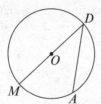

Ⓐ   40°
Ⓑ   50°
Ⓒ   60°
Ⓓ   80°
Ⓔ   100°

5. The figure below consists of four inscribed squares. The inner squares are inscribed in the outer squares so that their vertices are the midpoints of the sides of the outer squares.

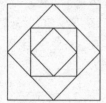

What is the ratio of the area of the innermost square to the area of the outermost square?

Write your fraction in the boxes below.

6. In $\triangle ABC$, $AB = BC$. Therefore, angles r and p each equal

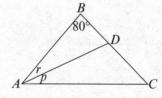

Ⓐ   50°
Ⓑ   25°
Ⓒ   20°
Ⓓ   10°
Ⓔ   cannot be determined

7. In the figure, $x =$

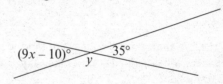

Ⓐ   15
Ⓑ   10
Ⓒ   9
Ⓓ   5
Ⓔ   4

8. What is the maximum number of cubes 3 inches on an edge that can be packed into a carton with dimensions as shown?

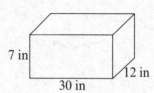

Ⓐ   70
Ⓑ   74
Ⓒ   80
Ⓓ   84
Ⓔ   88

9. Find the volume of a cube in cubic inches if the area of one of its faces is 49 square inches.

Ⓐ   49
Ⓑ   64
Ⓒ   125
Ⓓ   144
Ⓔ   343

10. Square $ABCD$ is inscribed in circle O with a radius of $\sqrt{2}$, as shown. Find the area of square $ABCD$.

Ⓐ   1
Ⓑ   2
Ⓒ   4
Ⓓ   8
Ⓔ   16

11. If the five angles of a pentagon are in the ratio 2:3:4:5:6, what is the degree measure of the largest angle?

Ⓐ   27°
Ⓑ   54°
Ⓒ   108°
Ⓓ   162°
Ⓔ   180°

12. Circle O intersects circle Q only at point K. $PQ = 13$, and the radius of circle O is 5. What is the area of circle Q?

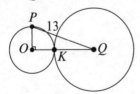

Ⓐ 144π
Ⓑ 100π
Ⓒ 81π
Ⓓ 64π
Ⓔ 49π

13. In the diagram, circle O inscribed in square $ABCD$ has an area of 36π square inches. What is the area of the shaded regions of the square? (Use $\pi = 3.14$.)

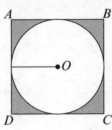

Ⓐ   24
Ⓑ   29.16
Ⓒ   30.96
Ⓓ   144
Ⓔ   200

14. A regular cylindrical tank is to be $\frac{2}{3}$ filled with water. If its height is 9 feet and its diameter is 12 feet, how many cubic feet of water will be needed?

Ⓐ 144π
Ⓑ 216π
Ⓒ 256π
Ⓓ 324π
Ⓔ 720π

15. In the figure, what is the area of the shaded region?

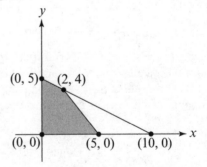

Ⓐ   15
Ⓑ   18
Ⓒ   20
Ⓓ   21
Ⓔ   25

16. Using the figure to determine the values of q and p, the product qp must equal

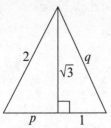

Ⓐ $\dfrac{1}{2}$

Ⓑ 1

Ⓒ 2

Ⓓ $2\sqrt{3}$

Ⓔ $3\sqrt{2}$

17. How many degrees are there in each interior angle of a regular decagon?

Write your answer in the box below.

18. The length and width of a rectangle are integers and the width is from one-third to two-thirds of its length. If the perimeter of the rectangle is 40, then which of the following could be the area of the rectangle?

Select **all** that apply.

Ⓐ 36

Ⓑ 64

Ⓒ 75

Ⓓ 80

Ⓔ 96

19. If a square has the same perimeter as a rectangle with sides 2 and 16, what is the area of the square?

Ⓐ 4

Ⓑ 9

Ⓒ 16

Ⓓ 36

Ⓔ 81

20. In the diagram, if one side of the regular hexagon $ABCDEF$ is 10, find the area of the entire hexagon.

Ⓐ 75

Ⓑ $75\sqrt{3}$

Ⓒ 150

Ⓓ $150\sqrt{2}$

Ⓔ $150\sqrt{3}$

21. If, at point P, l_2 bisects the angle formed by l_1 and l_3, what is the degree measure of x if z equals $100°$?

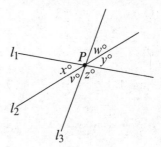

Ⓐ 30°

Ⓑ 40°

Ⓒ 45°

Ⓓ 80°

Ⓔ 90°

22. In circle O, if chord $SP = 6$ and the radius of circle $O = 5$, find the length of chord $\overline{RS}$.

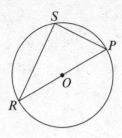

   Ⓐ   3

   Ⓑ $\sqrt{11}$

   Ⓒ   6

   Ⓓ   8

   Ⓔ   cannot be determined

23. In the figure, side $AB = 6$ and side $BC = 8$. Find the area of $\triangle ADC$.

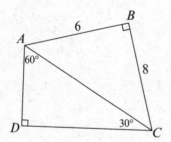

   Ⓐ $25\sqrt{3}$

   Ⓑ   24

   Ⓒ $\dfrac{25\sqrt{3}}{2}$

   Ⓓ   20

   Ⓔ $20\sqrt{2}$

24. On the coordinate grid, what is the length of segment AB if the coordinates at point A are (7, 9) and the coordinates at point B are (13, 17)?

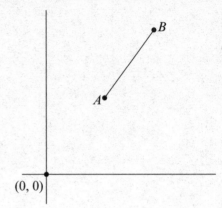

   Ⓐ $7\dfrac{1}{2}$ units

   Ⓑ $8\dfrac{1}{2}$ units

   Ⓒ   9 units

   Ⓓ   10 units

   Ⓔ $12\dfrac{1}{2}$ units

Question 25 refers to the following figures.

Rectangle Tile Figure A	**Parallelogram Tile** Figure B

25. Which of the following statements correctly expresses the relationship between the ceramic tiles pictured in Figure A and Figure B above?

Select **all** that apply.

   Ⓐ   The two figures have the same perimeter.

   Ⓑ   The two figures do not have the same perimeter.

   Ⓒ   The two figures have the same area.

   Ⓓ   The two figures do not have the same area.

   Ⓔ   The two figures are similar.

26. The figure represents the end of a garage. Find, in feet, the length of one of the equal rafters $\overline{AB}$ or $\overline{CB}$ if each extends 12 inches beyond the eaves.

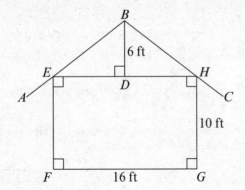

Ⓐ 10
Ⓑ 11
Ⓒ 13
Ⓓ 22
Ⓔ 33

27. The figure represents a rectangle, whose dimensions are l and w, surmounted by a semicircle, whose radius is r. Express the area of this figure in terms of l, w, r, and π.

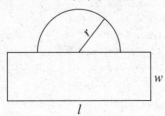

Ⓐ $lw + \dfrac{\pi r^2}{2}$
Ⓑ $lw + \pi r$
Ⓒ $lw + \pi r^2$
Ⓓ $\dfrac{\pi}{2} - r^2 lw$
Ⓔ lwr^2

28. The width of the ring (the shaded portion of the figure) is exactly equal to the radius of the inner circle. What percent of the entire area is the area of the shaded portion?

Ⓐ 25
Ⓑ 50
Ⓒ $66\dfrac{2}{3}$
Ⓓ 75
Ⓔ 90

29. By what number is the area of a circle multiplied if its radius is doubled?

Ⓐ $2\pi r$
Ⓑ 2
Ⓒ 3.1416
Ⓓ 4
Ⓔ 6

30. In the figure, $m\angle 1 = 27°$ and $m\angle 3 = 67°$. Find the measure of $\angle 2$.

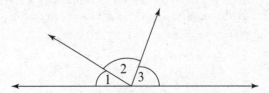

Write your answer in the box below.

Word Problems

1. Jose purchased three items for his new car—a steering-wheel grip, a floor mat, and a seat cushion. The steering-wheel grip cost three times the seat cushion. The floor mat cost exactly $5.75 with tax. Which of the following can be derived from the above information?

   I.   the cost of all three items
   II. the cost of the seat cushion
   III. the cost of the steering-wheel grip
   IV. the cost of the floor mat without the tax

   Ⓐ   I only
   Ⓑ   II only
   Ⓒ   III only
   Ⓓ   IV only
   Ⓔ   none of these

   John's car is 1 year older than Sue's car. Maria's truck is 1 year newer than John's car. Sue's car, a 2009 model, is newer than Maria's truck.

   ---

2. Fred is given the information above in a problem in his math class. With just the information given, Fred should be able to determine the approximate age(s) of

   Ⓐ   Sue's car
   Ⓑ   Sue's car and Maria's truck
   Ⓒ   Sue's car and John's car
   Ⓓ   Sue's car, Maria's truck, and John's car
   Ⓔ   Maria's truck

3. Harold is given the following information about the class treasury.

   I.   The current balance is $5 less than last year's final balance, which was $10.
   II. This year's balance of $10 is $5 more than last year's balance.
   III. Ten percent is half of this year's goal, which is $100.

   Which of these statements can be calculated by subtracting 5 from 10?

   Ⓐ   I
   Ⓑ   II
   Ⓒ   III
   Ⓓ   I and II
   Ⓔ   I, II, and III

   Arnold's Scores on Four Tests

   Test 1: 83%
   Test 2: 85%
   Test 3: 100%
   Test 4: ?

   ---

4. If Arnold's score on Test 4 was weighted double that of each of the previous three tests, and if his overall average was 90%, how could Arnold determine his score on Test 4?

   Ⓐ $(83 + 85 + 100 + x) = 90$
   Ⓑ $(83 + 85 + 100 + x + x) = 90$
   Ⓒ $\dfrac{(83 + 85 + 100 + x)}{4} = 90$
   Ⓓ $\dfrac{(83 + 85 + 100 + x + x)}{4} = 90$
   Ⓔ $\dfrac{(83 + 85 + 100 + x + x)}{5} = 90$

> 27,456 may be represented as P.
> 845 may be represented as Q.

5. Based on the above information, $27,456 \times 846$ may be expressed as

Ⓐ $PQ + 1$
Ⓑ $(P + 1)(Q)$
Ⓒ $P(Q + 1)$
Ⓓ $(P + 1)(Q + 1)$
Ⓔ $(P)(Q + 845)$

6. Dustin has 12 pounds of ground coffee valued at $8.50 per pound. Which of the following amounts (listed in pounds) of ground coffee valued at $4.00 per pound, when added to the 12 pounds of $8.50 per pound ground coffee, would yield a mixture worth from $5.50 to $6.00 per pound?

Select **all** that apply.

Ⓐ 12
Ⓑ 15
Ⓒ 18
Ⓓ 20
Ⓔ 22
Ⓕ 24

7. When Francisco multiplies $(x + 1)(x + 2)$, he gets $x^2 + 3x + 2$ as an answer. One way to check this answer would be to

Ⓐ divide $(x + 1)$ by $(x + 2)$
Ⓑ divide $(x + 2)$ by $(x + 1)$
Ⓒ plug in a positive integer for x
Ⓓ square $(x + 1)$
Ⓔ use reciprocals

> The sum of two numbers equals one of the numbers.

8. If the above statement is true, which of the following best represents the relationship?

Ⓐ $x + y = y + x$
Ⓑ $(x)(y) = 1$
Ⓒ $x + y = 1$
Ⓓ $x + y = y$
Ⓔ $x + y = x + 1$

9. Last year, Jorge was 3 years less than twice Teresa's age now. If Jorge is 10 years old now, which equation will enable Jorge to correctly find Teresa's present age, T?

Ⓐ $10 + 1 = 2T - 3$
Ⓑ $9 - 3 = 2T$
Ⓒ $9 = 2T - 3$
Ⓓ $11 = 2T - 3$
Ⓔ $10 = -3 + 2T$

10. If a tie costs T dollars and a suit jacket costs four times the price of the tie, which of the following best expresses the cost of two ties and three suit jackets?

Ⓐ $4T$
Ⓑ $T + 4(T)$
Ⓒ $2(T) + 3(T)$
Ⓓ $T + 3(4T)$
Ⓔ $2(T) + 3(4T)$

> Rosanna knows that a geometric figure is a rectangle and that it has sides of 18 and 22.

11. How can Rosanna compute the area of a square that has the same perimeter as the rectangle above?

Ⓐ Add 18 and 22, double this sum, divide by 4, then multiply by 2.
Ⓑ Add 18 and 22, double this sum, divide by 4, then multiply by 4.
Ⓒ Add 18 and 22, double this sum, divide by 4, then square the quotient.
Ⓓ Add 18 and 22, double this sum, then multiply by 4.
Ⓔ Add twice 18 to twice 22, divide by 2, then square the quotient.

Answer Key

The page number(s) in parentheses following each answer will direct you to the basic review section(s) for that specific problem.

Arithmetic

1. E (pp. 23, 47)
2. B (p. 20)
3. C (pp. 45–46)
4. D (p. 26)
5. C (p. 41)
6. C (p. 52)
7. B (p. 59)
8. D (p. 68)
9. A (p. 187)
10. A B, E, F (p. 62)
11. D (p. 52)
12. D (p. 27)

13. C (p. 52)
14. A (p. 56)
15. C (pp. 31–32)
16. A (p. 46)
17. A, B, C, E, G (p. 64)
18. 131 (p. 303)
19. B (p. 187)
20. D (p. 187)
21. A (p. 68)
22. D (p. 68)
23. 0.56 (p. 200)
24. B (p. 52)

25. B, C, D (p. 311)
26. A (pp. 187–188)
27. C (p. 306)
28. E (p. 54)
29. C (p. 290)
30. B (pp. 45–46)
31. C (pp. 48, 52)
32. C (pp. 187–188)
33. C (pp. 52, 311)
34. C (pp. 52, 311)
35. C (pp. 54, 57)

Algebra

1. E (p. 88)
2. C (p. 90)
3. A (pp. 90, 97)
4. D (p. 88)
5. C, D (p. 167)
6. 11 (pp. 99–100)
7. E (p. 163)
8. E (p. 99)
9. C (p. 122)
10. A (pp. 90, 94)

11. E (p. 88)
12. E (p. 88)
13. D (p. 123)
14. C (p. 90)
15. D (p. 90)
16. E (p. 107)
17. C (p. 143)
18. E (p. 16)
19. E (p. 88)
20. D (pp. 132, 139)

21. A (p. 90)
22. $\frac{11}{16}$ (pp. 199, 204)
23. C, E (pp. 104, 160)
24. D (pp. 90, 107)
25. A (p. 96)
26. D (p. 306)
27. B (p. 96)
28. C (p. 53)
29. D (pp. 143, 224)
30. C, D (p. 122)

Geometry

1. E (p. 226)
2. E (pp. 221, 233)
3. D (p. 233)
4. B (p. 265)
5. $\frac{2}{16}$ or $\frac{1}{8}$ (pp. 256–257)

6. E (p. 238)
7. D (p. 222)
8. C (p. 267)
9. E (p. 267)
10. C (p. 260)
11. D (pp. 255–256)

12. E (pp. 242, 262)
13. C (p. 262)
14. B (pp. 267–268)
15. A (p. 256)
16. C (p. 245)
17. 144 (pp. 232, 255)

18. C, E (p. 256) **23.** C (pp. 242, 245) **28.** D (p. 262)

19. E (pp. 256–257) **24.** D (p. 242) **29.** D (p. 262)

20. E (pp. 233, 256) **25.** B, C (p. 256) **30.** 86 (p. 223)

21. B (pp. 222–223) **26.** B (p. 242)

22. D (p. 242) **27.** A (p. 256)

Word Problems

1. E (p. 303) **5.** C (p. 86) **9.** C (p. 300)

2. D (p. 300) **6.** B, C, D, E, F (p. 296) **10.** E (p. 86)

3. D (p. 86) **7.** C (p. 115) **11.** C (p. 256)

4. E (p. 187) **8.** D (p. 86)

Answers and Explanations

Arithmetic

1. **E.** The pair in choice E is not equal. Dividing 7 by 11 gives 0.63+. Dividing 72 by 112 gives 0.64+.

2. **B.** Since the last two digits are divisible by 4, the number is divisible by 4, choice B. The sum of the digits is 19, so the number is not divisible by 3 or 6 (choices A or D). Because the number does not end in a 0 or 5, it is not divisible by 5 (choice C). Since the last three digits are not divisible by 8, the number is not divisible by 8 (choice E).

3. **C.** Change the terms into fractions and then multiply:

$$\frac{3}{2} \times \frac{2}{5} = \frac{6}{10} = \frac{3}{5}, \text{ choice C}$$

4. **D.** The greatest common factor is the largest factor that divides into all the numbers. Of the choices, 16 (choice D) is the largest number that can divide evenly into 32, 48, and 64.

5. **C.** To divide by a fraction, you invert the divisor and then multiply. Thus, 5 divided by $\frac{8}{2}$ is the same as multiplying by $\frac{1}{4}$.

$$5 \div \frac{8}{2} =$$

$$5 \times \frac{2}{8} =$$

$$5 \times \frac{1}{4} =$$

6. **C.** 0.25% is 0.0025; therefore, 0.25% of 2,000 equals $0.0025 \times 2,000 = 5$, choice C.

7. **B.** $(9.3 \times 10^7) - (2.1 \times 10^2) = 93,000,000 - 210 = 92,999,790$, choice B.

8. **D.** Multiply 72,000 births by 7 (days in a week) = 504,000 for Country A. Multiply 3 by 1,440 (minutes in a day) = 4,320 for the daily rate of births for Country B. Then multiply 4,320 by 7 for a weekly total of 30,240 for Country B. To find the positive difference subtract 30,240 from 504,000, which equals 473,760, choice D.

9. **A.** The average equals the sum divided by the number of items, average = $\dfrac{\text{sum}}{\text{number of items}}$. To find the sum, simply multiply the average times the number of items: $50 \times 30 = 1,500$ for Data Set A. Data Set B has a total of 25 times 100, which is 2,500. To find the positive difference, subtract the small number from the larger number to have a positive answer. Therefore, $2,500 - 1,500 = 1,000$, choice A.

10. **A, B, E, F.** The units digit, 3, in 73^n, will determine the units digit of 73^n for all positive integers n. Since $3^1 = 3$, $3^2 = 9$, $3^3 = 27$, and $3^4 = 81$, the units digits will repeat the same pattern indefinitely: $3^5 = 243$, $3^6 = 729$, $3^7 = 2,187$, $3^8 = 6,561$, and so forth. Hence, the 1, 3, 7, and 9 (choices A, B, E, and F, respectively) are the only possible units digits of 73^n.

11. **D.** To find any part of a simple percentage problem, use $\dfrac{\text{is}}{\text{of}} = \%$.

Plug in the given values:

$$\frac{24}{?} = 20\%$$

$$\frac{24}{x} = \frac{20}{100}$$

Cross multiply:

$$20x = 2,400$$

$$x = 120, \text{ choice D}$$

12. **D.** Since the ratio of males to females is 4 to 5, the males must be a multiple of 4 and the females must be a multiple of 5. Therefore, the total number of people at the party must have been $4 + 5 = 9$, or a multiple of 9. Similarly, adding adults and children means that $3 + 2 = 5$. The number of partygoers must also be a multiple of 5. The only choice that is both a multiple of 5 and a multiple of 9 is choice D, 45.

13. **C.** Twenty percent off the original price of $850 is a discount of (0.20)($850), or $170. Therefore, the new selling price is $850 - $170 = $680, choice C.

14. **A.** Notice that each change was an increase of 1,500 points. Therefore, the largest percent increase will have the smallest starting point (denominator). Thus, 13,000 in 2012 will be the smallest denominator or starting point:

$$\text{percent increase} = \frac{\text{change}}{\text{starting point}} = \frac{1,500}{13,000} \approx 11.5\%$$

The greatest percent increase was between 2012 and 2013, choice A.

15. **C.** Use a common denominator of 24:

$$\frac{1}{3} + \frac{1}{8} + \frac{5}{6} = \frac{8}{24} + \frac{3}{24} + \frac{20}{24} = \frac{31}{24}, \text{ choice C}$$

16. **A.** Changing the decimals to the nearest fraction gives

$$0.26 \times 0.67 \times 0.5 \times 0.9 = \frac{1}{4} \times \frac{2}{3} \times \frac{1}{2} \times \frac{9}{10}$$

Canceling leaves

$$\frac{1}{4} \times \frac{\cancel{2}}{\cancel{3}} \times \frac{1}{\cancel{2}} \times \frac{\cancel{9}^{3}}{10} = \frac{1}{4} \times \frac{3}{10} = \frac{3}{40} = 0.075 \approx 0.08, \text{ choice A}$$

17. **A, B, C, E, G.** Since $\sqrt{xz} = 10$, $xz = 100$, and the possible values of x and z are

$$
\begin{array}{rcl}
1 \text{ and } 100 & \rightarrow & 1 + 100 = 101 \\
2 \text{ and } 50 & \rightarrow & 2 + 50 = 52 \\
4 \text{ and } 25 & \rightarrow & 4 + 25 = 29 \\
5 \text{ and } 20 & \rightarrow & 5 + 20 = 25 \\
10 \text{ and } 10 & \rightarrow & 10 + 10 = 20
\end{array}
$$

Therefore, the correct answer choices are A, B, C, E, and G.

18. **131** Since the four numbers are consecutive odd integers, let

$$
\begin{aligned}
x &= \text{1st odd integer} \\
x + 2 &= \text{2nd odd integer} \\
x + 4 &= \text{3rd odd integer} \\
x + 6 &= \text{4th odd integer}
\end{aligned}
$$

There sum is $(x) + (x + 2) + (x + 4) + (x + 6) = 512$. Solve for x to find the value for each integer:

Their sum is
$$
\begin{aligned}
(x) + (x + 2) + (x + 4) + (x + 6) &= 512 \\
4x + 12 &= 512 \\
4x &= 500 \\
x &= 125 \\
x + 2 &= 127 \\
x + 4 &= 129 \\
x + 6 &= 131
\end{aligned}
$$

Therefore, 131 is the greatest of the four odd integers.

19. **B.** One method to solve this problem is to compute total percentage points. For the boys, 20×82 percentage points each = 1,640. For the girls, 10×85 percentage points each = 850. Adding gives 2,490 total percentage points. 2,490 total percentage points divided by 30 students gives an average of 83% per student, choice B.

Another method is to realize that, for every two boys averaging 82%, there is one girl averaging 85%. So the problem is simply, what is the average of 82, 82, and 85? Again, the answer is 83%.

20. D. If the average of four numbers is 14, then their sum must be 4(14) or 56. Since three of the numbers (10, 14, and 16) sum to 40, the fourth number must be 56 – 40, or 16, choice D.

21. A. Before the price reduction, $30 would purchase six times two dozen apples, or $6 \times 2 \times 12 = 144$. After the price reduction, $30 will buy five times three dozen apples, or $5 \times 3 \times 12 = 180$. Therefore, $180 - 144 = 36$ more apples can be purchased now, choice A.

22. D. One way to solve this problem is to set up a proportion using ratios:

$$\frac{mm}{cm} = \frac{mm}{cm}$$

$$\frac{28}{2.8} = \frac{x}{50}$$

Cross multiply:

$$1{,}400 = 2.8(x)$$

Divide each side by 2.8:

$$\frac{1{,}400}{2.8} = x$$

$$500 = x, \text{ choice D}$$

Another way to solve this problem is to realize that the number of millimeters is 10 times the number of centimeters. Thus, 10 times 50 centimeters equals 500 millimeters.

23. 0.56 A die has six sides. If it is rolled three times, there are $(6)(6)(6) = 216$ possible outcomes. Some of these result in all three rolls being different, and some rolls include duplicates. The probability of rolling all different numbers is the quotient between favorable outcomes divided by the total number of outcomes. The first roll can be any of the six sides, since it will not match anything. The second roll is limited to five choices, since one has already been selected by the previous roll. The third roll is limited to four choices, since the first two rolls have selected two of the choices.

The probability of all rolls being different is $\dfrac{(6)(5)(4)}{(6)(6)(6)} = \dfrac{120}{216} = 0.56$.

24. B. To determine an equivalent for $\dfrac{3}{8}$, simply divide 3 by 8.

$$8\overline{)3.000} \quad 0.375$$

Therefore, $\dfrac{3}{8}$ is equal to 0.375 (I), which may also be expressed as $\dfrac{37\frac{1}{2}}{100}$ (III) or $37\frac{1}{2}\%$ (II). Therefore, the answer is choice B (I, II, and III).

25. B, C, D. To find the cost of the food before tax, divide by (1 + tax). First, test the minimum value of $15.01:

$$\frac{\$15.01}{1.0875} \approx \$13.80$$

Now divide by 3 since we are looking for the cost per combo meal:

$$\frac{\$13.80}{3} \approx \$4.60$$

Repeat for the maximum value of $19.99:

$$\frac{\$19.99}{1.0875} \approx \$18.38$$

Now divide by 3:

$$\frac{\$18.38}{3} \approx \$6.13$$

Therefore, the cost of each combo meal, before tax, is between $4.60 and $6.13. Choices B ($4.65), C ($5.75), and D ($6.10) are all correct.

26. A. To determine the arithmetic mean (average) of the items in question, simply determine the total for all players, and then divide by the total number of players. For example,

Six Tigers each averaging 0.280 = 1.680.

Four Padres each averaging 0.250 = 1.000.

Together, the players average 1.680 + 1.000 = 2.680.

Now, divide the final total of 2.680 by the total number of players (10):

$$\frac{2.680}{10} = 0.268 \text{ average for all ten players, choice A}$$

27. C. To determine simple interest, use the equation $I = prt$, or Interest = (principal)(annual rate)(time in years). From the problem, 2% quarterly = 8% annually and 4 months = $\frac{1}{3}$ year.

Now plug in the given values:

$$I = (\$3,000)(0.08)\left(\frac{1}{3} \text{ year}\right)$$

$$I = (\$1,000)(0.08)$$

$$I = \$80, \text{ choice C}$$

28. **E.** To find the total number of paintings, use the following equation:

$$\frac{\text{is}}{\text{of}} = \%$$

The question is essentially, 24 is 30% of how many? Therefore, 24 is the "is," 30 is the percent, and "how many" (the unknown) is the "of." Plugging these values into the equation, you get

$$\frac{24}{x} = \frac{30}{100}$$

Note that the fractional percent is used to simplify the math.

Cross multiply:

$$30x = 2{,}400$$

Divide both sides by 30:

$$\frac{30}{x} = \frac{2{,}400}{30}$$

$$x = 80, \text{ choice E}$$

29. **C.**

Use $d = rt$

Going: 120 miles $= (60 \text{ mph})(t_1)$

2 hours $= t_1$

Returning: 120 miles $= (40 \text{ mph})(t_2)$

3 hours $= t_2$

Entire trip: 240 miles $= (r)(5 \text{ hours})$

48 mph $= r$, choice C

30. **B.** Since Albert stops after 0.8 km, he may run half that distance, 0.4 km, before stopping again, after which he may run 0.2, then 0.1, then 0.05 km. After his 0.05 km distance, he will make his fifth stop and must stop running. Adding the distances: $0.8 + 0.4 + 0.2 + 0.1 + 0.05 = 1.55$ km, choice B.

31. **C.** The original price, $7.00, is first discounted 20%: $7.00 − 0.20(7.00) = $7.00 − $1.40 = $5.60. Then the price is discounted an additional 10%: $5.60 − 0.10($5.60) = $5.60 − $0.56 = $5.04, choice C.

32. **C.** To find the average percentage for the three tests, you would find the sum of the three percentage scores and divide this by 3. In order for this average to be 85%, the sum of the percentages must be $3 \times 85\%$, or 255%. Because the student scored 80% on each of two tests, he has accumulated 160% and, thus, needs 95% more (choice C) to get the total of 255%.

33. **C.** Suppose you begin with a list price of $100.

$100 List price	$60 First selling price	$60	$100 List price
× 0.40	× 0.20	−$12	−$48 Selling price
$40.00 First discount	$12 Second discount	$48 Second selling price	$52 Total discount

$$\frac{\$52}{\$100} = 52\%, \text{ choice C}$$

34. **C.** In this problem, the words *at least* and *not more than* play an important role. Note that *at least 30%* means *30% or more.* And *not more than 20%* means *20% or less.* Requirement for orange juice = 30% of 400 cups = (0.30)(400) = 120 cups of orange juice. Note, however, that this is only the minimum. The punch bowl may contain 120 *or more* cups of orange juice. Ginger ale may be 80 cups or less. Of the choices given, only choice C (150 cups of orange juice, 70 cups of ginger ale) fits these parameters.

35. **C.** To solve this problem, use the following formula:

$$\frac{\text{is}}{\text{of}} = \text{percent}$$

From the information given, "is" becomes $\dfrac{1}{2^3} = \dfrac{1}{8}$ and "of" becomes $2^3 = 8$.

$$\frac{\text{is}}{\text{of}} = \frac{\frac{1}{8}}{8} = \frac{1}{8} \div \frac{8}{1} = \frac{1}{8} \cdot \frac{1}{8} = \frac{1}{64} = 0.016 \approx 1.6\%, \text{ choice C}$$

Algebra

1. **E.** Substituting $x = -3$ leaves

$$y = (-3+5)(-3-5)$$
$$y = (2)(-8)$$
$$y = -16, \text{ choice E}$$

2. **C.** First, circle $x + 1$ because that's the ultimate question. Solving the given equation, subtract 4 from both sides:

$$9x + 4 = -32$$
$$\underline{\quad -4 \quad -4 \quad}$$
$$9x = -36$$

Divide both sides by 9:

$$\frac{9x}{9} = \frac{-36}{9}$$
$$x = -4$$

Therefore, plugging in the value −4 for x gives $x + 1 = -4 + 1 = -3$, choice C.

3. **A.** Notice that (4)(4)(4) = 64 and (8)(8) = 64. Therefore,

$$(4)(4)(4)(4) = \frac{(8)(8)}{p}$$
$$(64)(4) = \frac{64}{p}$$

Cancel 64 on each side:

$$4 = \frac{1}{p}$$

Cross multiply:

$$4p = 1$$

$$p = \frac{1}{4}, \text{ choice A}$$

4. **D.** Plug in the given values for a, b, and c:

$$a^{bc} =$$

$$2^{(3)(2)} =$$

$$2^6 = 64, \text{ choice D}$$

5. **C, D.** One approach to solving this problem is to build a table of the values given and see where, or if, $*x > **x$.

x	$*x$	$**x$	$*x > **x?$
8	68	94	No
10	104	118	No
12	148	142	Yes
14	200	166	Yes

Choices C and D are correct.

Another approach (but a bit more algebraic and time-consuming) is to set up an inequality and solve:

$$x^2 + 4 > 12x - 2$$
$$x^2 - 12x > -6$$
$$x^2 - 12x + 36 > -6 + 36$$
$$(x - 6)^2 > 30$$
$$x - 6 > \sqrt{30}$$
$$x > 5.5 + 6$$
$$x > 11.5$$

In this solution, we used the completing the square technique to solve. Only the approximate positive square root was used since only positive values greater than 1 were presented as answer choices. Since x is greater than 11.5, the only answer choices that meet this requirement are 12 and 14, choices C and D.

6. **11** The traditional approach is to solve for each variable, and then determine the value of $x + y - z$. This can be done as follows:

From the second equation, we get that $x = -z$. Substitute $-z$ for x in the first equation, giving $-z + 2y = 10$. Combining this with the third equation gives

$$-z + 2y = 10$$
$$-2z + y = 11 \quad \text{(Multiply by } -2)$$

$$-z + 2y = 10$$
$$4z - 2y = -22 \quad \text{(Add these two equations)}$$

$$3z = -12$$
$$z = -4$$
$$x = 4 \quad \text{(Since } x = -z)$$
$$y = 3 \quad \text{(Since } x + 2y = 10)$$

Now, substitute these three values for x, y, and z into $x + y - z$, giving $4 + 3 - -4 = 11$.

But, there is a much more direct way to solve this problem: Add the second and third equations together:

$$x + z = 0$$
$$\underline{y - 2z = 11}$$
$$x + y - z = 11$$

We get the value of 11 without actually solving for any of the variables.

7. **E.** The square root of a number is always assumed to be a positive answer unless the square root symbol has a negative sign preceding it. Only choice E, when replaced for x, produces a negative answer for the square root, and thus cannot be the value for x in the given statement.

8. **E.** If t and p both equal 4, then $\frac{1}{4} + \frac{1}{4} = \frac{1}{2}$. In this case, $t + p$ would equal 8. But t could equal 1 and p could equal -2, which would also make

$$\frac{1}{t} + \frac{1}{p} = \frac{1}{2}$$
$$\frac{1}{1} + \frac{1}{-2} = \frac{1}{2}$$

In this case, $t + p$ would equal -1. Therefore, the sum of $t + p$ cannot be determined, choice E.

9. **C.** Since a and b are positive integers, they must be 6 and 5, respectively, because they are the only integers whose difference of their squares will equal 11 ($36 - 25 = 11$). Therefore, twice 6 plus twice 5 is $12 + 10$ or 22, choice C.

10. **A.** $x - 2$ is exactly four less than $x + 2$. Because $x + 2$ equals y, you know that $x - 2$ will be four less, or $y - 4$, choice A.

11. E. $(a + b)^2 = a^2 + 2ab + b^2$. If $ab = -5$, then $2ab = -10$. Plug in -10 for $2ab$:

$$(a + b)^2 = a^2 - 10 + b^2$$

Plug in the given $(a + b)^2 = 16$:

$$16 = a^2 - 10 + b^2$$
$$26 = a^2 + b^2, \text{ choice E}$$

12. E. The key phrase in this problem is *must also be an even integer.* A multiple of an even integer will result in an even number. Thus, adding or subtracting 1 from any even multiple will result in an odd number, eliminating choices A and B. In choice C, if you were to select x as 2, $\dfrac{x}{2} + 1$ would produce an even answer. But if you were to select x as 4, $\dfrac{x}{2} + 1$ would produce an odd answer, thus choice C is eliminated. In a similar manner, choice D can be eliminated. Therefore, only choice E will *always* produce an even integer.

13. D. Factoring the quadratic expression $m^2 + 11m + 30$ gives $(m + 5)(m + 6)$. Noting that the 5 and 6 represent y and z (or z and y), $yz = 5(6)$ or 30, choice D.

14. C. Notice that $4x + 10y$ is exactly twice $2x + 5y$. Therefore, the answer is twice 32 or 64, choice C.

15. D. Start with $25q^2p^2 = 8x$. Since you want an expression for $\dfrac{q^2p^2}{4}$, begin by dividing each side of $25q^2p^2 = 8x$ by 25. Then multiply each side of that result by $\dfrac{1}{4}$.

$$25q^2 p^2 = 8x$$
$$\frac{25q^2 p^2}{25} = \frac{8x}{25}$$
$$q^2 p^2 = \frac{8x}{25}$$
$$\frac{1}{4}(q^2 p^2) = \frac{1}{4}\left(\frac{8x}{25}\right)$$
$$\frac{q^2 p^2}{4} = \frac{8x}{100} = \frac{2x}{25}, \text{ choice D}$$

16. E. Either n or $(n + 1)$ may be even and the other odd. Since you're looking for what "must be true," this eliminates choices A and B. Since n and $(n + 1)$ are consecutive integers, they may be 1 and 2, or 2 and 3, or 3 and 4, or 4 and 5, and so on. Notice that their product will always be an even integer, choice E.

17. C. The coordinates of point C (choice C) are both negative. Thus, the product of two negative numbers will be positive. All the other points will either have a negative or a zero product.

18. E. First, try using 1, 2, and 3 as the three integers because these integers usually illustrate the exception to the rule. Using these three integers reveals that choices A, B, and C are incorrect because they will not be true with 1, 2, and 3. Choice D will be true with 1, 2, and 3, but it may not be true with many other integers (say, 5, 10, and 15). Notice that no matter what positive integers are inserted in choice E, the largest of the integers will always be greater than the middle integer divided by the smallest.

19. E. To find the greatest possible value of $\left(\dfrac{a}{b}\right)^2$, use the largest possible value for a (as the numerator) and the *smallest* possible value for b (as the denominator). Thus, $\dfrac{a}{b}$ would equal $\dfrac{0.05}{0.01}$, which equals 5. Therefore, $\left(\dfrac{a}{b}\right)^2$ will be 5^2 or 25, choice E.

20. D. The necessary condition refers to the denominator not equaling 0 because you cannot divide by 0. Therefore, $xyz \neq 0$ (III), choice D.

21. A. Multiplying each side of the equation $\dfrac{1}{5} + \dfrac{1}{2} + \dfrac{1}{x} = 7$ by the common denominator $10x$ gives $\dfrac{10x}{5} + \dfrac{10x}{2} + \dfrac{10x}{x} = 7(10x).$

Reduce the equation:

$$2x + 5x + 10 = 70x$$
$$7x + 10 = 70x$$

Subtract $7x$ from both sides:

$$7x + 10 = 70x$$
$$\underline{-7x \qquad\quad -7x}$$
$$10 = 63x$$

Divide by 63:

$$\frac{10}{63} = x, \text{ choice A}$$

22. $\dfrac{11}{16}$ The long (time-consuming) method would be to write out all the possible outcomes for flipping a coin four times and count how many consist of at least two heads.

$$\text{HHHH} \quad \text{HHHT} \quad \text{HHTH} \quad \text{HHTT}$$
$$\text{HTHH} \quad \text{HTHT} \quad \text{HTTH} \quad \text{HTTT}$$
$$\text{THHH} \quad \text{THHT} \quad \text{THTH} \quad \text{THTT}$$
$$\text{TTHH} \quad \text{TTHT} \quad \text{TTTH} \quad \text{TTTT}$$

Eleven out of the sixteen possibilities contain at least two heads; therefore, the probability of getting at least two heads is $\dfrac{11}{16}$.

A faster method is using binomial probability. Like with the coefficients of the binomial expansion in algebra, the values from the fifth row of Pascal's triangle give us all we need to answer the question. The values are 1, 4, 6, 4, 1. So, there is 1 way of getting all four heads, 4 ways of getting three heads and one tail, 6 ways of getting two heads and two tails, 4 ways of getting one head and three tails, and 1 way of getting all four tails. Add 1 plus 4 plus 6 to get 11 out of 16 possible outcomes.

Another way to solve this problem: We know that there are $2^4 = 16$ total outcomes (four tosses, two outcomes for each). Each of the outcome choices is a combination:

$$\text{Four heads: } {}_nC_r = {}_4C_4 = \frac{4!}{4!(4-4)!} = \frac{4!}{4!0!} = 1$$

$$\text{Three heads: } {}_nC_r = {}_4C_3 = \frac{4!}{3!(4-3)!} = \frac{4!}{3!1!} = 4$$

$$\text{Two heads: } {}_nC_r = {}_4C_2 = \frac{4!}{2!(4-2)!} = \frac{4!}{2!2!} = 6$$

Add 1, 4, and 6 to get 11 out of 16.

23. **C, E.** If one-fourth of the guests received the plate, then three-fourth of the guests received the vase.

Therefore, the number 24 represents three-fourths of the guests. If x is how many guests there were, then $\frac{3}{4}x = 24$, which means that $x = 32$. One-fourth of 32 is 8. So now we have 8 guests receiving the plate at \$16 and 24 guests receiving the vase at \$12. This gives $(8)(\$16) + (24)(\$12) = \$416$. Therefore, \$416 (choice C) is a possible choice. For each guest who receives an additional plate, the host will spend an additional \$16. Thus, $\$416 + \$16 = \$432$ (choice E) is also a possible value.

24. **D.** Set up an equation:

Let x be the unknown amount of the original solution. Solutions will be expressed in terms of concentration of water: 90% orange juice implies 10% water and one-fourth water implies 25% water.

$$\text{(water at the beginning)} + \text{(water added)} = \text{(water at the end)}$$
$$0.10(x) + 2 = 0.25(x + 2)$$
$$0.10x + 2 = 0.25x + 0.50$$
$$1.5 = 0.15x$$
$$10 = x$$

x is the number of liters in the original solution. Because the final solution is 2 additional liters of water, the final solution will contain 12 liters, choice D.

25. **A.** Ernie first purchased a certain number of apples (x) for a certain price per apple (y). Therefore, he paid xy, which equals \$5. He later learned that by purchasing 20% more apples ($1.2x$), he would have been given 20% off the per item price ($0.8y$). So, he would have paid $(1.2x)(0.8y) = 0.96xy$. Since $xy = \$5.00$, Ernie would have paid a new total of $0.96(\$5.00) = \$4.80$, which equals 20¢ less than the original total, choice A.

26. **D.** Set up an equation. Let x be the amount at 12%. Then $(\$2,000 - x)$ is the amount at 7%.

$$0.12x + 0.07(2,000 - x) = 200$$
$$0.12x + 140 - 0.07x = 200$$
$$0.05x + 140 = 200$$
$$0.05x = 60$$
$$\frac{0.05x}{0.05} = \frac{60}{0.05}$$
$$x = \$1,200, \text{ choice D}$$

27. B. To solve this problem, use the formula $\dfrac{\text{number}}{\text{cost}} = \dfrac{\text{number}}{\text{cost}}$.

If x represents the cost of n pencils, then we have, by substitution,

$$\frac{p}{c} = \frac{n}{x}$$

$$px = cn$$

$$x = \frac{cn}{p} \text{ cents, choice B}$$

28. C. To solve this problem, use the formula selling price = original price – discount.

If x = the original price, we substitute

$$165 = x - 0.40x$$

$$\frac{165}{0.60} = \frac{\cancel{0.60}x}{\cancel{0.60}}$$

$$275 = x, \text{ choice C}$$

29. D. Adding the x values together and y values together of points A and B, we have

$$(1,8)$$
$$+ (9,4)$$
$$(10,12)$$

Dividing each by 2 to find the midpoint leaves $(5, 6)$, choice D.

30. C, D. The expression $a^2 - b^2$ can be factored, and then the fraction can be simplified.

$\dfrac{a^2 - b^2}{a - b} = \dfrac{(a+b)(a-b)}{(a-b)} = a + b$ as long as $a - b \neq 0$. Since $a > b$ or $a < b$ implies that $a - b \neq 0$, answer choices C ($a > b$) and D ($a < b$) will guarantee that the given relationship is true.

Geometry

1. E. If l_1 and l_2 are parallel, then $z = 20°$. Therefore, supplementary angle x equals $160°$, as does vertical angle y, which means $160° + 160° = 320°$, choice E.

2. E. Since angle x and angle $5x$ are supplementary (their sum is a straight line or $180°$), then $5x + x = 180°$, and therefore, $x = 30°$. So the third angle of the triangle within the intersecting lines is the vertical angle of x or $30°$. The three angles of the triangle are thus $30°$, $40°$, and y: $30 + 40 + y = 180$; therefore, $y = 110°$, choice E.

3. D. Totaling the sum of the three angles in large $\triangle ABC$,

$$2x + 3x + (x + 3x + x) = 10x$$

Since there are $180°$ in a triangle, $10x = 180°$ and $x = 18°$.

Thus, in small $\triangle CEB$,

$$x + 3x + p = 180°$$
$$4x + p = 180°$$

Since x is 18°,

$$4(18) + p = 180°$$
$$72 + p = 180°$$
$$p = 108°, \text{ choice D}$$

4. **B.** Chord $\overline{MD}$ is a diameter cutting the circle in half. Therefore, $m\overset{\frown}{MD}$ is 180°. Since $m\overset{\frown}{AD}$ is 80°, that leaves $m\overset{\frown}{MA} = 100°$. $\angle MDA$ is an inscribed angle intercepting $\overset{\frown}{MA}$, 100°. Since an inscribed angle equals half its intercepted arc, $m\angle MDA$ is 50°, choice B.

5. $\dfrac{2}{16}$ or $\dfrac{1}{8}$

There are several approaches you can take to solve this problem. A visual solution is the easiest. Redraw the figure inserting horizontal and vertical dotted lines as follows:

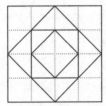

The dotted lines form dotted squares. The area of the outermost square is a total of 16 small dotted squares. The area of the innermost square is a total of 2 dotted squares (actually 4 half-squares).

Therefore, the ratio of the areas is $\dfrac{2}{16}$ or $\dfrac{1}{8}$. Either answer would be okay. It is not necessary to simplify answers on fill-in type problems.

A more mathematical solution would be to assign a value to the length of the side of the outermost square. For example, assign a value of 4; therefore, each dotted square has a side length of 1. The innermost square is made up of four right isosceles triangles. The legs of these right triangles have a length of 1. Therefore, the hypotenuse would have a length of $\sqrt{2}$. This is the length of the side of the innermost square. Thus, the area of the innermost square would be $\left(\sqrt{2}\right)^2 = 2$. Since the outermost square had a side length of 4, its area is 16. The ratio of the area of the innermost square to the outermost square would be $\dfrac{2}{16}$ or $\dfrac{1}{8}$.

6. **E.** $\triangle ABC$ is an isosceles triangle, so the base angles are equal, but nothing in the information given in the problem allows you to draw any conclusions about the relationship of r to p. $\overline{AD}$ is not necessarily an angle bisector. Therefore, the measures of angles r and p cannot be determined, choice E.

7. **D.** Since vertical angles are equal,

$$9x - 10 = 35$$
$$9x = 45$$
$$x = 5, \text{ choice D}$$

8. C. Ten cubes can be fitted across. Four cubes can be fitted along the depth. Only two cubes can be stacked along the height. Thus, $10 \times 4 \times 2 = 80$ cubes, choice C.

9. E. Since the area of one face of a cube is 49, its edges must each be 7 (as each face is a perfect square). Knowing each edge is 7, you can determine its volume, which equals length times width times height, or $7 \times 7 \times 7 = 343$, choice E.

10. C. Since the radius of circle O is $\sqrt{2}$, its diameter is $2\sqrt{2}$, which is also the diagonal of the square. The side of a square and its diagonal are always in a 1 to $1\sqrt{2}$ ratio. Therefore, if the diagonal is $2\sqrt{2}$, a side of the square must be 2. Hence, its area is 2×2 or 4 (choice C).

11. D. First, find the total interior degrees in a pentagon:

$$\text{total interior degrees} = (\text{number of sides} - 2)(180)$$
$$= (5 - 2)(180)$$
$$= 3(180)$$
$$= 540$$

Now, let the angles equal $2x$, $3x$, $4x$, $5x$, and $6x$. Their sum is $20x$. Therefore,

$$20x = 540$$
$$x = 27$$

Therefore, the largest angle, $6x$, is $6(27) = 162°$, choice D.

12. E. Since $\angle POQ$ is marked a right angle, $\triangle POQ$ is a right triangle; its hypotenuse is 13 and one leg is 5 (the radius of circle O). Therefore, the other leg, $\overline{OQ}$, must be 12 (a 5-12-13 right triangle). Because line segment $\overline{OK}$ is a radius of circle O, that equals 5, leaving a distance of 7 for $\overline{KQ}$, the radius of circle Q.

Thus, the area of circle Q is

$$A = \pi r^2$$
$$A = \pi(7)^2$$
$$A = 49\pi, \text{ choice E}$$

13. C. Since you know the area of circle O, you can find its radius.

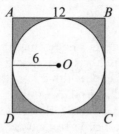

$$A = \pi r^2$$
$$36\pi = \pi r^2$$
$$36\cancel{\pi} = \cancel{\pi} r^2$$
$$6 = r$$

Now that you know the radius of the circle is 6, you can see that each side of the square will be twice 6, or 12. Since each side of the square is 12, the area is 144. The area of the circle is (3.14)(36) = 113.04. Therefore, the area of the shaded regions of the square is 144 − 113.04 = 30.96, choice C.

14. **B.** The volume of the cylindrical tank is

$$V = \pi r^2 h$$
$$V = \pi (6)^2 (9)$$
$$V = \pi 36(9)$$
$$V = 324\pi$$

However, the tank must be filled only $\frac{2}{3}$ full. Therefore,

$$\frac{2}{3}(324\pi) = 216\pi, \text{ choice B}$$

15. **A.** To find the area of the shaded region, first find the area of the larger triangle. Then subtract the area of the smaller, unshaded triangle. The area of the large triangle is $\frac{1}{2}bh$, or $\frac{1}{2}(10)5 = 25$. Now, find the area of the small, unshaded triangle:

$$A = \frac{1}{2}bh$$
$$A = \frac{1}{2}(5)(4)$$
$$A = 10$$

Subtracting, 25 − 10 = 15, the area of the shaded region, choice A.

16. **C.** The larger triangle is actually two 30°-60°-90° triangles whose sides are in the ratio $1 : \sqrt{3} : 2$. Therefore, $p = 1$ and $q = 2$. Their product is (1)(2) = 2, choice C.

17. **144** A regular decagon has 10 sides of equal length and 10 interior equal-sized angles. If n is the number of sides in a polygon, the total number of degrees in the interior angles of the polygon is $(n − 2)180°$. Since all 10 angles are equal in measure, the number of degrees in each interior angle is as follows:

$$\frac{(n-2)180°}{n} = \frac{(10-2)180°}{10} = \frac{(8)180°}{10} = \frac{1,440°}{10} = 144°$$

18. **C, E.** Remember, we are looking for integer values. Since the perimeter of the rectangle is 40, the length plus the width of the rectangle is 20. The width and length values of 1 and 19, 2 and 18, 3 and 17, and 4 and 16 are all eliminated since the width is less than one-third the length. A width of 5 and a length of 15 produces an area of 75 (choice C). A width of 6 and a length of 14 would work, but the product is not one of the answer choices. Same for 7 and 13. A width of 8 and a length of 12 produces an area of 96 (choice E), which is the other correct answer choice. The width of 8 and the length of 12 are acceptable since 8 is two-thirds of 12.

19. **E.** Since the rectangle's sides are 2 and 16, its perimeter is 2 + 2 + 16 + 16 = 36. Therefore, a square with the same perimeter, 36, has sides of 9 each; the area of the square is 9 × 9 = 81, choice E.

20. E. The hexagon is composed of six individual equilateral triangles, each having a base of 10.

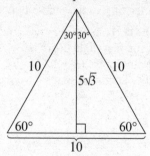

If a height is constructed within one of these triangles, then the height divides the triangle into equal 30°-60°-90° triangles. Thus, the height may be quickly calculated using the relationship of the sides of any 30°-60°-90° triangle: 1, $\sqrt{3}$, 2. The area of one triangle is, therefore, $\frac{1}{2}bh$ or $\frac{1}{2}(10)(5\sqrt{3}) = 25\sqrt{3}$. The area of the hexagon is six times this, or $150\sqrt{3}$, choice E.

21. B. If z equals 100°, $x + v = 80°$, since x, v, and z together equal 180° (a straight angle). Since l_2 bisects the angle composed of x and v, each must equal 40°, choice B.

22. D. Since $\overline{RP}$ passes through center O, chord $\overline{RP}$ is a diameter. Thus, inscribed angle RSP intercepts 180° of arc. Therefore, $\angle RSP$ measures 90°. $\triangle RSP$ is, therefore, a right triangle with hypotenuse of 10 (its diameter) and one leg of 6; it is a 3-4-5 right triangle. The other side must be 8, choice D.

23. C. $\triangle ABC$ is a 3-4-5 right triangle. Because $AB = 6$ and $BC = 8$, you know that $AC = 10$. Notice that $\triangle ADC$ is a 30°-60°-90° triangle. Its sides are always in the ratio of $1 : \sqrt{3} : 2$. Therefore, since the "2 side" here is 10, each side is actually multiplied by 5. Hence, the other two sides are 5 and $5\sqrt{3}$. Now the area of $\triangle ADC$ may be computed.

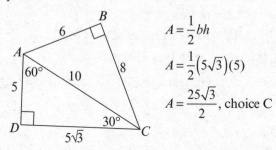

$$A = \frac{1}{2}bh$$

$$A = \frac{1}{2}(5\sqrt{3})(5)$$

$$A = \frac{25\sqrt{3}}{2}, \text{ choice C}$$

24. D. Using the coordinates of the points given, a right triangle may be constructed as shown below. Notice that the horizontal length of the triangle is 6; its vertical leg is 8. Therefore, it is a 3-4-5 right triangle. Its hypotenuse (side AB) must be 10, choice D.

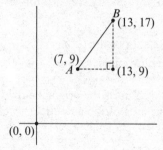

25. B, C. In each of the figures, the upper horizontal length can be found using the Pythagorean theorem since these are right triangles with a leg of length y and a hypotenuse of length x. The length then becomes $\sqrt{x^2 - y^2} = $ length z. Now the corresponding areas and perimeters of each figure can be expressed in terms of x, y, and z. In the rectangle tile (Figure A), the perimeter is $2(y + z)$. In the parallelogram tile (Figure B), the perimeter is $2(x + z)$. Notice that these perimeters are not equal; therefore, choice B is a true statement. The two figures have the same area, yz; therefore, choice C is a true statement.

26. B. First mark the diagram with the given values:

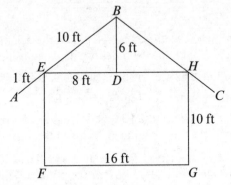

Since $FG = 16$ feet, $EH = 16$ feet. (Opposite sides of a parallelogram are equal.) Since $\overline{BD}$ is an altitude, $ED = DH = 8$ feet. (The altitude of an isosceles triangle is also the median.)

$$(EB)^2 = (BD)^2 + (ED)^2 \text{ (right triangle)}$$
$$(EB)^2 = 6^2 + 8^2 = 100$$
$$EB = 10 \text{ feet}$$
$$AB = BE + EA \text{ (given: } EA = 1 \text{ foot)}$$

Therefore, $AB = 11$ feet, choice B.

27. A. This figure represents both a rectangle and a semicircle. Use the following formulas:

area of a rectangle $= lw$

area of a semicircle $= \dfrac{\pi r^2}{2}$

Therefore, the area of this figure $= lw + \dfrac{\pi r^2}{2}$, choice A.

28. D. Given that $r = $ width of the ring (shaded portion) and $r = $ radius of the inner circle, $2r = $ radius of the entire circle. The area of a circle $= \pi r^2$. The area of the entire circle minus the area of the inner circle equals the area of the shaded portion. By substitution, $\pi(2r)^2$ or $4\pi r^2 - \pi(r)^2$ or $\pi r^2 = 3\pi r^2$ (area of shaded portion).

$$\frac{\text{area of the shaded portion}}{\text{area of the entire circle}} = \frac{3\pi r^2}{4\pi r^2} = \frac{3}{4} = 75\%, \text{ choice D}$$

29. D. The area of a circle $= \pi r^2$. If $x = $ radius of the original circle, then $2x = $ radius of the new circle. The area of the original circle $= \pi x^2$. The area of the new circle $= \pi(2x)^2 = 4\pi x^2$. Therefore, the area of the original circle has been multiplied by 4, choice D.

30. 86 Since the three angles $\angle 1$, $\angle 2$, and $\angle 3$ form a straight line, their sum is $180°$ and

$$\angle 1 + \angle 2 + \angle 3 = 180°$$
$$27° + \angle 2 + 67° = 180°$$
$$\angle 2 + 94° = 180°$$
$$\angle 2 = 180° - 94°$$
$$\angle 2 = 86°$$

Word Problems

1. E. Since the steering-wheel grip cost three times the seat cushion, call the seat cushion x, and the steering-wheel grip will then be $3x$. Notice that you do not have any other information except the price of the floor mat with tax. You have no way of determining in terms of dollars any of the statements, I, II, III, or IV. Deriving an answer in terms of an unknown (for example, $3x$) is not determining a value; therefore, the answer is choice E.

2. D. The only concrete piece of information from which you can begin is that Sue's car is a 2009 model. Therefore, you can first determine the approximate age of Sue's car (by subtracting 2009 from the year it is now). When you know the age of Sue's car, you can find the age of John's car because the information given states that his car is 1 year older than Sue's car. Then you can find the age of Maria's truck since it is 1 year newer than John's car. So, you can determine the approximate age of Sue's car, Maria's truck, and John's car, choice D.

3. D. Statements I and II are equations finding a balance by subtracting 5 from 10. In statement I, since the current balance is $5 less than last year's balance, $10, the current balance equals $10 − $5. In statement II, the same equation will also work to calculate last year's balance. Statement III cannot be calculated by 10 − 5 because 10 *percent* equals 0.10. Therefore, the answer is choice D, I and II.

4. E. To find the average of a number of items, you must find the sum of the items and then divide by the number of items. Note that since Test 4 is weighted double, it will actually count as *two* scores (hence, as tests 4 and 5). Set up the equation and solve:

$$\frac{\text{sum of the scores}}{\text{number of scores}} = \text{average}$$
$$\frac{83 + 85 + 100 + x + x}{5} = 90, \text{ choice E}$$

Note that since Test 4 is weighted double, the number of scores is 5, not 4.

5. C. Since 845 equals Q, then 846 equals $Q + 1$. Therefore, $27{,}456 \times 846$ may be expressed as $(P)(Q + 1)$, choice C.

6. B, C, D, E, F. Calculate the amount needed for each of the two extremes. Set up equations in terms of cost.

For the $5.50 per pound coffee,

$$(12)(8.50) + (x)(4.00) = (12 + x)(5.50)$$
$$(12)(85) + (x)(40) = (12 + x)(55)$$
$$1{,}020 + 40x = 660 + 55x$$
$$360 = 15x$$
$$24 = x$$

For the $6.00 per pound coffee,

$$(12)(8.50)+(x)(4.00)=(12+x)(6.00)$$
$$(12)(85)+(x)(40)=(12+x)(60)$$
$$1,020+40x=720+60x$$
$$300=20x$$
$$15=x$$

So, the range of amounts needed to yield coffee worth from $5.50 to $6.00 per pound is from 15 to 24 pounds; choices B, C, D, E, and F are correct.

7. C. To check $(x + 1)(x + 2) = x^2 + 3x + 2$, Francisco merely needs to plug in any positive value for x, choice C. If the equation balances, it is correct. For example, using 1 for x,

$$(x+1)(x+2)=x^2+3x+2$$
$$(1+1)(1+2)=1^2+3(1)+2$$
$$(2)(3)=1+3+2$$
$$6=6$$

The equation balances. Plugging in 1 enables Francisco to check his answer.

8. D. The word *sum* indicates addition. The sum of two numbers is, therefore, $x + y$. If this sum equals one of the numbers, then the equation will be either $x + y = x$ or $x + y = y$.

9. C. If Jorge is 10 years old now, then last year he was $10 - 1$. The question states that Jorge's age last year (9) is 3 years less than twice Teresa's age now. Therefore, letting T equal Teresa's age now, 3 years less than twice T can be represented as $2T - 3$. Thus,

$$10-1=2T-3$$
$$9=2T-3, \text{ choice C}$$

10. E. If a tie costs T dollars, then each tie $= T$. If a suit jacket costs four times the price of a tie, then each suit jacket $= 4T$. Hence, the cost of two ties and three suit jackets is $2(T) + 3(4T)$, choice E.

11. C. To determine the area of a square that has the same perimeter as a rectangle 18 by 22, Rosanna must take the following steps, as described in choice C:

Step 1: Find the perimeter of the rectangle by adding 18 and 22.

Step 2: Double the sum found in Step 1.

Step 3: Divide the result by 4 to find the side of a square of the same perimeter.

Step 4: Square the sum found in Step 3 to find the area.

Chapter 7

Quantitative Comparison

Quantitative Comparison Strategies

This unique problem type appears on the GRE, among others. It tests your ability to compare two given quantities using your knowledge of mathematics. After you compare two quantities, you must decide which quantity is greater, if the quantities are equal, or if a comparison cannot be determined from the information given.

Complex computation is not required. In fact, mathematical insight allows you to solve this type of problem more quickly than you can solve the more common math reasoning problems (see Chapter 6, "Mathematical Reasoning").

Directions

You will be asked to compare two quantities—Quantity A and Quantity B. Using the information centered above each quantity (if information is provided), determine a relationship between the two quantities and select one of the following answer choices:

- Ⓐ Quantity A is greater.
- Ⓑ Quantity B is greater.
- Ⓒ The two quantities are equal.
- Ⓓ The relationship cannot be determined from the information given.

NOTE: Memorize and practice this type of question using the four answer choices. The answer choices for questions on the actual computer version of the GRE and other standardized tests are not labeled with letters. This guide labels each answer choice with a letter choice, A, B, C, or D, for clarity. These letter labels will not appear on the computer screen when you take the test.

Example:

Quantity A	Quantity B
8×4	8^4

Analysis

In this example, the solution to Quantity A is $8 \times 4 = 32$. The solution to Quantity B is $8^4 = 8 \cdot 8 \cdot 8 \cdot 8 = 4,096$.

Since Quantity B is larger than Quantity A, the correct answer is choice B.

The purpose here is to make a comparison; therefore, exact calculations are not always necessary. (***Remember:*** In many cases, you can tell whether you're taller than someone without knowing that person's height. Comparisons such as this can be made with only partial information—just enough to compare.)

Notice that there are only four possible choices here, not five. To solve this type of problem correctly, you must quickly make a decision about the "relative values" of the two quantities provided. Apply your knowledge of mathematical insight, approximations, simple calculations, and common sense as you solve the problem.

Suggested Approach with Examples

Quantitative comparison problems emphasize shortcuts, insight, and quick techniques. Long and/ or involved mathematical computations are unnecessary and are contrary to the purpose of this question type.

Use the Process of Elimination

You can eliminate choices immediately to narrow down your answer.

- If you get different relationships, depending on the values you choose for variables, you can eliminate choices A, B, and C; the answer is choice D, "the relationship cannot be determined from the information given."
- If there are *values* in each quantity, because you can always compare values, eliminate choice D. The answer must be choice A, B, or C.

Cancel Out Equal Amounts

Note that you can add, subtract, multiply, and divide both quantities by the same value and the relationship between them will not change. *Exception:* You should *not* multiply or divide each quantity by negative numbers because the relationship reverses. Squaring both quantities is permissible, as long as each side is positive.

Example:

Quantity A	Quantity B
$21 \times 43 \times 56$	$44 \times 21 \times 57$

Canceling (or dividing) 21 from each side leaves you with:

43×56	44×57

You should do the rest of this problem by inspection—Quantity B is obviously greater than Quantity A without doing any multiplication. Each number in Quantity B is larger than the corresponding number in Quantity A. You could've reached the correct answer by actually multiplying out each quantity, but you save valuable time if you don't. The correct answer is choice B.

Make Partial Comparisons

Partial comparisons can be valuable in providing insight into finding a comparison. If you can't simply make a complete comparison, look at each quantity part by part.

Example:

Quantity A	Quantity B
$\dfrac{1}{3} - \dfrac{1}{65}$	$\dfrac{1}{58} - \dfrac{1}{63}$

Because finding a common denominator would be too time-consuming, you should first compare the first fraction in each quantity (a partial comparison). Notice that $\dfrac{1}{3}$ is greater than $\dfrac{1}{58}$. Now compare the second fractions and notice that $\dfrac{1}{65}$ is less than $\dfrac{1}{63}$. Using some common sense and insight, if you start with a larger number and subtract a smaller number, it must be greater than starting with a smaller number and subtracting a larger number, as shown here:

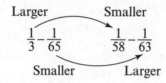

The correct answer is choice A.

Keep Perspective

Always keep the quantity in perspective before starting any calculations. Take a good look at the value of each quantity before starting to work on one or the other.

Example:

Quantity A	Quantity B
7^2	2^8

First, note that the answer cannot be choice D because there are values in each quantity. After looking at each quantity, compute the value of Quantity A: $7^2 = 49$. There is no need to take 2 out to the 8th power to compute the value of Quantity B. Just do as little as necessary: $2^2 = 4$, $2^3 = 8$, $2^4 = 16$, $2^5 = 32$. Stop. You can tell now that 2^8 is much greater than 49. The correct answer is choice B. Approximating can also be valuable while remembering to keep the quantities in perspective.

Plug In 0, 1, −1

If a problem involves variables (without an equation), substitute in the numbers 0, 1, and −1. Then try $\dfrac{1}{2}$, and 2 if necessary. Using 0, 1, and −1 will often tip off the answer.

Example:

Quantity A	Quantity B
$a + b$	ab

391

Substituting 0 for a and 0 for b gives

$$0 + 0 \qquad\qquad 0(0)$$

Therefore,

$$0 \quad = \quad 0$$

Using these values for a and b gives the answer: choice C. But any time you multiply two numbers, it isn't the same as when you add them, so try some other values.

Substituting 1 for a and -1 for b gives

$$1 + (-1) \qquad\qquad 1(-1)$$

Therefore,

$$0 \quad > \quad -1$$

and the answer is now choice A.

Anytime you get more than one comparison (different relationships), depending on the values chosen, the correct answer must be choice D (the relationship cannot be determined). Notice that if you had substituted the values $a = 4$ and $b = 5$, or $a = 6$ and $b = 7$, or $a = 7$ and $b = 9$, and so on, you would repeatedly have gotten choice B and might have chosen the incorrect answer.

Simplify the Comparisons

Often, simplifying one or both quantities can make an answer evident.

Example:

$$a, b, c, \text{ all greater than } 0$$

Quantity A	**Quantity B**
$a(b+c)$	$ab + ac$

Using the distributive property on Quantity A to simplify gives $ab + ac$; therefore, the quantities are equal, choice C.

Look for a Simple Way

Sometimes you can solve for a quantity in one step without solving and substituting. If you have to solve an equation or equations to give the quantities values, take a second and see if there is a very simple way to get an answer before going through all the steps.

Example:

$$4x + 2 = 10$$

Quantity A	**Quantity B**
$2x + 1$	4

You should be able to spot that the easiest way to solve for $2x + 1$ is by dividing $4x + 2 = 10$ by 2, leaving $2x + 1 = 5$.

Therefore,

5	>	4

Solving for x first in the equation, and then substituting, would also have worked, but it would have been more time-consuming. The correct answer is choice A.

Draw Diagrams

Drawing diagrams can be very helpful for giving insight into a problem. Remember that figures and diagrams are meant for positional information only. Just because something *looks* larger isn't enough reason to choose an answer.

Example:

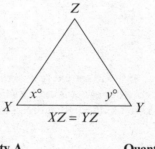

$XZ = YZ$

Quantity A	**Quantity B**
x	y

If you try to visually compare $\angle x$ to see if it is greater or less than $\angle y$, it is not enough.

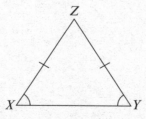

In this example, by quickly drawing hash marks on the diagram, you can see that the sides are equal measure. Because angles opposite equal sides in a triangle are equal, $x = y$. The correct answer is choice C.

Use Easier Numbers

If you're given information that is unfamiliar to you and difficult to work with, change the number slightly to something easier to work with (but remember what you've changed).

Example:

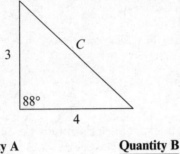

Quantity A	Quantity B
5	c

Since the 88° shown in the figure is unfamiliar to work with, change it to 90° for now, so that you may use the Pythagorean theorem to solve for c.

Solving for c:

$$a^2 + b^2 = c^2$$
$$3^2 + 4^2 = c^2$$
$$9 + 16 = c^2$$
$$25 = c^2$$
$$5 = c$$

But because you used 90° instead of 88°, you should realize that the side opposite the 88° will be slightly smaller or less than 5. The correct answer is choice A, 5 > c. (You may have noticed the 3-4-5 triangle relationship and not needed to use the Pythagorean theorem.)

A Patterned Plan of Attack

Quantitative Comparison

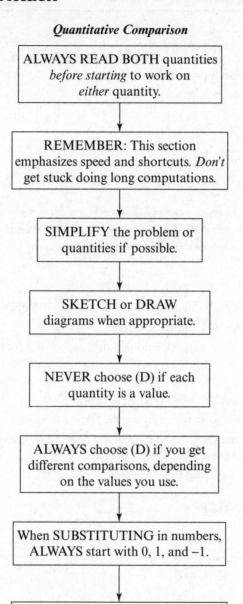

ALWAYS READ BOTH quantities
before starting to work on
either quantity.

REMEMBER: This section
emphasizes speed and shortcuts. *Don't*
get stuck doing long computations.

SIMPLIFY the problem or
quantities if possible.

SKETCH or DRAW
diagrams when appropriate.

NEVER choose (D) if each
quantity is a value.

ALWAYS choose (D) if you get
different comparisons, depending
on the values you use.

When SUBSTITUTING in numbers,
ALWAYS start with 0, 1, and −1.

When in DOUBT, plug in numbers.

Quantitative Comparison Practice

Directions

You will be asked to compare two quantities—Quantity A and Quantity B. Using the information centered above each quantity (if information is provided), determine a relationship between the two quantities and select one of the following answer choices:

- Ⓐ Quantity A is greater.
- Ⓑ Quantity B is greater.
- Ⓒ The two quantities are equal.
- Ⓓ The relationship cannot be determined from the information given.

> **REMINDER: The answer choices for questions on the actual computer version of the GRE and other standardized tests are not labeled with letters. This guide labels each answer choice with a letter choice, A, B, C, or D, for clarity. These letter labels will not appear on the computer screen when you take the test.**

Common assumptions:

- Information centered above both quantities refers to one or both quantities.
- All numerical values used are real numbers.
- Figures are intended to provide useful positional information, but they are not necessarily drawn to scale and should not be used to estimate sizes by measurement unless they are data displays (graphs and charts) or coordinates on coordinate axes. These will always be drawn to scale.
- Lines that appear straight can be assumed to be straight.
- A symbol that appears in both quantities represents the same value or object for each quantity.
- On a number line, positive numbers are to the right of zero and increase to the right, and negative numbers are to the left of zero and decrease to the left.
- Distances are always either zero or a positive value.

Arithmetic and Statistics

1.

Quantity A	Quantity B
$\dfrac{2}{5} \times \dfrac{1}{9} \times \dfrac{3}{8}$	$\dfrac{2}{11} \times \dfrac{2}{5} \times \dfrac{3}{8}$

2.

Quantity A	Quantity B
$\dfrac{1}{8} \times \dfrac{1}{4} \times \dfrac{1}{9}$	$0.125 \times 0.25 \times 0.1$

3.

Quantity A	Quantity B
The average of 12, 14, 16, 18, 20, and 22	The average of 11, 13, 15, 17, 19, and 21

4.

Quantity A	Quantity B
The average speed (in miles per hour) of a car that travels 8 miles in 15 minutes	30

5.

Quantity A	Quantity B
0.004	0.04%

6.

Quantity A	Quantity B
$\dfrac{1}{79} - \dfrac{1}{81}$	$\dfrac{1}{71} - \dfrac{1}{80}$

7.

Quantity A	Quantity B
The percent increase from $400 to $500	20%

8.

Quantity A	Quantity B
The price of 2 pounds of candy at 42¢ per pound	The price of 3 pounds of candy at 32¢ per pound

9.

Quantity A	Quantity B
4% simple interest on $2,000 for 1 year	8% simple interest on $1,000 for 2 years

10.

Quantity A	Quantity B
$9^5 - 9^4$	9^4

11.

Quantity A	Quantity B
$7\sqrt{3}$	$3\sqrt{7}$

Question 12 refers to the following diagram.

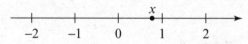

12.

Quantity A	Quantity B
1	$\dfrac{1}{x}$

13.

Quantity A	Quantity B
$9^2 + 8 \times 10^4 - 6^{10}$	$9^2 + 8 \times 10^4 + 6^{10}$

14.

Quantity A	Quantity B
$\dfrac{8 \times 10^4}{2 \times 10^2}$	400

15.

A hat contains 3 blue pegs,
2 red pegs, and 1 white peg.

Quantity A	Quantity B
The probability of randomly picking a blue peg	The probability of randomly picking something other than a blue peg

16.

Quantity A	Quantity B
The number of multiples shared by both 8 and 10 between 13 and 323	The number of prime numbers less than 19

17.

Quantity A	Quantity B
The cost per square inch of a circular pizza of diameter 12 inches for $10	The cost per square inch of a circular pizza of diameter 6 inches for $2.50

Question 18 refers to the following diagram.

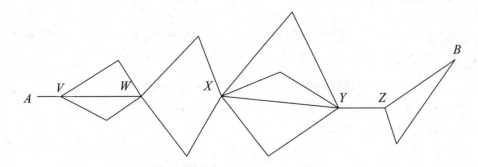

18.

Quantity A	Quantity B
The number of different paths from *A* to *B* without retracing any paths	$\dfrac{7!}{4!3!}$

19.

Events A, B, and C are independent events.

The probability of event A happening is $\frac{2}{3}$.

The probability of event B happening is $\frac{3}{8}$.

The probability of event C NOT happening is $\frac{3}{4}$.

Quantity A

The probability of
events A, B, and C happening

Quantity B

The probability of
events A, B, and C NOT happening

Question 20 refers to the following diagram.

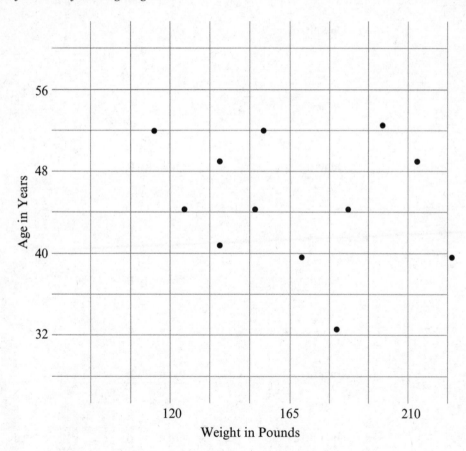

20.

The dots on the graph represent
the age and weight of the
12 members of the club.

Quantity A

The probability of randomly selecting
a member who is older than 44 and
weighs more than 180 pounds

Quantity B

The probability of randomly selecting
a member who is younger than 52 and
weighs less than 165 pounds

Algebra

1.

$$x > 2$$

Quantity A	Quantity B
$3x + 2$	$2x + 3$

2.

$$\frac{2x}{7} = 8$$
$$3y = 87$$

Quantity A	Quantity B
x	y

3.

$$\frac{s}{r} > \frac{3}{5}$$

Quantity A	Quantity B
s	r

4.

x is a negative fraction

Quantity A	Quantity B
$\dfrac{1}{x}$	$-x$

5.

Quantity A	Quantity B
$-(r - s)$	$-r + s$

6.

Quantity A	Quantity B
$(a^4 + b^3)^2$	$(a^3 b^6)^3$

7.

$$x < 4$$
$$y > 4$$

Quantity A	**Quantity B**
$x + 4$	$y - 4$

8.

$$x \neq 0$$
$$y \neq 0$$

Quantity A	**Quantity B**
$1 + \dfrac{x}{y}$	$\dfrac{x + y}{y}$

9.

$$y > 0$$

Quantity A	**Quantity B**
The average of $3y$, $5y$, 3, and 5	The average of $2y$, $6y$, 4, and 10

10.

$$0 < y < x$$

Quantity A	**Quantity B**
$(x + 2)(y + 3)$	$(x + 3)(y + 2)$

11.

15 is 30% of x
12 is 25% of y

Quantity A	**Quantity B**
x	y

12.

$$m > 0$$

Quantity A	**Quantity B**
m^3	$2m^2$

13.

$$\frac{r}{3} = \frac{s}{5}$$

Quantity A	**Quantity B**
$5r$	$3s$

14.

$$x > 0$$
$$y > 0$$

Quantity A	Quantity B
$\sqrt{x+y}$	$\sqrt{x} + \sqrt{y}$

15.

$$x + 3y = 7$$
$$4x + 12y = 28$$

Quantity A	Quantity B
x	y

16.

Line l passes through $(-2, 3)$ and $(0, 5)$.
Line w is perpendicular to line l.

Quantity A	Quantity B
slope of w	0

17.

$$G = \{1, 2, 2, 5, 6, 8\}$$
a = mean of G, b = median of G,
c = mode of G, d = range of G

Quantity A	Quantity B
$\dfrac{a}{d}$	$\dfrac{c}{b}$

18.

The ratio of m to n is 4:5.

Quantity A	Quantity B
m	n

19.

The permutation of n things
taken 2 at a time is 56.

Quantity A	Quantity B
The combination of n things taken 3 at a time	56

Geometry

Question 1 refers to the following diagram.

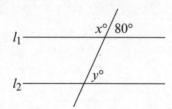

l_1 and l_2 are parallel lines.

1.

Quantity A	Quantity B
x	y

2.

Quantity A	Quantity B
The circumference of a semicircle with radius 4 inches	The perimeter of a pentagon with each side 4 inches long

Questions 3–5 refer to the following diagram.

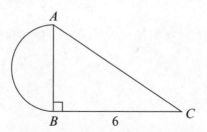

$\overline{AB}$ is a diameter of the semicircle.

$\triangle ABC$ is an isosceles right triangle.

3.

Quantity A	Quantity B
Area of the semicircle	Area of the triangle

4.

Quantity A	Quantity B
Length of $\overset{\frown}{AB}$	AC

5.

Quantity A	Quantity B
$m\angle A$	$45°$

Questions 6–9 refer to the following diagram.

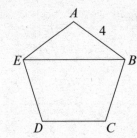

ABCDE is a regular pentagon.

6.

Quantity A	**Quantity B**
AB	*EB*

7.

Quantity A	**Quantity B**
The sum of interior angles of pentagon *ABCDE*	360°

8.

Quantity A	**Quantity B**
$m\angle AEB$	$m\angle ABE$

9.

Quantity A	**Quantity]**
$m\angle D + m\angle C$	180°

Questions 10–12 refer to the following diagram.

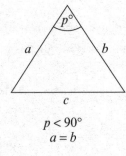

$p < 90°$
$a = b$

10.

Quantity A	**Quantity B**
$b + c$	a

11.

Quantity A	Quantity B
c^2	$a^2 + b^2$

12.

Quantity A	Quantity B
a	$c - b$

Questions 13–15 refer to the following diagram.

Vertices of square $ABCD$ lie on the circle.

13.

Quantity A	Quantity B
$m\angle DAC$	$m\angle BCA$

14.

Quantity A	Quantity B
Radius of circle	$\dfrac{\sqrt{2}}{2}$

15.

Quantity A	Quantity B
$2 \times$ area of square $ABCD$	Area of the circle

Answer Key

The page number(s) in parentheses following each answer will direct you to the basic review section(s) for that specific problem.

Arithmetic and Statistics

1. B (p. 38)
2. A (pp. 38, 45)
3. A (p. 187)
4. A (p. 290)
5. A (p. 49)
6. B (p. 31)
7. A (p. 56)

8. B (p. 297)
9. B (p. 306)
10. A (p. 57)
11. A (p. 65)
12. B (p. 16)
13. B (p. 14)
14. C (p. 61)

15. C (p. 199)
16. A (p. 27)
17. C (p. 262)
18. A (p. 204)
19. B (p. 199)
20. B (p. 199)

Algebra

1. A (p. 88)
2. B (p. 90)
3. D (pp. 94, 139)
4. B (p. 88)
5. C (p. 18)
6. D (pp. 88, 113)
7. D (p. 88)

8. C (p. 135)
9. B (pp. 112–113)
10. A (pp. 88, 114)
11. A (p. 52)
12. D (p. 88)
13. C (p. 97)
14. B (p. 165)

15. D (p. 99)
16. B (p. 156)
17. C (p. 96)
18. D (p. 204)
19. C (p. 204)

Geometry

1. A (p. 225)
2. B (pp. 232, 262)
3. B (pp. 244, 262)
4. A (pp. 244, 261)
5. C (p. 244)

6. B (pp. 238, 255)
7. A (p. 255)
8. C (p. 238)
9. A (p. 255)
10. A (p. 238)

11. B (p. 242)
12. A (p. 238)
13. C (p. 265)
14. C (pp. 244, 265)
15. A (pp. 256, 267)

Answers and Explanations

Arithmetic and Statistics

1. **B.** Dividing out equal fractions from both sides $\left(\dfrac{2}{5}\text{ and }\dfrac{3}{8}\right)$ leaves Quantity A with $\dfrac{1}{9}$ and Quantity B with $\dfrac{2}{11}$. Cross multiply:

    $$\overset{\textcircled{11}}{\underset{9}{1}}\bbox{\times}\overset{\textcircled{18}}{\underset{11}{2}}$$

    Since the larger product is always over the larger fraction, Quantity B is greater.

2. **A.** Change the decimals in Quantity B to fractions:

    $$\frac{125}{1,000}\times\frac{25}{100}\times\frac{1}{10}$$

    and reduce to the simplest form, and you get this comparison:

    $$\frac{1}{8}\times\frac{1}{4}\times\frac{1}{9}\qquad\qquad\qquad\frac{1}{8}\times\frac{1}{4}\times\frac{1}{10}$$

    Canceling out the $\dfrac{1}{8}$ and $\dfrac{1}{4}$ from each side leaves

    $$\frac{1}{9}>\frac{1}{10}$$

    Therefore, Quantity A is greater.

3. **A.** The fastest way to determine which average is greater is to notice that each of the numbers in Quantity A is one larger than its corresponding number in Quantity B. Therefore, Quantity A's average must be greater than Quantity B's average.

4. **A.** To find the average speed of the car in miles per hour, multiply 8 miles by 4, since 15 minutes is $\dfrac{1}{4}$ of an hour:

    $$8 \times 4 = 32$$

    32 miles per hour is the average speed and $32 > 30$. Quantity A is greater than Quantity B.

5. **A.** Expressed as a percent, Quantity A equals 0.4%, which is greater than Quantity B.

6. **B.** This problem is best solved by inspection. Notice that the values in Quantity A are very close together; therefore, their difference would be very small. Quantity B's values are farther apart, having a greater difference.

7. **A.** To find percent increase, use the percent change formula, $\dfrac{\text{change}}{\text{starting point}}=\text{percent change}$, and then convert to a percent:

    $$\frac{500-400}{400}=\frac{100}{400}=\frac{1}{4}=25\% \text{ and } 25\% > 20\%$$

    Quantity A is greater than Quantity B.

8. **B.** Quantity A equals 2 times 42¢, or 84¢. Quantity B equals 3 times 32¢, or 96¢. Therefore, Quantity B is greater.

9. **B.** The simple interest in Quantity A equals $2,000 times 0.04 times 1 year, or $80. The simple interest in Quantity B equals $1,000 times 0.08 times 2 years, or $160. Therefore, Quantity B is greater.

10. **A.** 9^5 is 9×9^4, so if 9^4 is subtracted from 9^5, the remainder is obviously greater than 9^4. Here is an alternate method:

$$\underbrace{\frac{9^5}{(9\times9\times9\times9\times9)}}_{59,049} - \underbrace{\frac{9^4}{(9\times9\times9\times9)}}_{6,561} = 52,488$$

$$52,488 > 6,561$$

Therefore, Quantity A is greater than Quantity B.

11. **A.** The fastest and most accurate way to compare two terms, each of which contains a square root, is to change each term to a single term under a radical.

$$7\sqrt{3} = \sqrt{3\times 49} = \sqrt{147} \qquad\qquad 3\sqrt{7} = \sqrt{7\times 9} = \sqrt{63}$$

Since $\sqrt{147}$ is greater than $\sqrt{63}$, Quantity A is greater than Quantity B.

12. **B.** On the number line, x is between 0 and 1; therefore, x is a positive fraction less than 1. Plugging in a simple value for x (use $\frac{1}{2}$, an easy-to-work-with fraction less than 1), we find Quantity B equals $\frac{1}{\frac{1}{2}}$, which equals 2. Quantity B is greater than Quantity A.

Every other fraction less than 1 will also make Quantity B greater than 1; therefore, Quantity B is greater than Quantity A.

13. **B.** Note that the only difference in the two quantities is the signs of the last values, 6^{10}. Because Quantity B is positive ($+6^{10}$) and Quantity A is negative (-6^{10}), Quantity B is greater than Quantity A. Actually calculating the numerical values is a waste of time and not necessary.

14. **C.** Canceling in Quantity A gives

$\dfrac{8\times 10^4}{2\times 10^2}$	400
4×10^2	400
4×100	400
400	400

The quantities are equal.

15. **C.** In Quantity A, the probability of randomly selecting a blue peg is 3 out of a total of 6, or $\frac{3}{6}$ or $\frac{1}{2}$. In Quantity B, the probability of randomly selecting a color other than blue is 2 + 1 out of 6, or again, $\frac{3}{6}$ or $\frac{1}{2}$. The quantities are equal.

16. **A.** Numbers that are multiples of both 8 and 10 are numbers that are multiples of the least common multiple of 8 and 10, which is 40. Quantity A consists of multiples of 40 between 13 and 323, or 40, 80, 120, 160, 200, 240, 280, and 320. There are 8 multiples of 40 between 13 and 323. Another way is to see how many 40s there are in 320 is to divide 320 by 40, which is 8. Now calculate the value of Quantity B. The prime numbers less than 19 are 2, 3, 5, 7, 11, 13, and 17. There are 7 of them. Therefore, Quantity A is greater than Quantity B.

17. **C.** To find the cost per square inch, take the cost and divide by the area. The area of a circle is found using $A = \pi r^2$, where r is the radius of the circle.

The pizza with a diameter of 12 inches has a radius of 6 inches and an area of 36π square inches. Its cost per square inch is, therefore, $\dfrac{\$10}{36\pi \text{ in}^2} \approx 8.8$ cents/square inch.

The pizza with a diameter of 6 inches has a radius of 3 inches and an area of 9π square inches. Its cost per square inch is $\dfrac{\$2.50}{9\pi \text{ in}^2} \approx 8.8$ cents/square inch.

Notice that if you were to take $\dfrac{\$2.50}{9\pi}$ and multiply by 1 in the form $\dfrac{4}{4}$, you can show the values are exactly the same: $\dfrac{2.50}{9\pi} \times \dfrac{4}{4} = \dfrac{10}{36\pi}$.
The two quantities are equal.

Alternative approach. This alternative approach makes use of the fact that the costs are directly proportional to the areas of the pizzas. Since the pizzas are circles, they are similar figures. The areas of similar figures compare like the squares of any two corresponding lengths; in this case, diameters.

Since the diameter of the larger pizza is two times as long as the smaller pizza's diameter, its area will be $\left(\dfrac{2}{1}\right)^2 = \dfrac{4}{1}$, or four times as large, and, therefore, would cost four times as much.

Multiplying, $4 \times \$2.50 = \$10.00$; therefore, the cost per square inch of pizza is the same for both quantities.

18. **A.** To find the value of Quantity A, make a table to organize the information given in the figure.

from to	A to V	V to W	W to X	X to Y	Y to Z	Z to B
# of paths	1	3	2	4	1	2

The number of different paths = $(1)(3)(2)(4)(1)(2) = 48$. Now calculate the value of Quantity B as shown:

$$\frac{7!}{4!3!} = \frac{7!}{3!4!} = \frac{(7)(6)(5)\,\cancel{(4)(3)(2)(1)}}{(3)(2)(1)\,\cancel{(4)(3)(2)(1)}} = 35$$

Therefore, Quantity A is greater than Quantity B.

19. **B.** The probability of an event *not* happening = 1 − probability of it happening.

The probability of a series of independent events happening is the product of their respective probabilities.

Event	Probability of happening	Probability of not happening
A	$\dfrac{2}{3}$	$1 - \dfrac{2}{3} = \dfrac{1}{3}$
B	$\dfrac{3}{8}$	$1 - \dfrac{3}{8} = \dfrac{5}{8}$
C	$1 - \dfrac{3}{4} = \dfrac{1}{4}$	$\dfrac{3}{4}$

The probability of events A, B, and C happening $= \dfrac{2}{3} \times \dfrac{3}{8} \times \dfrac{1}{4} = \dfrac{6}{96}$.

The probability of events A, B, and C *not* happening $= \dfrac{1}{3} \times \dfrac{5}{8} \times \dfrac{3}{4} = \dfrac{15}{96}$.

Therefore, Quantity B is greater than Quantity A.

20. **B.** On the age scale, there are two bars for every 8 years; hence, the age goes in increments of 4 years. On the weight scale, there are three bars for every 45 years; hence, the weight goes in increments of 15 years. The first bar above the 40 years is, therefore, 44 years, and the first bar to the right of 165 pounds is 180 pounds. There are three dots that are above the 44 years and to the right of 180 pounds. Therefore, the probability of selecting a member who is older than 44 and weighs more than 180 pounds is $\dfrac{3}{12} = \dfrac{1}{4} = 0.25$.

In a similar manner, there are four dots that are below age 52, the bar between 48 years and 56 years, and to the left of 165 pounds. Therefore, the probability of selecting a member who is younger than 52 and weighs less than 165 pounds is $\dfrac{4}{12} = \dfrac{1}{3} \approx 0.33$. Quantity B is greater than Quantity A.

Algebra

1. **A.** First, subtracting 2 from both sides gives $3x$ in Quantity A and $2x + 1$ in Quantity B. Since $x > 2$, start by plugging in values greater than 2 for x. Trying 3, then 4, then, say, 10, you'll find that Quantity A will always be greater than Quantity B.

2. **B.** Solve each equation:

$$\dfrac{2x}{7} = 8 \qquad\qquad 3y = 87$$

$$\dfrac{7}{2} \times \dfrac{2x}{7} = \dfrac{8}{1} \times \dfrac{7}{2} \qquad\qquad \dfrac{3y}{3} = \dfrac{87}{3}$$

$$x = 28 \qquad\qquad y = 29$$

$$28 < 29$$

Therefore, Quantity B is greater than Quantity A.

3. **D.** Trying some values in the equation gives different outcomes. For example, when $s = 4$ and $r = 5$,

$$\dfrac{4}{5} > \dfrac{3}{5}$$

$$s < r$$

When $s = -4$ and $r = -5$,

$$\dfrac{-4}{-5} > \dfrac{3}{5}$$

$$s > r$$

The relationship cannot be determined.

4. B. Substituting a value for x and considering the given condition (x is a negative fraction) makes it evident that Quantity B will always be positive and Quantity A will always be negative. For example, let $x = -\dfrac{1}{2}$:

$$\dfrac{1}{-\dfrac{1}{2}} \qquad\qquad -\left(\dfrac{-1}{2}\right)$$

$$-2 < +\dfrac{1}{2}$$

Therefore, Quantity B is greater than Quantity A.

5. C. This is really an example of the distributive property and can be solved by inspection. Or using an alternate method, let $r = 3$ and $s = 2$.

$$\begin{array}{ccc} -(3-2) & & -3+2 \\ -1 & = & -1 \end{array}$$

Therefore, both r and $s = -1$, so the quantities are equal.

6. D. Let $a = 0$ and $b = 0$, then both quantities are obviously equal. If $a = 1$ and $b = 0$, Quantity A is greater than Quantity B; therefore, the relationship cannot be determined.

7. D. Because x must be less than 4, Quantity A ($x + 4$) can equal any value less than 8. Because y must be more than 4, Quantity B ($y - 4$) can be any value more than 0. Therefore, between the range of 0 and 8, Quantity A and Quantity B could be equal or one quantity could be greater than the other. Hence, no relationship can be determined.

8. C. By changing the value of 1 in Quantity A to equal $\dfrac{y}{y}$, Quantity A can also equal $\dfrac{y}{y} + \dfrac{x}{y}$, which, combined into one fraction, equals $\dfrac{y+x}{y}$. Therefore, the two quantities are equal. Likewise, Quantity B could've been broken into two fractions: $\dfrac{x}{y} + \dfrac{y}{y}$, which is the same as $\dfrac{x}{y} + 1$ and, thus, equal to Quantity A.

9. B. Find the averages and simplify:

$$\begin{array}{cc} \dfrac{3y+5y+3+5}{4} & \dfrac{2y+6y+4+10}{4} \\[2mm] \dfrac{8y+8}{4} & \dfrac{8y+14}{4} \\[2mm] \dfrac{8y}{4} + \dfrac{8}{4} & \dfrac{8y}{4} + \dfrac{14}{4} \\[2mm] 2y+2 & 2y+\dfrac{14}{4} \end{array}$$

Subtracting $2y$ from both:

$$2 < \dfrac{14}{4}$$

Therefore, Quantity B is greater than Quantity A.

10. **A.** Simplifying each quantity leaves

$$xy + 3x + 2y + 6 \qquad\qquad xy + 2x + 3y + 6$$

Subtracting xy, $2x$, $2y$, and 6 from both sides leaves

$$x > y$$

From the condition given, $0 < y < x$, Quantity A is greater than Quantity B.

11. **A.** Solve each problem, first for x: 15 is 30% of x.

$$\frac{30}{100} = \frac{15}{x}$$

$$\frac{3}{10} = \frac{15}{x}$$

Cross multiply:

$$3x = 150$$

$$x = 50$$

Now solve for y: 12 is 25% of y.

$$\frac{25}{100} = \frac{12}{y}$$

$$\frac{1}{4} = \frac{12}{y}$$

Cross multiply:

$$y = 48$$

Since $50 > 48$, $x > y$, Quantity A is greater than Quantity B.

12. **D.** Trying the value $m = 1$ gives

$$(1)^3 \qquad\qquad 2(1)^2$$

$$1 < 2$$

Now, letting $m = 2$ gives

$$(2)^3 \qquad\qquad 2(2)^2$$

$$8 = 8$$

No relation can be determined because different values give different answers.

13. **C.** Cross multiply the given equation:

$$\frac{r}{3} = \frac{s}{5}$$

$$5r = 3s$$

Therefore, the two quantities are equal.

14. **B.** Substituting $x = 1$ and $y = 1$ gives

$$\begin{array}{cc} \sqrt{1+1} & \sqrt{1}+\sqrt{1} \\ \sqrt{2} & 1+1 \\ 1.4 & 2 \end{array}$$

$$1.4 < 2$$

Trying other values gives the same result; therefore, Quantity B is greater than Quantity A.

15. **D.** By inspection, the two given equations are the same: $x + 3y = 7$ is the same as $4x + 12y = 28$ if the second equation is simplified by dividing by 4. Because the two equations are equivalent, no definite values for x and y can be determined. Therefore, no relationship can be determined.

16. **B.** When two lines are perpendicular, their slopes are opposite reciprocals of one another. The slope of line l can be found using the formula $m = \dfrac{y_2 - y_1}{x_2 - x_1}$, where (x_1, y_1) and (x_2, y_2) are any two different points on the line.

$$\text{slope of } l = \frac{5-3}{0-(-2)} = \frac{2}{2} = 1$$

Therefore, the slope of line w is -1. Quantity B is greater than Quantity A.

Alternative approach. Whether the slope of a line is positive or negative can also be determined by the direction that the line slants. If a line slants up toward the right, it has a positive slope; if it slants down toward the right, it has a negative slope. When sketching the location of the given points and connecting the points, it can be seen that line l has a positive slope.

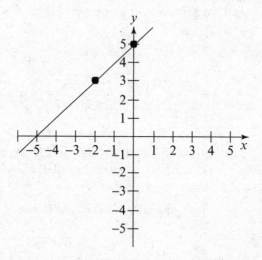

The slope of line l is a positive value; thus, the slope of line w must be a negative value. Quantity B is greater than Quantity A.

17. C.

The mean of G (the average) $= \dfrac{1+2+2+5+6+8}{6} = \dfrac{24}{6} = 4 = a.$

The median of G (the middle value) $= \dfrac{2+5}{2} = \dfrac{7}{2} = b.$

The mode of G (the value repeated most often) $= 2 = c.$

The range of G (maximum value − minimum value) $= 8 - 1 = 7 = d.$

$$\dfrac{a}{d} = \dfrac{4}{7} \qquad\qquad \dfrac{c}{b} = \dfrac{2}{\dfrac{7}{2}} = \dfrac{2}{1} \times \dfrac{2}{7} = \dfrac{4}{7}$$

The two quantities are equal.

18. D. Since there are no restrictions on m and n, they could both be positive or both be negative. Suppose $m = 4$ and $n = 5$; then $\dfrac{m}{n} = \dfrac{4}{5}$ and $m < n$. Now suppose $m = -4$ and $n = -5$; then $\dfrac{m}{n} = \dfrac{-4}{-5} = \dfrac{4}{5}$ and $m > n$. The relationship cannot be determined from the information given.

19. C. The permutation of n things taken 2 at a time is represented by $\dfrac{n!}{(n-2)!}$.

This can also be represented as $\dfrac{n(n-1)(n-2)!}{(n-2)!}$, which reduces to $n(n-1)$.

Therefore, $n(n-1) = 56$. By observation, $n = 8$ since $(8)(7) = 56$. The two quantities are equal.

Alternative approach. $n(n-1) = 56$ could also be solved by multiplying out the left side, setting the equation equal to zero, then factoring the left side to get possible values of n to be either 8 or −7, but since n is a positive integer, only 8 works.

The combination of n things taken 3 at a time is represented by $\dfrac{n!}{3!(n-3)!}$.

With $n = 8$, this becomes $\dfrac{8!}{3!(8-3)!} = \dfrac{8!}{3!5!} = \dfrac{(8)(7)(6)\,\cancel{(5)(4)(3)(2)(1)}}{(3)(2)(1)\,\cancel{(5)(4)(3)(2)(1)}} = 56$. The two quantities are equal.

Geometry

1. A. From the diagram and the rules of a transversal through parallel lines, it is evident that $y = 80°$. You know that $x = 100°$ because $x + 80$ must equal a straight line of 180°, or $180 - 80 = 100$. Since $100 > 80$, $x > y$; therefore, Quantity A is greater than Quantity B.

2. B. Because the circumference of a circle equals $2\pi r$, the circumference of the semicircle in Quantity A equals $\dfrac{1}{2}(2\pi r) = \dfrac{1}{2}(2)(\pi)(4) = 4\pi.$

Because π equals about 3, Quantity A equals approximately 12 inches. In Quantity B, if each side of a pentagon equals 4 inches, its perimeter equals 5 times 4 = 20 inches. Therefore, Quantity B is greater than Quantity A.

3. **B.** $AB = 6$ because $\triangle ABC$ is isosceles. The radius of the semicircle is $\frac{1}{2} AB$ or 3. Using the area formula for the circle:

$$A = \pi r^2$$
$$= \pi(3)^2$$
$$= \pi(9)$$
$$\approx 28$$

Taking $\frac{1}{2}$ of this leaves the area of the semicircle as approximately 14.

Now, using the area formula for the triangle:

$$A = \frac{1}{2} bh$$
$$= \frac{1}{2}(6)(6)$$
$$= \frac{1}{2}(36)$$
$$= 18$$

Since $14 < 18$, Quantity B is greater than Quantity A.

4. **A.** Using the circumference formula for a circle of diameter 6:

$$C = \pi d$$
$$= \pi(6)$$
$$\approx 18$$

Taking $\frac{1}{2}$ of this leaves 9 as the length of $\overset{\frown}{AB}$. Now, using the Pythagorean theorem to find AC:

$$(AB)^2 + (BC)^2 = (AC)^2$$
$$(6)^2 + (6)^2 = (AC)^2$$
$$36 + 36 = (AC)^2$$
$$72 = (AC)^2$$
$$\sqrt{72} = AC$$

Since $\sqrt{72}$ is approximately 8.5, $9 > \sqrt{72}$; therefore, Quantity A is greater than Quantity B.

5. **C.** Since $\triangle ABC$ is an isosceles right triangle, $m\angle A = m\angle C$ and $m\angle B = 90°$. This leaves 90° to be divided evenly between $m\angle A$ and $m\angle C$; therefore, $m\angle A$ is 45°. The quantities are equal.

6. **B.** Any diagonal of a regular pentagon is greater than any of the sides; therefore, Quantity B is greater than Quantity A.

   Alternative approach. An alternate method is to use the formula for finding the interior degrees of a polygon: $180(n-2)$ using 5 for n (number of sides of a pentagon):

   $$180(n-2)$$
   $$180(5-2)$$
   $$180(3)$$
   $$540$$

   There are 540° in the interior angles of the pentagon. Dividing this by 5, for the number of equal angles, leaves 108° in each angle. $m\angle A$ is 108° in $\triangle ABE$ and, therefore, is the greatest angle in the triangle. The longest side of a triangle is across from the largest angle, so $AB < EB$.

7. **A.** As you know from the previous problem, the sum of the interior angles of pentagon $ABCDE$ is 540°, and 540° > 360°. Therefore, Quantity A is greater than Quantity B.

   Alternative approach. Using an alternative method, the sum of the interior degrees of a pentagon can be derived by dividing the pentagon into triangles as shown:

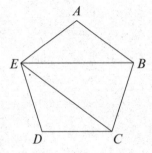

   Because there are three triangles and 180° in a triangle, there are $3 \times 180° = 540°$ in the pentagon.

8. **C.** The pentagon $ABCDE$ is a regular pentagon and its sides have equal lengths. Therefore, $AB = AE$ and $m\angle AEB = m\angle ABE$ because angles opposite equal sides in a triangle are equal. The quantities are equal.

9. **A.** As shown in the previous problems, each angle of the pentagon is 108°. Therefore, $108° + 108° = 216°$ and 216° > 180°, making Quantity A is greater than Quantity B.

10. **A.** The sum of any two sides of a triangle is greater than the third side; therefore, Quantity A is greater than Quantity B.

11. **B.** If $p = 90°$, then $c^2 = a^2 + b^2$. But since $p < 90°$, the opposite side, C, gets smaller. Therefore, $c^2 < a^2 + b^2$, making Quantity B greater than Quantity A.

12. **A.** The sum of any two sides of a triangle is greater than the third side, making the difference of any two sides of a triangle less than the third side. Solving algebraically, $a + b > c$. Subtracting b from both sides leaves $a > c - b$. Therefore, Quantity A is greater than Quantity B.

13. **C.** Since all sides of a square are equal and each corner of a square is 90°, $\triangle ADC$ and $\triangle ABC$ would each become isosceles right triangles. The acute angles in an isosceles right triangle each have measures of 45°. Therefore, $m\angle DAC = m\angle BCA$; the quantities are equal.

14. C. Using the Pythagorean theorem to find the length of diameter AC gives

$$(AB)^2 + (BC)^2 = (AC)^2$$
$$(1)^2 + (1)^2 = (AC)^2$$
$$1 + 1 = (AC)^2$$
$$2 = (AC)^2$$
$$\sqrt{2} = AC$$

Since the radius is $\dfrac{1}{2}$ of the diameter, $\dfrac{1}{2}$ of $\sqrt{2}$ is $\dfrac{\sqrt{2}}{2}$ and $\dfrac{\sqrt{2}}{2} = \dfrac{\sqrt{2}}{2}$; the quantities are equal.

15. A. Use the proper formulas:

$A = s \times s$ (area of a square)

$A = \pi r^2$ (area of a circle)

Substitute $s = 1$ and $r = \dfrac{\sqrt{2}}{2}$ from the previous problem:

$2 \times$ area of square $ABCD$	Area of circle
$2 \times (1 \times 1)$	$\pi \left(\dfrac{\sqrt{2}}{2} \right)^2$
	$\pi \times \dfrac{2}{4}$
	$\approx 3.14 \times \dfrac{1}{2}$
	≈ 1.57

$$2 > 1.57$$

Therefore, Quantity A is greater than Quantity B.

Chapter 8

Data Sufficiency

Data Sufficiency Strategies

Data sufficiency is a unique problem type that appears on the GMAT. Data sufficiency problems test your ability to determine whether enough information is present in order to solve the given questions. This question type emphasizes your knowledge of mathematical insight, approximations, simple calculations, and common sense.

Math calculations are not necessarily required to answer specific questions.

Directions

Each of the problems below consists of a question and two statements, labeled (1) and (2), in which certain data are given. You must decide whether the data given in the statements are *sufficient* to answer the question. Using the data given in the statements *plus* your knowledge of mathematics and everyday facts (such as the number of days in July or the meaning of *counterclockwise*), you are to click on the oval that represents the correct answer:

    ⬭   Statement (1) ALONE is sufficient, but statement (2) alone is not sufficient to answer the question asked.

    ⬭   Statement (2) ALONE is sufficient, but statement (1) alone is not sufficient to answer the question asked.

    ⬭   BOTH statements (1) and (2) TOGETHER are sufficient to answer the question asked, but NEITHER statement ALONE is sufficient.

    ⬭   EACH statement ALONE is sufficient to answer the question asked.

    ⬭   Statements (1) and (2) TOGETHER are NOT sufficient to answer the question asked.

Analysis

Your task is to examine problem sets, draw upon your math skills, and reason deductively to decide if the information provided will solve the problem. The purpose here is to determine whether the information given is *sufficient* to answer the question; therefore, *do not solve the problem* unless it is absolutely necessary.

The following memory aid, 12-TEN, will simplify the directions, making them easier to memorize and/or reference.

12-TEN Method

12-TEN Method	Answer Choice Letter	Say to Yourself
1 One	A	Statement **(1)** alone is sufficient.
2 Two	B	Statement **(2)** alone is sufficient.
T Together	C	Both statements (1) and (2) must be used **together** to be sufficient.
E Either	D	**Either** statement (1) or (2) alone is sufficient.
N Neither	E	**Neither** statement (1) nor statement (2) is sufficient—either alone or taken together. Additional data specific to the problem is needed to answer the question.

12-TEN is a mnemonic for 1, 2, together, either, or neither. (***Note:*** *Either* means select choice D, *not* E.) Because of the structure of this type of question, you should always be able to eliminate some of the answer choices.

On the actual GMAT exam, the five possible answer choice statements will appear with the question on the computer screen. Although we use letters in this guide as a strategy and for easy reference, no letters or numbers will be assigned to the answer choices on the actual GMAT. To select your answer, you must click on the oval that matches your selected answer choice.

Sometimes geometric figures are included. Use them only for positional value; don't measure them because they aren't necessarily drawn to scale.

Suggested Approach with Examples

Memorize the Sequence of Answer Choices

Memorize and practice the five possible answer choices *before* your exam. Many successful test-takers learn the lettered choices (A, B, C, D, and E) associated with the 12-TEN method as a memory aid. This will save you time the day of the test. These choices will always be presented in the exact order shown in the directions above.

Determine the Necessary Information

Quickly decide what is the necessary basic information to answer the question. Then see if the data supplies that information.

Example:

What is the area of circle *O*?

(1) The circumference is 12π.

(2) The diameter is 12.

To find the area of a circle, it is necessary to have the radius. Statement (1) gives enough information to find the radius by substituting into the circumference formula, $C = 2\pi r$, and getting $12\pi = 2\pi r$. Then you could solve for *r* (which is 6; thus, the area is 36π). Solving the problem isn't necessary, though—all you need to know is that you needed the radius and could find it from the information given. Statement (2) also gives enough information to find the radius; therefore, the answer is the fourth choice (D): Either statement alone is sufficient.

Don't Solve Unless Necessary

Don't solve the problem unless it is absolutely necessary. Avoid unnecessary calculations.

Example:

What is the value of *x*?

(1) $83x + 12 = 360$
(2) $25x + 3y = 16$

This problem is most easily solved by inspecting the first bit of data and quickly noticing that statement (1) is enough to answer the question (one variable, one equation, solvable), and statement (2) does not answer the question, which you can also determine by inspection (two variables, one equation, not solvable for a single value). The correct answer is the first choice (A), yet no actual solving had to be done.

Use a Simple Marking System

Use a simple marking system to assist you in making your decision.

Examples:

What is the average height of Tom, Bob, and Luke?

(1) Bob is 4 inches shorter than Luke, and Tom is 4 inches taller than Luke.
(2) Luke is 5 feet 6 inches tall.

Since the GMAT is a computer-adaptive test, you will need to abbreviate your markings. Each time you eliminate a choice, just write down the number with a slash through it.

Statement (1) is not sufficient because no actual height is given; therefore, write down the number 1 with slash through it. Note that the answer is immediately narrowed to second, third, and fifth choices (B, C, or E). Statement (2) by itself is also not sufficient, because the other two, Tom and Bob, aren't mentioned; therefore, write down the number 2 with a slash through it. For example,

What is the average height of Tom, Bob, and Luke?

(𝟙̸) Bob is 4 inches shorter than Luke, and Tom is 4 inches taller than Luke.
(𝟚̸) Luke is 5 feet 6 inches tall.

Notice that the answer is now narrowed to the third or fifth choices (C or E). Now, trying them together, they are sufficient. The answer is the third choice (C). In writing down the data, if you're not sure whether it's sufficient, put a question mark next to number and try the next bit of data. Don't waste time trying one bit of data for more than about 30 seconds.

Use Only Common Knowledge

Don't read in specialized knowledge. Use only the information given and common, or general, knowledge.

Example:

What is the runner's average speed in running around the track?

(1) One lap took 49 seconds.

(2) He ran 5 seconds faster than his previous best time.

Someone familiar with track and field might quickly assume that one lap is the standard 440 yards and would then *incorrectly* answer the first choice (A). This sort of assumption cannot be made because it is from specialized knowledge in the area and, therefore, is not common knowledge. The correct answer is the fifth choice (E), because the distance around the track is not given in either bit of data.

Watch for *Yes* and *No* Questions

Questions that are set up as *yes* or *no* questions can be tricky. Remember that you are *not necessarily trying to calculate a specific mathematical solution* to find the right answer choice; you are determining whether the question can be answered using the information provided. For example, if the question asks, "Is *x* positive?" and you know that *x* is –3, then *you do have sufficient information* to answer the question.

Draw Diagrams

If a geometric diagram is discussed but no figure is given, draw a simple diagram.

Example:

If the legs of a trapezoid are equal, what is the area?

(1) The smaller base is 8 inches and the legs are 6 inches.

(2) The height is 5 inches.

Drawing a diagram helps give important insight into what is needed to answer the question.

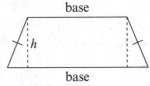

The formula for the area of a trapezoid is $A = \dfrac{1}{2}h(b_1 + b_2)$ or $A = \dfrac{h(b_1 + b_2)}{2}$.

Statement (1) does not give sufficient information to find the larger base or the height. Statement (2), by itself, does not give enough information to find the bases. Statements (1) and (2) together give enough information to find the bases and the height. The answer is the third choice (C). The Pythagorean theorem would be necessary to find the length of the difference between the smaller and larger bases. Adding this difference to the length of the shorter base would give the longer base. You now have the necessary information. Notice the markings on the diagram below; adding markings to your diagram will assist you in deciding what you have to work with.

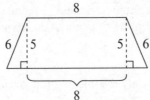

Practice, Practice, Practice

Data sufficiency questions require a shift in your ability to conceptualize math problems. Approximately one-third of the quantitative problems on the GMAT relate to data sufficiency, so it is important that you are comfortable with this type of question before you take the test. Consistent practice is critical if you are to succeed on this section of the test.

A Patterned Plan of Attack

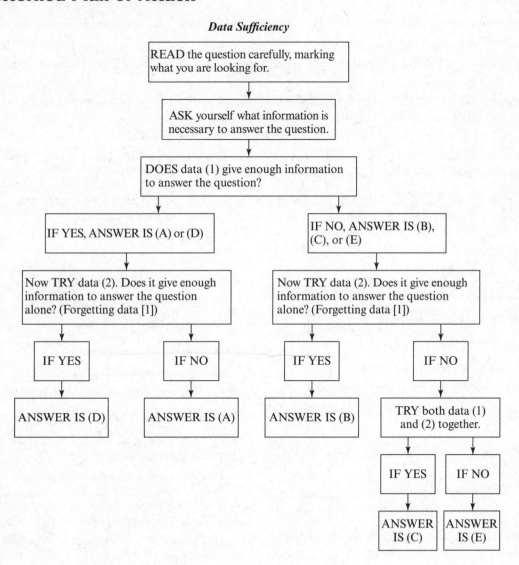

Data Sufficiency

Data Sufficiency Practice

Directions

Each of the problems below consists of a question and two statements, labeled (1) and (2), in which certain data are given. You must decide whether the data given in the statements are *sufficient* to answer the question. Using the data given in the statements *plus* your knowledge of mathematics and everyday facts (such as the number of days in July or the meaning of *counterclockwise*), you are to mark

Ⓐ if statement (1) ALONE is sufficient, but statement (2) alone is not sufficient to answer the question asked.

Ⓑ if statement (2) ALONE is sufficient, but statement (1) alone is not sufficient to answer the question asked.

Ⓒ if BOTH statements (1) and (2) TOGETHER are sufficient to answer the question asked, but NEITHER statement ALONE is sufficient.

Ⓓ if EACH statement ALONE is sufficient to answer the question asked.

Ⓔ if statements (1) and (2) TOGETHER are NOT sufficient to answer the question asked, and additional data specific to the problem is needed.

Note: Letter choices (A, B, C, D, E) are included above for your reference in answering the practice questions. On the actual GMAT exam, no letters will be assigned to the answer choices.

Arithmetic

1. The product of two integers is 6. What are the integers?
   (1) Both integers are positive.
   (2) One integer is 2.

2. How far did the airplane travel?
   (1) It flew from east to west for 9 hours.
   (2) It flew at a rate of 300 miles per hour for the first 8 hours.

3. The average of two numbers is 5. What are the numbers?
   (1) 7 is one of the numbers.
   (2) 3 is one of the numbers.

4. What must Maria's salary increase be in order to meet a 6% cost-of-living increase?
   (1) Maria's current salary is $15,000.
   (2) Maria's new salary will be $15,900 if her raise meets the increase in the cost of living.

5. John can jump half his height. How tall is he?
   (1) John is shorter than his brother.
   (2) John's brother can jump 5 feet.

6. What two fractions add to 1?
   (1) The fractions are equal.
   (2) The reciprocal of the first fraction is 2.

7. How many people at the party are men?
   (1) There are twice as many men at the party as there are women.
   (2) There are nine women at the party.

8. How many ounces does a full water bottle hold if 12 ounces of water remain?
   (1) The full bottle holds an even number of ounces.
   (2) 25% of the bottle has been used.

9. Bob can read 25 pages an hour. How long will it take him to finish the book?

(1) Bob has read half the book by midnight.

(2) Bob reads consistently from 8 p.m. until he finishes the book.

10. How much taller is Alice than her brother?

(1) Her brother is 5 feet 4 inches tall.

(2) Alice is 180 centimeters tall. (1 inch = 2.54 cm)

11. How many miles per gallon did Bruce get on his 300-mile trip?

(1) He used $\frac{3}{4}$ of a tank of gas.

(2) The tank holds 12 gallons.

12. Two integers are in the proportion 1 to 5. What is the larger number?

(1) The smaller integer is one digit and prime.

(2) The larger integer is greater than 30.

Algebra

1. What is the value of a if $3a - 2b = 4$?

(1) $a = 2b$

(2) a and b are integers.

2. John is twice as old as his brother, who is older than his sister. How old is John?

(1) John's brother is 2 years older than their sister.

(2) Their sister is 3 years old.

3. What is the value of x?

(1) The square of x is three more than twice x.

(2) x is negative.

4. If $a^n a^m = a^{15}$, what is the value of n?

(1) n is even and m is 3.

(2) n is four times as large as m.

5. What is the value of p?

(1) $p + 3h = 10$

(2) $9 + h = 15 - h$

13. What is Hal's average weekly salary?

(1) Hal's monthly salary is over $800.

(2) Hal's average daily salary is $40.

14. What is the annual rate of simple interest in Arlene's bank?

(1) Arlene receives $36 in interest for 2 years on savings of $120.

(2) If Arlene was to open an account with $50, after 1 year she would receive $7.50 in interest.

15. If the volume of a mixture doubles every 20 minutes, at what time was its volume 1 cubic meter?

(1) At 8 p.m., its volume was 64 cubic meters.

(2) Twenty minutes ago, its volume was 16 cubic meters.

6. If $\sqrt{ab} = 4$ and $a > 0$, what is the value of a?

(1) $ab = 16$ and b is even.

(2) $a = b$

7. John's first long jump was 1 foot short of the school record. His second jump exceeded the school's record by a foot. What was the old record that John broke by 1 foot?

(1) The average of John's two jumps was 18 feet.

(2) The sum of John's two jumps was 36 feet.

8. John has x dollars and Mary has y dollars. Together, they can buy a $45 ticket. How much money does John have?

(1) After the purchase, they have a total of $3 left.

(2) John started with less money than Mary.

Question 9 refers to the following figure.

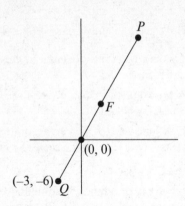

9. In the figure above, what are the coordinates of point P?
   (1) The midpoint of $\overline{QP}$ is at point F (2, 4).
   (2) $\overleftrightarrow{QP}$ passes through origin (0, 0).

10. For all integers a and b, the operation $\odot$ is defined by $a \odot b = \dfrac{a}{b}$, where $b \neq 0$. If x and y are integers, is $x \odot y$ an integer?
    (1) $x = y^2$
    (2) $x = 0$

11. What is the average of a, b, and c if $a + c = 20$?
    (1) $a - c = 12$ and $a + b = 18$
    (2) $b = 2$

12. How tall is Larry?
    (1) Three years ago, Larry was 4 inches shorter than his brother, Bill.
    (2) Larry has grown 3 inches in the last 3 years. Bill has grown only 2 inches.

13. Is $y > \dfrac{1}{y}$?
    (1) $y > 0$
    (2) $y > 1$

14. If x is an integer multiple of 7, what is the value of x?
    (1) $x = 5y$, where y is an integer.
    (2) $27 < x < 43$

15. What is the value of $xy - 8$?
    (1) $x + y = 5$
    (2) $xy - 10 = 22$

Geometry

Question 1 refers to the following figure.

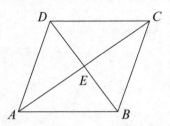

1. In parallelogram $ABCD$ above, what is the length of $\overline{AE}$?
   (1) $AB = 10$ and $m\angle AEB = 90°$
   (2) $AC = 12$

Question 2 refers to the following figure.

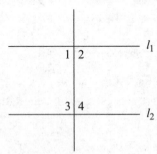

2. In the figure above, are lines l_1 and l_2 parallel?
   (1) $m\angle 1 = m\angle 2$
   (2) $m\angle 1 + m\angle 3 = 180°$

Question 3 refers to the following figure.

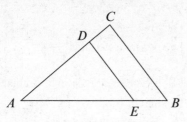

3. In the figure above, is $\triangle AED$ similar to $\triangle ABC$?
   (1) $m\angle ACB = 90°$
   (2) $DE = \frac{2}{3}CB$

Question 4 refers to the following figure.

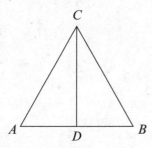

4. Is $\triangle ABC$ above an isosceles triangle?
   (1) $\overline{CD}$ is perpendicular to $\overline{AB}$.
   (2) $\angle ACB$ is bisected by $\overline{CD}$.

Question 5 refers to the following figure.

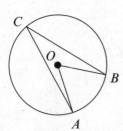

5. What is the measure of $\angle ACB$ in circle O above?
   (1) $CA = CB$
   (2) The length of $\overset{\frown}{AB}$ is $\frac{1}{5}$ the circumference of the circle.

Question 6 refers to the following figure.

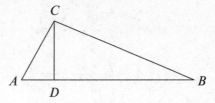

6. What is the area of $\triangle ABC$ above?
   (1) $AC = 6$
   (2) $BD = 10$

Question 7 refers to the following figure.

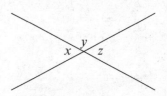

7. In the figure above, what is the measure of $\angle x$?
   (1) $m\angle y$ is twice $m\angle x$.
   (2) $m\angle x = m\angle z$

Question 8 refers to the following figure.

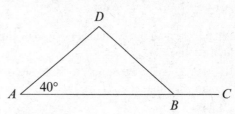

8. In the figure above, what is the measure of $\angle DBC$?
   (1) $m\angle ADB = 100°$
   (2) $AD = DB$

Question 9 refers to the following figure.

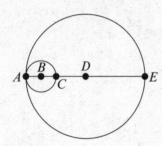

9. In the figure above, Circle *B* is tangent to Circle *D*. What is the area of the Circle *B*?
   (1) The large circle has area 9π and *CD* = 1.
   (2) *BD* = 2

Question 10 refers to the following figure.

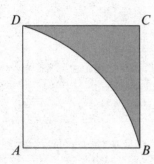

10. What is the area of the shaded portion of the figure above?
    (1) *ABCD* is a square and $\overset{\frown}{DB}$ is an arc of a circle with center *A*.
    (2) *AD* = 2

11. The volume of a box is 216 cubic inches. What are the dimensions of the box?
    (1) Length, width, and height are equal.
    (2) The length and width are each 6 inches.

12. What is the length of the hypotenuse of a 45°-45°-90° triangle?
    (1) The area is 8.
    (2) The perimeter equals $8 + 4\sqrt{2}$.

13. What is the volume of the right circular cylinder?
    (1) The height is 4.
    (2) The radius is an integer that is less than the height.

Question 14 refers to the following figure.

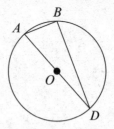

14. Circle *O* above has $\overline{AD}$ passing through *O*. What is the radius of the circle?
    (1) *AB* = 1
    (2) *BD* = 2

Question 15 refers to the following figure.

15. Does *AB* = *CD*?
    (1) *C* is the midpoint of $\overline{AE}$.
    (2) *BC* = *CD*

Answer Key

The page number(s) in parentheses following each answer will direct you to the basic review section(s) for that specific problem.

Arithmetic

1. B (p. 8)
2. E (p. 290)
3. D (p. 187)
4. D (p. 52)
5. E (p. 316)

6. D (p. 31)
7. C (p. 316)
8. B (p. 52)
9. C (p. 316)
10. C (p. 68)

11. C (p. 38)
12. C (p. 8)
13. E (p. 187)
14. D (p. 306)
15. A (p. 296)

Algebra

1. A (p. 99)
2. C (p. 300)
3. C (p. 88)
4. D (p. 88)
5. C (p. 99)

6. B (p. 65)
7. D (pp. 86, 90)
8. E (p. 316)
9. A (p. 143)
10. D (p. 167)

11. D (p. 99)
12. E (p. 316)
13. B (p. 88)
14. C (p. 25)
15. B (p. 90)

Geometry

1. B (pp. 242, 251)
2. B (p. 225)
3. E (p. 232)
4. C (p. 234)
5. B (pp. 261, 265)

6. E (p. 256)
7. A (p. 222)
8. D (p. 239)
9. A (p. 262)
10. C (pp. 256, 262)

11. D (pp. 232, 267)
12. D (p. 244)
13. E (p. 267)
14. C (pp. 242, 261)
15. E (p. 224)

Data Sufficiency Answers and Explanations

Arithmetic

1. **B.** 6 can be shown as the product of two integers in the following manner: (1)(6), (–1)(–6), (2)(3), or (–2)(–3). Statement (1) says that both integers are positive, but that still leaves two choices. Statement (2) says that one of the integers is 2; therefore, the other must be 3. Statement (2) alone suffices.

2. **E.** Without knowing the rate at which the airplane flew, statement (1) does not suffice. Statement (2) provides more information but does not say how long the total travel time was or the speed after 8 hours. The statements together do not provide sufficient data to answer the question because you don't know the speed for the final hour.

3. **D.** Knowing that the two numbers average 5, you can use either statement alone to determine both numbers. For example, using statement (1), which says that 7 is one of the numbers, you can determine that the other number must be 3 because the average of the two numbers is 5. The same process works for statement (2) alone.

4. **D.** Statement (1) is sufficient to determine an answer. Just multiply $15,000 by 0.06. Statement (2) is also sufficient to determine an answer. Just divide $15,900 by 1.06.

5. **E.** John's being shorter than his brother has nothing to do with John's jump; so statement (1) alone does not solve the problem. Because no information is given about how John's jump compares to his brother's jump, statement (2) is not useful either.

6. **D.** Statement (1) implies that the fractions are both $\frac{1}{2}$. Statement (2) implies that the first fraction is $\frac{1}{2}$; therefore, the second is $\frac{1}{2}$. Each statement is separately sufficient.

7. **C.** Statement (1) gives the ratio of men to women, but because no numbers are given, it is insufficient to determine the number of men. Statement (2) alone is insufficient to determine the number of men. If you take them together, however, you know that the number of men is twice the number of women, 9. Therefore, there are 18 men at the party.

8. **B.** Statement (1) tells you nothing of value for this problem. Statement (2) suffices. Since 75% of the total is 12 ounces, then $0.75T = 12$, or $T = \frac{12}{0.75}$.

9. **C.** Statement (1) tells you that Bob has read half the book by midnight. But because you don't know when he started or how long he has been reading, you can't calculate when he'll finish. Statement (2) alone is also insufficient, but together with statement (1), it allows you to calculate that it takes Bob 4 hours to read half the book; therefore, he will finish in 4 more hours. The answer is (C). Note that your knowledge of Bob's reading speed is useless; you don't know the page length of the book.

10. **C.** Statement (1) gives the brother's height in feet and inches. Statement (2) gives Alice's height in centimeters. Neither statement alone will suffice. Converting centimeters to feet and inches and subtracting the height in statement (1) from that in statement (2) shows the answer is choice C.

11. **C.** To answer the question, you need to know how much gas was used. Statement (1) says how much of the tank was used but not how much gas. Statement (2) says how much gas is in a full tank. Neither statement alone is sufficient, but taking the statements together, you find that Bruce used 9 gallons. You can then divide 300 miles by 9 gallons of gas.

12. **C.** From statement (1), you know that the smaller integer must be 2, 3, 5, or 7 because those are the only one-digit prime numbers. This statement alone is insufficient. From statement (2), you know that 5 times the smaller integer will give the second integer, greater than 30. Statement (2) alone is insufficient. Together, however, the statements provide the information that only 7 could be the smaller integer, because $5 \times 7 > 30$.

13. **E.** Because you know only that Hal's salary is *over* $800 per month, no precise average weekly salary can be determined from statement (1). Statement (2) is also insufficient because you don't know how many days each week Hal works.

14. **D.** By using the simple interest formula ($I = prt$), either statement alone will suffice to determine the rate of interest (15% in this case).

15. **A.** Statement (1) alone allows you to extrapolate back 20 minutes at a time to determine when the mixture's volume was 1 cubic meter. (Each previous 20 minutes the mixture is halved.) Statement (2) is insufficient because you aren't given any information regarding what is the *present* time.

Algebra

1. **A.** The problem states that $3a - 2b = 4$. Statement (1) gives $a = 2b$, resulting in two equations in two unknowns, which leads to a unique solution. Statement (2) does not lead to a unique solution, however, because many pairs of integers a and b will satisfy $3a - 2b = 4$.

2. **C.** Let x = John's brother's age, and $2x$ = John's age. Statement (1) tells you that John's brother is 2 years older than their sister. Hence, $x - 2$ = the sister's age. But you have no value for x. Thus, statement (1) alone is insufficient. Statement (2) tells you the sister's age, 3 years old, but you have no exact relationship between the sister and either of her brothers. So statement (2) alone is insufficient. Taking the statements together you have

   x = John's brother

   $2x$ = John

   $x - 2 = 3$ = sister

   Thus, you can solve for x (5 years) and find John's age, 10.

3. **C.** Statement (1) says that $x^2 = 3 + 2x$; so $x^2 - 2x - 3 = 0$, which factors to give $(x - 3)(x + 1) = 0$. This has two answers, $x = 3$ or $x = -1$, which in data sufficiency problems does not constitute a solution. Statement (2) says that the answer is negative, which alone does not suffice; however, taken together, the data are sufficient to determine a unique solution, $x = -1$.

4. **D.** Because $a^n a^m = a^{15}$ and you know that $a^n a^m = a^{n+m}$, you have $n + m = 15$. Statement (1) says that n is even and m is 3, which results in $n + 3 = 15$, or $n = 12$, a solution. Statement (2) says $n = 4m$. This together with $n + m = 15$ gives two equations in two unknowns, which lead to a solution also.

5. **C.** Statement (1) alone is not sufficient because it is an equation with two unknowns. Statement (2) allows you to solve for the unknown, h, which you may then plug into statement (1) to determine the value of p. Both statements taken together will answer the question.

6. **B.** The fact that $\sqrt{ab} = 4$ implies that $ab = 16$. Statement (1) says $ab = 16$ and b is even. This does not allow you to find a, because several choices are possible: (2)(8), (4)(4), and so on. If statement (2) is used, you have $a^2 = 16$, and there is only one positive integer solution, 4.

7. **D.** If you let x represent the original school record, John's first jump was $x - 1$ feet and his second jump was $x + 1$ feet. Statement (1) says that the average of the two jumps was 18 feet. This means that

$$\frac{(x-1)+(x+1)}{2} = 18$$

$$\frac{2x}{2} = 18$$

$$x = 18$$

18 feet was the old record. Statement (1) will suffice. Statement (2) says that $(x - 1) + (x + 1) = 36$. Solving this for x gives 18 feet. So this, too, gives a solution.

8. **E.** The question implies that $x + y$ must be 45 or larger. Statement (1) implies that $(x + y) - 45 = 3$. So $x + y = 48$, which does not allow you to find x. Statement (2) implies that $x < y$, but neither this nor the previous piece of information allows you to determine x.

9. **A.** Statement (1) alone is sufficient to determine the coordinates of point P. Because the coordinates are given for endpoint Q $(-3, -6)$, using the midpoint, you can derive coordinates for the other endpoint, P. (The midpoint coordinates are the averages of the endpoint coordinates. Thus, coordinates of point P are (7, 14). Statement (2) tells you nothing of value.

10. **D.** Either statement (1) or (2) alone is sufficient to answer the question conclusively. Statement (1) tells you that $x = y$ or $x = -y$. In either case, $x \odot y$ (or $\frac{x}{y}$) will be an integer, as it will equal either 1 or –1.

    Statement (2) tells you that $x = 0$; therefore, $x \odot y = \frac{0}{y} = 0$, which is also an integer.

11. **D.** The average of a, b, and c is $\frac{a+b+c}{3}$.

    Statement (1) and the information in the question give you three equations:

    $$a + c = 20$$
    $$a - c = 12$$
    $$a + b = 18$$

    If you add the first two equations, you get $2a = 32$, so $a = 16$. This allows you to find b and c. So statement (1) is sufficient. Statement (2) says $b = 2$. So this together with $a + c = 20$ allows you to find $a + b + c = 2 + 20 = 22$. Thus, statement (2) will suffice.

12. **E.** If you let x represent Larry's height 3 years ago and y represent Bill's height 3 years ago, statement (1) says $x = y - 4$. This does not allow you to find x or Larry's present height. Statement (2) gives no relationship between the heights. Putting both statements together allows you to write the second condition as

    $(x + 3) =$ Larry's height now

    $(y + z) =$ Bill's height now

    Since Larry was 4 inches shorter, he is now only 3 inches shorter than Bill, so

    $$(x+3)=(y+z)-3$$
    $$x = y - 4$$

    Thus, no new information is gained, and the problem cannot be solved.

13. **B.** Statement (1) alone is insufficient. Substituting 1 and 2 as values of y will result in a "no" then a "yes" answer for the original question. Statement (2), however, is alone sufficient. Any value of y greater than 1 will yield a consistent "yes" answer to the question.

14. **C.** Statement (1) allows you to know that x is a multiple of both 5 and 7. Thus, x may be 35, 70, 105, and so on. Since statement (2) alone tells you that x may be 28, 35, or 42 (all multiples of 7), it, too, is insufficient. Both statements taken together, however, will suffice to determine that x is 35.

15. **B.** Statement (1) is insufficient because it contains two unknowns. Statement (2) is sufficient alone. Although it contains two unknowns, notice that $xy - 10$ is simply two less than $xy - 8$. Therefore, if $xy - 10$ equals 22, $xy - 8$ equals 24.

Geometry

1. **B.** The key here is that the diagonals of a parallelogram bisect each other. Statement (1) does not provide enough information to compute the length of $\overline{AE}$. The fact that $\triangle AEB$ is a right triangle with a hypotenuse that measures 10 does not determine the lengths of $\overline{AE}$ or $\overline{EB}$. However, statement (2) allows you to determine $\overline{AE}$ at once.

2. **B.** Although statement (1) allows you to conclude that both $\angle 1$ and $\angle 2$ are right angles, this does not suffice to conclude that l_1 and l_2 are parallel. You can conclude from statement (2), however, that l_1 and l_2 are parallel because $\angle 1$ and $\angle 3$ are supplementary angles.

3. **E.** In order to conclude that the triangles are similar, you would need to know that $\overline{DE}$ and $\overline{CB}$ are parallel. Neither statement (1) nor statement (2) gives enough information to allow this conclusion.

4. **C.** An isosceles triangle has two sides of equal length. To conclude this, the information provided in statement (1) does not suffice because no conclusions about the sides AC and BC can be drawn. Similarly, statement (2) alone is insufficient. The information combined, however, leads to the conclusion that $\triangle ACD$ and $\triangle BCD$ are congruent (angle-side-angle); hence $AC = BC$.

5. **B.** $\angle ACB$ is an inscribed angle, so its measure is equal to one-half of $\angle AOB$. Statement (1) gives no information about the number of degrees in $\angle ACB$. Statement (2), however, tells you that $m\angle AOB$ is $\frac{1}{5}$ of 360°. This, together with the initial observation that $\angle ACB$ is an inscribed angle, is sufficient to answer the question.

6. **E.** The area of a triangle is equal to one-half the product of a base and an altitude. Neither statement (1) nor statement (2) allows you to determine the altitude of the triangle.

7. **A.** The key here is that $\angle x$ and $\angle y$ are supplementary angles. Thus, statement (1) implies that $m\angle x$ is 60° and $m\angle y$ is 120°. Statement (2) is always true (because vertical angles are equal); it is not sufficient.

8. **D.** $\angle DBC$ is an exterior angle of $\triangle ABD$ and, hence, it is equal to the sum of the angles BAD and ADB. Since $m\angle BAD$ is given as 40° and statement (1) tells you that $m\angle ADB$ is 100°, you can determine $m\angle DBC$. Statement (2) tells you that $\triangle ABD$ has two equal sides; therefore, it is an isosceles triangle, making $m\angle BAD = m\angle ABD$. Because $\angle ABD$ and $\angle DBC$ are supplementary, you can determine $m\angle DBC$ based on statement (2) alone.

9. **A.** You would need either the radius or the diameter of Circle B (small circle) to find its area. Statement (1) tells you that the radius of Circle D (large circle) (AD or DE) is 3 (because the area is π times the square of the radius). Because AE must, therefore, be 6 and $CE = CD + DE = 1 + 3 = 4$, you know that $AC = 2$, and you can find the area of Circle B. Statement (2) does not give you any information about the relationship between BD and the other parts of the circle.

10. **C.** Statement (1) tells you that if you know the radius of the circle (or equivalently the length of the side of the square), you could find the area of the shaded portion by subtracting the area of one-quarter of the circle from that of the square. However, statement (1) does not alone suffice. Statement (2) alone is of little use because you know nothing of the nature of the geometric figures. You need both statements to solve the problem.

11. **D.** Statement (1) tells you that your box is a cube. From the known volume, the length of its edge can be found. So statement (1) is sufficient. Statement (2) tells you that $(6)(6)(h) = 216$; therefore, you can find the third dimension—the height.

12. **D.** The right triangle is isosceles and, thus, its sides are in the proportion of $1:1:\sqrt{2}$. Statement (1) tells you that if you multiply one-half the length of a base times the altitude, you get 8. Because the legs in this case give you a base and an altitude, you can solve for the length of a leg and, hence, find the hypotenuse.

$$\frac{1}{2}(s)(s) = 8$$

$$s^2 = 16$$

$$s = 4$$

$$\text{hypotenuse} = 4\sqrt{2}$$

Using statement (2), you know that $s + s + s\sqrt{2} = 8 + 4\sqrt{2}$.

Thus, $s = 4$ and, again, hypotenuse $= 4\sqrt{2}$.

13. **E.** The volume of a right circular cylinder is $\pi r^2 h$, where r is the radius of the base and h is the height. Hence, statement (1) does not give sufficient information to compute the volume. Statement (2) does not specify the radius.

14. **C.** Because $\overline{AD}$ is a diameter, $\triangle ABD$ is inscribed in a semicircle and is, therefore, a right triangle because $m\angle ABD = 90°$. You can find the radius OA if you can determine AD (the diameter). Statement (1) gives you one leg of the right triangle. Statement (2) gives you the second leg. The Pythagorean theorem allows you to find AD and, hence, the radius.

15. **E.** Although statement (1) shows you that $AC = CE$, even taken with statement (2), no relationship may be derived between AB and CD. Note that with both pieces of data, a diagram may be drawn as follows.

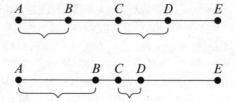

Final Suggestions

Now that you have completed this guide, you should

1. Obtain the CliffsNotes preparation guide for your specific test. A test-specific CliffsNotes guide will hone in on the specific math problem types on the test you're preparing for, offer more practice problems, and prepare you for any nonmathematical questions on the exam.
2. Practice solving multi-step reasoning problems that focus on practical applications for everyday problems.
3. Practice working problems under time pressure. Now that you've reviewed the basic skills, the next hurdle is being comfortable using them in a timed test setting.
4. Use this guide as a reference should problems arise.